ISAAC LEESER
AND THE
MAKING
OF
AMERICAN
JUDAISM

Isaac Leeser, 1868. (Courtesy of the Center for Judaic Studies,
Annenberg Research Institute, University of Pennsylvania,
Philadelphia.)

ISAAC LEESER

AND THE

MAKING

OF

AMERICAN

JUDAISM

LANCE J. SUSSMAN

 WAYNE STATE UNIVERSITY PRESS DETROIT

AMERICAN JEWISH CIVILIZATION SERIES
A complete listing of the books in this series can be found at the back of this volume.
EDITORS
Moses Rischin
San Francisco State University

Jonathan D. Sarna
Brandeis University

Library of Congress Cataloging-in-Publication Data

Sussman, Lance Jonathan.
Isaac Leeser and the making of American Judaism / Lance J.
Sussman.
p.   cm. — (American Jewish civilization series)
Includes bibliographical references and index.
ISBN 0-8143-1996-3 (alk. paper)
1. Leeser, Isaac.   2. Rabbis—Pennsylvania—Philadelphia—
Biography.   3. Philadelphia (Pa.)—Biography.   4. Judaism—United
States—History—19th century.   5. Orthodox Judaism—United States—
History—19th century.   6. Jews, European—United States—
History—19th century.   I. Title.   II. Series.
BM755.L397S84   1995
296.8'32'092—dc20
[B]   95-10952

Designer: Joanne Elkin Kinney

To Liz,
Benjamin,
Joshua,
Micah,
Judah,
&
Chana

CONTENTS

ACKNOWLEDGMENTS

My interest in writing a biography of Isaac Leeser (1806–1868) originated in my studies with Professor Jacob R. Marcus at the Hebrew Union College–Jewish Institute of Religion (HUC-JIR). The subsequent appointment of Jonathan D. Sarna to the HUC-JIR faculty proved providential. No doctoral student could have asked for finer advisors than Professors Marcus and Sarna. They are both exemplary teachers and generous scholars.

Thanks to their encouragement, I also conducted a broad search for new materials, including holographs and references to Leeser in the secular press during the Jacksonian and Antebellum periods. I discovered that, although scattered, hundreds of letters written to Leeser are extant. Letters from Leeser, on the other hand, are more rare.

At the Center for Jewish Studies (formerly Dropsie College), a division of the University of Pennsylvania, I found remnants of Emily Solis-Cohen's research notes and unpublished manuscripts on Leeser. Working during the 1930s, Solis-Cohen still had access to living oral traditions about the hazzan (cantor). During the last few years, the Leeser Papers at the Center for Judaic Studies have been properly catalogued by Arthur Kiron, who alerted me to a number of important documents. The archival materials used in this study are described in the Bibliography.

My search for archival materials brought me in touch with many other research institutions and a host of generous scholars. In particular, I thank Dr. Abraham Peck, Mrs. Fannie Zelcer, and Kevin Proffitt, archivists, and the large support staff at the American Jewish Archives for their patient assistance. In 1984, the Archives further assisted my work on Leeser by granting me a Summer Fellowship. Similarly, I am grateful to the staff of the Hebrew Union College–Jewish Institute of Religion's Klau Library, Cincinnati campus, especially those who secured materials from the Rare Book Room and assisted in computer checks on the Library of Congress holdings.

Personal and professional thanks are due to my friend Dr. Murray Friedman, regional director, American Jewish Committee (Philadelphia), for taking an early interest in my work and remaining a steadfast supporter. Through his office, Murray arranged for much-appreciated financial support from the Kevy K. and Hortense M. Kaiserman Foundation.

Many individuals at the following institutions also provided invaluable service: American Jewish Historical Society, Leo Baeck Institute (New York), the Historical Society of the Episcopal Church (Austin, Texas), the Historical Society of Pennsylvania, Jewish Historical Society of Maryland, the Jewish Museum (New York), Jewish Theological Seminary, National Museum of American Jewish History (Philadelphia), and the New York Public Library. Professor Abraham J. Karp (Rochester, New York) and Mr. Maxwell Whiteman (Philadelphia) also made important suggestions in the early stages.

I owe a debt of gratitude to Ellen Brand, a doctoral student in English at Binghamton University, who helped retype my manuscript. Her sensitivity to style, content, and argument greatly improved the literary quality of the project. Special thanks are also extended to Dr. Sylvia Horowitz for her assistance in the final stages of preparing this book for publication. The director of Wayne State University Press, Arthur Evans, has been extremely gracious in bringing my manuscript to press, for which I am very grateful. I also appreciate the many helpful suggestions of Moses Rischin, who read the manuscript at various stages.

I also want to thank a number of other people who, through friendship and generosity of spirit, have helped me bring this work to completion. My personal thanks are due to the members of Temple Beth Sholom (Middletown, Ohio) for allowing me countless hours away from the "job" to pursue my graduate studies at HUC-JIR, and to my friends at my second congregational home, Temple Beth El (Endicott, New York). The Board and Officers of Temple Concord (Binghamton, New York), where I now serve as a congregational rabbi, have been extraordinarily supportive of my academic interests, commitment to scholarship, and teaching responsibilities at Binghamton University, State University of New York.

A special word of gratitude is also due to my colleagues and friends in the History and Judaic Studies departments at Binghamton University. They have provided me with an intellectually stimulating environment in which I was able to complete my dissertation, rewrite it for publication, teach a wide variety of courses, and pursue my rabbinic vocation as well.

Finally, I thank my family for their constant support and interest in my work. My mother's dedication to Jewish life has always been exemplary. My father encouraged me to study and read widely; more than anyone else, he also urged me to complete my work on Leeser. The high price of advanced graduate work, writing, university teaching, and attending to the needs of an active synagogue, however, has fallen primarily on my wife, Liz, and five children, Benjamin, Joshua, Micah, Judah, and Chana. In honor of their patience and unequivocal love, I dedicate this book to my family, who have brought balance, depth, and intensity to my life.

INTRODUCTION

In many other countries the Hebrew is oppressed and despised; here he is upon an equality with other citizens, and is unmolested in the exercise of his religion. Yet in tyrannical countries the Jew has always been a true believer, and a zealot in his faith even to martyrdom. Let us then prove, that in a free country the Jew is no less zealous, no less animated with the love of Heaven, although the rod of persecution no longer compels him to seek shelter from the sword of man under the protection of the Almighty.

—Isaac Leeser, "Obedience and Repentance," September 28, 1832

VIEWED BROADLY, THIS BOOK is more than a biography of an individual. Its aim is to tell an important part of the story of Judaism's response to the challenge of political freedom and social acceptance in a new, modern society: the United States. As it came to terms with America, Judaism itself was transformed. This transformation was brought to completion in the decades just prior to the Civil War, and the key figure in this process was an Orthodox religious leader, Isaac Leeser (1806–68).

The story really began in 1654, when Jews first started arriving in America. Initially of Sephardic descent, they organized a tiny network of synagogues and in the course of daily life created a new tradition that was simultaneously American and Jewish. By 1776, the Jewish population of the new nation was still under three thousand and largely Ashkenazic in personal origin, although the vast majority followed Sephardic customs. Thereafter, restrictions imposed by European governments blocking emigration and the nearly constant war conditions in the Atlantic greatly limited the volume of immigration to America for a generation.

In their isolated state and in an environment of general religious laxity following the Revolution, American Jews continued to preserve their religious heritage. Judaism, however, did not flourish in America. American Jews depended on Europe for rabbinical guidance and religious books. No properly ordained rabbi settled in America until 1840. Services were conducted by semitrained cantors (hazzanim) who, with few exceptions, were held in low esteem by their congregations. At the end of the War of 1812, Judaism in American remained perilously weak.

In 1824, Isaac Leeser, a young Jewish orphan from the Westphalia region of Germany, arrived in Richmond, Virginia, at the invitation of his prosperous maternal uncle. He concluded that the religious freedom Jews enjoyed in America presented Judaism with an unprecedented opportunity for spiritual revitalization and cultural excellence. "This country," he wrote later, "is emphatically the one, where Israel is to prepare itself for its glorious mission of regenerating mankind." The immigration of nearly one hundred thousand Jews from Central Europe to the United States during the Antebellum Period greatly buoyed Leeser's hopes for a vital Judaism in America.

Leeser occupied a unique position in the American Jewish community of his day. Because he was thoroughly Americanized before the first period of mass Jewish immigration to the United States between 1830 and 1854, he was able to serve as a bridge between the old, native-born and the new, immigrant American Jews. Among the former, he inspired a handful to work for the revitalization of Judaism in America. To the latter, he was a spiritual leader, champion of tradition, and a guide to life in a new land.

During the course of his thirty-nine-year career, Leeser had a decisive impact on American Judaism. He was the outstanding Jewish religious leader in America prior to the Civil War, and should also be considered a primary shaper of both the American Jewish community and American Judaism. His contributions to Judaism in America were threefold. First, his extensive religious and journalistic publications helped make American Jewry a culturally independent community. Second, his advocacy of Jewish communal responsibility had a profound effect on shaping the local, national, and international agendas of the organized American Jewish community. Finally, he served as the leading spokesman for Orthodoxy in the United States for an entire generation—just at the time when Reform Judaism began to take root in the country. Edwin Wolf and Maxwell Whiteman did not exaggerate when they called the period in "American Jewish history from 1830 until the close of the Civil War, the 'Age of Leeser,' "[1]

Leeser's list of accomplishments is so long and far-reaching that it is difficult to imagine how one person could have been so productive.

"If he could have done only one thing," writes Bertram W. Korn, "and we were to decide from the perspective of these many decades later, we would have to single out Leeser's publication of his monthly 'newspaper,' *The Occident and American Jewish Advocate* (1843–69)."[2] The *Occident* was the first successful Jewish serial publication in the United States. In its columns, Leeser promoted Jewish cultural activity in America, transmitted information about Judaism in other parts of the world, and provided a public forum for communication and debate among America's widely scattered Jews.

In addition to publishing the *Occident*, Leeser took several other steps to promote unity among America's Jews.[3] He was the first to advocate a national ecclesiastical organization (1841); he participated in the founding of the first American Jewish defense organization, the Board of Delegates of American Israelites (1859); and, late in life, he helped broaden the appeal of B'nai B'rith among American Jews.[4] Through his friend and agent Gershom Kursheedt, Leeser was instrumental in securing a $200,000 bequest from Judah Touro of New Orleans. This legacy not only benefited various Jewish agencies and institutions in the United States and the Land of Israel but it revolutionized Jewish philanthropy in America and greatly contributed to American Jewry's growing self-awareness as a national community.[5]

In Jewish religious life, Leeser played a major role in the transformation of the traditional office of hazzan into an American Jewish ministry and thereby helped lay the foundations of the contemporary rabbinate in the United States.[6] Most important in this regard was his work as the pioneer Jewish preacher in America. Through his preaching and the publication of his own sermons as well as sermons of other leading Jewish religious leaders in the United States and Europe, Leeser established the sermon as a basic feature of the American synagogue. Moreover, he singlehandedly translated into English the entire Hebrew Bible (1853) and the Sephardic and Ashkenazic prayer books (1837 and 1848), as well as Moses Mendelssohn's *Jerusalem* (1850). He also edited and published the first Hebrew Bible with vowels in the United States (1845).[7]

In the field of Jewish education, Leeser played a crucial role in the creation of the Jewish Sunday school (1838), the first Hebrew "high" school (1849), and the first American Jewish theological seminary, Maimonides College (1867). He published various textbooks for these schools, including an original *Catechism* (1839) and the first Hebrew primer in the United States (1838). To promote Jewish learning among adults, Leeser also founded the American Jewish Publication Society in 1845.[8]

13

At the local level, in Philadelphia, where he lived during his entire active career, Leeser was among the first to recognize the need for such institutions as Jewish hospitals, orphanages, and community-wide charity federations. He also organized the first local board of rabbis.[9]

Finally, Leeser played a leading role in defending Judaism and Jewish rights in the United States and abroad. A letter he wrote to the Richmond *Whig* in 1829, to refute charges made in a scurrilous attack on Jews and Judaism in a London quarterly, was widely applauded by American Jews and directly led to his appointment as hazzan of Congregation Mickveh Israel. In 1840, he gained national prominence by leading the protest against the charges of ritual murder leveled at Jews in Syria and Rhodes known as the Damascus Blood Libel. Similarly, he relentlessly fought to protect Jewish civil rights in the United States. In particular, he was concerned with Sunday Laws, religion in public schools, and various attempts to "baptize" the Constitution.[10]

Despite the leading role he played in the Jewish community of his day and his many contributions to Judaism in America, Leeser faded from public view after his death. The "Protestantized" Orthodoxy he championed did not survive the nineteenth century and was broadly replaced after 1881 by an Orthodoxy primarily fashioned in East Europe. Moreover, neither his journal, the *Occident*, nor Maimonides College proved able to survive without him. Finally, his literary magnum opus, his English translation of the Bible, was superseded by the Jewish Publication Society's own translation in 1917.

Today, except in scholarly circles and perhaps in the Philadelphia Jewish community, Leeser remains an unsung hero in the history of Judaism in America. His name often goes unmentioned in standard cultural and religious histories of the United States, and to most historians of American society he is an unknown figure.[11] Until now, the scholarship on Leeser has consisted of little more than a handful of articles, mostly brief biographical sketches, and a dozen unpublished doctoral and rabbinic theses. This study, the first full-scale biography of the man and his times, thus seeks to fill a significant gap in both American and Jewish historical literature.

1

WESTPHALIA:
GERMAN BEGINNINGS, 1806–1824

I well remember the time when scarcely nine summers had
passed over my head, that you [Rabbi Abraham Sutro] arrived
among us; and how the first sermon I ever heard
delivered, the one you addressed to our congregation,
made a powerful impression upon us all,
not excepting the little unconscious boy I then was.
—Isaac Leeser, *Discourses,* 1836

ISAAC LEESER WAS BORN in the tiny rural village of Neuenkirchen near Rehine, Westphalia, on December 12, 1806, on the eve of Jewish emancipation.[1] "The Jewish townsfolk of Neuenkirchen," writes Maxwell Whiteman, "would never have believed that he was destined to become a religious leader of remarkable importance on the distant American Jewish scene."[2] He was not the descendant of great rabbis or prosperous "court Jews." He was, however, heir to the ancient and rich heritage of German Jewry, which at the time of his birth was rapidly changing to meet the new, radical demands placed upon it by the complex processes of modernization.

Jews had lived in the Westphalia region of Germany since the end of the twelfth century. The original Jewish settlers had wandered north from Cologne, where they lived under the protection of the Church and found residence in the various towns of the province, including Dortmund, Minden, and Münster. "Jews and other merchants" had been placed under the authority of the bishop of Madgeburg in 965 by Otto the Great, founder of the Holy Roman Empire, which at that time consisted of a "confused association" of more than three hundred autonomous and virtually sovereign states.[3]

The Church, however, was unable to protect the Jews in all cir-

15

cumstances. At best, its attitude toward Jews and Judaism was ambivalent: on the one hand, it served as the legal guardian of the Jewish community; on the other, it continued to charge the Jews with the crime of deicide. In the wake of the Black Death, from 1348 to 1349, Jews were seized as scapegoats and expelled from towns throughout Europe, including the region of Westphalia. Not until the end of the fourteenth century did Jewish life slowly begin to revive in the Westphalian countryside.

With the rise of absolutism, *Landjudenschaften*, self-governing Jewish communal institutions, were set up throughout the Holy Roman Empire. Their function was to govern numerous aspects of Jewish communal life. Most importantly, the state charged the *Landjudenschaft* with responsibility for the assessment and collection of taxes on its own behalf. In turn, most of the *Landjudenschaften* selected *Landrabbiner*, district rabbis, who were responsible for the equitable apportioning of the tax load.[4] In Westphalia, a *Landjudenschaft* was organized in 1650.

Court Jews (*Hofjuden*), whose financial skills and liquid capital were highly valued by the absolutist state, were often appointed as the titular leaders of the Jewish communities and served as their most important liaisons with the government. The court Jews, writes historian Michael Meyer, "were accepted because they served the interests of monarch or noble, not because there had been any change in thinking about the Jew."[5] Guilds still viewed Jews as business competitors and put heavy pressure on local governments to restrict Jewish economic activity.

One court Jew, Behrend Levi, an army purveyor and diplomatic agent of Frederick William, elector of Brandenberg, received a patent in 1650 to serve as overlord of the Jews in the elector's principalities west of the Elbe. Seven years later, after considerable controversy, when his patent was renewed, he helped gain the appointment of his brother, Nini, as the communal head of the Jews in Münster, where the prince-bishop, Christoph Bernhard von Galen, was eager to enlist Court Jews in the expansion of his mercantilist interests.[6]

In the Münster district of Westphalia, Court Jews also served as *Landrabbiner*. The last *Landrabbiner* of Münster during the waning years of the Holy Roman Empire were the *Hofjuden* Michael Mayer Breslauer (1771–89) and his son David (1789–1815). The Breslauers also served as mint suppliers to the bishop of Münster. Because between 1350 and 1815 Jews were not allowed to be officially registered as residents in the city of Münster or to openly practice Judaism, the seat of the *Landrabbiner* was located in Warendorf.[7]

The restructuring of the Jewish polity in the Holy Roman Empire during the age of absolutism did not radically alter the essentially medieval lifestyle of most Westphalian Jews. Not until the middle part of the eighteenth century did the winds of change begin to reach little villages like Neuenkirchen. Only then, more than half a century before French armies conquered Germany in 1806, did the ideas of the French Enlightenment and the turn toward acculturation to German society begin to have an impact on German Jewish life.[8]

This *Haskalah*, an Enlightenment movement and ideology that began in Jewish life during the 1740s, advocated assimilation in language, dress, and manners as a precondition for, and integral element in, Jewish emancipation. Moses Mendelssohn (1729–86), the symbolic leader and most important philosopher of the German *Haskalah*, attempted to demonstrate that Judaism was a religion of reason and that no conflict existed between adherence to the Jewish religious tradition and full participation in the modern state. The *Haskalah* had a direct effect on Isaac Leeser himself—his father had some leanings toward the *Haskalah* and occasionally even demonstrated some "freedom of thought and boldness of action."[9]

The year of Leeser's birth, 1806, marked a watershed in the history of the emancipation of West European Jewry. In May of that year, Napoleon convened the Assembly of Jewish Notables to meet for the first time to clarify relations between the Jews and the Napoleonic state. The French emperor made it clear to the notables that the Jews would have to renounce their communal distinctiveness and that Judaism would have to be relegated to matters of faith and ritual in lands under his control. The assembly had little choice but to appease Napoleon. "A French Jew," wrote a committee of twelve of the notables, "considers himself in England as among strangers, although he may be among Jews."[10]

Less than two weeks after Napoleon called the assembly, pressure from French diplomatic and military factions led to the dissolution of the Holy Roman Empire on August 6, 1806, after a history of a thousand years. Two months later, Napoleon routed Prussian armies at the battles of Jena and Auerstadt, and on October 27 he occupied the Hohenzollern capital city of Berlin. Thereafter, a new political order was established in Central Europe under French hegemony. As in France proper, Jewish corporate status was quickly terminated, and thousands of Jews in Central Europe were emancipated.

When Leeser was only a few months old, Napoleon established the Kingdom of Westphalia for his brother Jerome. On January 27, 1808, the Jews of Jerome's kingdom were the first in Germany to gain their civil rights. Now, by law, they could settle anywhere in the kingdom and were free to engage in the profession of their choice. Jews in other parts of Germany were immediately attracted to Jerome's enlightened kingdom, leading to a modest increase in Westphalia's Jewish population. According to one report, the Jewish population of Jerome's kingdom reached 19,039 by 1810.[11]

Just a few months after the emancipation of the Jews of Westphalia, a consistory, modeled on the French prototype developed by the Assembly of Notables, was established at the Westphalian capital, Kassel, to govern the internal affairs of the Jewish community and to promote the integration of the Jews into general society. "The wealthy, enlightened, somewhat autocratic" Israel Jacobson (1768–1828), a financial advisor to King Jerome Bonaparte and the founder of the Reform movement in Judaism, was appointed its president.[12]

The consistory, officially known as the Königlich Westphälisches Konsistorium der Israeliten, involved itself in a wide variety of issues. It divided the region into seven geographic districts, each with its own rabbi and assistant. Jews were ordered to choose family names, and Jacobson immediately undertook the task of restructuring Jewish life in Westphalia.[13]

Jacobson's most controversial activities affected education and religion. In 1810, he opened a consistory school in Kassel for training teachers and rabbis. At the school's synagogue, he introduced several radical innovations, including the reading of prayers in German, vernacular preaching, a confirmation ceremony, and the use of organ music. However, in the remote towns and villages, Jacobson's innovations were not well received by the more tradition-minded Jews of Westphalia. Even rabbis employed by the consistory as teachers were determined to preserve Judaism's ancient beliefs and practices and continued to instruct their students accordingly.[14]

The collapse of Napoleon's empire in the autumn of 1813, and along with it the fall of Jerome's kingdom and Jacobson's consistory, ushered in an era of political reaction. Almost immediately, the civil rights Jews had received from the French were jeopardized. In 1815, opponents of Jewish emancipation at the Congress of Vienna succeeded in creating a loophole in the constitution of the German Federation permitting states to independently review their Jewish populations' civic status. The clear intent of the new legislation was to restore Jews to their pre-emancipatory status as resident aliens.[15]

"Anti-Jewish feelings revived in the post-Napoleonic period," writes Samuel N. Stern, "not only because the political and economic emancipation of the Jews was regarded as one of the Napoleonic reforms that had to be removed, but also [because] of a spiritual and cultural reaction, an expression of a Christian-Teutonic, Romantic, and nationalist *Weltanschauung*."[16] Jews, the Romantics argued, were not Germans as long as they retained either their ethnic or religious distinctiveness. The intellectual, political, and spiritual challenges to the Jewish community seemed overwhelming. In fact, an entire generation passed before German Jews began to systematically incorporate Romanticism into their own justification for self-preservation as a unique entity. By that time, however, Leeser had already left the continent and resettled in America, where Jewish civic equality was more certain, having been guaranteed as part of the grander concept of "religious freedom" written into federal and state constitutions alike.[17]

How much Leeser knew of the sweeping changes in Jewish life that occurred during his childhood in Germany is difficult to determine. First, he was only seventeen when he left Europe for America. Second, in the vast body of literature he produced during his lifetime, he wrote very little about his childhood. Perhaps he did not want to be reminded of this painful period in his life or the unfortunate circumstances that compelled him to leave his family in Europe to seek a new life, alone, in the United States. Or he might have downplayed his background, as did other Jewish religious leaders in the pre-Civil War era trying to conceal their lack of training. A few, such as Isaac Mayer Wise, the most important leader in American Reform Judaism, simply invented academically respectable pasts for themselves. And yet, although Leeser said little about himself, what he did report was largely accurate.

Leeser was named for his mother's father, Isaac Ha-Cohen (that is, of priestly descent). His mother's name was Sarah; he never reported the name of his maternal grandmother. His mother's brother, Zalma, who adopted the name of his hometown, Rehine (pronounced "Rhine"), as his surname, emigrated to America in 1788. Leeser's mother longed to join her successful brother in America and planted favorable ideas about the United States in young Isaac's mind.[18]

Leeser chose the name of his grandfather on his father's side, Eliezer, as his family name (Eliezer, Liezer, Leeser). His paternal grandmother, Gitla, had a profound influence on him, especially after his mother died in 1814. Leeser's father, who did not remarry, asked his own mother to come to Dulmen, where the family had lived since 1810, to raise his three children. Emily Solis-Cohen, an unpublished biographer of Leeser who had access to oral information from those who knew him, called his Grandmother Gitla a "sage among women."

19

Isaac, she writes, "remembered how he sat gravely by her side while she answered questions brought by her neighbors. Jewish women consulted her on matters of religious procedure, Christian women on the ordinary affairs of life. She was pious, intelligent, charitable and beloved." In later years, Leeser was taunted by his detractors for practicing a "grandmother's religion."[19]

Eliezer and Gitla had four children: Jacob, Hyman, Abraham, and Leeser's father, Uri, who adopted the surname Lippman. Leeser was close to his cousins, especially the children of Jacob. One of Jacob's sons, Hayyim, later became a minister at Lübeck and published a modest Hebrew grammar, *Halichoth Leshon Ha-Kodesh* (1864).[20] Another, Selig, who also went by his Hebrew name, Salomon, became an obstetrician and settled in Berlin during the 1840s.[21] When their father died, Leeser's cousins were taken into custody by their uncle, Abraham, a hazzan and shochet (ritual butcher).[22] Hyman was a businessman who lived in Elberfeld, a town in the Rhineland.[23]

Leeser's father, Uri Lippman, was a merchant of humble means who did not enjoy good health, especially during the last nineteen years of his life.[24] All three of his children were born in Neuenkirchen. Isaac was the middle child. The oldest, Leah, married a shochet and unsuccessful exporter, Hirsch Elkus, and settled in Denekamp, Holland, a small town situated near the German border north of Enschede.[25] Jacob, the youngest of the three, was born in 1809 and, like his brother, emigrated to America at the request of Zalma Rehine, in 1832.[26] (Unfortunately, he died two years later at the age of twenty-five.[27])

When Leeser was four years old, his family left Neuenkirchen and resettled in Dulmen, a slightly larger town that lay on a main road to the provincial capital of Münster. Leeser never offered an explanation for the move. Emily Solis-Cohen, however, suggests that "Neuenkirchen had neither *melamed* [private Hebrew teacher] nor rabbi, and Uri [Lippman] did not trust himself as his children's teacher," whereas Dulmen had a *heder* with a good reputation. It is also possible that Leeser's father's business was adversely affected by the Napoleonic campaigns, which drained Westphalia of men and money, and that the family moved to Dulmen in search of new economic opportunities.[28]

Jewish scholarship played little part in the Leeser household. Leeser described his father as a "pious" but not a learned Jew. One book Leeser mentioned as present in his childhood home was a German translation of the Bible prepared for women and "printed in the year 5439 of the Jewish era," which corresponds to 1679.[29] Most likely, the folio edition Bible to which Leeser referred was a translation by either Jekuthiel Blitz or Joseln Witzenhausen. Both works appeared simultaneously at Amsterdam in the years 1676–79, and both received rabbinical endorsements. Rabbi Jacob ben Isaac Ashkenazi's *Tsena U-Rena*, the most popular religious book among Jewish women of the period, was also mentioned by Leeser. It was first printed in Krakow in 1620.[30]

Leeser lived in Dulmen for ten years, from the age of four through fourteen, and considered it his hometown. "The people," he later recalled, "were pious without running into extravagances."[31] In 1810, his father enrolled him in Dulmen's Jewish school. Leeser's first teacher, Rabbi Benjamin Jacob Cohen (Katz), made a lasting impression upon him. Twenty-four years later, when Leeser published his first work, under the title *The Jews and the Mosaic Law*, he intended to dedicate it to "this excellent guide of my infancy" when he learned of his mentor's death in 1833.[32] "From the simple school, the *Heder* so-called of Dulmen," Leeser wrote in 1861, "has spread the great progress in Hebrew literature not so universal in Westphalia, and there is another besides us in this country, our friend James K. Gutheim, of New Orleans, who has profited by the same spirit which impelled us onward."[33] So Leeser revealed the scope of this early influence.

Rabbi Cohen, although an inspiring teacher, was not a scholar of great distinction. In fact, very little is known about him. According to Moshe Davis, he was a native of Amsterdam and had once studied with Ezekiel Landau (1713–93), also known as the *Noda Bi-Yehuda*,[34] of Prague, an accomplished halachic authority. Perhaps it was via Rabbi Cohen that Leeser inherited some of Landau's proclivities. Landau vigorously opposed Hasidism and the study of kabbalistic (mystical) literature, supported the traditional element among the *maskilim* (proponents of the *Haskalah*), and even gave his approbation to books on history, grammar, and the natural sciences. In one of his best-known halachic rulings, he granted permission to shave during the intermediate days of a festival, a decision that caused a storm of controversy among his less lenient colleagues.[35]

On Saturday afternoons, Rabbi Cohen gave a *shiur* (lesson) on the Torah portion of the week. Fond of the *midrashim*, rabbinic legends that expound on Biblical texts, the *melamed* also familiarized his students with such homiletical works as *The Vintage of Ephraim* (1590), by "the celebrated Rabbi Ephraim Luntshetz," a traveling preacher whose works flourished in late-sixteenth-century Prague as well as in cities in Galicia and Poland. Later, Leeser regretted that the tradition of giving such *shiurim* was not continued in America.[36]

To a large extent, Leeser's early education was typical of that of the *heder* of the pre-emancipation period. It consisted, on the elementary level, of Torah translated into the spoken language and, on the secondary level, of Rashi's widely accepted eleventh-century commentary on the Torah. At the age of ten, students began to study *Mishnah* and, at fifteen, *Gemara*, the two principal strata of the *Talmud*. Thus, the basics of Judaism were acquired through a study of classical sources. The catechetical approach to the study of "religion" was just beginning in Jewish circles, and Leeser, who later translated German Jewish catechisms into English, never indicated that he was familiar with this new form of pedagogy while he lived in Europe.[37]

"Since the child attended class from morning until evening," writes Herman Pollack in his *Jewish Folkways in Germanic Lands (1648–1806)*, "the *heder*, or elementary school, had considerable influence on his most formative years from the age of five to thirteen." Pollack continues:

> During the winter months, the child rises one or two hours before daybreak and proceeds to school, held in the teacher's home. He is in class until it is time for the morning prayers, and after services, when there is a recess, he goes home for a snack. At the "fifth hour," or eleven o'clock, the pupil has another recess, lasting an hour, during which he returns home for his noonday meal. A short afternoon break takes place at three o'clock, the "ninth hour," so that he can again go home to eat and refresh himself. Following the recess, he remains in school until evening, attends services, and returns home. In summer months, he awakens in the early morning and after the morning prayers goes to school.[38]

Moshe Davis reports a quaint story from this period. As a new student in Rabbi Cohen's *heder*, Leeser paid close attention to the older students' repetition of the Torah portion *Ha'azinu* (Deuteronomy 32:1–52). At the examination, one of the upperclassmen forgot a verse. Leeser promptly supplied the missing words by whispering them to the embarrassed student. The teacher overheard Leeser and asked him how he happened to memorize the difficult passage. Leeser told his teacher that he had memorized *Ha'azinu* in its entirety simply by listening to the other students. He then proceeded to recite and translate the portion. Pleased by this demonstration, Rabbi Cohen gave his star pupil an honored seat by his side along the eastern wall of the *heder*.[39]

While Davis's story cannot be confirmed, Leeser was most likely an excellent student as a youth, and it is certainly true that as an adult he displayed a remarkable memory. This can be partly explained by the fact that he had very poor eyesight: it is possible that to compensate for this weakness he developed both his auditory skills and his ability to memorize vast amounts of information.

It is difficult to determine to what extent, if any, Jacobson's educational reforms in the Westphalia Consistory affected the school in Dulmen. According to Mordecai Eliav, a leading historian of Jewish education in Germany, the consistory's new program reduced Jewish studies to one-third of the curriculum in its schools and introduced many secular subjects, including German writing, French, mathematics, history, geography, nature, and drawing. Additional courses, such as Latin and logic, were also available if parents requested and paid for them. In many instances, local gentiles were employed by the consistory to teach some of the new classes. Though in some places the changes were accepted, many Jews in the small towns and villages (*Stockjuden*) were opposed to the reforms. In nearby Paderborn, for instance, parents insisted that rabbis continue to teach their children up to the age of thirteen.[40]

In 1813, when Leeser was seven, Germany was liberated from French rule, and the last of Napoleon's troops returned to the west bank of the Rhine. Jerome's kingdom was absorbed by Prussia, which had emerged as the most powerful of the German states. The Prussians dismantled the consistory, but they did not reinstate the *Landjudenschaft*. The Jews of Westphalia were then left without any organizational structure. The result was chaos, especially in the schools, where neither a tax base nor a supervisory staff existed to restore the former status quo.[41]

Abraham Sutro (1784–1869), a rabbi who had previously taught at the consistory school at Beverungen, was appointed to the new position of district rabbi (*Landesrabbiner*) of Münster and Mark in 1815 by a provisional government to restore order in the Jewish community. According to Sutro's most recent biographer, Lawrence Grossman, the new *Landesrabbiner* "was part of the first generation of German rabbis who combined strict traditionalism with certain innovations. . . . He wore an old-fashioned beard, and was one of the first rabbis to deliver German sermons."

Born near Erlangen, Bavaria, Sutro attended the renowned Fürth Yeshiva, where he studied Jewish law under Rabbi Wolf Hamburg. Later, he received full rabbinical ordination from Rabbi Menahem Mendel Steinhardt, a leading religious authority in the Westphalia Consistory. In 1836, Sutro published a scathing attack on Reform Judaism, *Sefer Milhamot Adonai* ("Book of the Wars of the Lord"), and although some of his legal decisions were lenient, he always remained an Orthodox Jew and well within the "fence around the Torah."[42]

Sutro's role as *Landesrabbiner* was highly problematic. The government limited his political power in the Jewish community and refused to give him funds to operate Jewish schools in his district, and many of the Jews in the city of Münster objected to his appointment because of his traditionalism and refused to recognize his authority. In addition, the borders of his jurisdiction were disputed in the confusion that followed the Prussian absorption of Westphalia. For the most part, he served as a bureaucrat and oversaw Jewish religious and educational activity in the outlying districts, especially in the *heder* schools, or *hadarim*.[43]

Leeser initially came into contact with Sutro in Dulmen in 1815. "I well remember the time," Leeser recollected in 1836, "when scarcely nine summers had passed over my head, that you arrived among us; and how the first sermon I ever heard delivered, the one you addressed to our congregation, made a powerful impression upon us all, not excepting the little unconscious boy I then was."[44] Leeser adds later, "We can yet remember how [Sutro] denounced the indifference of the rich who are satisfied that the poor should be religious, and compared them to Catholics, who urge their servants and poorer classes to attend public processions while they themselves disdain to mingle with the promiscuous throngs."[45]

Leeser also recalled Sutro's activity as superintendent of Westphalia's schools. "Mr. Sutro at once set about improving the school-system of the congregations in his district," Leeser writes in 1861, and "for several years travelled about every summer to examine the various schools, bringing scholars of the several towns and villages, situated near each other, together, that the proficiency in one might stimulate all; and he only ceased when the work was in hopeful progress."[46]

It is unlikely that Leeser studied Talmud with Sutro on a formal basis or that the district rabbi encouraged him to be a preacher, yet in the "dedication" to his first volume of sermons, Leeser wrote to Sutro, "You always seconded the efforts of my blessed teacher."[47] Whereas Leeser occasionally wrote about what he studied with Rabbi Cohen in Dulmen, he did not report anything specific about his alleged student-teacher relationship with Sutro.[48] Indeed, Bernhard Brilling, a historian of Westphalian Jewry, reports that in 1824, when the Prussian authorities suggested to Sutro that he serve as a classroom teacher to help relieve the shortage of Jewish instructors in the area, he refused on the grounds that his role as rabbi was contractually limited to *Zeremonialgesetzen*.[49] In any event, Sutro and Leeser developed a lifelong friendship.[50]

In 1820 tragedy led Leeser to leave Dulmen and resettle in Münster, the seat of the *Oberrabbiner*, the regional, administrative rabbi. First Leeser's father and then his grandmother "were borne to the grave in the course of three weeks and left us orphaned in a double degree in the wide world."[51] Later, in 1829, when Leeser responded to a series of articles first published in the *London Quarterly Review* that attacked Judaism—asserting that it offered none of its adherents, neither sinners nor saints, the comfort of the world to come—he described his last moments with his father to demonstrate the deep consoling powers of his ancestral faith:

> He had been confined to his bed for three weeks previous; and I left him to go to the house of one of my uncles, who did not live far off. About nightfall my father felt all at once his strength failing fast, and therefore sent for me to give me his last blessing and his last injunctions, as it is customary among us. I cannot describe my feelings, which were very acute, though I was but fourteen years old, when I approached his bed. He laid his hands upon my head, and pronounced the blessing with which the dying patriarch Jacob had prophesied the Israelites should always bless their children, and the blessings which, by the ordinance of God, the family of Aaron are commanded to bless the congregation (Numbers 6). My father saw how much I felt, and how deeply I was affected; and he therefore said to me in the most collected and calm manner: "Weep not for me; for my being longer in this world would be painful to me, and of no use to you, though I would recover. As for yourself, be an honest man and a good Jew, and God will never forsake you. Now go, my son; for your remaining any longer with me might disturb me, and distress you too much." I then left his presence . . . Soon after I was gone, the members of the Jewish congregation began to assemble to pray at the couch of their dying brother. He prayed with them as long as he was able, then laid himself composedly down, and departed this life without a struggle. Those who saw his death, those who heard of it, said, "May my end be like this." Thus died my father, and though poor, he left a reputation unsullied, and a memory respected by Jews and Christians alike.[52]

As an adult, Leeser championed the cause of orphans and destitute children, not only because he himself had suffered as a child but because an anonymous benefactor had rescued him and his siblings. On Thanksgiving Day in 1836, Leeser told the Society for the Education of Poor Children at Shearith Israel Congregation in New York about the desperate situation in which he found himself after his father's death. "Was [this orphan] now left to struggle in hopelessness and sickening toil for a scanty and tearful support? No; for there was a man, beloved of God and honored of all that knew him, who, though blest with but small means, had yet always a mite for those that were needy. He felt for the orphan-boy, took him as his own child, watched over his youth with paternal care, instructed him in the way of righteousness, and taught him to fear the Creator, and to look to Him for support in all his afflictions."[53]

Leeser's benefactor also arranged for him to continue his studies at a "university" in Münster. Permission for Jewish students to enroll at the local *gymnasium* was one of the benefits secured during the brief French occupation of Westphalia. However, the Prussians stripped the school in Münster of its university status, which it had obtained in 1771 through the efforts of the Münster secretary of state, Franz Friedric von Koningsegg-Rothenfels. In 1818, the school was temporarily closed after a debate about its Catholic status erupted. The Protestant government decided to establish a new university under its own auspices in Bonn but allowed the Münster school to reopen as an "institute" with a limited faculty.[54]

What led Leeser to pursue a secular education is unknown. "At fourteen years old," he stated simply, "I left Hebrew school and learned worldly things."[55] By 1820 there already was a trend among modernizing Orthodox Jews to seek a secular education. Samson Raphael Hirsch (1808–1888), the great champion of neo-orthodoxy, attended the University of Bonn for a year (1829). And even ultraorthodox rabbis, such as Isaac Bernays (1729–1849) and Jacob Ettlinger (1798–1871), studied at the University of Würzburg.[56]

Even with its reduced status, the school at Münster demanded that its students follow a rigorous course of studies. During the two and a quarter years he attended the Münster Institute, Leeser studied Latin, Greek, history, geography, trigonometry, and physics.[57] In a letter to Rabbi Benjamin Cohen, he described the difficult routine:

> Here there is much to be done. The headmaster requires that each day's task be completed. I have to keep myself awake every night until the hour of midnight if I am to finish my work with satisfaction. Were I to fail, I would be asked, 'Why did you not complete your work either yesterday or today?' Then I should be beaten with the rod of fools. This has happened to many of my companions, but to me only once.[58]

However, Leeser felt no resentment toward his teachers, some of whom were Jesuit priests. "The Jewish young men," he wrote, "were just as much honored as any of the Christian students."[59] In fact, the school even had a Jewish *Privatdozent* (assistant professor), Alexandar Hainsdorf (1782–1872), who taught in the medical sciences.[60]

In 1825 (after Leeser had left Münster) Hainsdorf founded an institute for the advancement of crafts among Jews and for the training of Jewish elementary school teachers. Its principal, also one of its instructors, was a friend of Leeser's, Rabbi Baer S. Cohen.[61] Leeser's first cousin, Hayyim, was one of the school's earliest graduates, and proudly wrote to America about its program.[62] Hainsdorf even won the endorsement of the *Oberrabbiner* for providing modern training for Jews. However, Rabbi Sutro strongly objected to Hainsdorf's more radical aspirations "to promote the amalgamation of Judaism and Christianity."[63]

Joseph L. Blau correctly concludes about Leeser that "to the extent that he developed at all as a [Jewish] scholar, [he] was self-taught."[64] In Germany, he received only the rudiments of Jewish education. To friends and detractors he freely admitted, "I do not pretend to be a great Talmudist," and "[I] had not the best opportunities of acquiring [Jewish] knowledge."[65] Leeser's distinction from the other American hazzanim, at least during the 1830s, was that he had received a solid, secular education. Moreover, he was by nature intellectually tenacious and continued to study both Jewish and general literature throughout his life.

In a highly idealized "Personal Recollection" of Leeser written in 1901, Rosa Mordecai sheds additional light on Leeser's last years in Europe, she maintains that he completed his studies at the university in 1822 and then spent two years "of a rather wandering life, teaching what he had acquired to those even younger than himself and receiv[ing] in return, sometimes, only food and shelter, at others, a small pittance that was always spent upon his little stock of books."[66] While the scenario she portrays is uncorroborated by any primary source, it rings true.

Being neither adventurous or robust, Leeser, to have agreed to his uncle Zalma Rehine's invitation to join him in the States, must have despaired of any personal success in Germany. For his part, Zalma must have supplied the pull by promising his nephew a good life in Richmond, Virginia.[67] Zalma's invitation and Leeser's acceptance reflected a growing interest on both sides of the Atlantic in encouraging immigration to the United States. On June 1, 1822, the Verein für Cultur und Wissenschaft der Juden, a society of young, Jewish intellectuals in Berlin, wrote a letter to Mordecai Manuel Noah (1785–1851), the best-known Jewish American citizen, "about the means of promoting the emigration of European Jews to the United States." Noah published the letter in the *Commercial Advertiser*, an influential New York newspaper, which added an encouraging prefatory note: "The wealth and enterprize of the Jews would be a great auxiliary to the commercial and manufacturing, if not agricultural, interests of the United States."[68] Other factors, such as the loosening of governmental restrictions to emigration, the return of peace to the North Atlantic, and technological advances in ocean travel, all added to the rising tide of immigration during the 1820s.[69]

Leeser's decision to go to America electrified his family. After complaining of her life as "a housekeeper . . . in charge of seven children," Leeser's sister Leah expressed her approval and added, "I, too, am not disposed to remain here." His uncle Abraham added that he also "should much like to make the journey with you, provided of course that it meets with your wishes."[70] In the end, however, Leeser voyaged alone; neither his uncle nor his sister ever left Europe.

Securing the necessary releases from his obligations in Münster, Leeser started his journey to the United States in late February, 1824.[71] It took nearly three months to cross the ocean. The long and difficult passage terrified the young traveler. Fifteen years later he described his transatlantic trip in a eulogy at the funeral of his friend and mentor Isaac B. Seixas. "When I had crossed the broad Atlantic Ocean," Leeser reminisced, "and had escaped by the almost miraculous interposition of Providence from the fury of the equinotical [sic] storm and the raging of the mountain billows, and when I recovered from a painful illness after my arrival on these shores, and when I repaired to the house of God: it was Mr. Seixas' voice I first heard lifted up in prayer to the throne of Grace, and in his presence it was that I returned thanks for the undeserved mercy that had been shown to me."[72]

Now that Leeser had come to America he was in the custody of his sixty-seven-year-old maternal uncle. Rehine assisted Leeser in his Americanization and quickly became a trusted source of personal advice and reassurance to the young foreigner. He introduced his nephew to his friends and made him feel welcome in his home.

"It may be," Lawrence Grossman has suggested, "that Leeser's fundamental ideas on matters of religion were part of the intellectual baggage that he brought across the Atlantic."[73] Without question, Leeser already was a modernizing orthodox Jew when he emigrated to the United States. Like his Jewish teachers, especially Rabbi Benjamin Jacob Cohen, he remained loyal to traditional Jewish beliefs and practices. Within that context, he was willing to accommodate non-Jewish practices that did not contravene Jewish religious law or touch on the traditional doctrines of Judaism. However, his willingness to modernize Jewish life exceeded that of his childhood mentors. He had received a solid foundation in the sciences and the humanities. Like Jacobson,

he envisioned new forms of Jewish self-governance in an age of republican ideology. Like Hainsdorf, he favored developing a modern system
of Jewish education.

America, and particularly antebellum Richmond, had a still more
decisive, liberating impact on Leeser. In five years, he was transformed
from a shy, studious schoolboy into a public spokesman for his ancestral faith. "I waited," he wrote in 1829, "but found no one in this
country, older than myself, attempting to enlighten the minds of my
brethren; I could therefore no longer remain silent—I felt called upon
to act, and I obeyed the inward call, not unmindful of what Hillel the
ancient said: 'And in a place, where there is no man, try even thyself
to be a man.' "[74]

2

RICHMOND:
AMERICAN REBIRTH, 1824–1829

Mr. Isaac Leeser, is a young gentleman who has resided a few years among us, I can confidently recommend as a person of steady habits, of moral worth, a strict observer of our religious rites, possessing a cultivated mind, capable of instructing your children in Hebrew and with a little practice will be enabled to discharge the duties of hazzan.
—Jacob Mordecai, letter to Raphael de Cordova, June 10, 1824

"ISAAC LEESER," OBSERVES MALCOLM H. Stern, was "a product of 1820s thinking."[1] He arrived in the United States on May 5, 1824, and by the end of the decade was thoroughly Americanized.[2] His uncle Zalma Rehine and the Jewish community of Richmond, Virginia, served as his guides to life in a new land. Not only did they teach him about America but they also recognized his potential as a leader in the Jewish community and directed him toward a career in the "ministry."

By 1824, America was a vast country whose population exceeded ten million. Most of the leaders of the Revolutionary period had died and the Jeffersonian Republican Party was breaking up into factions. When none of the four contenders for the presidency obtained a majority in the electoral college that year, the matter was sent to the House of Representatives to be resolved. A deal between John Quincy Adams of Massachusetts and Henry Clay of Kentucky, called the "corrupt bargain" by its opponents, resulted in the former being elected president and the latter receiving the position of secretary of state in the Cabinet. President Adams was a supporter of Clay's "American system," a proposal to arrange sectional interests in a national harmony. However, the majority of Americans preferred a laissez-faire approach to internal improvements. Thus, the new administration immediately found itself caught in a political stalemate that lasted for four frustrating years.[3]

A majority of Americans were also ambivalent about the changing economic structure of their society. While they wanted to preserve the virtues of Jeffersonian republicanism and tended to romanticize the agrarian way of life, they also threw themselves into the economic scramble of their day. To harmonize their world view, they seized on the idea of self-reliance. The ordinary man, it was widely believed, through hard, honest work, could achieve anything he wanted whether he was a farmer or a mechanic.[4]

Whatever his personal convictions, Andrew Jackson, the hero of New Orleans (1815), became the symbol of the new egalitarian movement. His mass appeal lay in the fact that he was both a great and an ordinary person. In 1828 he successfully ran against Adams in an election disgraced on both sides by vicious character assassination, hyperbole, and lies. The coalition of forces that brought him to power remained intact for a generation, and its democratic philosophy revolutionized American life.[5]

The new egalitarianism had its greatest impact on suffrage. At the beginning of the nineteenth century, only three of the fifteen states granted the vote to all white men regardless of property. By 1860, all but seven states in a Union of thirty states extended the ballot to white males, rich and poor. Moreover, governors and members of the electoral college were chosen by popular vote instead of by state legislatures. Most striking of all, between 1846 and 1853, thirteen states made various judicial posts subject to the direct pleasure of the people.[6]

Certain social changes also reflected "the rise of the common man." Concern for the improvement of the ordinary citizen led to the beginning of the free-school movement, an interest in adult education (through lyceums), and the slow spread of secondary education. Beginning in the 1830s, penny newspapers were appearing whose editors made a concerted effort to bring political news to the attention of the "common man." Even the effort to disestablish churches in several states revealed a dislike of special privileges.[7]

Egalitarianism strongly influenced religion in America also. Resurgent Protestantism sought to make Americans a church-going people. Missionary activity increased at home and abroad, with striking results. During the first three decades of the nineteenth century, church membership in the United States doubled. Between 1807 and 1834 Presbyterian communicant membership increased from 18,000 to 248,000. The American Bible Society (1816) and the American Tract

31

Society (1825) succeeded in broadly disseminating religious literature in all sectors of American society. Members of leading Protestant denominations established numerous seminaries and colleges to fortify Protestantism's intellectual foundations and spread its teachings. Alexis de Tocqueville observed upon his arrival in the Unites States in 1831 that "there is no country in the world in which the Christian religion retains a greater influence over the souls of men than in America."[8]

From his vantage point in Richmond, Leeser observed and internalized the great issues of the day. Jeffersonian republicanism was so appealing to him that he ascribed divine origins to it. Writing in 1828, he asserted: "It has been intimated that the institutions of the *republic* of the North American confederacy are of modern invention; but this cannot be admitted as altogether founded on fact, for the Mosaic code was evidently intended to form a republic of *freemen*, who were all equally entitled to protection from the government."[9]

To Leeser, "protection from the government" meant, above all else, freedom from religious coercion. "The chief excellence" of the American plan of government, he wrote, was that it "recognizes the broad principle of universal equality in the eyes of the law of all its citizens, and maintains the right of each individual to think for himself on matters of belief and religion." For the Jews, he continued, the doctrine of the separation of church and state meant safety "from molestation from the combined forces of the enemies of Israel and those of equal rights."[10] Of course, to Leeser, like other peers of his generation, "equal rights" only applied to white males and not to women, blacks, or Native Americans.

Leeser endorsed the idea that the true function of religion was "to lead the individual soul [and] not to interfere in politics." He also believed that political discussion had no place in religion.[11] He even sought to separate "temporal and spiritual" functions within the synagogue itself. Thus, he fought against the notion of a "national religion" in America, and strongly objected to the introduction of secular politics into Jewish religious discourse. "In the Synagogue and congregational meetings," he wrote, "we want Jews; in public matters, only American citizens."[12] Consequently, he rarely stated any particular political views of his own, except for such stray comments as an endorsement of the policies of the Democratic Party in the late 1850s.[13]

Leeser was also deeply influenced by egalitarianism. He fostered the development of schools, introduced preaching into the American synagogue as a form of religious education for adults, and established the first successful Jewish "newspaper" in the United States. He insisted that no matter how great his personal accomplishments, he was just an ordinary person. In a eulogy for the late president William Henry Harrison, Leeser summarized his American credo: "that virtue and moderation, joined to a straightforward line of conduct, are well calculated and will pre-eminently conduce to acquire for use the favour of God and man."[14]

Finally, Leeser was profoundly influenced by antebellum Protestantism. He was even willing to adopt some of its practices and theological emphases that did not conflict with traditional Judaism. While in Richmond, he helped organize the Jewish Sunday school. To those in the Jewish community who objected to this "imitation of gentile practice," Leeser later replied, "It is the first duty of Israel to instill knowledge of divine things in the hearts of the young, and this institution [the Sunday school] was eminently calculated to bestow this necessary blessing alike upon rich and poor without fee or price."[15] Later, he helped establish the sermon in the American synagogue, largely in imitation of Protestant practice, and called for the development of a Jewish ministry in the United States distinct from the traditional rabbinate.

Leeser learned about Jeffersonian republicanism, Jacksonian egalitarianism, and American Protestantism during his years in Richmond. Although he had non-Jewish friends, he spent the majority of his time with Zalma, his family, and the Jewish community in the city. He prayed with them, taught in their school, and discussed intellectual matters with the more learned individuals among them. From the Jews of Richmond he also learned about the realities of Jewish life in America and about his potential role in the American Jewish community.

The Richmond Jewish community of 1825–29, of which Leeser was a part, typified the American Jewish community in general. In 1820, the total Jewish population of the United States was 2,700 to 3,000. Through marriage, American Jews had nearly become one large family, and even though they had not created a single national organization, they were in constant communication with one another. Unlike the general population, of whom less than 10 percent lived in towns of more than 2,500 people, the vast majority of Jews lived in five cities: New York, Philadelphia, Richmond, Charleston, and Savannah. They engaged in commerce and generally achieved a level of affluence that allowed them "the time and the means to advance themselves culturally and educationally."[16]

33

During the course of the next ten years, American Jewry began to expand dramatically, both numerically and geographically. By 1830, the Jewish population of the country had grown to between four and six thousand as the result of immigration. Leeser himself was in the vanguard of the movement. Along with other pioneers, individual Jews began to move into the vast interior of the continent. Chain migrations and random settlement resulted in the founding of new communities. In 1824, the first congregation west of the Alleghenies, Bene Israel, was established in Cincinnati. Four years later, Congregation Shaarei Chesed was chartered in New Orleans.[17]

The possibility of mass Jewish immigration to the United States inspired a few individuals to draw up plans for large-scale Jewish colonies on the American frontier. Their schemes were inspired by a combination of religious messianism and a more mundane hope to reap personal profit through land speculation and real estate development. The most celebrated plan for "an Asylum for the Jews" was proposed by Mordecai Manuel Noah in 1820. He petitioned the New York legislature, "requesting that it survey, value, and sell him Grand Island in the Niagara River to serve as a colony for Jews in the New World." He named his project Ararat, for the mountain where Noah's ark came to rest after the flood and where the rebuilding of civilization began. After five years of inactivity, an opening ceremony took place at St. Paul's Episcopal Church in Buffalo with Noah presiding as "judge of Israel." Except for local newspapers, which hoped Ararat would attract people and capital to their region, it was widely ridiculed, especially by American Jews.[18]

The Sephardic elite certainly had a different understanding of Jewish communal life in America than that embodied in Noah's Ararat scheme. To them, Jewish life was primarily urban. They believed in managing but not planning Jewish group life. Unlike Noah, they maintained but did not trumpet their identities as Jews. In private, they were generally lax in their religious observance. During the Colonial Period, they established a strong tradition of lay dominance. Their synagogue-communities were governed by a "junta" or "adjunta," a board of trustees that hired religious functionaries to lead services, teach their children Hebrew, and provide the community with kosher meat. The board itself was presided over by a "parnass," usually a leading Jewish citizen, who had extensive power in the government of the congregation. To define the duties of the various officers, determine eligibility for membership, and comply with state law, the congregations wrote and adopted "constitutions" during the early decades of the nineteenth century.[19]

In the absence of ordained rabbis in America (a condition that prevailed until the 1840s), the hazzan, a semitrained religious offici- ant, had already become the principal Jewish religious specialist in the American synagogue prior to the Revolution. The office of hazzan was not held in high esteem by the Jewish laity. Hazzanim served under the direct control and strict supervision of the congregational board of trustees, which expected the religious functionaries to comply with their wishes. Although the hazzan was expected to perform a wide range of duties, his salary was meager, and frequently he had to peti- tion the congregational board for additional funds or goods to cover the basic needs of his family.[20]

To some extent, the eighteenth-century American hazzan was more like a Protestant minister than a traditional rabbi. Several factors contributed to this early evolution of the American Jewish ministry. First, Jews frequently had to be represented to the general public by a clergyman, and the hazzan was the only official who could serve in that role. Second, early American Jews had very little Jewish knowl- edge, and however poorly trained their hazzanim were, they were still the only available resident experts in Jewish law. (Questions that could not be answered by the hazzanim or learned laymen were sent to rab- bis in Europe, especially England.) Finally, in 1784 New York author- ized the performance of the marriage ceremony by only a minister of religion or a justice of the peace. State laws of incorporation for reli- gious societies often specified other ministerial functions as well.[21]

Gershom M. Seixas (1746–1816), by virtue of his exceptional per- sonality, was the first to demonstrate the full potential of the office of hazzan in America. He was respected by the two congregations he served, Shearith Israel (New York, 1768–76 and 1784–1816) and Mickveh Israel (Philadelphia, 1780–1784) and was considered a col- league by many Christian clergymen. He also served as a trustee of Columbia College.[22]

Seixas, like other hazzanim of the period, also acted as the teacher of the congregational school. Jewish education during the Colonial and Early National periods was "a rather haphazard affair," in the words of historian Jacob R. Marcus. Teaching materials were of poor quality and the book holdings of the schools insignificant. The schools were plagued by financial problems. An unsteady flow of income from tuition and congregational and state subsidies made the administration of the small institutions very problematic. There was a nearly constant turnover of teachers, and each instructor had his own curriculum. Seixas, for example, "taught not only Hebrew but also secular subjects, reading, writing, and cyphering."[23]

The sad state of affairs in the synagogues and the congregational schools did not remain unchallenged. On December 23, 1824, a group of forty-seven Jews in Charleston, South Carolina, met under the leadership of a thirty-six-year-old educator and dramatist, Isaac Harby (1788–1828), and his friend, Abraham Moise. On behalf of the group, Moise drew up a petition requesting a variety of changes including shorter services, use of the vernacular during worship, improved instruction for their children, and the replacement of public solicitation of "offerings" with annual dues. The board of the local synagogue, Beth Elohim, determined that the petition was unconstitutional and took no further action on the suggested reforms. Undeterred, Harby and his followers organized the Reformed Society of Israelites (1824–33) and appointed a committee to prepare a new prayer book reflecting their religious sensibilities.[24]

At the first annual dinner of the Society, Harby gave a fiery address in which he explained the historical necessity of a Reform movement in Judaism and predicted its quick triumph among American Jews. A copy of the address was sent to Jacob Mordecai, an important leader in the Richmond Jewish community and a staunch traditionalist. Mordecai prepared a lengthy refutation and showed it to Leeser. Leeser later recalled, "We thought then, inexperienced though we were, that Mr. M. had the best of the argument."[25]

When Harby died in December 1828, Moise emerged as the central leader of the Reformed Society of Israelites. Although it liquidated its building fund in 1833, Moise kept the spiritual torch of the Reform movement lit until the end of the decade, when he again proposed major revisions in Jewish worship. However, during the 1820s and 1830s, the work of Harby and Moise was isolated. A more pervasive tension in the Jewish community at that time was ethnic and not religious.[26]

During the 1820s several incidents occurred that revealed the growing tension between the old, Americanized Jewish community and the new arrivals from Central Europe. In 1823, for instance, Congregation Mickveh Israel of Philadelphia stiffened requirements for an individual to become a full member (as opposed to a seatholder) of the synagogue community. The intent of the constitutional revision was to preserve the political power of the native-born Jews in the congregation by slowing down the absorption of new, Ashkenazic immigrants from Central Europe.[27]

For their part, many Ashkenazim were less than satisfied with the Sephardic congregations. In 1825, while the Reform controversy raged in Charleston, fifteen Ashkenazic members of New York's Shearith Israel formed an organization, Hebra Hinuch Nearim ("The Society for the Education of Youth"), and petitioned the trustees for the privilege to conduct their own services. The board immediately rejected the proposal. The dissidents held a series of meetings and on October 18 formally resolved to establish their own congregation, B'nai Jeshurun. In 1828, a second Ashkenazic synagogue, Ansche Chesed, was formed, and during the course of the 1830s still another three, bringing the total number of synagogues in New York City to six.[28]

The same pattern was repeated in Richmond, Virginia, but at a much slower pace. The Jewish population of the Virginian capital was small, even by American standards, and also physically isolated from the major centers of Jewish settlement in the country. In 1839 German Jews organized among themselves a group called Hevra Ahavat Yisrael ("The Love of Israel Society") that in 1841 was formally constituted as Congregation Beth Ahaba. A third congregation was not organized until 1856.[29] Thus, during Leeser's years in Richmond, 1824–29, the Jewish community was relatively free from internal strife along ethnic lines and still represented the heyday of Sephardic hegemony in American Jewish life.

The early history of the Jews of Richmond is well known. In their 1917 study, *The History of the Jews of Richmond*, Herbert T. Ezekiel and Gaston Lichtenstein report that by 1769 Isaiah Isaacs had already settled in Henrico County. In 1781 he formed a partnership with Jacob I. Cohen, dealing in merchandising, real estate, and slaves. They employed Daniel Boone to survey a large parcel of land they had purchased in Kentucky, and in 1782 they advanced James Madison "fifty pounds of currency" so he could attend the Federal Congress that year. In 1790 Cohen himself was chosen as a city councilman and thereby established a tradition of Jewish involvement in local politics that remained particularly active throughout the Early National Period.[30]

Congregation Beth Shalome was organized in 1789 and immediately joined four other synagogues in congratulating George Washington upon his inauguration as first president of the United States. In his reply to the Jewish congregations, Washington observed that "the liberality of sentiment toward each other, which marks every political and religious denomination of men in this country, stands unparalleled in the history of nations. . . . The affectionate expressions of your address excite my gratitude and receive my warmest acknowledgement."[31]

Although the twenty-nine original members of the congregation were enthusiastic about the great events of the day, they were less zealous in their religious observances. For thirty years, they met for worship at each other's homes or in a rented room at the Union Hotel.[32] Myron Berman, a historian of the Richmond Jewish community, has pointed out that "the isolation of Richmond's small Jewish population from the larger concentration of coreligionists was a factor inhibiting the celebration of the various festivals in the Jewish calendar."[33] Joseph Marx (1772–1840), a prominent merchant and acquaintance of Thomas Jefferson, even thought that the Jews should change their Sabbath to alleviate the problem: "Nothing has so seriously caused us to reject our religion as the Christian policy of adopting a different Sabbath. The force of example, at least, would carry Jews to the synagogue, when Christians mass to the Churches, nay there would not be the same clashing of interests, nor a day of labour lost."[34]

By 1820, there were approximately forty-one Jewish households in the city, or about two hundred individuals, enough people to sustain a more permanent arrangement for the practice of Judaism.[35] In 1822, the congregation erected its first building after successfully appealing to Jews throughout the country for funds. The modest brick structure stood on Mayo Street on the west side of the Shockoe Valley. In 1891 the building was sold to Sir Moses Montefiore Congregation, a newly formed Russian synagogue, and subsequently it was demolished to allow the rebuilding of Richmond's downtown area.[36]

Leeser's years in Richmond were among the happiest of his life. He made several life-long friends, read widely, and developed a sense of confidence in himself and about his future. In short, Leeser came of age in Richmond. His most cherished friend and guide was his uncle, Zalma Rehine.

Zalma Rehine was born in 1757 and at the age of thirty-two left his native Westphalia for a new life in America. He landed in Baltimore on the eve of Yom Kippur, the Day of Atonement, and from there made his way south to Richmond, where he went into the dry goods business. On October 25, 1799, he bought a lot and house near Bloodly Spring.[37] He was one of the original members of Beth Shalome and later served as a grand master of the Royal Arch of Masons. He also joined a local militia, the Richmond Light Infantry Blues, under the command of Capt. William Richardson, in 1789.[38]

In June 1807, at the height of the "Impressment Controversy" with Great Britain, the Blues volunteered to fight. On June 22, 1807, an English vessel, sailing in the tidewater section of the Chesapeake Bay, hailed an American ship, the Chesapeake. The British commander, Capt. Salisbury P. Humphreys, demanded to be allowed to muster the crew and search for four deserters. When the Americans resisted, the

British opened fire. Unprepared for action, the Chesapeake surrendered. The violation of American sovereignty in U.S. territorial water outraged the country. The public clamored for war.

The news of the Chesapeake Affair reached Richmond on June 27. Two days later, the Blues met and "tendered their services to President Jefferson." On July 8, eighty-three militiamen left Richmond for a five-day march to Portsmouth. Besides Rehine, three of his brothers-in-law joined in the expedition.[39] Realizing that the American soldiers were no match for the British, Jefferson contented himself with ordering the British out of American waters. To retaliate, he signed an ill-conceived Embargo Act, which had catastrophic effects on the American economy. Rehine and his compatriots returned home without having fired a single shot at a British soldier.[40]

As a businessman, Rehine was both financially successful and involved in local booster activities. In December 1804 he joined in an "annexation" campaign to extend the City of Richmond's western boundary. At the same time he signed a petition to the Virginia legislature that protested the behavior of "many Captains of the Northern trading vessels which frequent the Rivers and inlets of this Commonwealth." The boat operators were accused of having "established clandestine and marauding intercourse and traffic with the slaves," encouraging insurrection, and slave snatching. In 1815, he also signed a petition in favor of improving navigation on the James River.[41]

On January 15, 1800, Rehine married Rachel Judah. Rachel's large family—she was one of eleven children—was deeply involved in the Jewish communities of New York, Baltimore, and, especially, Richmond. Her mother, Abigail Seixas Judah, was a sister of Rev. Gershom Mendes Seixas. Rachel's brother, Isaac H. Judah, a prominent "vendue master" (auctioneer) in Richmond, served as the first reader of Beth Shalome. Her sister Rebecca married Isaac B. Seixas, a first cousin, who was the hazzan of Beth Shalome during Leeser's first four years in Richmond. Finally, another brother, Baruch Hillel Judah, was librarian of the Richmond Library Company. He took an interest in Leeser's studies and supplied him with a steady flow of books.[42] Thus, while Zalma taught Leeser about life in American society, Rachel's family helped him become an integral part of Jewish religious and cultural life in the United States.

Isaac B. Seixas (1781–1839) was very fond of Leeser. He taught the young German immigrant the Sephardic mode of worship and asked Leeser to assist him in teaching at the congregations's Sabbath and day school, the first of its kind. "A great part of my usefulness as a minister," Leeser gladly acknowledged, "was owing to his instruction."[43] However, Seixas was not much of a scholar. In an 1824 letter sent to Congregation Mickveh Israel in Philadelphia, the parnass of Beth Shalome, Jacob Mordecai, wrote without equivocation that Seixas "does not possess a Grammatical knowledge of the Hebrew language."[44] In 1828, he left Richmond to become the hazzan of Shearith Israel Congregation in New York, a post he held to his death in 1839. In Richmond, he was succeeded by Abraham Hyam Cohen, the son of Jacob Raphael Cohen, hazzan of Philadelphia's Mickveh Israel from 1784 to 1811. Besides his ministerial work, Seixas was also a merchant. Like other Jews in Richmond, he served in the Blues during the War of 1812 and was active in local politics.[45]

Jacob Mordecai (1762–1838), the parnass of Beth Shalome, had an even greater impact on Leeser than Seixas. "If Isaac Leeser qualified as the first authentic Jewish scholar in America because of his published works," observed Myron Berman, "certainly Jacob Mordecai was a legitimate precursor."[46] Mordecai took Leeser under his wing, introduced the young, eager student to contemporary English-language Christian theological literature, and discussed grammatical problems in biblical Hebrew with him. He was widely viewed by the Richmond Jewish community as the champion of Jewish traditionalism, and, as already mentioned, he wrote a refutation of the radical ideal of the Reformed Society of Israelites.

Besides Leeser, other young, scholarly Jews were attracted to Mordecai. Among them was Jacob Ezekiel, who moved to Richmond in 1834. In 1898, he recalled that

> Mr. Mordecai was always admired on account of his brilliant intellect, being well versed in Biblical research, the Hebrew language, and its literature; in fact, he was considered authority on many questions pertaining to Judaism and Biblical interpretations. I always found him very genial in deportment, and we became so much attached to each other that I felt it a pleasure to visit his home on Church Hill on Sabbath afternoons, and this became one of my weekly resorts.[47]

Mordecai was born in Philadelphia and was only thirteen years old when the Revolution broke out. In 1782 he moved to Richmond, married Judith Myers, and went into business. Unable to make a living in the city, he wandered in search of opportunity. The hardships proved too much for his frail wife. Judith died in 1796. Three years later, Mordecai married his sister-in-law, Rebecca. By that time, he had already settled in Warrenton, North Carolina. In 1809, he opened the Warrenton Female Seminary, which he ran successfully for ten years.

"Strange as it may seem," Herbert T. Ezekiel reflected in 1917, "hundreds of Southern girls received their education during the early part of the last century at a nonsectarian seminary conducted by a Jewish family."[48]

In 1819, the Mordecais returned to the Richmond area and bought a farm. Jacob Mordecai, an observant Jew throughout his life, began to take a prominent role within Richmond's Jewish community. He was chosen as parnass and on September 15, 1822, gave a lengthy sermon at the consecration of Beth Shalome's first building. He exhorted the members of the congregation to live as proud Jews, to pray with sincerity, and "to consider the whole human family" as the children of the same God.[49]

Mordecai's private, scholarly work was largely an attempt to demonstrate theological contradictions in Christianity and to prove that only Judaism interpreted the Bible correctly. During the 1830s, he prepared several lengthy manuscripts, including a two-hundred-page polemic entitled "Introduction to the New Testament" as well as critiques of Harriet Martineau's 1832 missionary tract *Providence as Manifested Through Israel* and Rev. Alexander Keith's *Evidence of the Truth of the Christian Religion*. Although Mordecai's analyses of Christian doctrines and literature were often more detailed than Leeser's, their basic line of argument and emphasis on theology were quite similar.

During his first few months in Richmond, Leeser also became acquainted with Israel Baer Kursheedt (1766–1852), who, although not an ordained rabbi, was widely viewed as the leading expert in Jewish law in America during the Early National Period. "Mr. Kursheedt," Leeser recalled in 1852, "was one of the oldest acquaintances we had in America, as we met him on the first day of our arrival in Richmond."

Kursheedt was born in a tiny village in the Rhineland, studied at the yeshiva of Rabbi Nathan Adler in Frankfurt, and later became a purveyor to the Prussian army in their struggle against the French. With the defeat of the Prussians, he left Germany and made his way to the United States in 1796. He went first to Boston, but finding no organized Jewish life there, he decided to go to New York, where he remained until 1812. While in New York he married Sarah Abigail Seixas, a daughter of Shearith Israel's esteemed hazzan. From 1812 to 1824, Kursheedt lived in Richmond and served there as a lay leader at Beth Shalome. Thereafter, he returned to New York, where he was a founder and an active member of that city's first Ashkenazic synagogue, B'nai Jeshurun, and helped organize the Hebrath Terumath Hakodesh, a charity dedicated to aiding the Jewish community in the Holy Land.[50] One of Kursheedt's sons, Gershom, and Leeser developed

41

a strong friendship in Richmond that lasted until the former died in London in 1863.[51]

Leeser preserved few details about his initial encounter with America. Fragments of a diary he kept during his first few years in the United States illustrate the process of Americanization he underwent. The oldest extant entry, written in German, states: "Letter dispatched to the *Oberlandrabbiner* Abraham Sutro with Brig Brutus . . . [via] Bremen, Monday the 11th February 1825 or 26 Shebat 5585 after I have been 9½ months in the united Free States." On the same page, the next entry reads: "Johann Quincy Adams by the voice of 13 states elected president."[52]

Like many new immigrants, Leeser was deeply concerned about maintaining ties with the relatives and friends he left behind in the old country. He continued to correspond with a wide variety of people in Europe for the rest of his life and, at one point, even considered visiting his sister in Holland. At the same time, from the age of seventeen, he was faced with the difficult tasks of becoming an American and learning a new language.

Soon after Leeser's arrival in Richmond, Zalma made arrangements for him to be tutored privately. After only ten weeks, the teacher left to study medicine in Philadelphia. Leeser then resolved, Mayer Sulzberger wrote in 1867, "to learn business under his uncle's direction: wherefore, he entered definitively into his employ, and continued with him in that capacity for nearly five years. . . . He had never been endowed with riches, but his position in Richmond was, certainly, one of entire independence, and might have ultimately led to wealth and distinction, had he continued to pursue it with industry and patience."[53]

Like other young men of his age and place, Leeser reported for military duty. He was given the rank of private in Captain Prentis's Company, Nineteenth Regiment, Virginia Militia. However, he was extremely nearsighted and on April 13, 1826, was "recommended as a fit subject for exemption from military duty."[54]

During 1827 Leeser continued working with Zalma in the dry goods business. His command of English improved to a point where he could write highly literate letters to friends. In his spare time, he read widely and visited the Richmond Library on a regular basis. He also attended synagogue and frequently assisted the hazzan, Isaac B. Seixas, with his duties. Thus, in less than two years, Leeser had adapted himself to life in Richmond and was feeling at home in America.[55]

The turning point in Leeser's life came in the fall of 1828. A scurrilous article by Joseph Wolff (1795–1862), a well-known apostate and missionary, published in the *London Quarterly Review* as, "[The] Present State of the Jews," was brought to Leeser's attention. "Mr. L.," wrote Sulzberger, "had once an opportunity, before 1828, to appear in the papers in defence of our religion" but declined to do so.[56] He was also content not to respond a second time when Wolff's article was reprinted in a New York paper, on December 26, 1828. "I then thought it was high time to notice it," Leeser wrote on June 10, 1829, "as I verily believed that its circulating without a reply would be extremely injurious to the interest of my brethren in this country."[57]

Wolff was born in Weilerbach, Bavaria. His father was a rabbi. In 1812 he converted to Catholicism and, four years later, was admitted to the Collegio Romani. After being expelled for his heretical views, he moved to England and joined the Anglican Church. His career as a missionary began in 1821. He traveled extensively in Europe, the Middle East, Central Asia, and India. Years later, in 1836, he traveled to the United States, where he delivered a sermon before Congress in Washington, received a degree at Annapolis, Maryland, and was ordained as deacon in New Jersey.[58] Leeser went to hear him in a Philadelphia church in the fall of 1837 and was publicly humiliated by the clever speaker.[59]

Wolff's proselytizing activities were not unusual during the Antebellum Period. In 1816, the first society to proselytize Jews was organized in the United States. That same year another apostate-missionary, Joseph Samuel Christian Frederick Frey (1771–1850), came to America after being expelled from the London Society for Promoting Christianity Among the Jews in the wake of an ugly scandal. Frey, whose original name was Levy, was a native of Franconia and had converted to Christianity in 1798.

In 1820, the American Society for Meliorating the Condition of the Jews (ASMCJ) was organized in New York. "The Organization's list of officers reads like a Who Was Who of New York," writes historian Jonathan D. Sarna.

> Elias Boudinot, former president of the Continental Congress, stood at the helm. Below him sat many, obviously honorific vice-presidents, including John Quincy Adams, Jeremiah Day, Ashbel Green, Philip Milledoler (presidents respectively of Yale, Princeton, and Rutgers), William Phillips, and Stephen Van Rensselaer. Rounding out the list of officers was the treasurer, Peter Jay, son of diplomat John Jay.[60]

American Jews immediately responded to the challenge. In 1816, two British books were republished in New York refuting Frey's arguments: *Tobit's Letters to Levi; or A Reply to the Narrative of Joseph Samuel F. C. Frey* and *Koul Jacob in Defence of the Jewish Religion: Containing the Arguments of Rev. C. F. Frey*. The year the ASMCJ was organized, *Israel Vindicated: Being a Refutation of the Calumnies Propagated Respecting the Jewish Nation: In Which the Objects and Views of the American Society for Ameliorating the Condition of the Jews Are Investigated* was published by Abraham Collins. *Israel Vindicated* was allegedly written by "An Israelite," but recent scholarship has demonstrated that it was actually by George Houston, a non-Jewish ghost writer, with the help and financial assistance of Jews.[61] And finally, Solomon Jackson devoted his entire newspaper *The Jew* (1823–25), the first Jewish periodical in America, to "a defence of Judaism against all its adversaries."[62] "As far as Jews were concerned," concludes Sarna, "nothing was more important."[63]

Certainly, nothing was more important to twenty-year-old Isaac Leeser. Without assistance, he wrote a fiery reply to Wolff's article. He began his essay by defending Jewish honor. He systematically reviewed Jewish history, Talmudic literature, and the socioeconomic progress of the Jewish people since the Enlightenment. He also went on the attack. "How can any man then have the audacity to style our religion a false one," Leeser challenged his readers, "without at the same time admitting that he does not believe the sacred truths of the Bible."[64]

But Leeser was not content with merely stating a paradox. Judaism, he concluded, was historically and spiritually superior to Christianity.

> Whatever of moral beauties the Christian religion may have, ours is no less beautiful, no less effective in raising our ideas from nature to nature's Lord. To love Him, to confide in his goodness and special protection, is commanded to us in almost every page of Mosaic writings. To love our neighbor as ourselves is no new doctrine of the gospel, for this obligation was known already since the promulgation of the law, which commands: "And thou shalt love thy neighbor like thyself." Isaiah, Daniel, Ezekiel, spoke of the resurrection and the life everlasting, and reward for the righteous, and punishment for the wicked. What are the glorious truths which the Christian religion, for the *first time*, made known to a world sunk in darkness? I am absolutely unable to discover which and where they are, and I should, therefore, be much indebted to any *professor of Christianity* who could point out any moral doctrine which was not long previously taught by our prophets and Rabbins.[65]

Leeser's remarks were published in a Richmond newspaper, the *Constitutional Whig*, beginning on January 9, 1829. In introducing

Leeser to his readers, the editor, John Hampden Pleasants (1794–1846), added a few comments of his own. "Why should Christians despise and condemn the people of Israel?" he asked. Instead, "the Christian ought to respect the Jews as the living evidence of the holy origin of his own faith." He ended on a patriotic note: "We think it a glorious distinction to our country, that here the Jews have found a substantial fulfillment of the promise of being restored to the chosen Land."[66]

Pleasants was a well-known individual in Richmond. He was born in Goochland County, Virginia, and educated at the College of William and Mary, where he graduated in 1817. After practicing law for a few years, he turned to journalism and in 1823 became the acting editor of the Lynchburg *Virginian*. The following year, he moved to Richmond and immediately began publishing the *Whig* (1824–46). Pleasants, an ardent National Republican and supporter of John Quincy Adams, offered Richmond readers an option to Thomas Ritchie's *Enquirer*, the "Democratic Bible" of the Virginian press. In 1846 the *Enquirer* accused Pleasants of abolitionist leanings. His honor tarnished, Pleasants challenged Thomas Ritchie, Jr., to a duel in which the forty-nine-year-old editor lost his life.[67] Leeser grieved greatly over the loss of the friend of his youth.[68]

By allowing Leeser to raise the issue of the religious merit of Judaism, Pleasants, a good newspaperman, knew that he was precipitating a controversy. Jews and Judaism were interesting topics to antebellum Americans.[69] A local Quaker wrote a brief response to Leeser, which promptly appeared in the *Whig*. The anonymous "friend" asserted that Jews only applied the "golden rule" to one another and not to gentiles. On January 25, Leeser replied. "The Mosaic law," he attempted to demonstrate, "did enjoin universal love."[70] Again, he took the offensive and pointed out that the Gospels, particularly the Book of Matthew (5:43), falsely attributed the command "and hate thine enemies" to the Hebrew Bible. After publishing a second letter from the "professor of Christianity," Pleasants closed the issue. "I believe him to have been [moved] by the best motives," Leeser wrote of the *Whig's* editor, "in discontinuing the controversy."[71]

The matter was far from over for Leeser. First, Baruch Hillel Judah urged him to prepare an apologia for "our observing the proper day of the week as Sabbath."[72] Second, news of his bold initiative reached other Jewish communities in the country, and American Jews wanted to know who the "native of Germany" was who had stepped forward in their behalf. In Philadelphia, where the Sephardic congregation had been without a hazzan since late October 1828, following the death of

Rev. Abraham Keys, a committee of inquiry decided to write to Jacob Mordecai in Richmond to find out more about the young man. Mordecai kept Leeser informed of his correspondence with Congregation Mickveh Israel.[73]

Aware that his progress was now being observed from near and far, Leeser accepted Judah's challenge to continue writing. With a fervor he had never previously experienced, he began to prepare a broad defense of a traditional view of revelation. "I followed his suggestion," Leeser wrote six months later, "and began immediately to embody my thoughts relative to the truth of the mission of Moses; and though I intended to say but little, the subject grew by degrees under my hands."[74] His personal situation was "quite uncongenial to literature." Leeser writes, "Many a time after a day of active application to business have I spent the hours of night in writing."[75] Nevertheless, by the beginning of June he had completed a book-length manuscript and rescued his two letters to the *Whig* "from the perishable state in which they appeared" by including them as the second part of the work.[76]

Leeser called his book *The Jews and the Mosaic Law*. As it progressed, he showed it to Jacob Mordecai, Rev. Abraham H. Cohen, and John Pleasants.[77] His reviewers had "many valuable suggestions." Pleasants, in particular, tried to help him with "the difficulty that must always exist in the way of a person's writing with facility, for some time, a language other than his vernacular tongue."[78]

A far more serious problem involved the paucity of Jewish books in Richmond. "I never saw a book in the English language," Leeser wrote in the preface, that treated of the evidences of his religion, perhaps excepting David Levy's answer to Thomas Paine, and Rabbi de Cordova's little book *Reason and Faith*. "Yet," he noted, "this did not deter me from the attempt, it rather stimulated me more." Throughout the text Leeser also refers to Scholler, Cicero, Milton, Hume, and Gibbon, as well as esoteric works with which he had some familiarity.[79]

The use of classical and modern European literature was not accidental, nor was it an attempt to demonstrate his worldliness. Leeser, like Levy, wrote *Jews and the Mosaic Law* to convince unbelievers, especially deists, of the truth of biblical revelation and its Jewish interpretation.[80] Here, unlike his refutation of Wolff's article, "secular humanism," not triumphalist Christianity, was the target of his attack.

He began the work by firing a salvo at philosophy in general. He asked:

From what source does the philosopher derive the right to dictate laws to mankind from his study? How can he convince every one, that he is in

46

possession of more wisdom and virtue than every other human being . . . [and] whence proceeds his wisdom? Has he obtained it by intuition? Is his knowledge derived from himself, or from some superior Being? Do his superior endowments make him more than man? do they render him immortal? do they make him infallible? Is he no longer liable to err because he is wise, because he is learned? Is his virtue of that kind, that it never yields to temptation? In short, can he cease to be a man?[81]

Man, in Leeser's opinion, is simply not endowed with the ability to determine religious truth by himself. The human "conscience," the faculty enabling us to know right from wrong, "does not, cannot, *influence all alike*, and consequently cannot be the universal standard of right, since it leads different persons to different conclusions."[82] Therefore, he suggests that

unless there be a revelation, that is to say, a declared and known law proceeding from God, the world is left without the knowledge of right and wrong; and thus the deniers of revelation must accuse the Deity of the greatest injustice, in creating so many beings, endowed with reason, and leaving them to proceed without rule or guide, like a ship, tossed upon the billows of the tempestuous ocean, without rudder or compass.[83]

Leeser then asks the question: "Is the record of revelation reliable?"[84] In chapter 2, he asserts that Moses should be considered the author of the Pentateuch simply because he says he was. "You give credence to profane [Greco-Roman] history," Leeser argues, "and not even believe, that our blessed legislator was the author of his own books."[85] In chapter 3, Leeser adds that Moses is entitled to credibility as a historian because he was an eyewitness to the events he described. Moreover, "from the commencement of Genesis to the end of Deuteronomy, he merely relates the facts, as they occurred, without at any time commenting upon them."[86] "The Holy Spirit," Leeser maintains, "was Moses' instructor, which would have prevented him from committing any error."

In chapter 13 Leeser shifts from an "argument relative to the divine origin of our law, and proceed[s] to explain the Commandments themselves."[87] He begins with the Decalogue and discusses other *mitzvot* (commandments) such as phylacteries, festivals, and dietary laws. The last four chapters (23 through 26) argue against historical development in Jewish life?[88] Judaism, according to Leeser, has been consistent in its ritual and doctrine since the revelation at Sinai. Even in its dispersion, the Jewish people maintained the "purity of law," in part because of its retention of the Hebrew language in worship and its study of the Bible.[89] The book ends with a strong defense of the "Rabbins."

> The debates incident to a disagreement of opinion amongst the Rabbins called forth the most acute and close reasoning, and those persons at all acquainted with the Talmud must acknowledge this in spite of themselves. . . . They did not contend for the mastery in argument, nor the establishment of their own particular views; but only that the truth might be brought out by discussion, and all their differences were for the sake of Heaven, for the ultimate glory of the name of God. Such differences as these must raise the parties in our estimation, and compel us to respect the opinions of those men, who, with an eye solely to the advancement of religion and social virtue, braved persecutions, and poverty, and distress, to accomplish this noble object.[90]

Leeser was probably also responding to antirabbinism both in Christian literature and in the literature of the Enlightenment.

Leeser finished writing on June 10, 1829. He was full of pride in his accomplishment and hopeful that he would be able to find a publisher. Those plans had to be delayed, however, because word had just arrived from Philadelphia that Mickveh Israel was now seriously interested in hiring him as their new hazzan. By the end of the summer, the congregation finally made a firm offer. In all the excitement, the manuscript of *Jews and the Mosaic Law* was laid aside, and four long years passed before it was published.

On the same day that Leeser completed his book, Jacob Mordecai wrote a strong letter of recommendation to Mickveh Israel in his behalf. Mordecai knew that Leeser was their man, and did not equivocate in telling them just that.

> Mr. Isaac Leeser, is a young gentleman who has resided a few years among us, I can confidently recommend as a person of steady habits, of moral worth, a strict observer of our religious rites, possessing a cultivated mind, capable of instructing your children in Hebrew and with a little practice will be enabled to discharge the duties of hazzan. Our holy language is perfectly familiar to him, he renders Hebrew into English and English into Hebrew, with great facility and possesses a grammatical knowledge of both. . . . He pronounces agreeably to the [Sephardic?] mode. . . . With attention and experience the pronunciation will soon be perfect. He has a capable voice, but will require some instruction in the festival tunes.
>
> Mr. Peixotto [in Philadelphia] has kindly offered to instruct him, that gentleman has conversed with him on the subject. Mr. L. is extremely diffident of his powers to give satisfaction as a reader but is willing to

make an experiment. I have no hesitation in saying, take him all in all, that he will be a valuable acquisition to any congregation. He combines the qualifications of an instructor and an exposer of our laws and customs—possesses a decent classical knowledge, composes with facility and correctness, has an extensive historical knowledge and is a belles lettres scholar. . . . Tho' young, he is sedate, and with increasing years and his love of learning, and pious *conviction* of the truths of the religion he professes, he will, if blessed with length of days, become a shining light in Israel.

Mordecai also added a statement that haunted Leeser during the entire course of his employment at Mickveh Israel:

His pecuniary circumstances are perfectly easy and his relative and patron is able to make him in some degree independent of seeking office as a means of support. These observations proceed from myself and are not intended to influence your decision in relation to his compensation.[91]

Unfortunately, Mordecai's comment did influence some members of Mickveh Israel. During the course of his twenty-one-year career at the Philadelphia synagogue, Leeser and the congregation constantly argued over income and other contractual matters.

Mordecai's letter made "a most favorable impression in Philadelphia." On June 29, 1829, Raphael de Cordova, on behalf of Mickveh Israel, wrote directly to Leeser:

If it is your wish to become a Candidate for the office [of hazzan], it will be necessary for you to come to this City at an early period and to perform the services for the Judgement of the Congregation—the Salary attached to the office is one thousand Dollars [per] annum, with *Matanot* [perquisites] which are neither large nor frequent. But, it will be imperative on the Gentleman who may be elected that he shall undertake to teach the children of the Congregation our holy language. I have no doubt a well-conducted school will add something handsome to his Emoluments.[92]

Leeser was not predisposed to accept Mickveh Israel's invitation to run as a candidate for the office of hazzan. He was very comfortable in Richmond. He was earning a good living and was happy in the company of his family and friends. Perhaps he remembered the difficulties his uncle Abraham had faced as a hazzan in Westphalia. Certainly he was aware of the pecuniary problems of his friend and teacher Isaac B. Seixas. From Rev. Abraham H. Cohan, Jacob Mordecai, and others, he was able to learn about the politics in the Philadelphia Jewish community. In short, he had few illusions about the ministry, and although he was finally persuaded by Zalma and Jacob Mordecai to go to Philadelphia, he remained profoundly ambivalent about Mickveh Israel's invitation. Eleven years later he wrote, "I was not dazzled with the prospect of obtaining a high responsible office."[93]

According to Emily Solis-Cohen, Leeser left Richmond the day after the Ninth of Av, a Jewish fast day marking the destruction of the ancient Temples of Jerusalem, and traveled to Philadelphia by the steamer Long Branch.[94] He would return to the Virginian capital several times during his career. Richmond had become his home away from home. "We love this old commonwealth," Leeser wrote about Virginia in 1850. "It is the home of generous feelings, and the seat of true liberty of conscience."[95]

Leeser's departure from Richmond ended a chapter in his life. He was no longer a student, no longer a young immigrant. He was a twenty-two-year-old Americanized man. His talents as a Jewish spokesman had already been recognized by a few sympathetic individuals in Richmond. Now he was called upon to prove himself in another city, without the help of family or friends and in a profession not of his own choosing. He probably underestimated his own abilities and the extent of his knowledge of Judaism. His questions about the ministry, however, were well founded. The life of a hazzan was not an easy one, and the pulpit of Mickveh Israel would provide no exception.

3

PIONEER PREACHER, 1829–1834

It was perfectly clear that the people desired public instruction.
—Isaac Leeser, *Discourses*, 1837

IN 1829, WHEN ISAAC Leeser first arrived in town, Philadelphia stood on the verge of a major period of growth. In the course of the next few decades, the "City of Brotherly Love" was transformed from a provincial American town to a large, modern city. It had a rich colonial history and had served as the political capital of the revolutionary struggle. Some of the old charm was still visible, but it was quickly becoming evident that Philadelphia would be a radically different place than the town planned by William Penn in 1682.

The rapid increase in the number of residents and the vast expansion of Philadelphia's boundaries were the most visible signs of change. In 1795, Philadelphia, already a large city by American standards, had a population of 23,700; by 1820, its population had ballooned to 98,000; twenty years later, 258,000 people lived there. The physical growth of the city was just as dramatic. Originally the town was planned as a small grid of streets on the west bank of the Delaware River. In 1854, a consolidation movement resulted in the official amalgamation of twenty-nine separate municipalities into the city of Philadelphia.[1]

The transition of Philadelphia from a town into a city was accompanied by a host of problems. "Most historians agree," writes Michael

51

Feldberg, "that in the rapid expansion of the 1830s and 1840s, citizens of the American city lost social knowledge and physical contact with one another for the first time."[2] As a result, tensions among the myriad class, racial, religious, and occupational communities increased. As early as 1828, tension between German and Irish ethnics resulted in a bloody riot in nearby suburban Kensington. "The series of riots that began in 1834," writes Philadelphia historian Sam Bass Warner, Jr., "rose in intensity to a peak of violence in 1844 and then abated as organized politics assumed the place of fragmentary outbursts of frustration, prejudice, and anger."[3]

In addition to "organized politics," Jacksonian Philadelphia also saw the development of a number of important institutions. "Many of our [current] urban habits and institutions," Warner writes, "are survivals from innovations of the nation's first big city era—hospitals, charities, parks, water works, police departments, and public schools." Moreover, "the mid-nineteenth century was *par excellence* the era of the urban parish, the Lodge, the benefit association, the social and athletic club, the political club, the fire company, and the gang."[4]

In many ways, changes in the broad pattern of urban life in Philadelphia during the Jacksonian and antebellum periods were reflected in the Jewish community. In 1830, Philadelphia had a small Jewish population, between five hundred and one thousand, and had two Jewish congregations and three benevolent societies. Less than twenty-five years later, in their 1854 *Jewish Calendar*, Jacques J. Lyons and Abraham de Sola reported that Philadelphia had five congregations and seventeen societies.[5] By 1858, it is estimated that the Jewish population had grown to eight thousand.[6]

The early history of the Philadelphia Jewish community is well known. Jews first came to the Delaware Valley area during the 1650s as traders. Permanent Jewish settlement began in 1737 with the arrival of Nathan and Isaac Levy. The best-known Philadelphia colonial Jews, Bernard and Michael Gratz, brothers who developed a lucrative business that specialized in western trade, arrived in 1754. Their family also assumed a leadership role among the city's Jews, whose population finally surpassed one hundred by 1765.[7]

Jewish communal life began in 1740, when Nathan Levy secured a small parcel of land for Jewish burial on Spruce Street between Eighth and Ninth streets. Services, however, continued to be conducted on an informal basis for two more decades. For the High Holy Days in 1761, the local Jewish community obtained a Scroll of the Law from Congregation Shearith Israel in New York. "It may be assumed," write Edwin Wolf and Maxwell Whiteman, "that with a *Sefer Torah* on indefinite loan in Philadelphia, religious services became more regular. There was even a communal employee: Michael Gratz's account book for this period records a payment to a *Shammash*, or beadle." By 1773, the Philadelphia Jewish community had adopted *Mickveh Israel* ("The Hope of Israel") as its corporate name.[8]

The community grew slowly and steadily. Patterning themselves after Shearith Israel, which in turn had modeled itself after the great Sephardic congregations of London and Amsterdam, the Jews of Philadelphia elected a parnass, gabbai (treasurer), and a six-member adjunta (board of directors). At first they met in a rented house on Sterling Alley near Third Street. In 1776, they moved to Cherry Alley, where they assembled in a second-story room in a house owned by a gentile, Joseph Cauffman. According to Wolf and Whiteman,

> Cherry Alley was a little, cobblestone street, about fifteen feet wide, which began at Third Street and ran west between Race and Arch. An occasional tree threw some shade against the two-story brick houses in which some of the congregants lived. There were but few shops along its short length, for while it was surrounded by the business district, it was not part of it.[9]

The Revolutionary War completely transformed the Jewish community of Philadelphia. Following the departure of the British from the city in the spring of 1778, Philadelphia became a safe haven for Jewish civilians on the patriots' side who were fleeing from the ravages of battle. The largest number of refugees came from New York, including Gershom Mendes Seixas, the hazzan of Shearith Israel. Others came from Charleston, South Carolina, and Savannah, Georgia. Also among the many Jews who sought asylum in Philadelphia during the war was Haym Solomon (1740–85), a patriot who aided the cause of American independence by assisting Robert Morris, superintendent of the Office of Finance, in successfully selling bills of exchange and government notes on the Philadelphia market at a time when fiat continental currency was nearly worthless.[10]

By the end of the War of Independence, approximately one thousand Jews, more than a third of the total Jewish population of the United States, lived in Philadelphia. New quarters had to be found to house the congregation. In March 1782, a decision was made to build a new synagogue. A tiny edifice, erected on Cherry Street between Third and Fourth, was dedicated on September 13, 1782 with little fanfare.[11] Thus, after nearly fifty years of continuous Jewish settlement, Philadelphia's Jews had their own place of worship.

With the surrender of Cornwallis, Jews from New England, New York, and the South began to return home, including Gershom Seixas, who had been the congregation's hazzan since 1780. With great difficulty, the local community struggled to survive. A new hazzan, Jacob Raphael Cohen (1738?–1811), was hired, as were several other religious functionaries. Various parnassim, including Jonas Phillips (1736–1803), Manuel Josephson (1729–96), and Benjamin Nones (1757–1826), served the congregation with distinction. Phillips was the first parnass of Mickveh Israel after its reorganization in 1782. Josephson served as president for six years (1785–91) and spearheaded the drive among the scattered American synagogues to jointly congratulate George Washington on his election as president. Nones, a native of Bordeaux, France, was the head of the congregation for fifteen years (1791–99, 1805–1806, 1808–10, and 1820–1822) and championed a strict approach to Jewish law. He was well known in the general community for his outspoken support of Thomas Jefferson.[12]

The fledgling community established a clear Jewish presence in the political life of the city and in the new nation. In 1787, Jonas Phillips protested the Test Oath in Philadelphia, which prevented Jews from holding public office. The same year, when the new federal Constitution was ratified, the Philadelphia Jewish community furnished a table with kosher food so that its members could join in the public celebration of the event.[13]

Throughout the Early National Period, the Phillips family continued to play an important role in Mickveh Israel. Three of Jonas Phillips's sons served as parnass of the congregation: Naphtali Phillips (1799–1800), Benjamin I. Phillips (1811–15), and Zalegman Phillips (1806–1807 and 1822–34). Naphtali became the first American-born parnass of Mickveh Israel at the age of twenty-six. Thereafter, he moved to New York, where he served as parnass of Shearith Israel for ten years (1804–1805, 1815–24).[14]

Zalegman Phillips (1779–1839) was parnass of Mickveh Israel when Isaac Leeser was first elected hazzan in 1829. Phillips was a native Philadelphian and a graduate of the University of Pennsylvania. He was admitted to the bar in 1799 and was widely respected as a highly capable criminal lawyer with a large clientele. On October 23, 1805, he married Arabella Bush Solomons of Baltimore. Two of their sons, Jonas Altamont and Henry Myer Phillips, also had distinguished legal careers.[15]

Phillips had overseen the hiring of the previous hazzan, Abraham Israel Keys, after a transition period of seven years when the congregation functioned without benefit of a regular hazzan. Phillips was also president of the congregation when Mickveh Israel built its second sanctuary, a neo-Egyptian structure designed by William Strickland, the same architect who designed the Second Bank of the United States in Philadelphia. The new synagogue, completed in the autumn of 1824, had over 350 permanent seats, including a women's gallery. The success of the congregation during Phillips's presidency even resulted in numerous defections from Rodeph Sholom, Philadelphia's Ashkenazic congregation.[16]

As parnass, Phillips understood that one of the most important decisions a congregation faced was the selection of its religious leadership. When Mickveh Israel began searching for a new hazzan in 1829, the parnass opted for the appointment of Eleazar S. Lazarus (1788–1844), a native-born New Yorker and the grandfather of poet Emma Lazarus. In 1824, Lazarus had already been offered the position of hazzan at Mickveh Israel but refused, because he would not accept a contract "unless it be during good behavior and with a salary not extravagant but sufficient."[17] In other words, Lazarus wanted a life contract and an assurance of financial security. Phillips and the congregation would not meet his terms and instead turned to Keys.

Lazarus's boldness can be explained by the fact that he already had full-time employment in New York as a city assessor. He was also active in the Jewish community. He was affiliated with Shearith Israel and was a patron, but not a member, of B'nai Jeshurun, the city's first Ashkenazic congregation. In 1826 he edited the Hebrew text of Solomon H. Jackson's *The Form of Prayers According to the Custom of the Spanish and Portuguese Jews*. During the spring of 1829 he was persuaded to come to Philadelphia to lead services during the Passover holiday. However, he had no intention of staying, and returned to New York.[18]

A broad search for candidates for the office of hazzan resulted in three other possibilities: Isaac Leeser of Richmond, twenty-two years old; Abraham Ottolengui of Charleston, twenty years old; and Gompart S. Gomparts, who submitted his name at the last moment without presenting his credentials. Leeser was the most highly recommended of the three, and accepted the invitation from Mickveh Israel to come to Philadelphia "to perform the services for the Judgement of the Congregation."

The parnass was not impressed with Leeser and resolved to block his election. "Instead of an examination into [my] fitness, by previous study and the due achievements for the office to which [I] was called," Leeser complained, "[I] was merely required to read the service for three successive weeks."[19] "It has been my misfortune," Leeser later wrote to Zalma Rehine, "to have among the congregation a few persons who were opposed to my first coming hither and who left no means untried to prevent my being elected . . . and at every fitting opportunity they showed their darling scheme not to be abandoned, and that they were resolved to either make me retire or to render my stay unpleasant and dishonorable."[20]

Leeser's friend, John Hampden Pleasants, advised him to remain calm and let his merit speak for itself. On August 27, 1829, the editor of the *Whig* wrote to Leeser:

> I am sorry to hear that the prospect of thy success is not so certain as I was induced to believe, for though I am not personally interested in the result of the election, my feelings are so far excited as to desire the preference of one with whom I am in a measure acquainted, and who I have no doubt is qualified to fill the office in some very essential respects. But I am glad to perceive that thou will be satisfied, however the election may result; and not less so, at thy standing aloof from all interference in it. When promotion is voluntarily offered, there is a charm and gratification in success, which does not fall to our lot if we have used any active means to obtain it. I shall be pleased to hear from thee as soon as the matter is decided.[21]

Why the parnass and his faction opposed Leeser is not fully known. Several factors present themselves as the possible cause. First, Leeser was only twenty-two years old, and had neither experience nor substantial training as hazzan, especially in the Sephardic liturgy. Also, Leeser was ambivalent about the prospect of becoming a religious functionary. A third possibility is that Jacob Mordecai's suggestion that Leeser had the financial support of his uncle was interpreted by Phillips and others to mean that Leeser would be independent-minded and not fully responsive to the authority of the parnass and adjunta. Fourth, Leeser also had ideas about being a writer and an intellectual, prospects not necessarily viewed with favor by some members of the congregation. Fifth, Leeser's opponents might have simply detected something in his personality that they did not like. Finally, it is also possible that there was prejudice against Leeser because he was a German Jew. Phillips might even have found Leeser's close relations with John Hampden Pleasants, a Southern Whig, objectionable.

On September 6, 1829, the congregation met to elect a new hazzan. A motion to postpone the whole matter was quickly overridden. The terms of employment were then debated. Suggestions concerning length of contract ranged from one to five years, and from $600 to $1,000 per annum for salary. After considerable discussion and parliamentary maneuvering, the salary was fixed at $800 for a term of two years. The status of the potential candidates was then reviewed. Lazarus had not consented to stand for election. Ottolengui had withdrawn, and his name was dropped from contention. Only Leeser remained as a bona fide candidate. In the ensuing election, he received twenty-six votes, while seven ballots were cast to Lazarus, as a protest.[22]

Some years later, Leeser wrote to the chief rabbi of England about his bittersweet election: "Knowing my own want of proper qualification, I would never have consented to serve, if others more fitting in point of standing, information, or other qualities had been there; but this not being the case . . . I consented to serve."[23]

On September 7, 1829, Leeser officially accepted the position without questioning the fact that the income originally promised to him by de Cordova had been reduced by 20 percent. He informed the congregation of his decision by writing to two officials involved in the selection process, Joseph S. Cohen and L. M. Goldsmidt.

> Permit me to transmit through you, to the members of K. K. [holy congregation] Mickveh Israel, my acceptance of the office of hazan, to which office they did me the honor to elect me on yesterday. In accepting this highly responsible station, I am fully alive to the various, and in a measure, new duties which devolve upon me. No man can be more aware than myself of my want of qualifications to acquit myself properly; but it shall be my constant aim to merit the indulgence, if not the confidence, of this respectable congregation by attending strictly, as far as lies in my power, to the duties of my office so that I may never be accused of carelessness and negligence. It would be unbecoming in me to be more particular, as I do consider it wrong to make any promises which I might be unable to fulfill.
>
> Accept for yourselves, gentlemen, my sincere thanks of the highly flattering matter in which you announced to me the result of the election; and be assured that your prosperity, and the prosperity of the community you represent, will ever be gratifying to
>
> Yours and the congregation's very Obedient Servant
> Isaac Leeser.[24]

Leeser had little time to settle his personal affairs—the High Holy Days were close at hand. After they passed, Zalma Rehine came to Philadelphia to observe, first hand, how his nephew was adjusting to his new situation. Rehine was particularly pleased with the way his friends the Peixotto family, who had been providing Leeser a place to stay, were helping. Upon returning to Richmond, he wrote to Leeser with some sage advice: "My dear Isaac, I hope you will Try to Cultivate the friendship of every body in your Congregation and not mind some few kicks which now and then you might receive, never interfere with any difference between them, but be a peacemaker and make them friends."[25]

Unfortunately, the parnass and those who sided with him against Leeser did not relent in their opposition to the young hazzan. In a letter to the congregation written eleven years later, Leeser recalled that "during the first year of my residence here, various unpleasant things took place, which it is needless to call to mind again, and altho' matters were smoothed over again, *still the report reached a distant congregation,* that my situation was not very pleasant here. Therefore, overtures were made to me by several influential members from that place to take the office of Hazzan vacant there." Leeser, however, decided to stay and make Philadelphia his home. He remained with Mickveh Israel for twenty-one stormy years before resigning in anger and frustration.[26]

The predicament of the young hazzan was viewed sympathetically by Rebecca Gratz (1781–1869), a daughter of Michael Gratz, a leading Philadelphia businessman and early leader of the local Jewish community. She was the outstanding Jewish woman of her time, and exemplar of the "cult of true womanhood." Involved in numerous social welfare activities, in both the Jewish and general communities, she was secretary of the Female Association for the Relief of Women and Children in Reduced Circumstances in 1801, aided in the founding of the Female Hebrew Benevolent Society in 1819, was the moving force behind the establishment of the first Jewish Sunday school in 1838, and helped organize various orphanages in Philadelphia.[27]

Rebecca Gratz immediately recognized the importance of Leeser to the Jewish community and criticized the "horrible spirits" in the congregation who persecuted him. In her private correspondence, she also gives the earliest portrait of the young hazzan. In a letter to her sister-in-law, Maria Gist Gratz, on November 4, 1829, she writes that

> our young pastor is certainly more attractive to those who are indifferent to the *outer Man* looking sage, who in reply to a high born damsel's remark on the freak of nature in placing so much wisdom in so ugly a creature, demanded what kind of vessel her father kept his wine in—she said a common earthen, for wine kept in precious metal became sour—he observed wisdom is safest with ugliness—for there are few provokatives to vanity—which is an enemy to wisdom—this anecdote is most aptly applied to Mr. Leeser—who is ugly and awkward—but so sensible and pleasant as well as pious—that all the old ladies are charmed, while the girls are obliged to persuade themselves to be pleasant.[28]

The following April, she again wrote to her sister-in-law about Leeser and made several critical observations about him.

Before he came to Phila he had written some essays in "defence of the Jews and Mosaic law," which gained him some reputation among a small circle of friends. It was his first attempt at authorship and he fell in love with his work. . . . I have read it, and although it gives me a good opinion of his talents have advised him not to publish—but some other friends have encouraged him, and he issued proposals to publish it by subscription. . . . With these burthens on his shoulders, before he had got through the first difficulties of his new station, he had taken too much upon himself and does not seem to get along happily as if he had reserved his whole strength and attention to the duties of the reading desk. But youth is apt to be proved, experience will aid in checking, or rather directing enthusiasm to proper channels . . . he is certainly a very pious and worthy man and takes very hard the latitude allowed in matters of religion in this enlightened age. Fortunately he is a beardless youth. Did he wear the chin of a rabbi, he would be scoffed at by his congregation.[29]

Leeser's physical unattractiveness and personal frustrations with his congregation stood in stark contrast to the success of a local Unitarian minister, William Henry Furness (1802–1896), who enjoyed the friendship of many of Leeser's congregants, especially Rebecca Gratz. In January 1825, he had been installed as the minister in the church founded by Dr. Joseph Priestly in 1796. Furness quickly became a highly regarded preacher, scholar, and translator. Various Jews could be found in his congregation on Sunday mornings to hear his sermons. On August 9, 1831, Rebecca Gratz again wrote to Maria Gratz:

Your favorable opinion of Mr. Furness will be confirmed by a fact which has raised him in the estimation of his congregation, so much that they are at a loss to express their admiration. He had permission to accompany his family to New England and pass July and August away. He preached at Boston, and had a unanimous call to a church in that city, at a salary of $2,500—and an allowance of $200 more for fuel, and the perquisites which would add considerably to the richness of living—he receives here but $1,500—yet his love for his own congregation, and sense of duty to them was put in the balance, and outweighed the tempting offer—he returned home last week.[30]

Gratz also admired Furness's skill as a public speaker. In 1838, she again wrote her sister-in-law about Furness:

Our favorite orator gave a most beautiful lecture the other evening on Genesis—and verily—I thought he illustrated the subject most aptly—

the hall was crowded, and the most deep and fixed attention prevailed. I wished you could have heard him, for I never heard him more eloquent in the pulpit, and he managed popular lecture so as to abate nothing from the reverence and dignity of his clerical character.[31]

From the very beginning of his employment at Mickveh Israel, Leeser hoped to elevate the office of hazzan and to remodel it after the best aspects of the Christian ministry. The first and most important change, according to Leeser, was the establishment of regular preaching in the synagogue. Sermons, he wrote in 1845, could "exercise an influence over the mind of society, which we now can hardly have any idea of. What does one think would be the fate of protestant Christianity without the constant appeal to the fear and reason of its professors from the ten thousand pulpits which scatter information and admonition many times during every week."[32] Later, he also advocated the development of an American Jewish theological seminary to train "ministers" and championed substantial changes in the contractual relationship between the hazzan and his congregation.

Historically, preaching had its roots in the ancient synagogue. The need to translate and explain the meaning of the Torah was already felt in synagogues in the land of Israel during the first century. Specific rules of biblical exegesis, a variety of literary structures, and novel illustrative techniques were developed to teach, inspire, and comfort worshippers. During the Middle Ages, the *derashah* or homily was a regular feature of synagogue life. While formal preaching by rabbis was often limited to the Sabbaths before Yom Kippur and Passover, informal and often imaginative discussion of the Torah by *maggidim* (itinerant preachers) was a popular folk custom, especially in Eastern Europe. Even boys who had become Bar Mitzvah, and bridegrooms, were expected to give a *derashah*.[33]

At the beginning of the nineteenth century, interest in modern preaching developed among Jews in Germany and England. German reformers sought to replace the traditional *derashah* with a *predigt*, a vernacular sermon consciously modeled on the pattern of Christian homiletics. They even used Christian guides to the art of preaching. Subsequently, beginning in the 1840s, German Jewish preachers broadly began using rabbinic sources to illustrate their sermons. In England, on the other hand, where vernacular preaching also began among the Sephardim early in the nineteenth century, Jewish homiletics remained Bibliocentric.[34]

Modern Jewish preaching also began in the United States during the Early National Period on a limited basis. "It is true," Leeser wrote

PIONEER PREACHER, 1829–1834

in 1841, "that occasionally lectures were delivered . . . by the late Rev. Gershom M. Seixas, of New York, the late Rev. Emanuel N. Carvalho, of Philadelphia, Rev. A. H. Cohen of Richmond, Dr. Jacob De La Motta, of Charleston, and several other ministers, besides occasional volunteer lectures among laymen, if such a word can be with propriety used among Israelites; but no appointment was ever made with a view to sermons."[35] More traditional messages were delivered to American Jews by a handful of "Palestinian messengers" who already began visiting American synagogues in the eighteenth century to raise funds for Jewish communities and activities in the Land of Israel. However, the Saturday afternoon *shiur* (scriptural lesson) and the tradition of the *maggid* did not transplant themselves to America.

By contrast, preaching and public lecturing were important features of American culture in general. Early New England preachers such as Increase Mather (1639–1723), Cotton Mather (1663–1728), and Jonathan Edwards (1703–1750) helped establish the centrality of the sermon in American religion. During the nineteenth century, that tradition was continued by numerous preachers and revivalists including Horace Bushnell (1802–1870), Peter Cartwright (1785–1872), and Charles G. Finney (1792–1875). And, of course, there was Leeser's contemporary, William Henry Furness. Moreover, between 1826 and 1834, the same period when Leeser emerged as a preacher and lecturer, over three thousand lyceums were established in the United States as a form of adult education.[36]

"But even before being in office," Leeser wrote in a note in his first volume of sermons, published in 1837, "it had appeared to me as an incongruity, that words of instruction formed no part of our regular service." Whether Leeser thought the lack of preaching in the American synagogue to be "incongruous" with Jewish tradition or American culture or both is unknown. He certainly believed that American Jews were broadly in favor of restoring the sermon to the synagogue. "It was perfectly clear," he wrote, "that the people desired public instruction." He also received some "kind approbation and encouragement . . . by some intelligent ladies" from Mickveh Israel.[37]

The parnass and the adjunta, on the other hand, were content with the status quo. The authority to order a sermon on special occasions lay with the parnass. Late in life, Leeser recalled with disdain the original conditions of his employment at Mickveh Israel.

Our own position for twenty-one years, was simply that of hazzan, in which capacity we were only required to read the prayers in the original Hebrew according to the custom of the Portuguese Jews, on Sabbath Eve,

61

morning and night, and the same on Holy Days and festivals, to attend all funerals and subsequent mourning services and to perform at no time any marriages or funeral rites without the consent of the parnass or the adjunta. . . . It requires little reflection to understand that the ministry under such conditions is one of very limited functions and privileges and likewise demands only a very small amount of talent and information.[38]

Leeser had hoped that on account of his "literary" achievements in Richmond, the board of Mickveh Israel would have requested that "he give discourses on our religion in the language of the country." When they failed to take any such initiative, Leeser was "sadly disappointed." After nine months in office, he recalled, "I was induced to address a circular letter to the several members of the Board of the Adjunta, asking them whether my speaking in Synagogue would meet their consent." Again to his dismay, the board did not act officially on his proposal. Instead, they "signified, in unofficial letters, their approval of my intention." Thirteen years passed before the board formally sanctioned Leeser's work as a preacher.[39]

Leeser targeted the first Saturday in June 1830 (*Shabbat Naso*), as the date for delivering his first sermon. Preparing his first "discourse" was not an easy task for him. He needed nearly two weeks to write it. He began with a verse from the prophet Isaiah (25:9). Appropriately, he called his sermon "Confidence in God."[40] Twenty-two years later, Leeser recalled his anxiety on the Sabbath he began his career as a preacher.

> Few but those who have been placed as I was, can imagine the embarrassment I experienced when I commenced speaking. I will briefly state, that I, in all my life, never had heard but about a half a dozen addresses, either from the pulpit or elsewhere; I knew that I have a considerable heaviness of speech, almost amounting to a stammer, unless I speak very deliberately or rapidly; besides all this, a first attempt before an audience, whose judgements one has to respect, and individuals, whose taste is both refined and experienced, is not an easy or pleasant task.[41]

Waiting until the end of the service, he spoke after the singing of the closing hymn, "Adon Olam" ("Lord of the Universe"). Later in his career, he preached prior to the conclusion of worship.

He began "Confidence in God" with a confession of humility and by revealing "that only in obedience to the repeated solicitations of persons who really feel an interest in the welfare of our [Jewish] nation, I persuaded myself to attempt teaching that, which I deem to be

the essential part of our faith." Then he explained why he felt it was
necessary to preach at all.

> It is highly probable, that most of you, if not all, may have heard all of
> which I can advance; but then I must beg of you to consider, that known
> truths may often be faintly remembered, and that we may derive great
> and lasting benefits by having them presented to us in a light, in which
> perhaps we had never before viewed them. It is for this reason expedient,
> that occasional lectures on religious subjects should be delivered in our
> Synagogue.[42]

With that, Leeser gave the verse and commenced with his exegesis.
Peering through his heavy spectacles, Leeser reminded his congregation that it is "our duty to remain unshaken: in being God's servants.
The God of Israel is a faithful God and we should be mindful not to
be overcome with a false sense of self-sufficiency. Instead, we should
busy ourselves with the care of our souls." In a parable, Leeser illustrated his own pious conviction:

> A certain man had three friends, to one whom he was devotedly attached;
> to the second he was kind but he did not esteem him by far as much as
> the first; to the third, however, he paid but little regard, and scarcely
> ever thought of him. It happened one day, that this man was suddenly
> summoned to appear before the king; and not knowing the cause of the
> unexpected summons, or perhaps dreading to appear before the king
> without a powerful defender to assist him in case of necessity; he applied
> to the first of his friends, being sure, that he would not refuse him his
> countenance in the present emergency. The friend, however, did refuse,
> excusing himself, saying: "I really cannot go; I am so much occupied with
> my own concerns, that it is impossible for me to assist you now; besides
> this, I have no influence with the king." He then went to the second, who
> answered: "I can do but little for you; but as we have been friends so long,
> I will accompany you as far as the palace-gate; more than this I cannot
> do." Finding himself so rudely treated by his most intimate friends, he
> applied to the last, whom he had so long neglected. This one, who in fact
> had always loved him more than either of the others, received him with
> open arms, saying: "How glad I am, my dear friend, that you have given
> me this opportunity of serving you; I will go with you to the king, I will
> remain with you, and defend you if necessary."

The preacher then gave his interpretation.

> The moral of the foregoing is, that a man generally values his riches more
> than his relatives and friends, and these again more than his religion,
> which, alas! like the last friend in the parable, is too often neglected and

almost forgotten. He is finally summoned to appear before the King of kings, the Holy One, praised be He; his money avails him nothing—this must be left behind; his friends and relatives accompany him to the grave, there they must leave him, and thus his virtues and good deeds alone remain with him to the tribunal of the Judge of all to defend him and to plead in his favor.[43]

Having defined the "true aim of life," Leeser brought his remarks to a close with a *nehemta* (passage of consolation) and a prayer petitioning for Restoration in Zion.

The style and structure of Leeser's sermons quickly evolved after this first address. He rarely returned to the use of parables and tales from rabbinic literature, a practice soon to be popularized in Europe by the Viennese preacher Adolf Jellinek (1820–93). Instead, he primarily used the Bible to illustrate his talks. An original introductory prayer, often in the petitionary mode, became a standard feature of his preaching. This prayer was of variable length and not strictly tied to the major themes of the subsequent discourse. The place of the verse also shifted from the beginning to the middle or end of the sermon, at least during his first few years as a preacher, probably to distinguish his own remarks from those of contemporary Christian preachers, who often stated their scriptural passage before preaching. In discussing the organization of his sermons, Leeser later wrote:

> In place of giving out a text and stringing a sermon to the same, as is customary with most preachers, I have generally chosen to introduce it in the middle or even at the conclusion of my discourses; because I desired to illustrate a doctrinal point, and then show its consonance with the text of Scripture, believing this course less fatiguing and more interesting to the audience than the usual mode.[44]

The body of Leeser's sermons often did not follow any consistent organization pattern. He was aware of his tendency to ramble. Commenting in the middle of one sermon, he noted "as usual with me, I have wandered away from the subject which I first spoke of." Because the structure of his remarks was not well defined, his sermons were long, requiring thirty to forty-five minutes to deliver, but in the context of America in the mid-nineteenth century, this length was not unusual. An average Leeser sermon consisted of 5,300 words and was slightly over sixteen printed pages.[45]

The literary quality of Leeser's sermons has been a matter of some debate. His friend and assistant Mayer Sulzberger wrote warmly of Leeser's sermonic accomplishments:

The chief characteristic of his method is simplicity. He is never betrayed into an affectation, if even a show, of learning. There is no straining after rhetorical effect, or startling climaxes, or marvellous theories. He has a message to deliver, which he does straightway in a manner that is relieved from dryness only by his pronounced taste for illustrating what he has to say, for simplifying it to its last elements. Indeed, measured by ordinary standards, he rarely reaches the point which the schools call eloquence. But if true eloquence be to convince and impress, rather than to daze and electrify, he possesses that quality in a high degree. His subject always remains, at bottom, a monition, a warning, an instruction; it is never an essay or a philosophical treatise. It is informed by learning—not filled with it. The element of personality is therefore never prominent. One never stops to wonder at the beauty of the discourse or the eloquence of the preacher. There arises, rather, a feeling of the subject discussed, a realization of short-comings, a resolve to better one's self.[46]

Sulzberger was even more complimentary about Leeser's extemporaneous speaking, to which the hazzan increasingly resorted after leaving Mickveh Israel in 1850: "As a speaker, his command of language and of ideas enabled him to present well-digested thoughts in excellent shape, without previous preparation. Indeed, many of his extemporaneous discourses might well serve as elegant specimens of pulpit oratory."[47] Rosa Mordecai wrote in a similar vein, "These extemporaneous discourses seemed often to be inspired and it is impossible for me to make any one who had not the great privilege of hearing them understand their full force. . . . I never heard such a flow of language or rapidity of utterance, except from the late, lamented Bishop Phillips Brooks."[48]

Modern scholarly opinion, on the other hand, has taken a dimmer view of Leeser's sermons. The views of Joseph Blau and Salo W. Baron are typical:

At no time in his career, if we may judge by his published volumes of *Discourses*, was Leeser an inspired or inspiring preacher. His sermons, in his maturity as well as . . . in his youth, read like student essays. There is, too, a stiffness, almost a pomposity, in their style and language, with no touch of warmth and color or any originality of conception or freshness of exposition to them. He must have been very dull to hear. Perhaps the redeeming quality of his sermons, for the auditor as well as the reader, is the obvious sincerity with which Leeser struggled to express his simple faith and piety.[49]

During the course of his long career, Leeser published more than 250 sermons and addresses. Most of them appear in his ten-volume work, *Discourses in the Jewish Religion* (volumes 1 and 2 were first published in 1837, volume 3 in 1841, and volumes 4–10 in 1867). Additionally, many of his sermons appeared in his newspaper, *The Occident and American Jewish Advocate* (1843–69). A few of his sermons were also printed separately as pamphlets. To promote Jewish preaching in general, Leeser also published scores of "messages" by other Jewish preachers in America and Europe in the *Occident*, many of which he translated and edited himself.

Leeser did not give Sabbath sermons with great frequency compared to twentieth-century congregational rabbis in the United States. In 1830, the first year of his preaching, he spoke eleven times at Mickveh Israel. The following year, he gave eight sermons. During a three-year period, 1837–40, when his relations with his congregation were at a low ebb, he spoke a total of only six times, mainly during the High Holy Days. His peak year as a preacher was 1847, when he sermonized eighteen times.[50]

Thematically, Leeser limited himself to theological topics reflecting his belief in the strict separation of the spiritual and the temporal parts of existence. His favorite topics were God the Creator, providence, the Covenant, irreligion and sin, the Messiah, and the Restoration of the Jewish people to the Land of Israel. He often emphasized the importance of religious faith and placed a greater value on belief than on the performance of any one particular commandment. He was also careful to delineate the differences between Jewish and Christian doctrines and, beginning in the middle of his career, was critical of Reform Judaism's denial of the coming of a human Messiah and rejection of the hope of Restoration. Only on rare occasions would Leeser talk directly to his congregation about its internal problems or accomplishments.[51]

His sermons, however, were not mere abstractions unconnected to the daily course of events. Rather, Leeser attempted to interpret in a theologically orthodox manner the meaning of daily life. Thus, if the community was suffering from a "plague," he would talk about sin and retribution. If riots broke out in Philadelphia, he would talk about the value of divinely revealed "Law." If a member of the community—or, as happened in 1841, the president of the United States—died, he would offer his congregants the assurance of eternal life. Sometimes, in his published works, he added a note to explain the context of his remarks. His congregants most likely made the connections on their own.[52]

 Of all Leeser's accomplishments, his role as the pioneer Jewish preacher in the United States was closest to his heart. On being honored by friends in March 1861, he responded to a tribute by saying, "You have spoken of my sermons; and indeed, if I have any merit, it is to these that I point."[53] When Maimonides College, the first rabbinical seminary in America, finally opened in 1867, Leeser was gratified in being appointed not only provost but also professor of homiletics, belles lettres, and comparative theology. In fact, the last project Leeser undertook was the publication of his *Discourses*. On July 21, 1867, he wrote:

> It is confidently hoped, however, that all the various sermons, addresses, and prayers may be found to have sufficient interest to make them some-what valuable for future reference and use, and that they may be regarded hereafter as vehicles of information on many points, and be used for private devotion in the family circles of our people. If this wish be realized, I shall be amply compensated for the thought, labour, and care expended in preparing them for press, and presenting them to the public as my humble contribution to Jewish religious literature.[54]

Leeser's dedication to preaching as a form of adult Jewish education was matched by his interest in religious instruction for Jewish youth. During his first year at Mickveh Israel, he clearly established himself as an important Jewish educator. Simultaneously, he tried to resolve two fundamental problems: the need for properly organized Jewish day schools, and the lack of appropriate study materials.

On March 31, 1830, Leeser proposed to the board of Mickveh Israel that the congregation establish a Jewish school for both boys and girls with an enrollment of twenty students. He also requested $1,500 to begin the program. Apparently, the board did not grant him the money. Approximately one year later Leeser tried again and was able to start a small school at the house where he was then boarding. His seven students created all types of problems for him, and even damaged the landlord's furniture. On April 21, 1831, he asked the congregation to supplement his income ($80–100 per quarter) so that he could continue to run the school. The congregation wanted no part of it, and classes were suspended.[55]

Lack of appropriate Jewish study material in English was just as frustrating to Leeser as the refusal of the congregation to give him financial support. Familiar with modern Jewish schoolbooks written in Germany, Leeser decided to translate Joseph Johlson's *Unterricht in der Mosaischen Religion* (Frankfurt am Main, 1819) or *Instruction in the Mosaic Religion* sometime during his first year at Mickveh Israel. Johlson (1777–1851), the son of the rabbi of Fulda, was closely associated with the emerging Reform movement in Germany. His chief works were written in connection with his career as a classroom teacher, and in 1826 he also published a German translation of the twelve minor prophets.[56]

Leeser's willingness to associate himself with the work of a known reformer is not difficult to explain. According to Jakob J. Petuchowski, "the acceptance or rejection of the method of catechism per se had very little to do with the 'assimilationist' (or other) tendencies of the authors. It was primarily a matter of educational technique broadly used among Christians and Jews. Some arch-conservatives, like Salomon Plessner, wrote catechisms, while religious radicals, like Israel Ascher Francolm, preferred other styles of presentation."[57] Leeser himself wrote:

> In an age when science of every kind is pursued with avidity, no astonishment can be manifested at the attempt of an Israelite to give his brethren a clear knowledge of the religion which they have inherited from their ancestors; since, if it is of any importance whatever to any portion of the human family to profess a certain creed, it is also highly necessary that the principal features at least of this creed should be familiar to all who profess the same.[58]

Moreover, Johlson was a relatively obscure figure, and American Jews were not yet polarized into Reform and Orthodox factions except, perhaps, in Charleston. In general, the distance between Reform Judaism and Orthodoxy was still relatively narrow in 1830. The great German philosophical systematizers of Reform, Abraham Geiger and Samuel Holdheim, were only twenty and twenty-four years old, respectively, and neither had, to date, been appointed rabbis. Although Reform and Orthodox rabbis had already exchanged angry words in Germany, they had done so primarily in the form of traditional responsa, or rabbinic legal briefs written in Hebrew. Separationist tendencies on both sides had not yet fully developed.[59]

In explaining why he should undertake to translate Johlson's catechism, Leeser told his readers:

> Having been appointed lately a fellow-labourer in the vineyard of the Lord, I thought it best to transplant this foreign shoot into that part entrusted to my care. May then its branches spread over a wide surface, to shade and shelter the weary, and may its good fruit be plentiful, and refresh many a hungry traveller in the path of life. This is the sincere wish and only reason of the humble servant of his brethren.[60]

In preparing his translation of *Instruction in the Mosaic Religion*, Leeser generally adhered closely to Johlson's original German text.

I claim no great literary merit on the account of the present performance; for though the labour bestowed on it has been great, and considerable additions have been made (particularly to the *tenth* ["Of the Duties Towards Our Fellow-Men"] and *eleventh* ["Of the Duties Towards the State"] chapters), yet the road was already so clearly pointed out by the learned author of the original that I had nothing more to do than to make as good a use of the materials as my limited abilities and inexperience would permit.[61]

However, he did make several important changes in the book to give it an Orthodox character. When Johlson declared that "teachers of the people" can "in some cases act even against established customs, which have become of equal force with laws through public opinion," Leeser added a lengthy note of his own.

As the words of Mr. Johlson may perhaps be misunderstood, I beg leave to subjoin the following in explanation: From the whole tenor of our laws it is apparent, that no old established custom, which has become general, can be abolished for the benefit of *one* particular section of the country; as through such means the uniformity of our institutions would be annihilated. Let us, for instance, name the worship in the Hebrew language, which is now universal throughout all the dispersions of Israel. It is no doubt a great misfortune, that the Hebrew is so little understood by many persons; but it would nevertheless be more injurious to adopt as the *sole* language of public worship, any of the languages of the countries in which we live. . . . My limits will not permit me to enter at greater length into a discussion of this point, which would, besides, be also out of place here; but this one example will clearly prove that reform, such as our author recommends from time to time, must be confined to *excrescences* only, but should never be extended to *essentials*. . . . The remarks of our author, however, are directed against superstitious customs solely, and *these* should be abolished, no matter how sacred they may be regarded by the mass of our nation, since all superstition is contrary to the Mosaic Law.[62]

Furthermore, in the section on "immortality," where Johlson concluded on a highly universalist note and expressed a hope for a time of universal peace and brotherhood,[63] Leeser injected an Orthodox note of his own. "What is this period called?" he asked. "The time of the Messiah, who is to be a descendant of King David, and be the means of restoring the people of Israel to their own land, the sacrifices

69

at the temple in Jerusalem, and dispense justice and equity on the earth."[64]

Similarly, in a sermon, "The Consolation of Israel," given at Mickveh Israel on July 27, 1830, just one week before he finished working on *Instruction in the Mosaic Religion*, Leeser reiterated his traditional view of Restoration:

> May we all live to behold the consolation of Israel, the rebuilding of Jerusalem, and the restoration of the worship of the temple, and may we be held sufficiently deserving before our heavenly Father, to receive the crown of glory instead of ashes, and to participate in the joy of those who sincerely mourn for Zion, ardently look forward to the time, when the Lord, whom we seek, will suddenly come to his sanctuary.[65]

Leeser's friend and disciple Mayer Sulzberger went so far as to assert that "for him [Leeser], Palestine was still the country to which Jews had a divine right, which God, in his own good time, would assert—it might be in a day or in a millennium. He believed it necessary to hold one's self in readiness for the call, and this belief doubtless influenced the determination, to which he inflexibly adhered, never to become a citizen of the United States."[66]

Instruction in the Mosaic Religion, Leeser's first published book, was released late in the summer of 1830. He dedicated it "to His Beloved Uncle, Zalma Rehine of Richmond, Virginia." According to Maxwell Whiteman, it was Judah L. Hackenberg (1793–1862) "who was responsible for the publication of Leeser's first work."[67] Hackenberg, a native of Koblenz, Prussia, was a merchant "highly regarded for his many virtues."[68] Later, Abraham Hart (1810–85), a successful publisher and the outstanding lay leader in Philadelphia's Jewish community during the nineteenth century, as well as Hyman Gratz (1776–1857) aided Leeser in his various literary endeavors. Unfortunately, *Instruction in the Mosaic Religion* was poorly received by the public. Leeser later admitted that although intended for "the instruction of the younger part of Israelites of both sexes," the book was "better calculated for the instruction of advanced classes."[69]

Disappointment with the fate of his first book was less troublesome to Leeser than his growing dissatisfaction with the office of hazzan. By the time his first contract was up, he was in open disagreement with the congregation. One complaint regarded his income. On March 25, 1831, he wrote to the congregation that his contract would expire in September and suggested "the propriety of taking such *immediate* steps, as may best comport with the interest of the congregation according to the wisdom of your body."[70] On May 15, 1831, a committee was appointed by the board to meet with Leeser to discuss the renewal of his contract. They offered him a five-year contract at $800 per annum. Nine years later (during another contractual dispute with the congregation) Leeser recalled the difficult summer of 1831. Unsure of his position with Mickveh Israel, he entered into negotiations with Congregation Beth Elohim in Charleston, South Carolina.

> As this amount [$800] was evidently less than I had a right to expect, I did not think myself at liberty altogether to decline to proposals made to me from abroad; yet I made such exorbitant demands as almost to preclude any idea of their being agreed to; one was in election without being a candidate, or going on to be heard beforehand; second, an election for life; third, an absence of three months every year, and lastly to be permitted; to stay in this congregation three months after the expiration of my time of service, to enable them to provide a suitable successor. Strange enough, all but the two first demands (and they in a modified degree to correspond with the laws of the above Kahal [congregation]) would have been accepted, if I may put any confidence in the assertions of the heads of the congregation, if in case I had consented to accept office there.[71]

However, because the Charleston synagogue pressed Leeser for an immediate answer, he felt compelled to reject their offer. He decided to remain at Mickveh Israel.

On September 4, 1831, the congregation met to reelect Leeser as its hazzan. They empowered the parnass, Zalegman Phillips, to engage Leeser for five years at a salary of one thousand dollars per annum. The vote was fifteen "ayes" and eight "nayes." Phillips voted against Leeser. One week later, the parnass officially wrote to Leeser and asked if he accepted the terms or whether he desired any modification to the number of years. The hazzan agreed to the new contract as offered by the congregation, but clear battle lines had been drawn, and the wounds on either side would never completely heal.[72]

Besides income and tenure, another area of contention involved the authority of the parnass and the adjunta. The matter came to a head in November 1831, when a member of the congregation, Henry Weil (1793–1853), a native of Hesse-Kassel and a former cavalry lieutenant in Jerome Bonaparte's army, caused a disturbance at Mickveh Israel during services. In the process, he personally affronted Jacob Phillips, a member of the adjunta. Phillips, the segan (deputy presiding officer) in the temporary absence of the parnass, brought the matter before the board on November 13. The adjunta placed the offender in *herem* (excommunication) and ordered the hazzan to announce the censure from the pulpit for three consecutive Sabbaths "as a warning to all evil doers."[73]

In America, the use of a partial *herem* by a lay board was already established during colonial times, usually as a way of combating both disruptive behavior in synagogue and religious laxity.[74] An entry in the minutes of Shearith Israel from the year 1757 reads:

> The Parnassim and Elders having received undoubted Testimony that several of our Brethren in the Country have and do violate the principles of our holy religion, such as trading on the Sabbath, Eating of forbidden Meats and other Heinous Crimes . . . therefore whosoever for the future continues to act contrary to our Holy Law by breaking any of the principles command [sic] of the Sinagoge Conferred on him and when Dead will not be buried according to the manner of our brethren.[75]

However, the use of the *herem* as a coercive and punitive measure to combat religious laxity was generally ineffective, especially in post-revolutionary America. It violated the idea of voluntary religious association and thus embodied a mode of religious coercion that was generally unacceptable in republican America. Finally, with the breakdown of the all-inclusive *kehillah*, or synagogue-community, during the Early National Period, it became impossible to enforce a ban of excommunication.

To Leeser, the idea of a lay-imposed *herem* was anathema. He refused to read the censure of Henry Weil in the synagogue. His act of insubordination infuriated the board. They met on February 12, 1832 and

> *Resolved*, That the Parnas inform the Hazan of the great dissatisfaction of the Board, at his not having complied with directions of said resolution, and to enquire of him what reasons, if any, he had for non-compliance with orders of the Board of Managers.
>
> *Resolved*, That this Board will adjourn to meet on Sunday, 11th March, at 10 A.M., at which time the Hazan is required to attend before the Board on the subject of the foregoing resolution.[76]

One month later, the entire board met as planned. Leeser refused to appear before them. Instead, he wrote a letter to the Parnass and openly maintained that he would not "acknowledge the Board of Managers to be [my] constituted Judges." The board, in turn, passed two more resolutions. The first stated that it had "full power and authority to manage the affairs of the congregation and that all officers are bound by the orders of the Board and the directions of the Parnass, and that this Board will exact from the officers of the congregation a strict compliance with all their orders." The second resolution ordered Leeser to make a full report to the entire congregation at their next meeting. On April 8, 1832, the congregation met and reaffirmed the authority of the parnass and adjunta to "control" the salaried officers.[77]

The vote of the congregation was tantamount to a vote of censure. Apparently, Leeser never explained his "motive for refusing to obey a plain duty" to the satisfaction of the congregation. Leeser subsequently discussed the problem of the relationship between the hazzan and the government of the synagogue in the *Occident*. He consistently adhered to a belief in the radical separation of the secular management of the synagogue and its spiritual program. On January 11, 1841, in the preface to his third volume of *Discourses*, he wrote:

> Now it is all well and proper to leave the management of every temporal concern in the hands of the President and his assistants; but the minister should not be in the discharge of duties altogether subservient to the temporal managers, who ought to confine themselves strictly to their branch of duty, and leave the public worship in the proper hands of those elevated to conduct it.[78]

A third source of dissatisfaction for Leeser during his early years at Mickveh Israel was the general conduct of the congregation. On September 28, 1832, less than half a year after being censured, he gave an impassioned sermon, "Obedience and Repentance." "Let me entreat you, brethren," he pleaded, "in this perhaps my last address to you, to forget each of you the peculiar grievances he may have to complain of."[79] He complained not only of factionalism, the withholding of contributions, and a lack of punctuality but of a general laxity in the religious life of the congregation.

> I may, though I hope not to do so, offend by my present remarks; but long since have I felt deeply in spirit for the loneliness which our place of worship presents! No one can imagine how much grief it must cause any sincere lover of his religion, to see so little true respect paid to the sacred edicts, which have been the admiration of the heathens even; to see how we, in this free country, where we are at liberty to worship our God according to our holy faith, without molestation, show our stubbornness by seeking every pursuit but that of Heaven, frequent every place but the house of God! Brethren, this ought not to be; let us wipe this reproach from us; let it not be said, and said with truth, that the churches of other denominations are filled with attentive audiences, whilst our Synagogues are nearly empty![80]

73

Leeser earnestly believed that Judaism could thrive in America. He never abandoned that hope, and he dedicated himself to creating a thriving Jewish religious life in a society where individuals were free to practice or ignore their respective religious traditions. "In many other countries," Leeser reminded his congregation, "the Hebrew is oppressed and despised; here he is upon an equality with other citizens, and is unmolested in the exercise of his religion." He continued,

> In tyrannical countries the Jew has always been a true believer, and a zealot in his faith even to martyrdom. Let us then prove, that in a free country the Jew is no less zealous, no less animated with love of Heaven, although the rod of persecution no longer compels him to seek shelter from the sword of man under the protection of the Almighty.[81]

Leeser was neither naive nor quixotic in his aspirations for Judaism in America. He recognized both the deep inroads that secularization had made in the Jewish community and the way that emancipation had weakened Jewish identity. Secularization, Leeser believed, was basically the product of Enlightenment philosophy and its denial of revelation as the exclusive source of truth in favor of human reason. Thus, he again turned to the manuscript he had prepared in Richmond, *Jews and the Mosaic Law*. With the help of Abraham Hart, the book was finally published in August 1833.[82] Hart, a native of Philadelphia and, since 1832, secretary of Mickveh Israel, was already, at the age of twenty-three, a rising star in the publishing industry.[83]

The completed version of *Jews and the Mosaic Law* contained two parts: "A Defence of the Revelation of the Pentateuch, and of the Jews for their adherence to the same," containing twenty-six chapters and an appendix with notes; and "Four Essays on the Relative Importance of Judaism and Christianity," in which Leeser reproduced and elaborated on the letters he first published in the Richmond *Whig* in 1829. Unfortunately, like his first book, this second book was a commercial failure. "The first book I issued made no profit," Leeser wrote in 1837, "and the second caused a considerable pecuniary loss."[84]

For several months after the publication of this work, Leeser was relatively inactive. He only preached twice during the remainder of the year: once during the High Holy Days (on the theme "The Duty of Instruction"), and again on December 12, his twenty-seventh birthday, on "The Selection of Israel," in which sermon he defended the idea of the Chosen People.

It is possible that Leeser had become depressed. Not only was he unhappy as hazzan of Mickveh Israel but he had also suffered a personal setback. Late in 1832, Abraham C. Peixotto, Leeser's host and a friend of Zalma Rehine, asked the hazzan to find a different place to live. Apparently Leeser had fallen in love with one of his daughters and he did not approve. A concerned Zalma wrote to his nephew on December 18, 1832 from Baltimore.

> I wish you to let me know why Mr. Peixotto does not wish to have your letters directed to his care. Should it be on account of Miss Simha, and I think . . . it is on that account from some information I have had . . . let me know it by next Post. I also advise you not to visit too often During the Absent [sic] of Mr. Peixotto at his House. When I receive your answer I shall be more particular, till then I wish you not to say anything to anybody about it, and depend on it I [am] as much interested on your account with what ever depends on your Happiness as on any[thing] what Can interest me in this world.[85]

A heartbroken Leeser then found lodging in an apartment sublet by a gentile seamstress, Mrs. Deliah Nash Cozens, at 86 Walnut Street. Some members of Mickveh Israel did not approve of the arrangement. Rumors abounded that Leeser was not eating kosher food and also that he had become fond of Mrs. Cozens' daughter, Ellen. The situation was aggravated by the fact that a previous hazzan, Abraham H. Cohen, whom Leeser knew in Richmond, had married a gentile, Jane Picken.[86]

Late in 1833, while residing at Mrs. Cozens's, Leeser recalled, "I was seized with a fearful malady, which prevented me from continuing my labours till after a long and painfull interruption."[87] The "fearful malady" was smallpox, and it left Leeser physically and emotionally scarred for the rest of his life. Rebecca Gratz described Leeser's affliction to her sister-in-law on February 2, 1834:

> There is another evil under the sun that has been making havoc in our city varioloid—poor Mr. Leeser is one of its present subjects, and tho his life and eye sight have been spared I am told his countenance will bear many marks of its ravages—he has always been so sensitive on the subject of personal disadvantages—that his former humility will appear like vanity to his present state—and unless some Desdemona shall arise to see his visage in his mind—all future expectations must be confined to solitary studies.[88]

Mrs. Cozens served as Leeser's nurse. He never forgot her kindness during this trying period in his life and included an annual stipend for her in his will.[89]

Smallpox brought still further grief in its wake. Leeser's younger brother, Jacob, migrated to America early in 1833. Like Isaac, he came to the United States at the request of Zalma Rehine, who had by this time moved from Richmond to Baltimore. Against Isaac's wishes, Jacob went to Philadelphia upon learning of his brother's situation. When he arrived, the hazzan had already slipped into a coma. Little hope was held for his recovery. By a twist of tragic irony, Jacob caught the same disease and died. Leeser, on the other hand, slowly began to recover. With great anguish, he recalled that with his

> being supposed on the point of death my only brother hastened from a distance to my bedside. It pleased our heavenly Father to afflict him with the same disease. Although robust, and to all appearance of that physical construction, as to render his long surviving me almost a matter of certainty, he yet sunk under his sufferings, and tranquil and resigned he breathed out his pure spirit in the hands of Him who gave it, in the twenty-fifth year of his age, on the 14th of March [1834], beloved by many, and hated by none. The recollection of his death is doubly agonizing, because he had to receive from friendly strangers the kindness and attention that ought to have been rendered by his brother, who was kept from his couch of sickness by sufferings of unspeakable intensity and horror.[90]

Less than three months later, Leeser had recuperated to the point where he could preach again. On May 23, 1834, he spoke on "The Duty of Active Benevolence." He began with a prayer of deliverance: "O most merciful One! who sendest succour to the afflicted, and protectest the helpless, grant us thy protection and deliver us from evil, and judge us not according to our unworthy deeds, but according to thy goodness, which is everlasting." In the address itself, he reflected further on the ephemeral nature of human existence.

> We are taught in the books of Holy Writ not to look upon this life as the chief period of our existence; nor upon the goods of earth, the material possessions, as the greatest acquirement; nor lastly, upon sensual pleasures as the highest enjoyment. And seeing that every thing here below is transitory, even the most careless observer is very apt to acquiesce in the idea, that life is short and its pleasures uncertain; yet there are few, indeed, who are led on to a virtuous and godly life through a contemplation of the vicissitudes to which they are subject.[91]

Man, Leeser concluded, should resolve "to exercise charity to the poor, to comfort the afflicted, to love our fellowmen like ourselves, and to keep the festivals of the Lord, and to celebrate weekly with devotion and an abstinence from labour the Sabbath of rest, in honour of our God."[92]

Leeser's spiritual reaction to his illness typifies a basic mode of human religiosity. Fredrick J. Streng, a contemporary student of religion, explains that "when man feels anxiety and pain, religious insight can be awakened. Reflection on who man is . . . wells up from a concern deeper than that for a logically perfect system of philosophy. The question of the meaning of life is experienced as a personal challenge."[93]

Following his recuperation, Leeser felt the challenge of creating a vital Judaism in America grow inside him again. Two years later, in 1836, when he published his first two volumes of *Discourses*, the profound effect of his bout with smallpox was still in evidence.

> The first twenty Discourses were rewritten; because I could not suffer my first attempts to come before the public without a careful revision. The others, however, which were composed chiefly after the chastening hand of the lord had fallen heavily on me, were prepared with more care, and I therefore only corrected them thoroughly, and altered those parts which appeared objectionable or defective.[94]

During the rest of 1834, Leeser continued to recuperate. He spoke once every month (except August) at Mickveh Israel but apparently restricted his other activities in an effort to regain his strength. On June 12, 1834, he again spoke on "The Selection of Israel." During the summer months, he reflected on "The Blessing of Revelation" and "The Permanence of the Law" and thereby was able to contrast the social stability that Torah produced with the severe civil disorders that racked Philadelphia that summer. The last sermon he gave that year, "The Jewish Faith," was an attempt to summarize his basic theological position. He began with the premise, in part borrowed from Protestantism, that faith precedes works.

> Without a motive for action, we do not act, and consequently without a motive for religious conduct we would certainly not be religious; and therefore if we wish to be religious, or to speak more properly, if we are anxious to secure that great share of happiness which flows from an obedience to the divine law, we must fortify ourselves previously by an acquisition of such feelings as best conduce to such a desirable consummation; or what is the same, we must endeavor growth of good deeds; for faith alone can be the producer of outward actions, if these actions are to have the least claim to sincerity.[95]

He then listed three basic dogmas:

> In the first place we have, as the foundation of all religion, the belief in the existence of a God; secondly, we are to acknowledge that this God

77

made known to mankind his will for their guidance; and thirdly, that we are accountable to this God for a dereliction from, or to be rewarded by Him for an obedience to, his will as declared to us.[96]

Leeser's list corresponds exactly to that of Joseph Albo, a fifteenth-century Jewish philosopher and preacher, and represented a rejection of Moses Mendelssohn's more universal and rationalist emphasis on the immortality of the soul and free will. On the other hand, Leeser also viewed Moses Maimonides' (1135–1204) "Thirteen Principles of Faith" as the authoritative Jewish creed. Not a systematic thinker, Leeser did not find it necessary to harmonize the positions of the two Judeo-Spanish philosophers, as he believed that they expressed the same "truth" in different manners. His knowledge of both Maimonides and Albo was not based on extensive reading of medieval literature but rather derived from secondary sources. He eventually owned a German translation of Albo (published in 1844), and late in life, he developed a keen interest in Maimonides and even contemplated an English translation of the *Guide to the Perplexed* based on the French work of Solomon Munk.[97]

Leeser's creedal approach to Judaism resolved several problems. First, it put Judaism on a footing similar to that of Christianity and thereby simplified the work of defending Judaism as the "true religion" and demonstrating its reasonableness. Second, it gave Judaism a truly "orthodox" or "right doctrine" character in an age when basic tenets of Jewish belief were being challenged by religious reformers. Third, by drawing on sources from the Golden Age in Spain, Leeser both reinforced Sephardic Jewish identity in the United States and strengthened his case for the historical necessity of revitalizing Judaism in America. Finally, Leeser, who made no claim to being a rabbi, was personally more comfortable discussing Judaism in theological terms than from the perspective of *Halachah* (Jewish law), in which he had little formal training and no authority.

His theology was neither profound nor original. Yet it was representative of Judaism in America during the nineteenth century, especially in its emphasis on dogma and the centrality of the Bible. His fight both with Christianity and Reform Judaism is best understood in this context. His theology did not change significantly over the years. To Leeser, truth was revealed and immutable. The idea of the historical development of religion was simply not a part of his world view. What Leeser learned in Germany and reformulated in Richmond was most fully articulated in Philadelphia from the pulpit of Mickveh Israel.

By the fall of 1834, Leeser was fully recovered from smallpox and was actively at work on a number of projects. It is evident that in general his years as a young preacher were filled with frustration. Relations with the leadership of the congregation started poorly and degenerated into open and mutual hostility. His preaching, very important to him personally, was met with indifference. His publications brought him no glory. Even his meek efforts at romance were hampered by the disapproval of the girl's parents. Finally, illness weakened him and ravaged his already homely appearance.

A person of less inner strength might have been overwhelmed by this sad string of events. Even though he was subsequently subject to occasional periods of depression and despair, Leeser found the resolve to go on with his life and work. He became within a few short years a tremendous intellectual and cultural force in the American Jewish community, broadly recognized by 1840 as the most important American Jewish religious leader of his time. Unfortunately, his relationship with his congregation would not improve. It was to remain a source of personal and professional conflict.

4

EDUCATOR, AUTHOR, SCHOLAR, 1834–1840

*Brethren, the painful truth must force itself upon the convictions
of everyone who thinks, that the present age is not one of
religion, but that, on the contrary, the duties which the law
demands are daily more and more neglected.*
—Isaac Leeser, "The Spirit of the Age," *Discourses,* April 1, 1836

DURING THE LATTER PART of the 1830s, Isaac Leeser emerged as
the foremost American Jewish religious leader of his day, a role he
would continue to play for more than three decades. Although still in
his twenties, he was already without peer among American hazzanim.
The other Jewish religious leaders in the United States at that time
were a very unimpressive group; Leeser alone had the vision, ability,
and requisite determination to combat the wide array of problems con-
fronting Judaism in America during the late Jacksonian and Antebellum periods.

Central to Leeser's maturation as a religious leader during this
time was the realization that freedom in America offered Judaism un-
limited possibilities but that the democratic spirit of the young republic also weakened the Jewish community's ability to maintain a viable,
separate life of its own. Individualism, a central part of the credo of
the young nation, contributed to the weakening of the authority of
Jewish religious tradition and helped loosen the ties of many American
Jews to the organized Jewish community. Moreover, American Jews,
increasingly an immigrant community, sought to integrate themselves
into the social and cultural mainstream of American society.

Leeser hoped to overcome the forces detrimental to the preserva-

80

tion and further development of Jewish life in America by introducing a series of innovations that captured the spirit of America and preserved the letter of the law of traditional Judaism. He believed that the key to counteracting individualism and assimilation was Jewish education, augmented by the mass dissemination of Jewish information and literature. By offering adequate instruction to American Jews, adults as well as children, he hoped to simultaneously Americanize Judaism and "Judaize" American Jews.

The role of education in Leeser's developing program for American Jews was paramount. The need to improve Jewish education in the United States had been clear to him since his arrival in Richmond a decade earlier. The failure of his first two day schools in Philadelphia reinforced that perception. While Leeser believed in the intrinsic value of Jewish education and wanted to make it available to the masses of American Jews, he also clearly understood the challenge the public school movement posed to Jewish traditionalists in the United States. He knew that if a viable Jewish educational alternative was not developed, the majority of American Jews might never receive any formal training in their ancient religious heritage and ultimately drift away from the faith.

Beginning in the 1830s, an educational reform movement swept across the United States geared toward expanding and improving public education. Motivated by the same belief in the intrinsic goodness of the average citizen that led to a broadening of suffrage in Jacksonian America, educational reformers such as Horace Mann and Henry Barnard set out to resolve a plethora of problems afflicting education in America. "We want a COMMON and EQUAL education—also PUBLIC because it is of general concern," one radical Jacksonian newspaper demanded in 1835. The same cry echoed throughout the land, especially in New England and in several north central states.[1]

During the early decades of the nineteenth century, education in America had fallen into a period of general decline, a situation the reformers now sought to reverse. American education suffered from decentralization, insufficient funding, and a failure to recruit and train good teachers. By 1833, it has been estimated, out of a total national population of 13 million people in the United States, one million school-age children were not receiving any formal education at all.[2]

Although the majority of American Jews apparently supported the growing public school movement, religious leaders such as Leeser did not.[3] Foremost among his objections to the new "free schools" was the fact that their curricula were far from nonsectarian and usually

81

attempted to inculcate a nondenominational mode of Protestantism. (The battle to secularize public education did not begin in earnest until the 1840s, when state legislatures debated the constitutionality of using public funds for private educational institutions.) Jewish children, Leeser concluded, should be sent to Jewish schools, and not be unnecessarily exposed to a system that would challenge their identities as Jews and weaken their religious faith.[4]

Leeser's views paralleled to a large extent those of American Catholics, who also concluded that their children should receive parochial education. At the first provincial council of Baltimore in 1829, the Church declared it to be "absolutely necessary that [Catholic] schools should be established in which the young may be taught the principles of faith and morality while being instructed in letters."[5] The Catholic community, however, had resources at hand unavailable to American Jews. First, the Church itself supported and coordinated the development of the schools and directly supplied numerous teachers and administrators. Second, the Catholic population was large, especially in comparison to the total number of American Jews. By 1853, the American Catholic population exceeded 2 million, while Jews did not yet number one hundred thousand. Also driving the Catholic desire for parochial schools was the steadily growing anti-Catholicism in the United States that began in the 1830s. Catholic families, hoping to shield their children from religious bigotry and social discrimination, favored the development of parochial schools.[6]

American Jews, on the other hand, possessed no ecclesiastical hierarchy, were few in number, and were generally not viewed as a threat to the "American" way of life in the same way that Catholics were. In fact, most Jews supported the public schools on ideological grounds, and preferred to make them religiously neutral instead of building parallel institutions of their own. From the 1830s onward, only a minority of tradition-minded Jews sought a religious alternative to the public schools, and in the years following the Civil War, nearly all their institutions collapsed.[7]

From the beginning, Leeser knew he would face an uphill battle to convince American Jews of the value of general Jewish schools. Nevertheless, when "various respectable residents" of Philadelphia approached him in 1835 and asked him to open a general school for Jewish children, he gladly accepted the challenge.[8] His enthusiasm for the project was fired by reports from Münster about the Hainsdorf School, which had been established the year after his departure from Westphalia. "This is the favourable moment," Leeser wrote, "when the experiment should be tried, [to see] whether Israelites in this country are not able, not willing, to establish for themselves, like their brethren have done in towns in Europe, a seminary, whence the seeds of righteousness are to be scattered far and near."[9]

In looking to Europe for a model for his new school, Leeser was acting in a fashion typical of his time. American educators in general were mindful of European innovations in their field. Pestalozzian methods and Lancastrian plans had already been imported from Switzerland and England earlier in the nineteenth century. By the 1830s, American educators were even traveling abroad to observe European, and most particularly Prussian, schools. Some German educators, such as Dr. Julius of Hamburg, were also invited to the United States to describe their work to American audiences.[10]

Aware of these developments, Leeser envisioned a modern school with a broad course of studies. Initially, the curriculum would include Hebrew reading and translation, basic Judaism, English grammar, geography, history, arithmetic, and writing. Later, additional languages, natural history, philosophy, drawing, singing, and other courses would be added "if the capacity of the scholars would admit of it." Enrollment would be open to children from both Jewish congregations in Philadelphia and, in the egalitarian spirit of the period, would also be open "to such Christians as might be willing to send their children to such an institution." "I intend to begin with boys only," Leeser wrote, "but if the number of girls offered should be sufficient to pay an assistant teacher, a school for females will also be commenced."[11] (Similarly, Lomdai Torah, "Students of Torah," an educational association affiliated with Congregation Anshe Chesed of New York, which was organized in 1828, also invited children of both sexes to participate in its program.[12])

On March 8, 1835, Leeser issued a prospectus for the school and sent it "to the Jewish Inhabitants of Philadelphia." He hoped to enroll forty students. Tuition was set at ten dollars per quarter for boys more than five years of age and twenty-five dollars per annum for younger children, although Leeser did not specify the nature of the preschool program. He also hoped that affluent members of the community would make significant donations to the school for capital purchases and to subsidize the education of children from families too poor to pay the proposed tuition. "To the work then!" Leeser exclaimed to the local Jewish community, and he actively began seeking "scholars."[13]

An enthusiastic Leeser also wrote to Zalma Rehine in Baltimore about his plans for a Jewish school, but Rehine was not as sanguine about the school's prospects as his nephew. He quickly replied to Leeser and suggested that the curriculum be limited to a few select areas of study. He also felt a limited enrollment to be more prudent, at least when the school first opened. He fully appreciated the extent of the American Jewish community's indifference toward Jewish education and hoped to temper his nephew's expectations for the school's success.[14]

Leeser's new school opened on March 31, 1835, with classes meeting at his home at 86 Walnut Street. Initially, only seven students enrolled. When several additional students applied and asked for tuition scholarships, Leeser turned to Mickveh Israel for assistance. "There are several poor children in this city," he wrote to the congregation, "whose parents are anxious to give them a good education, better than can be obtained in a free school, where besides (as I am told) Jewish children are exposed to insults."[15] The congregation did not heed the request. And yet, instead of turning the children away, Leeser absorbed the cost of their materials himself.[16]

By June, the enrollment had reached sixteen boys, which was to be its peak. Thereafter, the number began to decline. Late in the summer of 1836, Leeser informed Mickveh Israel that he did not have "one paying scholar over the age of three." Thus, after eighteen months, he was forced to close the school. In desperation, he asked Mickveh Israel to subsidize the program and reopen it under their own auspices. Again, no support was forthcoming—for now, the experiment was over.[17]

Just as Zalma Rehine had suspected, Leeser's school was doomed to fail from the outset. The hazzan had neither independent financial backing nor a guaranteed minimal enrollment. Both the synagogues and the Jewish benevolent societies remained distant from the project and offered no material support, and the little interest expressed by families able to pay tuition was withdrawn after indigent children became the majority of the student body. In addition, middle-class Jewish families already showed a propensity toward public education and the chance to further their integration into the mainstream of American society.

In Leeser's mind the root cause of the school's failure was religious indifference. "Brethren," Leeser told his congregation on April 1, 1836 (in a sermon entitled "The Spirit of the Age"), "the painful truth must force itself upon the convictions of everyone who thinks, that the present age is not one of religion, but that, on the contrary, the duties which the law demands are daily more and more neglected." Widespread lack of support for Jewish education, failure to observe ritual commandments, and mixed marriage led Leeser to predict that "in less than the age of one man the name of Israelite will hardly be known in this land, save as an object of memory, to be referred to as something that has been."[18]

Leeser was particularly impatient with Jewish families who failed, largely out of indifference, to have their infant sons circumcised. On September 21, 1835, when Fredrick Henry Etting, the uncircumcised son of Benjamin and Harriet (née Marx) Etting, died at the age of ten months, the question was raised as to whether or not he could be buried in Mickveh Israel's cemetery.[19] Standard procedure was for the parnass to handle the matter. However, the new parnass, Lewis Allen (1793–1841), was unsure of Jewish law in regard to this matter and consulted with Leeser.

Allen had become parnass at Mickveh Israel in 1834, after Zalegman Phillips declined to run for a thirteenth consecutive year in office. Born in England and brought to the United States at the age of twelve, he was well known as a "respected merchant" in the dry goods business. During Leeser's early years at Mickveh Israel, Allen had already frequently served as acting parnass and, although typically autocratic, did not despise Leeser as his predecessor did. Therefore, he was willing to consult with the hazzan on a fine point of Jewish law.[20]

An empathetic but frustrated Leeser researched the problem in the halachic literature available to him and wrote a brief reply to the parnass:

> I feel fully the true force of your embarrassing situation with regard to the decision you have to make about the burial of the child of Benjamin Etting, who himself uncircumcised, had denied up to the last minute the holy rite of circumcision to his two sons, and the youngest of whom is now dead, and the subject of embarrassment which you and I and every other Jew must so justly feel. Were I to give you an opinion from my own notions and feelings, I would say that the child is not entitled to burial; but taking our liberal code of laws for my guide, I have come to the conclusion with the means of forming an opinion in my power, to maintain that the child be admitted to the burying ground . . . without the usual honors, since there can be no doubt in law that he is a Jew, and only defective in the great point of circumcision.[21]

Greatly relieved at the decision to bury the child in a Jewish cemetery, a member of the Marx family, perhaps Joseph Marx, the maternal grandfather and a wealthy merchant from Richmond, Virginia, offered Leeser an honorarium, which he refused. His decision was based solely on his reading of the Law, not any deference to the rich.[22]

Five years later, still concerned about adherence to Jewish law,

Leeser devoted an entire sermon to a discussion of "The Covenant of Abraham."

> Parents! Do you fear God? Do you dread to appear before Him with the sin of neglect, of apostasy, upon your conscience? Then hasten to initiate your children into the covenant, and let them not have occasion in after-life to accuse you of being the cause that they are not members of the Jewish community. It is true, that it is the duty of every Israelite to assume the covenant himself, if his parents have been neglectful of the commandment; but what reason have you to expect, that your children will be sufficiently strong in faith to submit to the law, when you thought it unreasonable and cruel, or unnecessary, in their infancy. Let me impress it solemnly on your mind, that it is no small crime to cut off an entire household, or an entire family, from communion with Israel.[23]

However, his admonishments did little to change people's minds. The problem of salutory neglect continued to grow.

Leeser realized that widespread religious indifference left American Jews vulnerable to attempts to convert them from Judaism. Sometimes, christian missionaries carried their activities to the front door of the synagogue. In 1836, Leeser published a letter in *The United States Gazette* and reported that an agent of the American Tract Society "visited our place of worship on last Sabbath. . . . After the conclusion of the service, he posted himself at the entrance, and as the congregation was leaving the synagogue, he handed copies of a tract . . . contravening the tenets which we profess, to ladies, gentlemen, and even children." Outraged by the incident, the hazzan gave notice that "much as we deprecate violence or disturbance, we cannot answer for the forbearance of the zealous ones among us, who might perhaps be induced in their honest indignation, to eject an impertinent intermeddler, mildly if they can, forcibly if they must."[24]

To combat missionaries and to help Jews defend themselves against more subtle attempts at being proselytized, Leeser began a series on the Jewish view of the Messiah on October 30, 1835. Although he had intended to speak just once or twice on the topic, its theological importance and his own need to fully understand it resulted in his developing the theme more completely than he had first anticipated. The series, the first of its kind in the history of the American synagogue, developed over a fourteen-month period.[25] However, Leeser also recognized the limitations of his work, and insisted that "the discourses on the subject of the Messiah not be viewed as a complete treatise, but merely as an illustration of doctrines therewith."[26]

Leeser's concept of the Messiah largely conformed to traditional Jewish belief. In his opinion, the Messiah existed before the creation of the world, and Moses predicted his coming in Deuteronomy 18:14–15. The Messiah, Leeser wrote, will be a human messenger, a well-endowed judge, who will herald a change in the moral order of the universe without revoking the Law or changing the metaphysical nature of man's soul. Israel will derive great benefits from the coming of the Messiah, particularly its Restoration to its own land. It is an article of faith in Judaism, Leeser concluded, to believe in the advent of the Messiah, a scion of the House of David, even though it is impossible to predict exactly when he will arrive.[27]

While his view of the Messiah was neither original nor unusual, Leeser's attack on the Christian view of the same was uncharacteristically bold. "I must do myself the justice to state," Leeser explained to the congregation, some of whom took exception to his raising the issue in the first place, "that although I thus undertake to attack, to a certain extent, the opinions of the majority of the people among whom we live: it is not done for the sake of making a display of our own views." Rather, Leeser maintained, the purpose of the sermons on the Messiah was "solely to instruct those among us who may entertain doubts, or not be well informed on this subject."[28]

Christianity, Leeser argued, held a view of the Messiah that could not be substantiated by a close reading of Scripture. In rapid succession, he attempted to demonstrate the indivisibility of God, the limited nature of original sin, the eternal nature of Israel's election, and the unequivocally human status of the Messiah. In Leeser's mind, Christian theology collapsed like a house of cards if one adhered to a close, grammatically correct reading of Hebrew Scripture.[29] For example, in response to the Christian claim that a Hebrew word for God, *Elohim*, is a plural noun and thus an important point of evidence for trinitarianism, Leeser explained that "the word *Elohim* is the plural of *El* in its signification of *power*, and should accordingly be *powers*, and as applied to God, He in whom all powers are centered."[30] Although Leeser's explanation is plausible, it probably neither swayed Christian opinion nor delighted his congregation, whose interest in Hebrew grammar was minimal at best.[31]

On December 3, 1836, at the end of his seventh sermon on the Messiah, Leeser reluctantly told his congregation that he would not continue the series even though he wanted to do so. He had made private arrangements to publish two volumes of *Discourses* and had to stop his preaching "almost abruptly . . . before these volumes had entirely gone to press" to edit his manuscripts for publication.[32] The time had arrived to share his reflections with a larger audience. "Let me hope," Leeser wrote on January 6, 1837, in the preface to his *Discourses*, "that the exertions I have made in the service of my Maker redound to diffuse the knowledge of his commandments among our people, and to contribute to cement strong the bond that unites us in our capacity."[33] He occasionally returned to the topic of the Messiah during his long career as a preacher.

The appearance of the first two volumes of Leeser's *Discourses* in 1837 marked another turning point in his career. Although he still did not have a commercial publisher to print and distribute his work, a network of family members and friends coalesced and sold his works throughout the country and in the Caribbean. The five hundred copies of the *Discourses* Leeser had printed were quickly disseminated, and requests for him to continue the series were made, much to his delight.[34] At least in some circles, American Jews had finally accepted the idea of a sermon as an integral part of Jewish practice and had discovered that sermons could serve as a valuable source of information about Judaism. Indeed, in the following decade, an increasing number of American synagogues began to look for skilled preachers as their religious leaders.

Leeser must have also been pleased by the favorable notice of his *Discourses* printed in Ludwig Philippson's *Allgemeine Zeitung des Judentums*, a leading German-Jewish newspaper published in Breslau. Philippson, a moderate reformer, wrote that the spirit of Leeser's works "may appear too orthodox, nevertheless, it is that orthodoxy, full of clarity and sublimity, which is so much admired in the works of Mendelssohn." Philippson continued, "Mr. Leeser," opposes indifference and dependence on mere formalism in religion, supporting his thesis by citing Scriptures and the teachings of the Rabbis. He has a delightful style, his opinions are comprehensive, and his knowledge, even though inferior to some great German scholars, is far above average."[35]

Leeser's *Discourses*, 590 pages long, was the first collection of Jewish sermons to be published in the United States—only individual sermons and addresses had been printed before, nothing this ambitious. Even the nonhomiletic works written and published by American Jews on topics of Jewish interest paled in comparison to Leeser's accomplishment. The *Discourses* thus evidenced Leeser's tenacity, even as their uniqueness bore silent testimony to the weakness of Judaism in America during the 1830s.[36] Altogether, Leeser included fifty sermons, as well as two addresses given in nonliturgical settings, in the *Discourses*.[37]

Another indication of Leeser's growing importance in the American Jewish community at this time was the role he played in the placement of a new hazzan in Charleston, in 1836. Beth Elohim, which had offered Leeser a position five years earlier, was again looking for a hazzan. This time Leeser took the initiative and nominated Gustavus Poznanski, then a religious functionary in New York, for the position. The Southern congregation hired him, satisfied with Leeser's unequivocal recommendation.[38]

Although Poznanski later became a source of embarrassment and consternation for Leeser when he endorsed several controversial reforms (including the use of an organ for Jewish worship[39]), what is important is that Leeser's recommendation was sufficient to influence the selection of a hazzan in a distant congregation. In time, Leeser would become an unofficial rabbinic placement office among traditional American congregations—a position that greatly enhanced his power on the national scene.

If Leeser was beginning to develop a following among American Jews in general, he still had few active supporters among the members and officers of his own congregation. Several factors contributed to their failure to rally behind their hazzan. Leeser was a difficult person: he had an inferiority complex and was, therefore, extremely sensitive. In addition, he was not much of a role model—especially not in appearance and demeanor. Some congregants resented his extensive outside interests, and preferred for him to attend to his ministerial duties. Furthermore, Leeser's independence of mind with respect to the role of hazzan led to frequent conflicts, which generally resulted in stalemate rather than compromise. As his second contractual period drew to a close, dissatisfaction began to turn into a nasty, but ultimately unsuccessful, campaign to prevent his reelection at Mickveh Israel.

At a meeting held just prior to the High Holy Days, a resolution to rehire Leeser "for three years at $1,000 per annum" was defeated. "There was," the hazzan wrote later, "properly speaking, no minister elected to office during the latter part of the holy days, a circumstance which evidently must be mortifying to one who had for seven years faithfully done his duty." Moreover, Leeser added that the situation was "highly prejudicial to the interest of the congregation, as it was thus in my power, if I had chosen to display a revengeful feeling, to leave the congregation absolutely unprovided at the very season of the holy festivals."[40]

The parnass of the congregation, Lewis Allen, then asked Leeser to continue acting as hazzan until the holidays passed, when the congregation could vote again on Leeser's future at Mickveh Israel. "I was only reelected," Leeser maintained, "as I heard a year afterward, by a bare majority, despite that there was no charge of misconduct or incompetence against me." The new contract was for only one year, and it did not include any additional income.[41]

The insecurity of his position at Mickveh Israel complicated Leeser's plans for the immediate future. He had decided to undertake a major literary project and publish the entire Sephardic liturgy in six volumes. Nearly two hundred subscribers from across the country backed the project, and Leeser also invested "several thousand dollars" of his own money, although it is unclear how he had accumulated such a large sum.[42] Leeser was aware that the slow process of translation and the printing of hundreds of pages in Hebrew would require nearly two years of ceaseless effort. Not surprisingly, he stopped preaching in January 1837 for ten full months to concentrate all his efforts on the project. Because he was not contractually obligated to preach, the board of the congregation did not officially challenge his decision to temporarily stop giving sermons. However, neither did they encourage his publication of the Sephardic liturgy.

Instead, the trustees of Mickveh Israel decided to advertise broadly for a new hazzan. Late in the summer of 1837, Jacques Judah Lyons (1813–77), a twenty-four-year-old South American hazzan, responded to the call and announced that he would arrive in Philadelphia in September, just prior to the holidays, to stand as a candidate in the coming elections. Lyons, a native of Surinam, Dutch Guyana, had served as the reader for Congregation Neve Shalom in his home town of Paramaribo since 1833.[43]

On August 22, 1837, nine members of Mickveh Israel petitioned the parnass "to hear Rev. Lyons perform the entire Sabbath Service, at an early date prior to the Coming Elections for Hazan."[44] Leeser was outraged by the request. Lyons had neither arrived in town nor personally requested to officiate on a trial basis at services. The next day, Leeser sent a strongly worded letter to the parnass. He maintained that the congregation had no right to ask him to "yield the *Tebah*" (pulpit), but that he would do so in "a mere spirit of courtesy, as I would not well refuse one who has been in office to read the service if he is earnestly desirous to do so." Leeser added that the entire congregation could be advised of the stance he had taken.[45]

Lewis Allen reacted coolly to Leeser's display of anger. He wrote, "As you have taken the liberty to address a letter to me explaining your motives for allowing the Rev. Lyons to read prayers, which explanation I never asked for, I take this method to tell you I have neither the time nor do I choose to make *your* sentiments known to the congregation."

Allen also wrote to the ad hoc committee that Lyons would be asked to read the service on the coming Shabbat.[46]

Lyons led services at Mickveh Israel on August 6. Two weeks later, twelve individuals asked Allen if Lyons could again read the service, since not everyone was able to attend the first time, and others wanted to hear him again before making a decision. This time Allen denied Lyons permission "owing to its being the last Shabbas of the Revd. I. Leeser's present engagement." He added, "I do not think it correct to deprive him of that honour—but for the satisfaction of all parties, the Revd. Mr. Lyons has permission [to read] on the first part of the next Shabbas morning prayer."[47]

On September 22, having already read once at Mickveh Israel, Lyons presented his credentials to the members of the synagogue and formally applied to run for the position of hazzan. His carefully constructed letter of introduction suggested that he was a strong candidate in precisely those areas where Leeser's performance was problematic. "He is solicitous to undertake the Holy Calling," Lyons deliberately wrote of himself, "and to contribute his sole time and exertion, to the duties devolving thereon." With respect to his work as a Hebrew teacher, Lyons added that "where the Parents are in reduced circumstances," he would teach "free of expense to them." Finally, he left the matter of compensation up to "the Wisdom of the Members" but added that "he is accompanied to this country by Aged Parents; who in duty he feels bound to protect with Filial Care."[48]

Lyons' strategy failed. The election was held on September 24, with only the yahidim (members with voting privileges) participating. Leeser was reelected by a solid majority: twenty-three "ayes" to ten "nays."[49] "After a very animated contest," Leeser wrote, "the congregation honoured me for the fourth time with their suffrage." Hyman Gratz and Solomon Moses were appointed to convey the good news to the hazzan. A relieved Leeser reportedly wrote to his family members that "the Lyon is subdued."[50]

The sweetness of victory, however, was spoiled for Leeser by the reduced terms the congregation offered him. Perhaps in light of the recent recession, the Panic of 1837, the congregation asked him to take a 20 percent cut in pay and to serve at the new rate ($800 per annum) for the next three years. The congregation also decided to enforce, for the first time since Leeser had arrived in Philadelphia, its twenty-seventh bylaw, which directed that "the Hazan and Shohet, shall enter into written contracts under a penalty for the faithful performance of their respective duties" (emphasis added).[51]

Leeser was indignant. He refused to comply with either condition.

91

"I can see no just ground for reducing the income attached to the office," he informed Allen. Furthermore, he observed, the bylaws "only prescribe a bond (under a penalty) for faithful performance of the office; but [are] silent in regard to any pledge as to continuance in such office." In addition, he revealed, "it would be out of my power to leave this year." In Leeser's opinion, the bond was both superfluous and degrading.[52]

On December 10, 1837, Allen announced to the board that Leeser had refused to sign the new contract. To break the deadlock, the trustees resolved to take the matter to the entire congregation. Lyons was still in Philadelphia, and it was possible that the congregation would call for a new election.[53] Leeser realized he was in a vulnerable position and wrote to his uncle for advice.[54]

"My own opinion," the hazzan wrote to the elderly Rehine (according to one of his early biographers), "is decidedly opposed to pledging myself to stay with the congregation as they have done so much to mortify me. . . . According to my views of the question I can lose nothing by leaving Philadelphia for the congregation who cannot treat me properly after an acquaintance of eight years deserves not to have me." Rehine replied, "If you are to be treated ill by them without cause, I shall be the last man to advise you to engage with them . . . to be their slave . . . but I hope that the case is not so bad as you mention that you have no friends among them."[55]

Rehine persuaded Leeser to sign the contract and the bond. An agreement was reached on December 27, 1837, and the congregational meeting was canceled.[56] Several days later, the treasurer of the congregation informed Leeser that he would not be able to pay the hazzan at the beginning of the quarter "from want of funds."[57] Clearly, synagogue "poverty" was in tension with the demands of the hazzan, a problem that would continue to grow at Mickveh Israel for thirteen more years.

Although finally reelected, the campaign to defeat him in 1837, the subsequent contractual dispute, and the failure of the congregation to promptly meet its financial obligations to him left Leeser bitter and disappointed. He resented both the legal constraints placed on him personally and the general disrespect shown to the office of hazzan. Only a few individuals at Mickveh Israel recognized the important role Leeser was starting to play in the American Jewish community. Most simply viewed him as a hireling with a disagreeable personality.

Remarkably, in the face of the hard-fought election, neither Leeser nor Lyons harbored any resentment, a tribute to both the former's sense of professionalism and the latter's diplomacy. On February 17, 1838, Leeser prepared a "Certificate . . . as to the qualifications of Rev.

J. J. Lyons as Hazan" and sent it to Congregation Beth Shalome in Richmond, Virginia, where his old friend, Jacob Mordecai, was still parnass. Lyons was offered the position and briefly served in Richmond. In 1840, he was invited to become the hazzan of New York's prestigious Shearith Israel, where he remained until his death in 1877.[58]

Nor did Leeser's conflict with his congregation delay his plans to publish the Sephardic liturgy. It is even possible that the hazzan intensified his publishing activities as a way of maintaining his self-esteem. "It was only on the twenty-seven of last July [1837]," Leeser wrote, "that the subject [of publishing the liturgy] was seriously agitated and the final resolve was not taken till the first of November."[59] He had imported Hebrew types, an admirer later recalled, and "was obliged to teach the Sacred language to the printers in order that they might set up the pages with tolerable correctness."[60] Leeser recollected, "There being no persons here acquainted with Hebrew composition, vexatious delays had to be submitted to, till novices had, by perseverance and highly commendable application, rendered themselves qualified to do the work creditably."[61]

Leeser originally undertook the task of publishing the liturgy because "it has hitherto always been necessary to procure every holyday book from England, generally at an enormous cost: and in addition to this, the supply had become completely exhausted." When the first volume of a newly translated British Sephardic liturgy, published by the Rev. David de Sola, hazzan of the Portuguese Congregation of London, appeared just as Leeser was about to go to press, he was forced to reevaluate the need for his own publication. After comparing his work with de Sola's, he concluded that his own translation was "superior" and that he should continue with the project.[62]

Leeser not only decided to complete his own work on the Sephardic liturgy but even strove to make it competitive with de Sola's work. Thus, he included both "A Prayer for the Royal Government" and "A Prayer for a Republican Government." A decade later, after considerable Jewish immigration from Central Europe to the United States had greatly expanded the domestic market, Leeser published a daily prayer book for Ashkenazic Jews, but omitted the "Prayer for a Royal Government."[63]

In preparing his translation of the Sephardic liturgy, Leeser strove to adhere as closely as possible to the literary style of David Levi (1742–1801), a scholarly British Jew whose English rendition of the Sephardic liturgy (1789–1793) was viewed as authoritative by both American and British Jews.[64] Leeser also frequently consulted Moses

Mendelssohn's German translation of the Bible in preparing his rendition of biblical passages in the prayer book. "Let it not, however, be thought that I have furnished a translation of a translation;" Leeser advised his readers, "only that the Hebrew has been rendered according to the great light shed upon it by the great philosopher and those who preceded him in the task of elucidating Scriptures, such as Yarchi [Rashi], Aban Ezra, and other bright luminaries of our people."[65]

Several months later, in September 1838, he began a translation of Mendelssohn's most important philosophical work, *Jerusalem.* "The work was merely done, to give a friend some idea of what M. thought on certain points," Leeser wrote. Curiously, he did not publish his English version of *Jerusalem* for fourteen years, because he felt he had done an unsatisfactory job, and yet he entertained no such doubts about his work on the Sephardic liturgy.[66]

Leeser was particularly proud of his translation of the numerous psalms contained in the liturgy. "It may also be left to the candour of all my readers," he asserted, "whether they are Hebrew scholars or not, to say whether this version, especially of the Psalms, is not more harmonious and intelligible than it was in the old books and the English Bible."[67] In fact, Leeser's psalms were stylistically inferior to the King James', although perhaps closer mechanically to the original Hebrew word order. The changes in the English text, however, did satisfy Leeser's readers that a new and authentically Jewish translation had been prepared. Thus the foundation for Leeser's most important literary project, an original translation of the entire Hebrew Bible, was laid.

The work on the liturgy was finished in February 1838. The six-volume, bilingual edition of the Sephardic prayer book appeared under the title *Siftei Tzadikkim* ("The Lips of the Righteous"). Volume 1 contained the "Daily Prayers," volumes 2 and 3, the High Holy Day liturgies. The final three volumes had the prayers for the three pilgrimage holidays: Tabernacles (Sukkot), Passover (Pesach), and the Feast of Weeks (Shavuot). Without question, *Siftei Tzadikkim* was the most ambitious Judaica publishing project in America since Jews first arrived in New Amsterdam in 1654. A second edition of the liturgy was published in 1845. It was reprinted in 1853 and 1878.[68]

With the prayer book completed after a year and a half of intensive work, Leeser fell into one of his periodic depressions, this one intensified by the exhaustion that followed upon achievement. "Now, I confess," he wrote, "I feel at a loss for something to do; a certain restlessness has overpowered me . . . but still, I have but one ultimate aim, the same which I trust my books display—an earnest desire for the dissemination of the truth, which I conceive to be the knowledge and practice of our religion."[69]

Luckily, it did not take long for the hazzan to find a new outlet for his energy. Rebecca Gratz, one of Leeser's few supporters at Mickveh Israel, decided in February 1838 to organize a Jewish Sunday school in Philadelphia.[70] Leeser took an immediate and deep interest in the Gratz Sunday School. Rosa Mordecai, who attended the school in the 1840s, recalled in 1901 that "Miss Rebecca Gratz found in him an able and untiring assistant in forming the Hebrew Sunday School."[71] "The establishment of the Sunday-schools," Dr. Abraham Rosenbach wrote in 1913, "touched the deepest chord of his [Leeser's] nature; he responded with full and unselfish devotion."[72]

By 1818, Gratz, Leeser's elder by twenty-five years, had already taken the initiative to sponsor private Hebrew classes in her home.[73] The new plan was much more ambitious. In part, it was based on the program Leeser and his teacher, Isaac B. Seixas, had developed in Virginia ten years earlier. But while the Seixas-Leeser school was ephemeral, the Gratz Sunday School quickly became the model for Jewish education in the United States.[74]

Although the idea of the Christian Sunday school can be traced back to seventeenth-century Puritan Joseph Alleine, the institution did not become popular until Robert Reikes (1735–1811), a Gloucester printer and journalist, established a "First Day" school in his hometown in 1780 and publicized the idea in the English press. Reikes was particularly concerned with the impact of the Industrial Revolution on disadvantaged children in England and hoped to curb juvenile delinquency by increasing literacy among the poor. His school emphasized both general and religious instruction. Similarly, Hannah More (1745–1833), an English religious writer who may have served as a role model for Rebecca Gratz, worked indefatigably on behalf of the indigent children in the mining districts of the Mendip Hills.[75]

When Sunday schools were transplanted to America, they also functioned as both general-charity and religious schools. The popularity of the Sunday school soared during the Early National Period, and it is estimated that by 1830 as many as 1.5 million children attended Sunday school in the United States. As general education became available to the masses during the first half of the nineteenth century, however, the role of the Sunday school narrowed. Its curriculum became oriented exclusively toward religious studies.[76]

Philadelphia, it should be noted, served as a leading administrative center for the Sunday school movement in America. In 1791, the first American Sunday School Society was founded there. Among the founders was Dr. Benjamin Rush, a patriot and leading medical doctor in Philadelphia. In 1824, the American Sunday School Union was also formed in Philadelphia, to promote the establishment of new Sunday schools and publish materials for their instructional program.[77]

Exactly what motivated Gratz to begin the Sunday school experiment in 1838 is difficult to determine. Certainly, she was aware of the dismal condition of Jewish education in the United States. But perhaps more important was the social crisis in American Jewry at that time. The second half of the 1830s witnessed a rapid intensification of Jewish immigration to the United States. The country's Jewish population grew from between 4,000 and 6,000 in 1830 to about 15,000 a decade later. Subsequently, immigration became even more intense, especially during the 1840s and the early years of the 1850s. Compounding the many problems involved in absorbing the flood of immigrants was the Panic of 1837—a panic that drove many into bankruptcy.[78]

Leeser, like Gratz, was painfully aware of the consequences of the depression for the thousands of new Jewish immigrants to the United States. In speaking to women's benevolent societies, he pleaded the case of the poor, the widow, and the orphan. In an address, "The Duty and Scope of Charity," delivered before the Female Benevolent Society of Philadelphia on November 6, 1836, Leeser ended with the request to "forget not the task, most delightful of all, to instruct the young mind, to awaken the tender soul to a knowledge of the Creator, and assist the distressed mother to enable her to rear up the children of the Lord that the Lord has given her, a joy to herself, an honour to you, and servants to their Maker."[79] A month later, he spoke before the Society for the Education of Poor Children at Shearith Israel in New York. It was the first time he had been invited to speak outside Philadelphia since first employed by Mickveh Israel. Leeser again linked the themes of "charity and enlightenment." "There are here and now present, those who are greatly blessed with means beyond their wants; he exhorted them. "Let them open their hearts, and give freely unto the treasury, whence the sufferings of many may be relieved, through which many may be rescued from ignorance, from ignominy, and irreligion."[80] The following year, Leeser was again invited to speak to the Female Hebrew Benevolent Society of Philadelphia at their November meeting. Again, he urged them to persevere in their relief work and, above all, to pay special attention to the needs of the immigrants.[81]

Leeser's close relationship with the Female Hebrew Benevolent Society was no accident. Rebecca Gratz had played a leading role in developing its program since its inception in 1819. Then, at the age of thirty-eight, she had already had considerable experience in women's

96

benevolent societies in the general community, and was ready to apply that knowledge to create parallel activities in the Jewish community. According to Edwin Wolf and Maxwell Whiteman, the Female Hebrew Benevolent Society was one of "the first separate, charitable organizations founded by Jews in Philadelphia," as well as one of the oldest Jewish charities in the United States to stay in continuous existence. Throughout its early history, it "remained under the direction of the women of the leading families of Mickveh Israel."[82]

At a meeting of the society held on February 4, 1838, it was resolved "that a Sunday-school be established under the direction of the board, and teachers appointed among young ladies of the congregation." Two committees were organized: one "to procure a school room," the other "to procure books and make all necessary arrangements." Rebecca Gratz, who served on both committees, was the driving force behind the project.[83] Writing to her Christian sister-in-law in Kentucky about the project, Rebecca commented, "If it succeeds I shall feel that I may have been useful in my generation."[84] In another note she amplified on these sentiments: "It will be a consolation for much lost time, if this late attempt to improve the degenerate position of a once great people shall lead to some good and induce wiser and better Jews to take the work in hand."[85]

Three weeks following the meeting of the Female Hebrew Benevolent Society in February 1828, Rebecca Gratz reported to her sister-in-law, "We have a room and expect to open next week."[86] An announcement of the school's opening was circulated in the Philadelphia Jewish community, attracting considerable attention. According to the announcement, the Sunday school would

> not be limited to any number or class of children. All who are hungry for the bread of life are welcome to this banquet; all who desire to read the Scriptures understandingly are invited to partake of instruction, given and received with reverence, and at no other charge than attention—no other cost than such free will offerings as it may be the pleasure of convenience of some to bestow. The school is opened every Sunday morning at ten o'clock and closed at twelve o'clock.[87]

On March 4, 1838, Rebecca Gratz's fifty-seventh birthday, the Sunday school opened with an all female faculty. The first session was held at Miss Peixotto's Private Academy, a school operated by Simha Cohen Peixotto at 97 Walnut Street above Fourth. Peixotto and Gratz were joined by five other members of the Female Hebrew Benevolent Society. According to their board minutes, "the school was this day opened with about sixty scholars, and, they trust, prosperously commenced."[88]

The operation of the Sunday school was closely patterned after the Protestant model. The curriculum emphasized Bible study and used the catechetical method. The children were grouped according to age and sat on "bright yellow benches with pastoral medallions." Only limited instruction in Hebrew reading was offered. It has also been reported that "a penny contribution box for the poor of Jerusalem" was kept at school.[89]

Assemblies played an important part in the first Jewish Sunday school. They were usually conducted by Rebecca Gratz. One student later recalled: "Her majestic figure rose high above all there collected—a hundred scholars or more—to hear her mild and firm voice read a chapter of the Holy Bible, and then they in unison, repeated a prayer written for them by herself which combined 'all prayer.' "[90] The principal would begin the devotion by saying: "Come ye children, hearken unto me, and I will teach you the fear of the Lord; lift up your hearts in prayer; in all your ways acknowledge Him, and He will direct your paths." To this the children would respond:

> O God, give unto us the help we need; give us bread to eat and raiment to put on, and instruction to understand thy mercies; may we be grateful for all Thy goodness; may we be dutiful to our parents; honest in all our dealings, true in our behavior to one another; attentive to our teachers, and above all ardent and devout in adoring Thee alone, the God of our fathers Abraham, Isaac, and Jacob; enlighten our faith, that we may daily repeat the acknowledgement of Thy unity. "Hear O Israel, the Lord our God is one Lord. Blessed be the name of the glory of His kingdom for ever and ever. Amen."[91]

The most important assembly of the year, the Annual Examination, took place on the Sunday that fell closest to Purim. Initially, it was held at Mickveh Israel. The elite of the Jewish community were invited to attend and were solicited for funds to defray expenses for the coming year. "The children were seated on the steps of the *hechal*, or ark," an early source reports. "Miss Gratz as superintendent conducted the exercises. After the examination and the distribution of premiums the children repaired to an adjacent building and received, for refreshment, a pretzel and orange." Prizes included the Ten Commandments, printed on silk, and religious books, usually Leeser's *Daily Prayers* and, later, his Bible.[92]

The success of the Sunday school was astonishing. During its second year of operation, eighty students enrolled. By 1843, Miss Peixotto's academy was no longer able to house the operation. The school then moved to Masonic Hall between Seventh and Eighth streets and occupied a room appropriated by the managers of the famous Franklin Institute. Ten years later, the school moved again, this time to the building of the Phoenix Hose Company and, finally, to the (old) building of the Hebrew Education Society, later known as Touro Hall. By 1913, the Hebrew Sunday School of Philadelphia had become a school system operating from thirteen different locations with an enrollment of more than four thousand pupils.[93]

Ironically, Leeser's chief reservations about the Sunday school, namely, the limited nature of its program, also constituted the reason for the school's success. The Sunday school enabled parents to provide their children with a formal introduction to Judaism without compromising their belief in public education. Moreover, the Sunday school reinforced the Americanist goals of the public schools by promoting a "Protestant" mode of Judaism.

The Sunday school was also popular with a wider circle of American Jews than those primarily interested in Jewish day schools because no tuition was charged. Teachers worked gratis, as they did in Protestant Sunday schools, and the Jewish community rallied to Gratz's cause because of her high social position in American Jewish circles. The school also had the institutional backing of the Female Hebrew Benevolent Society. Finally, the Sunday school was a lay-sponsored and lay-run institution, free from direct supervision of the clergy. Leeser and other hazzanim assisted the staff on an advisory basis and played a largely symbolic role at the various assemblies. Americanist in its orientation, undemanding on its students, inexpensive for parents, and securely controlled by the laity, the Sunday school proved to be the answer to Jewish educational needs in the 1830s.

In 1839, additional Sunday schools opened in New York and Charleston. Thereafter, the movement quickly spread. By the time the Civil War broke out, Jewish Sunday schools were operating in cities throughout the United States, Canada, and the Caribbean.[94] As in Philadelphia, the schools were largely organized by women from elite Sephardic backgrounds.

However, not all American Jews accepted the idea of Sunday instruction for their children. "Without exception," historian Leon Jick observed, "German Jewish congregations rejected the Sunday School." It was "not until the late 1860s," he added, that "German Jews [were] ready to settle for the Sunday Schools as a desirable or at least acceptable form of Jewish education."[95]

Perhaps the most important thing that Leeser, a traditional religious leader, did on behalf of the Jewish Sunday school movement was to give it his personal approval and counter the Ashkenazic opposition to the program. "As may be imagined," Leeser wrote in 1840, "some prejudice was at first manifested by various persons, who fancied that they discovered an objectionable imitation of gentile practices in this undertaking, forgetting that it is the first duty of Israel to instill knowledge of divine things in the hearts of the young, and this institution was eminently calculated to bestow this necessary blessing alike upon rich and poor without fee or price."[96] After 1843, he frequently reported Sunday school news in the *Occident* and wrote editorial articles in praise of its goals.

Leeser was also a conspicuous figure at the Gratz Sunday School. "To the teachers," Rosa Mordecai again recalled, "he was a walking Encyclopaedia, ever at their command. He knew every scholar by name and seldom passed in the street without a greeting. He led the Hebrew hymns, gave short discourses to the children, and handed them prizes at the Anniversaries."[97] On opening day, for instance, it was reported that "a donation of thirty copies of Mr. Leeser's *Instruction in the Mosaic Religion* was presented by Mr. Abraham Hart."[98] When it was discovered that the textbook was too difficult for most of the children, Leeser immediately began to prepare a new, more appropriate book for them.

In 1839, Leeser published his *Catechism for Jewish Children*, which quickly became known as the "Leeser Catechism."[99] Actually, the new work was based on Eduard Kley's *Catechismus der Mosaischen Religion* (Berlin, 1814). Kley (1789–1867) was a well-known Jewish religious reformer in Germany who preached at Israel Jacobson's private temple in Berlin and, later, at the radical Hamburg Temple. Influenced by the great Protestant theologian Fredrick Schleiermacher, he emphasized the devotional aspects of religion. He believed that the essence of Judaism could be reduced to the three fundamental principles suggested by philosopher Joseph Albo: belief in the existence of God, belief in revelation, and belief in divine retribution.[100] Leeser was probably attracted to Kley's *Catechismus* both because of its simplicity—and therefore applicability to the Hebrew Sunday School—and, perhaps more importantly, because of its availability.

As with his translation of Johlson's *Instruction in the Mosaic Religion*, Leeser felt free to depart from the original German work in order to make the English version conform with his own Orthodox beliefs. He added a second appendix, which he called "The Jewish Creed" to guarantee the work's Orthodoxy. Not only did he include Albo's three fundamental principles in the addendum, but he also listed Moses Maimonides' "Thirteen Fundamental Principles of the Jewish Faith." "This book is no translation," Leeser wrote in the preface to the *Catechism*, "because, in the first place, it contains fully double the quantity of the doctor's book; and, secondly, not to mention that several important points had been omitted or too obscurely given by him, he [Kley] had imparted a peculiar colouring to his ideas."[101]

Mindful of the problems encountered with his first textbook, Leeser attempted to prepare the *Catechism* specifically for eight- to fourteen-year-olds. He wrote at graduated levels of difficulty, so that the last chapters were written primarily for the older youths. He even suggested that certain chapters be put off for a second reading of the book.[102] Unfortunately, the book again proved too difficult for many of the Sunday school students who were still learning English as a second language. Nevertheless, it was reprinted five times, the last in 1872, for want of alternatives.[103] Leeser dedicated the book, originally completed in May 1839, to Rebecca Gratz.

Because Leeser's two catechisms could be used only by the better students in the more advanced classes, Rebecca Gratz needed to find additional materials for her school. Some Protestant works were used, including hymnals, the King James Bible, and the American Sunday School Union's *Child's Bible Questions*. Objectionable passages were either pasted over or torn out.[104] Rebecca Gratz donated thirty copies of Solomon Cohen's *Jewish Faith*, which, like Leeser's works, was probably too advanced for most of the Sunday school students. Jews from around the country also sent copies of pedagogical works. From New York, Mordecai Manuel Noah sent a copy of J. Van Oven's *Manual of Judaism*.[105] Later, several teachers at Gratz's school wrote texts of their own, including Simha Cohen-Peixotto's *Elementary Introduction to Scripture* and a rhymed catechism by her sister, Mrs. Eliezer Pyke, entitled *Scriptural Questions for the Use of Sunday Schools for the Instruction of Israelites*.[106]

Although the Gratz Sunday School did not include a systematic introduction to Hebrew in its program, Leeser also published *The Hebrew Reader* in 1838, which he intended to be the first of a series "calculated for the acquisition of Hebrew." It contained exercises, simple grammatical rules, aids for pronunciation and reading, liturgical selections with English translations, and directions for the teacher. Even though the proposed companion volumes were never published, *The Hebrew Reader* proved to be a valuable aid for teaching children.[107] The other available works, for example, E. N. Carvalho's *A Key to the Hebrew Tongue* (1815) and Joseph Aaron's *A Key to the Hebrew Language* (1834), were written primarily for Jewish adults and for Christians studying the language.[108]

*   *   *

By the end of the 1830s, Leeser was unquestionably the most prolific Jewish religious writer in the country. After nearly a decade of service at Mickveh Israel, he had published a general theological work, a two-volume collection of sermons, three textbooks, and a six-volume translation of the Sephardic liturgy. Privately, he had prepared an English-language rendition of Mendelssohn's *Jerusalem*, and had begun working on a translation of the Pentateuch. In February 1839, he also began publishing a series of letters in the *Philadelphia Gazette* defending Jews and Judaism. Two years later, he would publish them collectively in an expanded work entitled *The Claims of the Jews to an Equality of Rights* (1841).[109] All this established Leeser's name across the growing country and beyond. Mickveh Israel, however, felt increasingly neglected.

Few of the other hazzanim in the country at the time either were particularly articulate or had established reputations beyond the narrow confines of their respective congregations. Poznanski, prior to the controversies over reforms, performed his duties in New York and, later, in Charleston in an unexceptional fashion. Lyons, who had gone to Richmond, was preparing to leave for a new position at Shearith Israel in New York. He was a competent individual but had neither Leeser's vision of a vital Judaism nor his drive to help fashion it. Lyons saw his mission as basically congregational; Leeser viewed his in national terms.

Perhaps the one exception was Samuel Myer Isaacs (1804–78), a Dutch-born hazzan and preacher who had served in England, who was invited to serve the pulpit of B'nai Jeshurun, the leading Ashkenazic synagogue of New York, in 1839. Isaacs's brief appointment included the provision "to give lectures on *Shabbat Hagadol*, on *Shabbat Teshubah* and on every *Shabbat* preceding Rosh Hodesh and at other times when the Parnass and Trustees may so direct."[110] Many years later, Isaacs would edit a newspaper, the *Jewish Messenger* (1857–1902), that would successfully compete with Leeser's *Occident*. The New York hazzan would also serve as the moving force for the creation of the first Jewish defense organization in the United States in 1859, the Board of Delegates of American Israelites, and he was deeply committed to Jewish relief work in Palestine. But in 1839, Isaacs was still a newcomer who had to learn to deal with New York's complex and growing Ashkenazic community.

Although B'nai Jeshurun's decision to hire a preacher, the first appointment of its kind in American Jewish history, must have pleased Leeser in one way, it must have also deepened his frustration with his own congregation. Not only had they failed to grant him the official title of preacher but, early in 1839, they actually put severe limitations on his freedom to give public discourses in the wake of an unanticipated dispute with the president of the congregation.

In February 1839, on the evening preceding *Shabbat Zachor* (the "Sabbath of Remembrance" that precedes the holiday of Purim), Leeser was invited to the home of the parnass, Lewis Allen, for a social visit. Although he planned to preach the next day, the hazzan decided not to inform the Allen family in advance of his discourse, because, in his own words, "it was always repugnant to me to publish my purpose of giving a lecture, not wishing to draw people especially to listen to a discourse, and thus making preaching more of a consequence than the reading of the service."[111]

The next morning, Saturday, February 22, 1839, Leeser spoke on "Obedience to the Law" and urged his congregation to "receive all the commandments, being, as they actually are, the emanations of the same Wisdom, as equally obligatory." At the conclusion of the discourse, the parnass angrily approached Leeser and demanded an explanation why he had not given notice that he would speak so that others in his family, particularly the women, could have been present. The hazzan's response did not satisfy Allen, who then left in a huff.[112]

Several days later, Leeser received a written order from Allen that directed that the hazzan could preach only if he notified the parnass at least one day prior to giving the sermon. "Deeming this procedure a degradation of the ministry," Leeser later wrote, "as it would be in effect to render public teaching dependent on the preacher's subserviency to the temporal authorities, and not willing to act without their consent, I refrained from addressing the people until the president revoked his order."[113] The hazzan kept his word and did not preach again at Mickveh Israel until March 25, 1840. The only time he broke his silence was to give an invocation at the first anniversary of the Hebrew Sunday School.

Nearly forty years later, Isaac Mayer Wise, the great leader of American Reform Judaism during the nineteenth century, reflected on Leeser's 1839 clash with Lewis Allen. In Wise's eyes, Allen's position typified the autocratic and therefore unsatisfactory nature of the office of the parnass in the early American synagogue. Writing in his typically hyperbolic style, Wise noted:

A correct conception of the power and autocracy of the *parnass* in those days can be formed from the following occurrence: Isaac Leeser, who was the *lumen mundi* of American Jewry at that time, was not permitted to preach in his own synagogue without the permission of the *parnass* because he had been elected *chazan* [cant'n] and not *chakham* [sage] of the Portuguese congregation, and in truth there was once quite an uproar because Leeser preached without such permission. I formed the acquaintance of a number of autocrats of this ilk. Their demeanor was astonishingly pompous and ridiculous. These people were serious obstacles in the path of progress, because as a usual thing they were very ignorant and narrowminded. The eagerness to become *parnass* was the fundamental cause of the multiplication of congregations in the cities.[114]

In fairness to Allen, however, it should be noted that he was not telling Leeser what to preach; he only sought to advertise that a lecture would take place. Indeed, this was, in a sense, a compliment—though Leeser did not so interpret it.

Leeser's fight with Allen on the issue of "freedom of the pulpit" proved to be only a prelude to the ugly and protracted negotiations to renew the hazzan's contract with Mickveh Israel. Ironically, as his relationship with the congregation approached low ebb, Leeser's role as a national leader in the American Jewish community continued to increase. With little hope for harmony at home, Leeser seized upon the theme of Jewish unity early in the 1840s and made it his rallying cry for nearly two decades. Union, however, was as problematic in the American Jewish community as it was for American society in general during the Antebellum Period.

In the end, Leeser's indefatigable efforts would yield only a few tangible results. He demonstrated to American Jews that intercommunity cooperation and national Jewish institutions were essential to Jewish survival in America, but he was unable to bring about unity—either in his congregation or in the Jewish community at large.

5

EMERGENT NATIONAL LEADER, 1840–1841

*If we were united, few as we are yet in America and the adjacent
countries, what a noble and enviable people might we be.*
—Isaac Leeser, *Occident*, 1845

THE BEGINNING OF THE 1840s was a decisive period both in the
life and career of Isaac Leeser and in the evolution of the American
Jewish community. The time had arrived to begin development of a
coordinated national Jewish agenda in the United States, and Leeser
was determined to play a major role in shaping Jewish communal policy. By 1840, Jews could be found in every region of the immense new
country and could claim a total national population of approximately
15,000 people. Sixteen synagogues were functioning in cities across
the country, and there were even more informal congregations in
smaller towns. As a religious and ethnic group, the American Jewish
community had grown too large for responsible leaders not to begin
thinking about regulating and shaping it on a collective basis.[1]

The problems facing the organized American Jewish community
in 1840 were complex and numerous. One of the most important issues was the defense and expansion of their political rights and interests.[2] A second problem involved the religious life of American Jews,
which was becoming increasingly chaotic. On the one hand, a native
impulse toward reform and an increasing awareness of synagogue reforms in Europe emboldened religious liberals. On the other hand,
traditionalists, alarmed at the success of reformers in Charleston, in

105

their efforts in 1840 to take control of an established, "Orthodox" synagogue, sought to organize American Jews on a national basis on religious grounds that respected Jewish law. Finally, if any progress toward communal and intracommunity cooperation was to be achieved, the informal communication network among American Jews would have to be replaced by a more extensive and organized system.

At the age of thirty-four, Isaac Leeser was prepared to step forward to urge the Jewish community to unite and to begin a process that would result in the creation of a *kehillah* or consistory-type institution modified to meet the circumstances of American Jewish life. By the beginning of the 1840s, he had a clear idea of how he personally wanted to organize American Jewry and what institutions were needed at the national level. Religion, Leeser believed, provided the only valid basis for Jewish communal life, and he fought valiantly, although largely unsuccessfully, to realize his dream.

Leeser had also refined his position on Jewish political rights in the United States during the course of the 1830s. He viewed public legislation enforcing the Christian celebration of Sunday as a day of rest as both unconstitutional and discriminatory, and was very disappointed when a petition was not presented to "the members of the convention for amending the Constitution of the State of Pennsylvania." It had been prepared in 1838 by several "members of the Jewish persuasion" asking "for ever to prohibit any future legislation from imposing any fine, or other penalties, upon Jews or other observers of the Seventh day, for following their indoor occupations on the First day of the week."[3] The insecurities of Jewish life prior to emancipation, Leeser recognized, would be difficult to overcome, and meekness on the part of American Jews, as well as legal disabilities, was an important enemy to the promotion of Jewish interests in America.

Equally bothersome to the hazzan were the increasingly bold efforts of Christian missionaries to convert Jews, which were particularly intense in Philadelphia during the 1840s. In Leeser's mind, not only was proselytizing a malicious and unenlightened enterprise but it violated the basic American belief in the equality of all religions before the law. Claims of spiritual superiority were illogical and reprehensible to him. Nor was he afraid to challenge the defamatory claims of the missionaries in his public speeches and in his writing.

Beginning on December 12, 1839, Leeser published a series of six letters to the *Philadelphia Gazette* in an attempt to thwart the efforts of Christian missionaries, reveal their ignorance of Judaism, and establish Judaism as a full and protected sector of religion in America. Christians, Leeser argued, are "no privileged class. Liberty precludes the idea of *toleration*." He added, "We utterly deny the right of our Christian neighbours to bring up our people and religion as a constant topic of discussion; and what is more, to raise funds to bring about a defection of our members."[4] Nearly two years later, the letters were reissued by Leeser, together with an introduction and annotations, in a book with the impressive title *The Claims of the Jews to an Equality of Rights*.

While Leeser dedicated most of the remaining five letters to a defense of the character of the Jewish people and a review of biblical history from Abraham to the destruction of the First Temple, he returned to his main point on February 28, 1840, in his last letter to the *Gazette*. "As citizens with equal rights," he concluded, "we demand of our fellow-citizens to abate the causeless prejudice which so many entertain for us."[5] "Of one thing I can assure my associates in religion," Leeser boldly remarked. "I shall be ever ready to enter upon a defence of our people and faith."[6]

Unfortunately, the opportunity for Leeser to prove himself an unequivocal "defender of the faith" was already in the making in distant Damascus, then an administrative center in the declining Ottoman Empire. Widely viewed as a turning point in modern Jewish history, the Damascus Affair not only rallied international Jewish opinion in defense of a handful of Syrian Jews who were falsely accused of ritual murder, but it became one of the great test cases in the nineteenth century of whether or not modern, progressive societies had weaned themselves from the diabolic image of the Jew that perpetuated and intensified anti-Semitism during the late Middle Ages and the early modern period.

The crisis began on February 4, 1840, when an Italian Capuchin monk, Father Tomaso, and his Muslim servant, Ibrahim Amara, disappeared in the Syrian capital. Rumors were immediately circulated by other Capuchin monks that the two missing men, who in fact were involved in shady business deals, had been kidnapped and murdered by local Jews who needed their blood for Passover rituals.

Because Catholics in Syria were under French protection, the matter should have been investigated by the French consul, Ratti-Menton. The French consul, however, saw in the bizarre turn of events an opportunity to expand French influence in Syria. He successfully involved the governor-general of Syria in the affair, and together they conducted a mock investigation. After "an elaborate confession was bastinadoed out of an impoverished Jewish barber," twelve more Damascus Jews were named as conspirators, arrested, and tortured. Sixty-three Jewish children were also seized as a coercive measure to extort information from their parents. Meanwhile, throughout the East, blood accusations and anti-Jewish violence began to spread, the most serious incidents taking place on the island of Rhodes.[7]

The Damascus Affair had become a full-blown international diplomatic crisis. Nearly all the major foreign ministries in Europe, as well as the U.S. State Department, became involved in the subsequent power struggle. A leading American Jew of the period, Mordecai Manuel Noah, correctly suspected that the British hoped to use the Damascus Affair to embarrass France and thereby block the expansion of French imperial interests in the Ottoman Empire. With big power interests at stake, a quick resolution of the affair seemed unlikely.[8]

The Austrian general consul in Egypt, however, did make some progress. On April 25, 1840, two months after the disappearance of Father Tomaso and Amara, he succeeded in stopping the torture of the Jewish prisoners in Damascus. Still, justice had not yet prevailed. The heinous charge of ritual murder was not dropped by the Syrian officials.

Outraged Western Jews, led primarily by Moses Montefiore in England and Adolphe Cremieux in France, petitioned their respective governments to force the Syrian Turks to drop the charges and release the prisoners. On July 21, 1840, Montefiore and Cremieux headed a delegation of leading Jewish spokesmen to plead their case directly to Muhammad Ali in Egypt. Special prayers for the success of the mission were offered in synagogues throughout Europe. "Never before," Jonathan D. Sarna notes, "had the western world and the Jewish people been so united in defense of Jewish liberty."[9]

By contrast, American Jews were extremely slow in organizing their protest to the events in Damascus, even allowing for the slow transmission of news across the Atlantic. No public protest was held in the United States until the third week of August, 1840, more than two months after various European Jewish leaders had begun to meet and to plan their course of action. In short, the lack of organized Jewish leadership at the national level was now exposed as a glaring reality in American Jewish life.[10]

The American Jewish community was so disorganized that it was also completely unaware that the U.S. State Department had taken a very favorable view of the situation. On March 24, 1840, the American consular representative in Syria, a Macedonian named Jasper Chasseaud, wrote to the secretary of state, John Forsyth, and gullibly reported "some details of a most Barbarous secret, for a long time suspected in the Jewish Nation." Forsyth apparently was unpersuaded by Chasseaud and took no action. Subsequently, he heard from the

American minister in England, Andrew Stevenson, who maintained a more sympathetic position than Chasseaud. He had also been officially informed by the lord mayor of London of the resolutions passed on July 3 at a large protest meeting organized by the Jews of London.

In a letter dated August 14, the secretary of state informed a member of the diplomatic corps in the Near East that "in common with people of the U. States, the President has learned with profound feeling of surprise and pain, the atrocious cruelties which have been practised upon the Jews of Damascus and Rhodes, in consequence of charges extravagant, and strikingly similar to those, which, in less enlightened ages, were made pretexts for the persecution and spoilation of these unfortunate people." He continued, "The President has directed me to instruct you to do everything in your power . . . to prevent or mitigate these horrors."[11]

Leeser's first public comments on the Damascus Affair, perhaps the earliest expression of concern about the blood libel in the American Jewish community, were given in a sermon, "The Sorrows of Israel," on July 24, 1840. Apparently not yet fully informed of the recent actions taken by Jews in England, he mainly discerned in the events in Damascus a profound religious message, but not an occasion to rally American and world Jewry.

Modeling himself after the prophets of Israel, the preacher enumerated the sins of his community and then linked the persecution of the Jews in the East with a promise of divine retribution at home. Threatening his congregation with "fire and brimstone," he asked rhetorically:

> May it not be, beloved brethren, that evil is now impending over us for our manifold transgressions, for our repeated disregard of the duties demanded by our holy law? Even now persecution has again lighted her consuming torch, its lurid glare has already terrified many of our distant communities, nay some have bled under its visitation: and we fear not; we think the evil is too far removed for us to dread its approach . . . I fear, that our security is of a like uncertain tenure; for if even there should be no human persecution possible in lands where the rule of law is firmly established, God's power is not shortened, and He has in store exquisite pains of a new and unheard-of nature, perhaps, which may unawares strike deep into the heart of the obdurate sinner.[12]

While Leeser's theological interpretation of the Damascus Affair might have been appropriate in the context of a sermon, what was urgently needed was an effective, public way of demonstrating concern for the well-being of the Jews in the Ottoman Empire.

The first American protest meeting was held in New York at Congregation B'nai Jeshurun on August 19, 1840. The chairman of the event, Isaac B. Kursheedt, and the secretary of the organizing committee, Theodore J. Seixas, were both friends of Leeser whom he knew from his years in Richmond. Mordecai Manuel Noah, New York's leading Jewish citizen, was asked to be the main speaker at the event.

However, the New York meeting did not take place without controversy. The organizers of the event had originally hoped to hold the protest meeting at New York City's Sephardic congregation, Shearith Israel. The New York Sephardim questioned the wisdom both of petitioning the American government to intervene with a foreign nation on behalf of Jews who were not American citizens and of broadly publicizing their ties to "unenlightened" Jews in the Ottoman Empire. Consequently, they refused the protestors permission to use their synagogue building for the protest rally.[13]

According to Jacob R. Marcus, the refusal of Shearith Israel to host the Damascus protest rally was more than a simple matter of meekness or indifference. The congregation's decision not to open its doors, he observes, "may well be designated the moral abdication of Sephardic hegemony [in American Jewish life]. It was tantamount to a symbolic renunciation."[14] On the other hand, the leaders of B'nai Jeshurun, the leading Ashkenazic congregation in New York, were more than willing to host the event.

Despite the problems in organizing the New York meeting, other protest rallies were held in rapid succession in other cities in the United States. The most important demonstration took place in Philadelphia. The event caught the attention of the *Pennsylvania Inquirer and Daily Courier*'s editor who devoted two-thirds of his news page to the story. "We have been compelled," the editor wrote on August 31, "to crowd out several articles intended for this morning's paper, in order to make room for the official account of the recent meeting in this city, in relation to the persecuted Jews of Damascus."[15]

Unlike New York's group, Philadelphia's prestigious Sephardic congregation, Mickveh Israel, gladly opened its doors to a protest meeting, and from its ranks came all the leaders who organized the Philadelphia meeting. Not only was Leeser a member of the original planning committee, he was also asked to be the keynote speaker. The president of the committee was sixty-nine-year-old John Moss, a distinguished member of the congregation who had served as steward of the St. George Society and as a member of the Philadelphia City Council. The energetic and talented Abraham Hart, a close associate of

Leeser who would become president of Mickveh Israel in 1841, served as chairman.[16]

Joining Leeser, Moss, and Hart on the podium were several Christian clergymen, including Rev. Dr. H. W. Ducachet (Episcopalian), Rev. Willim Ramsey (Presbyterian), and Rev. Mr. Kennedy. The three ministers all agreed to give brief extemporaneous speeches at the rally. Although the texts of their remarks were not preserved, it is probable that they followed the lead of Dr. Ducachet, who had written to Hyman Gratz, a leading member of Mickveh Israel, that "it is not, sir, the cause of the *Jews* only you are about to espouse: it is the cause of humanity."[17]

Chairman Hart began the protest meeting after a regular evening service on August 27, 1840, by giving "a succinct history of the cruelties practised against our brethren, and concluded with an appeal to the feelings and sympathy of the audience."[18] He also apologized, "It is due to the Jews residing in Philadelphia to state, that a meeting was intended to be held on this subject at a much earlier date, but owing to the absence from this city of the worthy and highly respected presiding officer of this synagogue [Lewis Allen, Jr.], it was postponed till this evening."[19]

In contrast to the Sephardic Jews in New York, Hart was fully confident of the value of staging a demonstration on behalf of Jewish rights abroad: "Can there be any one who doubts or disbelieves that the free expression of opinion and outpouring of sympathy, from those who reside in this country where every one acts and speaks his judgements and conscience dictates, will tend greatly to inspire confidence in the sufferers, and to strike terror into their persecutors?"[20] The rostrum was then turned over to Leeser.

Leeser realized the importance of his presentation and seized the day. Jacobs writes that in his speech, Leeser "took the bold course of repudiating the blood-accusation by the simple argument that as both Christianity and Islam were derived from Judaism, if the last advocated ritual murder, the daughter-religions would be guilty of the same practice."[21] Next, he stressed the theme of world Jewish unity:

> We have no country of our own; we have no longer a united government, under the shadow of which we can live securely; but we have a tie yet holier than the community of one government: our tie is sincere brotherly love, our patriotism is the affection which unites the Israelite of one land to another.

Jewish unity, he asserted, transcended modern nationalisms.

> As citizens we belong to the country we live in; but as believers in one God, as the faithful adorers of the Creator, as the inheritors of the law,

111

the Jews of England and Russia and Sweden are no aliens among us, and we hail the Israelite as brother, no matter his home be the torrid zone, or where the poles encircle the earth with the impenetrable fetters of icy coldness.[22]

After concluding his speech with a brief prayer, Leeser read a preamble and series of resolutions that "were the joint production of different persons," presumably members of the ad hoc planning committee. Several practical measures were adopted, including the creation of a fund "to relieve the victims of unholy persecution." Thanks were also accorded both to European consuls and Jewish notables in Europe for their constructive efforts toward the resolution of the crisis. Finally, it was approved that "a letter be addressed to the President of the United States" asking him to help "to procure for our accused brethren at Damascus and elsewhere an impartial trial."[23] A Correspondence Committee was formed and was headed by John Moss. Leeser gladly became a member of the group, which remained active during 1840, and served as its liaison to the Delegates of British Jews in London.[24]

While the Philadelphia meeting had no immediate effect on the Sublime Porte, a liberation order was coincidentally issued by the sultan the day after the rally (August 28, 1840), and the Jewish prisoners in Damascus were set free. Unfortunately, several of the men had died in captivity, and a fourth had been forcibly converted to Islam. The seven-month ordeal was finally over. World Jewry had won an important battle in the fight against anti-Semitism and injustice. Jews had also come to the realization that international cooperation among all the diaspora communities was essential to Jewish security the world over.

Rebecca Gratz eloquently expressed the feeling of Jewish solidarity in a letter to Solomon Cohen, a nephew by marriage, on October 4, 1840:

The Damascus persecution has fallen in a time to put down all petty strife and make us all desire to act and pray for the oppressed. May not this "partial evil prove a universal good"? or in the language of scripture "by their strife we may be healed." We are in the hands of God, who suffereth not a sparrow to fall but according to his will and yet in the occasions of his providence, great and terrible things come to pass on earth.[25]

However, the creation of a permanent Jewish defense organization in the United States was still a distant dream.

For his part, Leeser had played a major role in rallying American

Jewish opinion. "In the course of the activity surrounding the Damascus Affair," historian Leon Jick concludes, "Isaac Leeser emerged as the preeminent spokesman for American Jewry."[26] As a contributor to an important local newspaper in defense of Jewish rights, he helped pave the way for bold, public demonstrations by Philadelphia Jews in behalf of their coreligionists. Along with lay leaders at Mickveh Israel, he played a key role in organizing the Philadelphia meeting. The subsequent publication and broad distribution of a pamphlet entitled *Persecution of the Jews in the East*, which contained the proceedings of the protest meeting in Philadelphia including his address, fortified Leeser's position as a national spokesman. Without question, the hazzan was gaining recognition as a "defender of the faith" and a leader of his people.

Another clear indication of Leeser's growing importance in the American Jewish community was the increasing interest other congregations began to take in him as a guest speaker. Throughout the 1840s and 1850s, he frequently visited other cities as America's leading traditional Jewish dignitary and was asked to dedicate numerous new synagogues. Because of the relatively short distance, he visited New York most often, but as early as 1841 he also made a brief tour of the South, and spoke in both Charleston, South Carolina, and Savannah, Georgia. The hazzan's travels were facilitated by improvements in the national transportation system, in which he took a keen interest.[27]

Early in September 1840, with the High Holy Days approaching, Leeser agreed to speak at New York's leading synagogues, B'nai Jeshurun and Shearith Israel. In the wake of the successful conclusion of the Damascus Affair, his sermons reflected a feeling of vindication and confidence in divine providence. On September 4, 1840, in his remarks at B'nai Jeshurun, "The Requirements of the Law," Leeser defended the reasonableness of biblical law and its power to save its adherents. Six days later, at New York's Sephardic congregation, he concluded that it is best to "be convinced THAT ALL THAT IS IS RIGHT, although you do not readily discover HOW this is."[28]

Upon returning home to Philadelphia, Leeser greatly increased the frequency of his preaching. From September 24, when he spoke on "The Way of Life," a reflection on the true meaning of "happiness," to the end of the secular year, he gave a total of six discourses. In 1839, he had spoken only twice, and in 1838, he preached four times. Yet, beginning in 1840 he gave numerous Sabbath discourses for a ten-year period. His activity as a preacher hit its high mark in 1847, when he gave eighteen sermons.

Several factors contributed to Leeser's intensification of his preaching activities. In general, Jewish preaching was becoming more popular in the English-speaking world. He also probably viewed his selection as the keynote speaker at the August protest meeting as a de facto endorsement of his abilities as a preacher and as a signal to speak more often. His dispute with the parnass of Mickveh Israel, Lewis Allen, over the requirement for the hazzan to give the president of the congregation prior notice of his intention to speak, slowly faded into the background.

Leeser's sermons also captured the attention of an aspiring Jewish author of great potential in England. Grace Aguilar (1816–47) wrote to Leeser in 1840 after reading his first two volumes of *Discourses*, and not only praised the hazzan's work but paid him a supreme compliment by asking him to serve as her literary mentor. Leeser felt greatly encouraged by her admiration of his writings, and he subsequently edited, annotated, and published several of her works.[29]

Also spurring his increase in preaching were Leeser's plan to publish a third book of *Discourses* early in 1841 and his desire to present a voluminous work to the public. Having always fancied himself a writer, he was more convinced than ever of the power of the written word, and he worked with great zeal to bring another book to the light of day.

The topic most on Leeser's mind in 1840 was education. Beginning on November 20, the hazzan gave a three-part series of sermons on religious education, directed largely at the young parents in the congregation. Similar to a high-minded address he had given five years earlier, on June 2, 1835, in which he largely focused on the education of young girls, Leeser, a childless bachelor, now offered extensive advice on how to rear preschool-age children. The absence of books on Jewish parenting during the Antebellum Period necessitated his comments, and although he urged discipline and obedience, his strictness was not unusual by Victorian standards.[30]

"Religious Education, Number One" primarily dealt with the special problems of the one- to three-year-old group, most particularly "the evil effects of indulgence." He cited the tragic example of Adonijah, a son of King David who "was slain by order of his brother [Solomon] as an enemy to the internal repose of the realm" because "he had never been reproved by his father, and this indulgence, unwisely extended, caused him in this weighty point also to regard his own will merely."[31]

According to Leeser, the primary responsibility for raising children belonged to the mother. He vigorously disapproved of asking servants to take care of young children. "It is," he insisted, "unwise for the mother to surrender her child into the care of servants, even at the tenderest age." Servants, he suggests, will indulge children to make their task easier—or worse, even resort to administering "sedative or stupefying medicines."[32] "It is the duty of the parents conjointly," he summed up, "to watch over the dispositions of their children from the earliest age; to check every fault, and to counteract every evil propensity; not to be moved by tears, by petulance or perseverance, but to act with their responsibility to the Lord before them."[33]

The following week, on November 27, 1840, Leeser discussed the religious education of young children in "Religious Education, Number Two." He condemned the practice of telling children ghost stories and other tales of the supernatural, because they might lead the child to hold superstitious beliefs or even to be "godless" in later life. (Tales of the supernatural were becoming increasingly popular at the time, as evidenced by Edgar Allan Poe's publication of *Tales of the Grotesque and Arabesque* in 1840, including one of his most famous stories, "The Fall of the House of Usher.")

"In the same manner," Leeser added to his list of prohibitions, "when you think proper to reward your child, do not employ the agency of a supernatural being to bring the gift to them."[34] The "supernatural being" most worrisome to Leeser in this regard was none other than Santa Claus.

By the early 1840s, the celebration of Christmas in the United States included the decoration of trees and extensive gift giving, especially to young children, as part of a general interest in "romantic religion." For American Jews, this presented a difficult religious problem, as Hanukkah was traditionally considered to be only a minor festival. Some American Jews, such as Mordecai Manuel Noah, saw nothing wrong in Jews celebrating the "birthday of that religion which spread monotheism throughout the world."[35] Leeser, on the other hand, saw no room for accommodation. In a note to "Religious Education, Number Two," he stated, "As an Israelite I must condemn the system of making presents on gentile festivals, and use the common phrases that such or such imaginary being has brought them. Israelites have nothing to do with those seasons and ideas, and they better omit giving presents then, reserve them for Purim or Pessach, and tell the young folks the reason for this procedure."[36] Later, American Jews developed a third response to Christmas—they magnified the importance and celebration of Hanukkah to give it an equally festive mood, complete with gift giving.[37]

115

The hazzan gave his third and longest discourse on religious education (twenty-six printed pages) on December 11, 1840. When children are ready for formal training, he asserted, "it is a bad system to send sons and daughters of Israel at an early age to schools where either no religion at all, or one of an opposite character of our own is taught."[38] He declared, "My advice is that schools for general education under Jewish superintendence should be established." Furthermore, although successful, Sunday schools should only be viewed as "an initiatory course of instruction."[39]

Anticipating some standard objections to Jewish day schools, Leeser maintained that "the sciences can well be blended with the study of religion; and do not imagine that the teaching of the former will be hurtful to the latter, or that careful study of Bible and commentators will retard the progress of science."[40] Furthermore, Leeser noted, Jewish education was itself undergoing profound changes. "In former years," he admitted, "there prevailed an error of teaching abstruse points of legal knowledge, to the exclusion, to a great extent, of pure scriptural knowledge."[41] Good teachers with a modern viewpoint and pedagogic method could also be obtained. "Let such inducements be held out that youths, whom the Lord has endowed with wisdom, will seek to qualify themselves for teachers in our academies, and to become lecturers and preachers of the Word in our Synagogues." The following year, he explicitly called for the establishment of a modern rabbinical seminary in America.[42]

Leeser's pleas for general education under Jewish superintendence again fell on deaf ears. Nevertheless, he did not abandon his dream of a modern Jewish school with a curriculum combining "science" and religion. Nor did he give up on his idea about training Jewish instructors for the new academies. He realized that if Judaism were to take root in America, Jewish schools would have to be organized. So far as he was concerned, the battle for the hearts and minds of American Jewry had just begun.

Another battle had to be fought, and Leeser dreaded it—the fifth renewal of his contract at Mickveh Israel. In Leeser's mind, more than the details of the terms of his reengagement were at stake. Beyond anything else, he resented being a "hireling," and wanted to dignify both his own situation and the office of hazzan in general. He felt that he had earned life tenure at Mickveh Israel and that he was, therefore, entitled to a perpetual contract with a guaranteed minimum salary. He also hoped that because of the prestige Mickveh Israel enjoyed in the American Jewish community, the congregation would attempt to set new and favorable precedents for rabbinic employment in the United States. The congregation, however, was generally satisfied with the status quo in their business relationship with Leeser, and merely sought to meet the conditions stipulated by their constitution with respect to hiring a hazzan. Furthermore, they probably believed that they could offer the hazzan a generous, although not extravagant, financial package.

The process to reengage Leeser quickly disintegrated into an ugly clash of wills. More than a year passed before the two parties came to an agreement. Leeser resented the congregation's refusal to meet his terms and, in turn, was often tactless during the protracted negotiations. Mickveh Israel, on the other hand, refused to recognize Leeser's growing role in the American Jewish community and appropriately reward him with job security and favorable financial terms.

Before the new contract was prepared by the officers of the congregation on December 11, 1840, the same day Leeser completed his talks on religious education, a series of events had already taken place that set the scene for a long and unpleasant stalemate in the negotiations. On May 15, two days before the congregation was to meet to vote to reengage Leeser, the hazzan addressed a long letter "To the Parnass and Members of the Congregation Mickveh Israel." Because only full "members" were allowed to attend the meeting, Leeser presented his point of view to the congregation in writing so that "every member of the congregation in proceeding to deliberate upon the matter of the meeting will discard every thing like prejudice and partiality, and *endeavor for once to throw personal dislike or friendship* aside and vote in a manner he can conscientiously hereafter look upon as the best conducive to the welfare of the congregation and to the promotion of the spread among us of that heavenly religion which we have received."[43]

Leeser began by giving "a short account of my stay in this city," in which he emphasized the various sacrifices he had made in order to serve Mickveh Israel, as well as the difficulties involved in negotiating his fourth contract with the congregation three years earlier. "An amicable arrangement between us can be easily arrived at," he suggested, "if you only endeavor to convince yourselves that the Hazan as an individual has some rights and consequently some little to say about the disposal of his services."[44]

Leeser then set forth his two conditions. He was willing to continue serving as hazzan at Mickveh Israel "if they allow me the yearly salary of *twelve hundred and fifty* Dollars, this amount never to be reduced whilst I continue in office," and "with regard to the continuance of office . . . the election to be . . . for an indefinite period." About his suggested salary, he noted that "other congregations not more numerous or at least not greatly so, and not having more extensive means, give their Hazan a house and from $1,200 to 1,800 salary per annum." As for his request for life tenure, he suggested that "it is high time that I be assured whether Philadelphia is to be my permanent home or not. I am now past thirty-three years old, and I ought to be no longer harassed about my future prospects." "It is in your power, gentlemen," he concluded, "to sweeten a little the course of life of one to whom sorrow is no stranger."[45]

On Sunday, May 17, 1840, the congregation met as planned to consider Leeser's contract renewal. No other candidates presented themselves as contenders. Only the terms of the renewal needed to be discussed. Abraham Hart offered the first motion, the exact terms the hazzan wanted: life tenure and $1,250 per annum. The measure was defeated ten to fourteen. Then, John Moss amended the proposal to reengage Leeser for a period of ten years, and the motion passed by a vote of fourteen to ten. The salary Leeser requested was then approved by a wide majority, twenty-one to three. A committee was appointed to inform the hazzan of the decision. On May 22, Leeser wrote to Lewis Allen, "I deem it both a duty and a pleasure to signify to you and the congregation that I accept the terms."[46] He made no attempt to have the congregation reconsider the ten-year renewal in hope of securing life tenure.

The entire summer passed without any further discussion of Leeser's contract, which was to take effect on September 29, 1840. Meanwhile, events in Damascus and other congregational affairs occupied the attention of the leaders of Mickveh Israel.[47] Apparently, no effort was made to write and sign a formal contract until the second week of December. Whatever the reason for the delay, it immediately became clear on December 9, when Leeser and Lewis Allen met to discuss the matter, that a significant obstacle stood in the way of their mutually agreeing on the hazzan's new contract.

Just as in 1837, the obstacle was the congregation's insistence that both parties secure a bond, this time "in the penal sum of *one thousand dollars*." The bond could be obtained for a minimal fee, and was to serve as a legal device to help enforce both parties' compliance with the terms of the contract. In case either Leeser or the congregation failed to live up to the letter of the agreement, the aggrieved side could "sue" the other party's bond for damages. And again, just as three years earlier, the congregation insisted that it was bound by bylaw 27 of its constitution to obtain a bond from the hazzan, and Leeser insisted that it was unnecessary, degrading, and not required by the constitution.[48]

Leeser and Allen met again on December 10. The hazzan agreed to "give a bond in accordance with the Bye-Law" but refused to sign the bond the parnass had prepared. The next day, the parnass called a board meeting and reported that the hazzan refused to sign the bond officially approved by the congregation. The board then wrote a letter of inquiry to the hazzan "requesting him . . . to give a written reply setting forth his reasons for such refusal." Leeser's answer, according to a hostile source who reported the events a decade later, was "indecorous and disrespectful . . . giving the most flimsy reasons for his disobedience, and casting the grossest imputation on the honor and veracity of . . . Allen, then Parnass of the congregation."[49]

In a letter dated December 17, 1840, Leeser explained that his "signing a bond three years ago has nothing to do with the matter at issue" and that as far as he was concerned, he did "not want a bond from the congregation . . . because the Resolution of May the 17th 5600 [1840] is sufficient guarantee." With his letter, he also sent a new contract that he had prepared himself. On the critical issue of the bond, the hazzan suggested that "for every infraction of the terms of this contract, he binds himself to the Congregation in the penal Law [?] of $25 to be deducted out of his Salary." Thus, he reduced the bond to an insignificant penalty clause, which could not be invoked in a general way to prove that he failed in the "due and faithful performance" of his duties.[50]

Leeser's letter to the board and his contract proposal served only to make the situation worse. A meeting of the congregation was called for January 3, 1841. The board of Mickveh Israel was determined to take charge of the situation and force Leeser to comply with its wishes. Three strongly worded resolutions were passed. The first motion censured the hazzan for being rude to the officers of the synagogue:

> Resolved, That in the opinion of this meeting the Rev. I. Leeser has been guilty of disrespect towards the Parnas and Adjunta of this congregation, in his communication with the Parnas, in relation to the contract of re-engagement as Hazan.

The second motion, offered by Abraham Hart, who now needed to balance his friendship with Leeser with his duties as a member of the board at Mickveh Israel, confirmed that the congregation had a constitutional responsibility to ask their hazzan to sign a bond:

> Resolved, That in the opinion of this meeting the contract tendered to the Rev. Leeser, by the Parnas and Adjunta for signature, is in strict accor-

119

dance with by-law 27 of this congregation, and as such is by this meeting deemed correct.

Finally, in an attempt to break the deadlock, the congregation unanimously passed a resolution that Leeser had until March 29, 1841, to sign the contract offered by Mickveh Israel, or "said bond or his re-engagement would be annulled and made void."[51]

Leeser decided to fight back and show his contempt for the resolutions. He took a vow, perhaps rashly, that he would never agree to the bond as formulated by the board of Mickveh Israel, and promptly informed members of the synagogue of his retaliatory action. So far as he was concerned, the congregation had twice overstepped the limits of its authority: first, by insisting on the bond, which he viewed as little more than "indentured servitude," and, more recently, by censuring him. In both instances, Mickveh Israel had, in Leeser's mind, failed to see "the Hazan as an individual [who] has some rights" and who has something "to say about the disposal of his services."[52] Thus, there was no choice but to stonewall his adversaries.

Leeser also wanted to express his feelings about the situation at Mickveh Israel to a broader audience. Perhaps, he felt, others would understand his refusal to sign the bond. His opportunity to formulate his opinion presented itself almost immediately. On January 11, 1841, just eight days after being censured by the congregation, he completed work on his third volume of *Discourses*. In the preface, he offered a detailed account of the development of Jewish religious leadership in modern times and pleaded the cause of the new Jewish ministry.[53] The temporal rulers of the synagogue, Leeser wrote, "have too much direct interference with the Hazan in every public act in which he can engage." As in general society, he then suggested, a clear separation should be made between religion and government.

> It is in the nature of man to desire freedom of action; and the same feeling therefore which renders us restive under political subjugation, will also create an uneasiness, far from promoting harmony, in the minds of ministers of religion if they are rendered subservient to persons who evidently cannot be more religious and better informed than they are themselves.[54]

In good republican fashion, Leeser suggested that the root of the problem lay in synagogue government in the Old World.

> No doubt this evil originated in former years in the large congregations of Europe, which were always provided with Rabbins and teachers in sufficient numbers to require of the Reader nothing more than certain

duties in the Synagogue, for which the chief requisites were, besides a correct moral and religious conduct, a thorough knowledge of accepted tunes and the manner of performing the service, and these qualities very often constituted the whole of the qualifications demanded or desired.

"But," he added, "the times have changed."[55]

The officers and members of Mickveh Israel who read the passage were unmoved by their hazzan's appeal to reduce "Trusteeism" in the synagogue. Frustrated by the continuing deadlock in the negotiations, Leeser decided to retain legal counsel for himself. E. D. Ingraham, a local attorney, advised Leeser that a $300 penalty would be sufficient. Leeser communicated this to Lewis Allen in a letter on February 7, 1841, and added, "I believe that any damage the congregation can possibly suffer by my neglect of duty will never amount to this sum." He also offered to adjust the amount of the penalty and submitted yet another contract that either he or his attorney had prepared.[56]

The parnass replied to Leeser the next day and rejected the new proposals on procedural grounds:

> You must be aware that according to a Resolution passed by the Congregation at their last meeting (of which I believe you have a Copy) that I am directed only to receive your signature to the Bond tendered you by me and no other. It is therefore out of my power to receive or sanction any other. I therefore respectfully return you the same also E. D. Ingraham, Esquire's written opinion which you have taken the trouble to procure.[57]

With the March 29 deadline approaching and little hope for a resolution to the situation, Leeser asked for and received permission to take a brief trip to officiate at a wedding and dedicate a new synagogue in Savannah.[58] The hazzan welcomed the chance to leave Philadelphia temporarily. The prospect of Southern hospitality was particularly attractive to the battle-weary Leeser, who still fondly recalled his days in Richmond, and perhaps even considered himself to be somewhat of a Southern gentleman. For the time being, the renewal fight was tabled, but larger battles were looming on the not-too-distant horizon.

En route to Georgia, Leeser stopped for a few days in South Carolina. Charleston's Jewish community had recently split over the installation of an organ in Congregation Beth Elohim's new building. Outraged by the violation of Jewish law, the traditional Jews in Charleston withdrew from the city's original synagogue and, early in 1840, organized their own congregation, Shearith Israel, named after the prestigious New York synagogue. Naturally, they prevailed upon Leeser to address them while he was in Charleston. For the Philadelphia hazzan, it was his first major opportunity to directly confront the growing Reform movement.[59]

Local efforts to reform Judaism were, as we have seen, not new in Charleston. In 1824, the year Leeser arrived in America, thirty-six-year-old Isaac Harby, a dramatist and teacher, and a young friend, Abraham Moise, led a group of primarily young, native-born members of Beth Elohim in an effort to modify both the worship and educational practices at the Sephardic synagogue. When their petition was summarily dismissed by the congregation's board, the dissidents organized the Reformed Society of Israelites (RSI). The RSI spawned a number of original prayer books that reflected its deist philosophy of Judaism. The RSI liturgies represented an American impulse toward religious reform, although Harby and others were aware—but not well informed—about developments in Germany. When Harby died prematurely in 1828, the RSI slowly disintegrated, and gradually, some of its members rejoined Beth Elohim.[60]

The decline of the RSI did not spell the end of Reform Judaism in Charleston. Harby's bright, young successor, Abraham Moise (1799–1869), remained committed to radical religious reform. By 1840, a narrow majority at Beth Elohim, including the tenured hazzan, Gustavus Poznanski, had joined the Reform camp. In a hotly contested battle, the congregation voted on July 26, 1840, by a margin of forty-six to forty, to install an organ in its new building. Unwilling at this point to fight the reformers in court, an action Leeser had advocated from his vantage point in Philadelphia, some of the traditionalists withdrew from Beth Elohim and organized a new congregation. Others remained within the parent congregation, greatly complicating the situation.[61]

In contrast to Beth Elohim's handsome new building, now in the hands of the reformers, the traditionalists initially met "on the upper floor of a warehouse on Meeting Street, which had been fitted up as a place of worship." There, on February 19, 1841, Leeser spoke to the members of Shearith Israel. His discourse, "The Dangers of Israel," consisted mainly of an angry denunciation of Reform Judaism and a warning about the perils of assimilation. He implored the members of the new congregation "to take the light of our own ancients, the manner of interpretation which has been handed down to us, to abide by the custom which long and well-established usage has sanctioned, in your mode of thinking and in your manner of acting through life." He concluded, "The opposite tendency . . . is the danger which threatens the peace and unity of the house of Jacob."[62]

While his remarks might have reassured the Orthodox secession-ists that their cause was just, Leeser's remarks had little impact on the reformers. Two days later, on February 21, 1841, the use of an organ at Beth Elohim was officially approved. A peace meeting convened later that year failed to produce a compromise between the parties, and ultimately the matter did go to court. By that time Leeser was already publishing the *Occident* and reported on the two trials in great detail. He was outraged when the courts twice ruled in favor of the reformers.[63]

The bitter fight in Charleston between the reformers and the tradi-tionalists sent shock waves through the American Jewish community. Within four months of his return to Philadelphia, Leeser was busy trying to organize American Jewry on a national basis. The primary purpose of the organization was to fight Reform and prevent its spread beyond the Charleston community.

Leeser was unable to begin to work on a "plan for unity" immedi-ately upon returning to Pennsylvania. First and foremost, he still needed to resolve his contractual dispute with the congregation. He had also agreed to be a speaker, along with Rev. Moses N. Nathan of Jamaica, at the third anniversary of Rebecca Gratz's Hebrew Sunday School, which by March of 1841 had grown to two hundred students.

In his remarks, "Dangers and Remedy," given to the Sunday school scholars and their guests, Leeser extolled the value of Jewish education in fighting assimilation and apostasy. He also reminded his listeners of "the necessity there exists of not confining education to one day in the week only."[64] Later that summer he also urged the members of the Young Men's Literary Association, at a meeting at the Crosby Street Synagogue in New York, "to leave no means untried to further a proper acquisition of the Hebrew, and to encourage every undertaking which promises to aid in this desirable result, and to promote the undefiled worship of the true God."[65]

Leeser's remarks to the Sunday school on March 28, 1841, im-pressed its principal, Rebecca Gratz. The following day, she wrote a letter to Mrs. Solomon Cohen of Savannah, Georgia. "Mr. Leeser [of-fered] an appropriate psalm and benediction and gave us an excellent Discourse." However, she also added that she was "exceedingly con-cerned about Mr. L.'s offices. . . . Mr. L. is of great importance to us—and he is sensible of it but there are some horrible spirits who have an influence on the board. . . . I know not what will be his fate." She also blamed part of the problem on Leeser's lack of "manage-ment."[66]

In fact, Leeser purposefully let the date for the signing of his contract (March 29) pass without taking any action. The congregation met on April 4, 1841, and in a conciliatory gesture extended the deadline to July 1. Leeser then began a letter writing campaign to bring the board around to his point of view.[67]

Before the controversy had fully resumed, a tragic event temporarily consumed the attention of the hazzan, the congregation, and the nation. Exactly a month after his inauguration, President William Henry Harrison died in office on April 4, 1841. Claiming to have offered the first address "spoken on the decease of the suddenly summoned chief magistrate of the land," Leeser told his congregation on April 9, "if we are bound by the religion we profess to pray for the welfare of the city in which we dwell, if even it be subject to a tyrannical ruler . . . how much more must we pray for the well-being of a land like this."[68]

Usually reticent about his political leanings, Leeser had difficulty in disguising his delight over the fall of the Jacksonians in his eulogy for Harrison. "I need not tell you," Leeser remarked, "how his [Harrison's] success was hailed as the guarantee of better times and returning to prosperity."[69] Leeser greatly admired Harrison's military career and viewed him as the personification of "the prowess of the civilized Caucasian race" in its struggle against the "fierce, untamable sons of the forest." To Leeser, Harrison's life was "a lesson that virtue and moderation, joined to a straightforward line of conduct, are well calculated and will pre-eminently conduce to acquire for us the favour of God and man."[70]

In light of the loss of the newly inaugurated president, Leeser's conflict with Mickveh Israel seemed unimportant and petty. Still, the hazzan persisted in his cause and sent four letters to the parnass. On May 11, Lewis Allen convened a meeting of the whole board of the congregation and presented Leeser's correspondence to all of its members. The board discreetly resolved to "decline taking any action on said letters, or giving any advice or opinion thereon." Instead, a special meeting of the congregation was called for May 16.

Although neither a transcript nor minutes of the meeting are extant, apparently a compromise was reached. Leeser agreed to serve for ten years at $1,250 per annum "under a penalty of eight hundred dollars."[71] He probably was not satisfied with the arrangement but agreed to meet the congregation's offer instead of risking his position at Mickveh Israel. It also might be assumed that his eighty-four-year-old uncle, Zalma Rehine, again persuaded Leeser to work with and not against the congregation. (Rehine died in 1843, and when his nephew's contract was to be renewed in 1850, no one was able to convince Leeser to pursue a moderate course in negotiating with Mickveh Israel and in a show of contempt he ultimately resigned his post. In the meanwhile, the 1840s proved to be among the most productive years of the hazzan's career.)

Because of a lack of documentation, it is impossible to fully assess why Leeser fought so relentlessly with the parnass and board of Mickveh Israel. From the beginning, it was clear that the congregation would not grant him tenure but would meet his request for a fixed salary. The fight over the penalty clause was largely symbolic on Leeser's part, and probably would have required an amendment to the congregation's constitution to circumvent. Ironically, Leeser neither raised the issue of freedom of the pulpit nor sought an official sanction of the board for his work as a preacher during the protracted negotiations.

In the final analysis, the hazzan's deepest anxieties and personal insecurities were aroused during the period in which his contract at Mickveh Israel was renegotiated. The fights over tenure and the penalty clause were probably more a matter of pride than anything else. Although the congregation continued to underestimate his real worth to them and American Jewry in general, ultimately Leeser himself was at fault for failing to respect the realities of synagogue life in America in 1840. A more skillful negotiator could have gained the same results with less pain on both sides of the table.

The fact that Leeser had essentially failed in his efforts to redefine and upgrade his position at Mickveh Israel did not deter him from seeking a solution of the problems of the American Jewish ministry at the national level. Nor did he believe that the problematic situation of American hazzanim was unconnected to the general problems of Jewish ignorance and ritual laxity in America. A national policy, Leeser reasoned, could accomplish what the fiercely independent American synagogues could not on their own: the proper regulation of Jewish religious life according to Jewish law, the professionalization of the ministry, and the establishment of Jewish schools in major centers of Jewish settlement throughout the country. What Leeser needed to do now was to galvanize public support for his position. He had to link the problems of the American Jewish ministry with other, broader issues.

The success of the reformers at Beth Elohim in Charleston, coupled with news of the steady growth of Reform in Germany and England, suggested to many traditional leaders, including Leeser, that the time had arrived to take direct action to contain the Reform movement in the United States. At Mickveh Israel, moreover, the specter of Reform Judaism making any further inroads into the American Jewish community simply outweighed any internal problems of the congregation. To fight reform, the laity and the hazzan could join together and jointly develop a plan to bolster Jewish traditionalism in America and contain the embryonic Reform movement.

Early in June 1841, an ad hoc committee met to plan a large public meeting to discuss and plan a national Jewish strategy that would, in part, attempt to contain the growth of Reform Judaism in America. It was decided that the meeting would be held at the newly formed Beth Israel Congregation in Philadelphia on June 27, 1841. Lewis Allen was named chairman of the event, and the treasurer of Beth Israel, Henry S. Cohen, was appointed secretary. Leeser, who had done an outstanding job at the protest rally during the Damascus Affair, was asked to give the keynote speech.[72]

The meeting was held as planned on the twenty-seventh, and before a large and excited crowd, Leeser "made an extemporaneous address of near an hour long" in which he proposed "a plan for a general union of all the Jews in America under one general church government." At the conclusion of the meeting it was resolved that a committee of seven "be appointed to consider the propriety of endeavoring to establish a plan of religious union of the different congregations of America."[73]

The committee promptly met on July 1, 1841, and empowered Isaac Leeser, Zadok A. Davis, and J. L. Hackenberg to work on a "Plan of Union." Leeser was selected as the principal draftsman. Within a week's time, he prepared a rough draft of a constitution for the proposed national religious organization and submitted it to the full committee. In a letter to Zalma Rehine, Leeser mentioned, "I was put upon the committee to mature the plan, and accordingly was delegated by them afterward to draw up rules and regulations." "I had to go to work accordingly," he continued, "and did what had been asked of me; and the committee had thereupon several meetings [July 11 and 12] to debate, alter, and amend my rough draft. In the main it was adopted."[74]

The plan was presented at a general "meeting of Israelites" at the Masonic Hall on Sunday, July 18. Leeser agreed that Louis Salomon, the hazzan of Beth Israel and a native of Metz in Alsace-Lorraine, "who is not acquainted with English," would be recognized as a co-architect of the plan to give it institutional strength, although Salomon had contributed little to the preparation of the document. The plan was clearly an epitome of Leeser's own thinking.[75]

The purpose of the plan was threefold. First, it sought to

strengthen Orthodoxy in the United States by using the democratic instrument of majority rule to clamp down on Reform. Leeser was certainly aware of the crisis in church government in American Protestantism during the late 1830s and, like the power brokers at nearby Princeton Theological Seminary, he wanted to fortify the position of the "old school." Second, the Plan of Union sought to upgrade and strengthen the role of Jewish religious leaders in the United States at home and with respect to their European counterparts. Finally, it attempted to make Jewish education the responsibility of the entire Jewish community and not just that of the students' families.

The preamble succinctly explained the need for a national Jewish religious organization and laid out its basic institutional structure:

> The Israelites of Philadelphia, in common with their brethren in other places of America, have long since been alive to the many evils under which they labour in the great downfall of religious observance, and the want of proper religious education among them. But deeming it their duty to leave no means untried to counteract the deplorable state of want of proper observance, and to promote a due knowledge of the blessed religion they have received from their fathers, to effect by a common effort, that which would evidently be beyond the power of accomplishing by any one of the small congregations in which the Israelites of this country are divided; they therefore offer the following suggestions . . . first, establishing a competent ecclesiastical authority . . . secondly, by establishing schools for general and religious education under Jewish superintendence . . . and, thirdly, by promoting harmony and a concert of action among all their brethren scattered over the western hemisphere.[76]

The keystone of Leeser's plan, the creation of a Central Religious Council, was discussed in Article I. Modeled directly on a traditional *bet din* (court of Jewish law), the council was to be made up of "three gentlemen of undoubted moral and religious character, who are duly learned in the written and oral law." Perhaps Leeser hoped that Abraham Rice (1802–1862), the first properly ordained rabbi to settle in America, who arrived in Baltimore in 1840, would head the council.[77] The Central Religious Council was to be strictly Orthodox in character, and would "determine all questions laid before them, according to the law, and the approved rabbinical authorities." Additionally, the council would examine and appoint all shochets and hazzanim and supervise all Jewish schools in America.

Limits were also placed upon the authority and jurisdiction of the council, primarily to respect the autonomy the American congregations claimed. Most importantly, the three members of the council were to be elected by delegates representing all synagogues in the country. The size of the delegation was calculated to reflect the size of the congregation it represented. As another concession to the principle of congregational autonomy, preachers were also required to give written notice to the parnassim before speaking, and congregations retained "the privilege of performing the marriage ceremony." Finally, Leeser made sure that the council would be forbidden to "exercise the power of excommunicating any one, for any offence whatever."[78]

Article II called for Jewish schools "to be established in every town where Israelites reside." Teachers were "to be paid out of a common local fund, and on no account to receive any pay or fee whatever from parents." Leeser also called for the development of regional high schools, in which young men could be educated to serve as hazzanim, preachers, and teachers, "and young women be educated for the high calling of female instructors."[79]

Finally, Article III mandated the establishment of a biennial assembly of congregational delegates. "The delegates in general assembly," Leeser wrote, "shall have the power to deliberate on all subjects, which may tend to the general welfare of the Israelites, with the exception of matters properly belonging to legal points of Mosaic law." Moreover, the general assembly was not to "interfere directly or indirectly in the internal affairs of the congregations." An executive or central board was to meet in Philadelphia on a regular basis, and local chapters were to be formed as well, in "each town."[80]

Four years later, Leeser was still excited enough about the plan to write about it in the *Occident*. "If we were united," he maintained, "few as we are yet in America and the adjacent countries, what a noble and enviable people might we be." He offered an idyllic vision of American Jewry:

> United among ourselves we might have beautiful places of worship, as the pride of our congregations, attentive and numerous assemblies filling the hour of our Father whenever the doors were opened for worship; noble schools, where all our youth, the rich and the poor together, might be taught the will and word of God, where they might imbibe the precious stream that sprung from Sinai, conjointly with the elegance of literature and refinement under God-fearing instructors.

His vision also included a wide variety of communal and welfare institutions:

> We might have our hospitals and houses of industry to prevent the poor from seeking relief from a grudging charity, and to support them during

their illness in a manner not repugnant to our laws. We might have our savings banks and loan offices, to enable the industrious Israelites to lay by their hard earnings in trusty hands, and to give aid to the deserving to commence business or set up in a mechanical trade, to earn an honest livelihood without the necessity of appealing to unwilling souls for a small advance to commence the world. We might also have our seminaries and high-schools whence should be sent forth the natives of the soil, instructed in the religion of Israel.[81]

Although many aspects of Leeser's plan were ultimately adopted by different constituencies in the American Jewish community, no immediate action was taken to have it implemented in 1841. Instead, the proposals met with resistance from many old guard Sephardic congregations and from the reformers. Shearith Israel of New York, according to Joseph Buchler, "refused to support the plan because they feared that the German Jews would outvote the Sephardim, and thus gain ascendancy in American Jewish life."[82] The reformers at Congregation Beth Elohim in Charleston took even greater exception to Leeser's plan. On August 10, 1841, they passed a resolution "that all conventions, founded or created for the establishment of any *ecclesiastical authority* whatever . . . are alien to the spirit and genius of the age in which we live, and are wholly inconsistent with the spirit of American liberty."[83]

Two days later, Abraham Moise, the leader of the Charleston reformers, wrote a long letter to Leeser. "I would not have you understand that I regret the institution of your plan; on the contrary, I am rejoiced at it." He continued, "I am highly pleased to discover that you have taken alarm, that you regard our progress as of sufficient importance to cause your apprehensions, by inducing the efforts you are now making [to prevent the people] from following in our footsteps."[84] Although Moise also overstated the threat of Reform to traditional Judaism in America in 1841, he was correct in essentially labeling Leeser's plan as stillborn.

Leeser, however, was undaunted by the fact that the American Jewish community was not ready for a national religious organization. He never tired of explaining the virtues and benefits of "religious union" to American Jews, and made repeated attempts to create a national organization responsible for the regulation of Jewish religious life in North America.

Perhaps the only tangible result of the plan was that it helped to relieve tensions between Leeser and Lewis Allen, who later died after a brief illness, in November 1841. At the end of the sheloshim (thirty days of mourning), the hazzan preached a sermon on divine justice in his memory. "Of late years," Leeser reflected, Allen had "given proof that he felt the solemn obligation of surrendering his interests to the calls of his religion; and every measure proposed, which promised to promote piety, met with his hearty approval and co-operation. . . . When he erred, we may freely assert, that it was never from bad intentions, such was the kindliness of disposition which he evinced on all occasions."[85]

The new parnass, Abraham Hart, was the brilliant and energetic friend of the thirty-five-year-old hazzan. Under his presidency, Leeser enjoyed the most productive and strife-free years of his career, until the professionally fatal contract dispute of 1849–50 brought Leeser's career at Mickveh Israel to an abrupt end. In the meanwhile, the problems of massive immigration, the progress of Reform, Christian missionary activity, and irreligion did not abate. Nor did Leeser's energy or motivation to create a dynamic Jewish center in America. Slowly, he warmed to the idea of a national Jewish "newspaper," and by April 1843 he had launched his most ambitious and ultimately most successful undertaking, the publishing of *The Occident and American Jewish Advocate*.

6

AN ADVOCATE FOR
AMERICAN JUDAISM, 1842–1846

*But by degrees it became manifest to us, that the age is more
inclined to receive information in the detached manner in which
journals treat the same, than by the slow process of deep
research, which formerly was considered the road to knowledge.*
—Isaac Leeser, *Occident*, 1843

THE 1840s WERE A PERIOD of tremendous expansion for the United
States—the prospect of cheap land, gold, and adventure attracted tens
of thousands of new immigrants to America and inspired native-born
Americans to uproot themselves in search of better lives. John L. O'Sul-
livan, a journalist, captured the mood of the country in a single sen-
tence. He wrote in 1845 that nothing can be allowed to interfere with
"the fulfillment of our *manifest destiny* to overspread the continent
allotted by Providence for the free development of our yearly multiply-
ing millions." The drive for expansion also resulted in a brief war with
Mexico and various treaties to redefine the borders of the growing
republic. Similarly, America's urban centers not only grew physically
and demographically during the 1840s but were increasingly beset by
social problems, including poverty, violence, and, periodically, rioting.[1]

Although still relatively few in number, American Jews were also
transformed by the rapid physical expansion of the country and the
steep rise in immigration during the administrations of presidents
Tyler and Polk. During the course of the 1840s, the Jewish population
of the United States zoomed from approximately 15,000 to 50,000.
Synagogues were organized and built in every section of the country

as Jews, like other Americans, explored and settled the vast interiors of the continent. In 1843, a secular Jewish fraternal organization, B'nai B'rith, was founded in New York, creating new options for Jewish self-identification in America. "The European unified communal structure, which had been shattered by the traumas of modernization and trans-plantation," writes Leon Jick, "could never be replicated in the United States." He concludes, "In its place, a far more complex and diversified entity began to emerge."[2]

American Jews, however, were still neither a community nor a polity. A well-established tradition of religious laxity and the chaotic conditions of immigrant life undermined the little social cohesion that existed among Jews in the United States. The failure of Leeser's Plan of Union to overcome ideological and subethnic differences was indic-ative of the condition in which American Jewry found itself.

Except for Leeser's single-handed efforts and those of a few other Jewish intellectuals, most books of Jewish interest still had to be im-ported from Europe. As late as 1842, neither a serial publication nor a national Jewish organization provided a sense of unity among Ameri-can Jews. What they needed, more than anything else, was intellectual and communal leadership.

Through his publications and role as a public orator, Leeser slowly emerged as the principal religious spokesman of traditional Judaism in American during the 1830s and, especially, during the critical years of 1840 and 1841. By 1842, his role as defender of the faith was clearly established. His belief that traditional Judaism could be maintained and would even flourish in America through a modest two-part pro-gram of modernization of external forms and the development of a pedagogically new mode of full-time Jewish education was becoming increasingly well known, though still not widely accepted.

Leeser's greatest assets as a religious leader were the sincerity of his religious convictions, his personal industry, and his devotion to Jewish causes. Unlike many American hazzanim during the 1840s, he was neither opportunist nor lackluster. His detractors frequently at-tacked him on theological grounds, but rarely for lack of integrity. Yet his appeal to the masses of American Jews was limited by flaws in his personality, his volatile relationship with Mickveh Israel, and his unshakable conviction that religion and not philanthropy or defense work formed the common ground for American Jewry. In fact, religion proved to be increasingly divisive among American Jews, especially in the 1840s and 1850s.

The failure of the Plan for Union suggested to Leeser that the best way to influence American Jewry and promote traditional Judaism was to proceed with his original plan to write and publish religious literature. Although he never succeeded in developing a felicitous style, he proved remarkably prolific and dedicated to his goal. By the end of the 1840s, his work as a religious writer not only had made him a household name among American Jews but had firmly established his place in the annals of Jewish literature.

Less than six months after his *Claims of the Jews to an Equality of Rights* appeared, Leeser edited and published Grace Aguilar's theological work for women, *The Spirit of Judaism*, in June 1842. Aguilar had sent Leeser her original manuscript in 1840 for his corrections and annotations, but the text mysteriously disappeared in transit. Forced to recreate her work from her notes, she again forwarded to Leeser her manuscript from her home in England. Because of numerous interruptions, Leeser needed thirteen months to complete his work on *The Spirit of Judaism* and publish and distribute it. By January 1842, the book was ready to be presented to the public.[3]

In introducing *The Spirit of Judaism*, Leeser went out of his way to mention that "our females will find in it many passages peculiarly calculated to win and arrest their attention by their elegant imagery and truly delicate portraiture." "I rejoice greatly," he added,

> that a gifted daughter of Israel has at length appeared, who does not disdain to stand forth as the champion of her ancient creed and who, forsaking for awhile the field of secular literature, where both fame and profit await the successful aspirant, links her fate with those ardent few who hesitate not to avow their abiding hope in the law of their Hebrew forefathers, and who seek for no better reward, than to see their own religion followed and its adherents honoured.[4]

As with his support of Rebecca Gratz's Sunday school and its all-female faculty, Leeser's endorsement and encouragement of Aguilar's work represented a mixture of traditional Jewish practice and contemporary Victorianism. In no way was Leeser a protofeminist; rather, he was able to emphasize those elements of American social customs that he believed to be in the best interest of Judaism. And why a theological book for Jewish women? Aguilar summed up the rationale herself: because "from their lips must the first ideas on all subjects be received."[5]

Leeser's praise of *The Spirit of Judaism*, however, was not unqualified. "The chief points of difference between Miss Aguilar and myself," he wrote, "are her seeming aversion to the *tradition*, and her idea that the teaching of mere formal religion opens the door to the admission of Christianity."[6] Aguilar generally equated the Hebrew Bible with Judaism and saw little value in the teachings of the ancient and medieval rabbis. Leeser countered in a note, "I am no advocate for any abuses introduced under Rabbinical rule, but I am far more opposed to the notion of certain moderns who would reject all for a few blemishes incident more to the *times* in which our teachers lived and taught, than to any absolute defects in their system."[7] He added that "it is not tradition which has shackled the Jewish mind, but the cruelty exercised by Christians, pagans . . . towards our bodies and spirits both."[8]

Leeser was particularly strong in his criticism of Aguilar's call for the abolition of Judaism's fixed liturgy. "Were we only to pray when our soul is altogether free from extraneous thoughts," Leeser asserted, "it would be but seldom indeed that the offering of prayer could be sacrificed upon the altar of the heart. It is, therefore, an admirable institution, that we have set forms of prayer."[9]

Finally, Leeser rejected Aguilar's suggestion that many Jews were converting to Christianity because they found Judaism's "formalism" to be spiritually unsatisfying. "The Jew embraces Christianity if at all," Leeser boldly maintained, "by his desire for some tangible advantages which his change is supposed to bring, or from a mere ignorance of his own belief." "Indifference," he concluded, "is a far greater enemy to us than conversion."[10]

Leeser's notes to *The Spirit of Judaism* help clarify his attitude toward rabbinic Judaism. Although a modernizer who often looked to Protestantism for new forms into which the traditional content of Judaism could be cast, he did not seek a "Reformation" of Judaism by returning to the Bible and abrogating centuries of religious development. "I insist," he wrote in the editor's preface, "in concert with all who have duly weighed the subject, that, without claiming infallibility for the sayings and decisions of our Rabbins, they are nevertheless entitled to be listened to with profound respect and to be obeyed as holy ancestral customs."[11] A correct English translation of Scripture, he further asserted, would vindicate rabbinic Judaism and show that it and not Christianity stood firmly on biblical foundations. Three years later, the hazzan published his English translation of the Pentateuch and, subsequently, the entire Bible.[12]

In a sermon, "The Prohibitions," delivered on August 5, 1842, that was primarily intended to promote stricter observance of Jewish dietary laws, Leeser also discussed the way Scripture should be interpreted and the biblical basis of Judaism. "We maintain," he told his congregation, "that the Bible can be explained only by the words of the context and the manner of interpretation as received from our fathers, which is at best nothing but an exposition of how they acted up to the words of Scripture."[13] Judaism, according to Leeser, was the only true biblical religion.

Not only did Leeser and Aguilar share a common concern with demonstrating the biblical basis of Judaism, they both were also highly critical of the way Judaism was observed in their respective places of residence. While Aguilar protested against "formalism," Leeser saw other abuses. In a letter addressed to the board of Mickveh Israel on August 28, 1842, he complained about the lack of attendance on Saturday mornings at the synagogue, the late hour at which services commenced, and the habit of several older members of the congregation of leaving the synagogue after the chanting of the *haftarah* (weekly prophetic reading) which, if the hazzan preached, was only the midpoint of Saturday morning worship.[14]

Leeser also suggested modifying synagogue finances. Apparently, Mickveh Israel found itself short of cash late in the summer of 1842. Leeser wrote that he would abolish money offerings altogether, because they "interfere in a great degree with the solemnity of the service," "open the door to the caprice of individuals," and tend to tax regular worshippers heavily while allowing less observant individuals to evade their fiscal responsibilities. Instead, Leeser suggested, "I would leave it to the good sense of the congregation to determine whether a mode of annual subscriptions could not be devised, which would effect a more equitable assessment," a modification originally suggested by the Reformed Society of Israelites in Charleston nearly twenty years earlier. In a sermon, "The Sanctuary," given a few days later, the hazzan again reminded the congregation that "circumstances have occurred which have rendered it imperative upon the heads of our congregation to demand a small additional annual contribution for the support of the public expenditures."[15]

Another way of raising funds, Leeser suggested, was to create a registry of all life cycle events in the congregation. To prove the idea feasible, he quantified his own pastoral activities during his first twelve years in Philadelphia. "Since my residence here," he noted, "I have recorded in the congregation book about 82 marriages, and in my private memoranda the interment of 118 persons, and the birth of 129 boys and 85 girls." Although unordained and more interested in writing than pastoral work, his activities at Mickveh Israel exemplified the new, modern rabbinate that was then taking shape.[16]

Finally, Leeser requested that the congregation formally give him the right to preach at Mickveh Israel. "It is known to you all that for the last 12 years, I have occasionally delivered English sermons at the conclusion of the service . . . ," he wrote, "and I have as yet only spoken under the general permission obtained from the Members of the Board of Adjunta of the year 5590 [1830]." "Tho 13 years ago sermons were not considered necessary," the hazzan added, "the case is very different now."[17]

Nearly a year passed before the congregation formally considered Leeser's various suggestions and his request to preach. On April 9, 1843, a series of resolutions was submitted to the board calling for voluntary annual contributions, a general direction for the hazzan "to give a moral or religious lecture in the English language every Sabbath morning," the organization of a congregational choir, and the development of a congregational registry. The measures were voted upon and passed during the summer. On September 17, 1843, Leeser wrote to the parnass, Abraham Hart, to thank the congregation "for the approval bestowed upon my sermons."[18]

A variety of reasons could explain the congregation's sudden willingness to take the advice of its hazzan. Most importantly, Hart was sympathetic to Leeser and had a great deal of influence on the board. In addition, Leeser's ideas no longer were novel—Jewish preaching in the vernacular was becoming increasingly acceptable, if not desirable, among Jews throughout the English-speaking world. Both British and numerous American synagogues were experimenting with voluntary annual contributions, and finally, Leeser had gained wide recognition beyond the Philadelphia Jewish community as the result of his public speaking and his writing. In fact, his most important publishing adventure to date, the monthly Jewish journal *The Occident and American Jewish Advocate*, was launched at the same time the four resolutions were originally placed before the board, in April 1843.

The *Occident* was not the first Jewish journal published in the United States. Twenty years earlier, in March 1823 (just one month after Leeser arrived in the country), Solomon Jackson (d. 1847) began publishing a monthly called *The Jew*. Unlike the *Occident*, which had a broadly conceived cultural and religious mission, the sole purpose of *The Jew* was to counteract the work of missionaries. Early in 1823, the American Society for Meliorating the Condition of the Jews (ASMCJ) had developed a periodical, with the deceptive name *Israel's Advocate; or the Restoration of the Jews Contemplated and Urged*. It was designed to promote missionary work among American Jews. The circulation of the paper quickly grew to two thousand.[19]

Jackson, a Jewish widower who had been married to the daughter of a Protestant minister and who, late in life, became a "repentant Jew," viewed the appearance of *Israel's Advocate* as a personal challenge. He responded to the ASMCJ by publishing *The Jew*. Issues generally contained a twenty-page polemical essay by Jackson in response to the missionary content of *Israel's Advocate*, as well as select materials by other contributors. Jackson's monthly journal appeared for only two years before the operation was disbanded.[20]

The Jew's lack of longevity has been explained in various ways. Hyman Grinstein maintains that Jackson's attention was diverted when he became involved in a political dispute internal to Congregation Shearith Israel that led to the establishment of B'nai Jeshurun, New York's first Ashkenazic synagogue. Malcolm Stern suggests that Jackson "felt he had achieved his major purpose" of neutralizing the missionary publication. Leon Jick offers a third explanation: "The appearance and rapid disappearance of this journal reflect the anxiety of a community concerned with threats to its survival but unable to muster sufficient resources and initiate a positive program of response." It is also possible that Jackson believed he had effectively countered the publication of the ASMCJ and so voluntarily ceased publishing *The Jew*.[21]

A second ephemeral American Jewish periodical appeared in Philadelphia in 1837. Published in German by Julius Stern, *The Israelite* failed after just two issues. Stern later became a contributor to the *Occident*, and in its first issue suggested that American Jews create their own colony in the United States. If the appropriate number of settlers (70,680) could be found, he felt, the colony could become a Jewish "state" in the Union. Leeser rejected the idea but "invite[d] a discussion on the subject."[22] While the discussion of various proto-Zionist and protoautonomist ideas continued, Stern disappeared from public view. No other attempts at publishing a Jewish paper in the United States after Stern's were made for six years.

The Jewish press in Europe, unlike that in America, was well developed by 1843. Jewish periodicals had already appeared in Germany in the middle of the eighteenth century. The most famous of the early papers was the enlightened Hebrew-language *Ha-Me'assef* or *The Gatheter* (Berlin, 1784–1811). A German paper, *Sulamith*, appeared in Dessau from 1806 to 1833. The longest-lived journal in the history of the German Jewish press—eighty-five years—was the weekly *Allgemeine Zeitung des Judentums*, founded in 1837 in Magdeburg by Reform rabbi Ludwig Philippson. During the same year, the *Hebrew Review and Magazine of Rabbinical Literature* appeared in England under the editorship of Morris Jacob Raphall. A pro–religious reform paper, *Les*

Archives Israëlites appeared in France in 1840 and was edited by S. Cahen.[23]

Leeser intensely followed the development of the European Jewish press. He wrote in his introductory remarks to the *Occident*, "We could not shut our eyes to the consideration that daily there was more demand for similar work in this country." But perhaps even more important than the growth of the Jewish press in Europe was Leeser's awareness of the size and effectiveness of the general religious press in the United States.[24] The first religious periodical in America was published during colonial times in 1743, however, it was not until 1789 that a denominational journal was printed for the first time. Francis Asbury served as one of the editors. Subsequently, the Methodist paper the *Christian Advocate* became one of the largest newspapers in the world. By 1829, it circulated 25,000 copies of each issue. From 1789 to 1830, nearly five hundred religious newspapers were established in the United States, although few survived for more than a few months.[25]

The secular American press was also in ascent during the first half of the nineteenth century. By 1812, New York alone had seven dailies. Circulation vastly increased in the 1830s with the rise of the penny press. In 1835, James Gordon Bennet began publishing the *New York Herald*, and by featuring scandal stories, Bennet built up a huge readership. By 1861, the *Herald* was the largest paper in the world, with a daily distribution of over 75,000.[26]

Leeser knew that he lived in an age of journalism but was hesitant to apply its form and methods to American Judaism. He wrote in the *Occident*:

> The plan of a religious periodical, did not originate with ourself, nor did we approve of it when it was first suggested to us. We thought then, and still think, that newspaper knowledge is at best superficial . . . much matter must be admitted which is more pleasing in its nature than instructive.

"But by degrees," he continued,

> it became manifest to us, that the age is more inclined to receive information in the detached manner in which journals treat the same, than by the slow process of deep research, which formerly was considered the road to knowledge.[27]

Ironically, the idea for the *Occident* originated with an unnamed religious reformer in Charleston. A nearly total disagreement over religious matters apparently did not prevent Leeser and his counterpart

from discussing other common interests, including the need to revital-
ize Solomon Jackson's antimissionary work. Leeser wrote in April
1846, "When the subject of starting a monthly religious magazine was
first presented to our notice, by a legal gentleman, a member and a
great admirer of the reform congregation . . . we did not deem the
project practicable." The practical issue that was of greatest concern to
the new editor was not the prospect of extended journalistic or religious controversies but the cultivation of an ample readership.[28]

Leeser worked on developing the *Occident* for an entire year before
the first issue went to press. First, he appealed to friends, family members, and various editors of Jewish papers in Europe to support his
project. On May 27, 1842, a notice appeared in the London paper The
Voice of Jacob, "that there is some idea of commencing a Jewish periodical . . . in America." Leeser wrote to the editor of the British biweekly
"of the want of uniformity . . . existing among the different bodies of
Jews" and the general ineffectiveness of Christian missions to the Jews
in the United States. Leeser also wrote to Ludwig Philippson in Madgeburg in October of the same year, expressing his intention to publish
a bimonthly Jewish paper in America.[29]

Leeser knew from the beginning that finding sponsors to make
publishing of an American Jewish paper economically feasible would
be difficult. Although he hoped only to cover his costs, he still wanted
to reach a broad cross-section of Jews in the Americas and West Europe. The initial subscription lists reveal that several hundred individuals were interested in the project. The mainstays of his support,
naturally, were Philadelphia and New York, but dozens of others, from
small towns such as Lebanon, Tennessee, and Liberty, Missouri, also
subscribed. He also had numerous readers in Canada and in the West
Indies, especially St. Thomas and Jamaica. Among his most illustrious
readers were Sir Moses Montefiore and Rev. Abraham de Sola of London. The *Occident* even reached the distant shores of Australia and
New Zealand.[30] Still, the total number of readers was eventually to
disappoint the editor. "The patronage bestowed upon us," he mildly
lamented after two years of publishing the paper, "has been much less
than we had a right to expect." By the end of his second year of publication, in March 1845, he could claim only "scarcely above 510" subscribers. Nevertheless, he was willing to continue the project
indefinitely.[31]

In introducing the *Occident* in April 1843, Leeser explained his
reasons for launching a Jewish paper and his philosophy of religious
journalism: "We will briefly state that we shall endeavor to give circulation to every thing which can be interesting to the Jewish inhabitants

in the western hemisphere." Thus, as the years passed, the pages of the *Occident* became not only an intellectual biography of its editor but the most important record of American Jewish life in the middle decades of the nineteenth century.[32]

The scope of the *Occident* was astonishingly broad. Leeser called for original articles to be submitted, and he promised to offer translations of the best of contemporary European Jewish literature and to review "new books as concern our people."[33] He also showed remarkable sensitivity to Jewish women by inviting them to publish in his national journal. He planned "to give accounts of public religious meetings" and offered "our pages to congregations and societies as a medium of giving publicity to their intended assemblings." Finally, he understood that the paper could be of lasting historical value and serve as a depository of information about the development of American Jewry. "We also request the respective presidents and secretaries of our American congregations especially to send us a condensed account of their first establishment, and of anything of interest connected to them."[34] He published scores of historical documents illustrating America's Jewish past, and even included lengthy, contemporary legal documents, especially those involved with the expansion or protection of Jewish rights.

Perhaps the most notable feature of the *Occident* was its editorial policy. It strongly represented the liberal American ideal of freedom of speech and, unlike most other religious papers in the United States, was not controlled by a church organization. Although Leeser admitted, "We have opinions of our own which we shall not hesitate to avow with becoming firmness upon every proper occasion," he also openly invited those with different views to use his paper as a responsible forum in which to express themselves. Years later, he wrote, "There is no need to treat our opponents in such a manner that reconciliation becomes impossible." Henry Englander, an early biographer of Leeser, summed up the editor's basic policy as being "temperate when attacking persons, severe when attacking principles."[35]

The complete title and motto of Leeser's journal also reveal his intentions in establishing the journal. The full name of the paper was *The Occident and American Jewish Advocate. A Monthly Periodical Devoted to the Diffusion of Knowledge on Jewish Literature and Religion.* Double titles were commonplace among antebellum religious journals. Leeser probably used the word "Occident" to emphasize his periodical's Americanist orientation, and for symmetry after *The Orient*, a weekly paper then currently published in Leipzig, Germany, by Dr. Julius Furst. The second part of the title, "American Jewish Advocate," suggested both a countermissionary policy (as *The Jew* was published in opposition to ASMCJ's *Israel's Advocate*) and, perhaps, a way of identifying the editor as a proponent of developing Judaism in the Western Hemisphere and in the United States in particular.[36]

The motto of the *Occident*, "To learn and to teach, to observe and to do," was taken from the traditional Jewish morning liturgy. It clearly identifies the periodical as being of a confessional and activist nature. In an essay, "Our Motto," Leeser explained:

We would therefore be truly happy could we induce our brethren, especially those in America, among whom our more immediate sphere of action is placed, to throw off their long sleep, their unaccountable apathy, and to prove to themselves and the world that they love and esteem their sacred birthright, that they feel the weight of the obligation which the observance of their religion places upon them, and they are fully aware of the exalted destiny of being the chosen servants of God.[37]

Not only did the purpose of the *Occident* remain the same for more than a quarter of a century, its format also went essentially unchanged during the periodical's entire life. It appeared monthly, octavo size, with the exception of a brief period when it came out weekly in a larger format. It usually included an editorial, sermons, short stories, original poetry, book reviews, correspondence from readers and contributors, and "news items." Long articles were often serialized. Occasionally entire books were printed, including Benjamin Dias Fernandes's *A Series of Letters on the Evidences of Christianity* and an original translation of Moses Mendelssohn's *Jerusalem*. Toward the end of the 1850s, Leeser attempted to transform the *Occident* into a weekly publication as the competition among American Jewish journals stiffened, but the exigencies of war, especially the loss of Southern readers because mail service was curtailed, forced him to return to the original monthly format.[38]

To some extent, the content of the *Occident* gradually narrowed during its many years of publication. As the debate over religious reform grew more intense during the 1840s and 1850s and the total number of American Jewish papers increased, "controversial" writing increasingly dominated the pages of the *Occident* at the expense of the purely literary pieces, that had been ubiquitous during its early years. Leeser, who was strongly committed to Americanization and the use of the English language by American Jews, occasionally printed German articles during this period, and a score of Hebrew letters also appeared in the *Occident*, exclusively on religious topics.[39]

A typical issue was fifty to sixty pages long and was complemented by an advertising supplement of an additional five or six pages, which included book advertisements, information on obtaining ritual items, notices from boarding schools, classified announcements, subscription information, and a table of contents. Other papers, particularly Robert

Lyon's *Asmonean* (1849–58), made business news an essential component of their operation, but Leeser kept the commercial aspect of the *Occident* secondary and segregated.[40]

"If he could have done only one thing," scholar and rabbi Bertram W. Korn writes about Leeser, "we would have to single out publication of his monthly journal, *The Occident*. Quite aside from its usefulness as a historic record of the time, *The Occident* was the first instrumentality to give a sense of national belonging to the widely scattered children of Israel in the United States."[41] In fact, for six years (1843–49), it was the only Jewish newspaper in the United States, and thereafter, when the American Jewish press slowly began to expand, it remained a leading monthly, especially among traditional Jews.

The *Occident* also reshaped Leeser's career. Until 1843, he had functioned primarily as a hazzan-preacher and writer. By 1840, he had emerged as religious leader of national consequence but still had no organizational support or direct means of communication to the masses of American Jews. The appearance of his journal changed all that.

The *Occident* immediately became the main focus of Leeser's work. Besides personally overseeing all the difficult technical aspects of publishing, and functioning as his own business manager, he also wrote or translated a large percentage of the materials that appeared in the *Occident*. Moreover, Leeser corresponded with hundreds of readers and contributors as well as the merely curious who became part of the journal's network. As editor of a Jewish journal, he was frequently in contact with his counterparts throughout the world and with many of the most important Jews of the nineteenth century. In short, the *Occident* kept him in the limelight of American and general Jewish life from its first issue to his death in February 1868. Only after his health began to decline during the 1860s was he willing to accept help in publishing the journal. First Jonas Bondi and later the young Mayer Sulzberger acted as co-editors with Leeser in the humble offices on Walnut Street.

The *Occident* quickly became an integral part of American Jewish life. Although a few readers complained that the periodical was "flat and uninteresting," the majority of its readers viewed it as a crucial link to contemporary Jewish cultural and intellectual life. The most exuberant letters praising the journal came from Jews who lived in remote, frontier areas. On May 28, 1853, for instance, Isaac Jalonick wrote to Leeser from Belon, Bell County, Texas.

> It will surprise you sir, to hear from such remoot part on the frontier of Texas. . . . I am surry to say that I am a poor scholar. I cane not express

my feeling with the pen, when I accidently came in posestion of such valuible inphomatin as containing in your Occident. May the leeving God spair you that you may accomplish which you have undertakin to do.[42]

The *Occident* also appealed to the American Jewish elite. Mordecai Manuel Noah, perhaps the most articulate and influential Jewish layman in antebellum America, used Leeser's periodical as a medium through which he could communicate his views to his coreligionists throughout the United States. An old newspaperman himself, Noah made many newsworthy contributions to Leeser's journal and, in turn, helped shape the thinking of both the neophyte editor and his readership about contemporary Jewish issues by provoking debate on a number of important topics.

Noah's first communication to the *Occident* appeared in the September 1843 issue. Animated by a desire to find a way to preserve and strengthen the Jewish identity of the young in a free society, he called for the establishment of "a HEBREW COLLEGE, where children of the Jewish persuasion can obtain a classical education, and at the same time, be properly instructed in the Hebrew language; where they can live in conformity to our laws, and acquire a liberal knowledge of the principles of their religion."[43] Leeser, of course, was delighted. In two subsequent issues, the editor tried to rally support for the proposal. In "Public Religious Education" (November 1843), he bemoaned the general ignorance of Judaism in western countries, and in "Jewish Children Under Gentile Teachers" (December 1843) he amplified the theme suggested by the title of the essay in much the same way as Noah in his letter to the *Occident*.

Leeser and Noah, however, did not always agree. While both sought to maintain traditional Judaism in the modern world, Leeser was more conservative in his approach to the problem. In October 1844, Noah again communicated with the *Occident*. This time he suggested that a chemical test be used to detect the presence of lard in vegetable oil. Leeser initially agreed in principle that this was a valid method to determine the *Kashrut* of that food product, but after hearing the reaction of several learned Orthodox Jews, especially that of Rabbi Abraham Rice of Baltimore, who ruled that "this mixed oil . . . is prohibited to any Israelite," he qualified his position. In the end, Leeser favored the inspection and sealing of the oil by recognized rabbinic authorities. Rice subsequently added that it was time for American Jews to elect a chief rabbi, following the British model, to deal with such problems.[44]

A third and final debate initiated by Noah in the early issues of the

143

Occident concerned the Restoration of the Jews to the Holy Land. In the final number of volume 2 (March 1843), Leeser wrote a lengthy literary notice reviewing Noah's "Discourse on the Restoration of the Jews." Delivered twice (October 28 and December 2, 1844) before distinguished audiences in New York, the "Discourse" called on Christians to "unite in efforts to promote the restoration of Jews [to Palestine] in their *unconverted* state, relying on the fulfillment of the prophecies and the will of God for attaining the objects they have in view after that great advent shall have arrived."[45]

Leeser detected several serious practical problems with Noah's flamboyant address. First, he suggested that "many of our people living under the iron sway of Russia, ardently desire the consummation of some project of the kind" and that as many as 2 million Jews would elect to resettle Palestine. The Jewish settlers, however, would insist on maintaining their independence in foreign affairs and, in their disorganized condition, would "be a prey to the designing powers of modern Europe."

Leeser also rejected the idea of a cooperative effort with Zionist Christian missionaries. "With conversionists, as such, we cannot, as Jews enter into any league," Leeser warned, and continued, "The Jews are abhorrent to them, and if they grant us any favours, they do it for the sake of a return." Israel will be restored, he concluded, "in spite of our enemies . . . and if they are to assist at all, it will be that they will be ashamed of their foolish efforts, and be urged by the impulse of the Lord to hasten . . . the returning captives to their former inheritance."[46]

Implicit in Leeser's critique of Noah's "Discourse" was a thoroughly modern view of the Restoration of the Jews to Zion. Although Leeser's belief was predicated on traditional Jewish theology, his vision of a Jewish homeland was more contemporary and realistic than eschatalogical in nature. A modern Jewish state in Palestine seemed a real possibility to Leeser as early as 1843, but only if circumstances would allow its security. The nationalist European revolutions of 1848 reinforced this view five years later.[47]

In the meanwhile, Leeser became increasingly concerned with the welfare of the Jews already resident in the Holy Land. From Palestinian messengers in America, such as Rabbi Jechiel Cohen of Hebron, who visited the States in the spring of 1847, and Americans who visited Palestine, such as the eccentric Warder Cresson, Leeser learned that "there is no fiction in the sufferings of the Jews in Judea." By improving the lot of Palestinian Jews through agriculture, industry, and the modernization of fund-raising on their behalf, Leeser believed that the infrastructure for a Jewish state could be developed. This work, Leeser believed, would certainly fulfill the ancient biblical prophecies on the Restoration of the Jews.[48]

The clash between Leeser and Noah over Restoration was not merely the collision of a defender of the faith with an "integrationist" but a premature collision of two very different modes of Zionism: practical and political. Practical Zionists, beginning in the late nineteenth century, called for the immediate settlement of the Land of Israel by Jews. Political Zionism, on the other hand, sought a diplomatic solution to the international problem of anti-Semitism prior to mass Jewish settlement in the Holy Land. Remarkably, Leeser was also able to foresee how practical Zionism and traditional Jewish Restorationism could be merged. Noah, on the other hand, like Theodor Herzl, dreamed of grand schemes and spectacular scenarios for the Jewish people.[49]

While Noah's proposals concerning a Jewish return to Zion were mainly speculative in nature, the rapid progress of Reform Judaism during the middle years of the 1840s was very real and particularly vexing to Leeser. Aware of the power of the press, Leeser used the pages of the *Occident* to track and, he hoped, contain the movement to liberalize Jewish practice and belief. "In the discharge of our duty as an editor of a Jewish periodical, and minister of our religion," he wrote plainly in February 1845, "we have been impelled to bear our decided testimony against all attempts lately made to establish a reform which will naturally cause a disruption to our communities, and lead to the establishments of sects in our bosom."[50] He added, "We will merely state we too are for progress, but it must be a progress, not for lopping off an observance here and there, and striking out a phrase of a passage or a portion of the prayers, simply because one does not like rabbinical portions, another not the metrical hymns, another does not approve the doctrines embraced in our ritual, or because a fourth finds some critical faults."[51]

In the first volume of the *Occident*, Leeser primarily focused his attention on the activities of the reformers in Charleston. In July 1843, he wrote a detailed review of the events that resulted in the reformers at Beth Elohim going to court (A. Ottolengui *vs.* G. V. Ancker) to disenfranchise several traditional members of the congregation. "Our sympathies are with the defendants," the editor wrote. "Nevertheless, we cannot think of being unjust to their opponents [and we] offer them our periodical for a rejoinder."[52]

The following month, Leeser published a lengthy letter he had written to Gustavus Poznanski, the spiritual leader of the Charleston reformers. As defender of the faith, the angry hazzan challenged the reformer to defend his suggestions to abrogate the second day of Jewish festivals, introduce instrumental music into the synagogue on Sabbaths and festivals, and remove references to both the coming of a Messiah and the resurrection of the dead in Jewish worship.[53] Poznanski, busy with his own affairs and unwilling to engage Leeser in a sustained debate, never answered. The battle to stop reform, however, was far from over.[54]

The year 1844 proved to be critical in the history of the Reform movement. In July, Leeser announced to his readers that Ludwig Philippson had proposed an annual meeting of German rabbis to discuss the establishment of a "Jewish Theological faculty," "the foundation of a Jewish hospital and school in Jerusalem," and the way to obtain unity "in reference to the improvement of public worship." "We hope," Leeser added, "that much good may result from the assembly of so many eminent men."[55] However, as it became increasingly obvious that the meeting would be dominated by Reform rabbis, his expectations for the conference diminished and his concerns grew.

By October 1844, news of the late-spring meeting at Brunswick began to reach Philadelphia. Leeser was outraged at the resolutions passed at the conference, and especially at the loophole the German reformers created to allow rabbinic participation at mixed marriages if the children of the couple would be raised as Jews. "It is indeed singular," Leeser railed, "that these great men did not consult the Scriptures before they pronounced judgement; one would be tempted to believe that they studied everything but Scripture."[56] The rabbinic tradition, Leeser added, was no less adamant in its opposition to interfaith weddings.

> We cannot imagine that a Rabbi, who must have Talmudic knowledge, would pretend to say, that he could pronounce the benediction over persons who have no faith in what he does, the words he pronounces, and the ceremony over which he presides. Besides it has always been a maxim with us, that properly speaking, "no Jew can marry a gentile," as the Kiddushin (the betrothment and marriage act) are a nullity between an Israelite and a gentile.[57]

"A Christian to marry a Jew in the law of Moses," the editor added with exasperation—only look at the absurdity of the thing!"

Leeser also kept a watchful eye on the development of Reform congregations in Frankfurt and Hamburg, as well as the Congregation of British Jews in London. He called the members of the Reform Society at Frankfurt "nothingarians." "In our estimation," Leeser added, "the above Society [at Frankfurt] is but an evidence of the deplorable state of irreligion in which many of the continental Jews are sunk." He also felt that Judaism was in a stronger position in America than in Europe. "There is now a greater religious sentiment here than in Europe," Leeser wrote with some qualifications, "and the little that has been left to us in our domestic and public relations is cherished with an ardour of which the European new-lights have but little conception."[58] The real reformation of Judaism, in Leeser's mind, should involve the invigoration of the tradition in a modern orthodox mode. He also fully expected that this reformation would be located in America.

The ultimate success of Judaism in America was predicated on preserving and expanding Jewish civil rights in the United States. The *Occident*, Leeser correctly understood, was able to play a vital role in the protection of Jewish rights in America and elsewhere, and as a defender of his people, the editor proved remarkably vigilant. The pages of his journal were frequently filled with news from courtrooms around the country. He reported on Sunday legislation, attempts to "baptize" the constitution, and Test Oath cases. He did not call for a total separation of church and state but insisted on the right of Jews to equality in American law. Morton Borden recently wrote that "Isaac Leeser, more than any other Jewish spokesman, was concerned with and would settle for nothing less than complete legal and religious equality."[59]

One of the first civil rights issues reported in the *Occident* involved Gov. James H. Hammond of South Carolina. In 1844, the governor proclaimed a day of "Thanksgiving, Humiliation, and Prayer." He exhorted "citizens of all denominations to assemble in their respective places of worship, to offer their devotions to God their Creator, and his Son Jesus Christ, the Redeemer of the world." The Jewish citizens of Charleston immediately protested the "obvious *discrimination and preference*" in Hammond's proclamation. Incensed, the governor replied, "I have always thought it a settled matter that I lived in a Christian land! And that I was the temporary chief magistrate of a Christian people! That in such a country and among such a people should I be, publicly, called to an account, reprimanded and required to make amends for acknowledging Jesus Christ as the Redeemer of the world, I would not have believed possible, if it had not come to pass."[60]

Leeser strongly rebuked Governor Hammond in the January 1845 issue of the *Occident*. "No doubt," he wrote, "he was clinging in his imagination to times never known in this country since its freedom was established, which proscribed persons for their speculative opinions, and hence he forgot that there were such people as Israelites within the bounds of the state of South Carolina." He then proceeded

147

to teach the governor (and his own readers) a basic lesson in American civics:

> A majority cannot do every thing; and among the prohibited things is the abridgement of any one's rights for opinion sake. It matters not in this respect whether the majority be Christian or Jewish; the constitution knows nothing of either; and it is well known that, in the fundamental charter of the United States, neither Christianity nor Judaism is mentioned by name . . . both therefore were placed upon such an equality that a preference was given to neither.[61]

The following year, a Jewish merchant in Charleston, Solomon Benjamin, was charged with selling gloves on Sunday, a practice allegedly outlawed by a state ban on retailing on the "Day of the Lord." When a local judge ruled that the ordinance was unconstitutional, the state appealed the case to the Supreme Court of South Carolina. Writing for the court, Judge John B. O'Neale wrote concerning the Jewish merchant that "he is compelled to keep two Sabbaths [Jewish and Christian]. . . . We say to him, simply respect us, by ceasing on this day [Sunday] from the pursuit of that trade and business in which you, by the security and protection given to you by our laws, make great gain."[62]

Leeser was outraged by the decision of the court. He published a letter in the *Occident* by an anonymous "Hebrew" who protested "against these terms, '*you*,' '*us*,' '*our laws*.' " "Such language is unworthy of an American judge," the angry correspondent wrote. Subsequently, in an editorial, "Freedom of Conscience," the editor urged American Jews to remember that "no special privileges should be asked, no special disqualifications should be voluntarily submitted to."[63]

American Jewish public opinion, however, was not monolithic. Mordecai Manuel Noah, for instance, rushed to Judge O'Neale's defense. In his *Sunday Times and Noah's Weekly Messenger*, he wrote that it was "a very able opinion" with which "we entirely agree." In contradistinction to Leeser, Noah suggested a strongly accomodationist strategy for American Jews, asserting that "respect to the laws of the land we live in is the first duty of good citizens of all denominations."[64]

Morton Borden, a leading scholar of Church-State issues in American Jewish history, has suggested that "Noah's views probably were more representative of Jewish opinion, but Leeser remained adamant." In time, especially during the twentieth century, the majority of American Jews came to agree with Leeser. In his mind, membership in a religious minority in America required not timidity but boldness. The

148

full realization of American democracy depended on Jews and others asserting their "claims to an equality of rights." More than a century later, Winthrop S. Hudson, a historian of religion in America, concurred with Leeser: "Perhaps one of the greatest contributions of Judaism to America will be to help other Americans understand how the United States can be a truly pluralistic society. . . . From the long history of Judaism, Americans of other faiths can learn how this may be done with both grace and integrity."[65]

Neither the importance nor the demands of Leeser's work on the *Occident* caused him to reduce his efforts or activities in other areas. In fact, he seemed energized by his new career in journalism. For instance, simultaneous with the appearance of the *Occident*, Leeser noticeably increased his preaching. His renewed vigor as preacher perhaps was linked to his need to publish contemporary sermons and addresses of interest to the Jewish community.[66]

The topics of Leeser's sermons did not change significantly from the 1830s. He continued to focus his preaching on theological defenses of traditional Jewish doctrines. Simultaneously, he attempted to demonstrate fallacies in Christian teachings and prove their lack of a legitimate biblical basis. Early in 1843, for example, he gave a three-part series on miracles in which he concluded that God used supernatural means to prepare the ancient Hebrews for the giving of the Torah, and that the report of miracles in the New Testament could not be used as proof that the Law had lost its divine sanction.[67]

Leeser also campaigned against Reform Judaism from the pulpit during this period. In "The Eternity of the Covenant" (June 2, 1843) and "The Consolation of Israel" (August 11, 1843), he spoke out against Reform's rejection of traditional Judaism's belief in the Restoration to Zion and the coming of a human Messiah, in a fashion similar to that of his epistle to Gustavus Poznanski that same summer. In "Our Religious Teachers" (June 21, 1844), he argued against the proceedings at the Brunswick Conference in Germany and reassured his congregation that Reform, although visible everywhere in Western Jewish life, was still a small movement.[68]

Nor did Leeser desist from working on other literary projects independent of the *Occident* after 1843. Indeed, his productivity soared. In just three years, he wrote a lengthy essay on American Judaism for a standard reference work, translated and published the Pentateuch, and organized the first American Jewish Publication Society.

When I. Daniel Rupp began compiling his *He Pasa Ekklesia. An Original History of the Religious Denominations at Present in the United*

States (Harrisburg, Penn., 1844), he chose Leeser, a fellow Pennsylvanian, to write the chapter on "The Jews and Their Religion." Not only was Leeser the best-known Jewish religious leader in the country at the time but, because of his work as editor of the *Occident*, he truly had a unique bird's-eye view of American life in 1844.[69]

Leeser's article in Rupp's book is divided into three parts: an apologia reviewing Judaism's contributions to Western civilization, a section on the doctrines of the Jews, and a description of the Jews in the United States. "When we endeavor to trace the origin of the civilization which rules with its benignant sway the mightiest nations of modern times and none more so than the people of the United States," he remarks in his explanation of Judaism's contributions to world culture, "we shall soon discover that it must be ascribed to a great *moral* influence which had its birth in the gray ages of antiquity." Of course, the "great *moral* influence" was the Hebrew Bible and, he added, the character of the Jewish people.[70]

In the second part of the article, Leeser notes that although Judaism posits no formal creed, because it "is not a theoretical system, but one of actions and duties," nevertheless, "pious men . . . have endeavoured to condense the biblical dogmas for the use of the nation at large." He proceeded to list Moses Maimonides' "Thirteen Principles of Faith," prefaced by Albo's three fundamental principles (God, Revelation, Retribution), as essential doctrines of Judaism. He was especially careful to point out that in Judaism "the King Messiah [is] simply a man eminently endowed, like Moses and the prophets in the days of the Bible."[71]

The most important part of "The Jews and Their Religion" is the final section, a modest four-page description of American Jewry in 1845. In it, Leeser briefly describes the first settlements of Jews in different parts of the United States and the nature and extent of Jewish communal organization. Although he did not suggest what the total Jewish population of the country was in 1845, he did estimate that "the number of Jews in the city of New York is said to be about 10,000 [and] is rapidly increasing by emigration from Europe." He suggested that the Jewish population in Philadelphia numbered between 1,500 and 1,800. During the course of the next fifteen years (up to the outbreak of the Civil War), the American Jewish population grew at a record pace, and by 1860 was 150,000, a tenfold increase in less than two decades.[72]

To help meet the religious needs of America's rising Jewish population and promote the Americanization of the new immigrants by providing them with important English literature, Leeser published his original translation of the Pentateuch in 1845 under the title *The Law of God*. Later, he recalled that his interest in translating the Bible was "a desire entertained for more than a quarter of a century, since the day he quitted school in his native land to come to this country, to present to his fellow Israelites an English version, made by one of themselves, of the Holy Word of God."[73]

The Law of God is best understood as part of Leeser's plan to provide American Jewry, in the words of Bertram W. Korn, "with every kind of publication essential to Jewish survival." "My intention," Leeser wrote in the preface, "was to furnish a book for the service of the Synagogue, both German and Portuguese." The final work, therefore, included a vocalized Hebrew text, notes, and the *haftarot* (prophetic readings), "given according to the various customs, with necessary directions." Each of the Five Books of Moses was published in a separate volume. Three years later, in 1848, he published a complete *Biblia Hebraica* with vowels, the first of its kind in the United States. In 1853, he completed his magnum opus, an original English translation of the entire Hebrew Bible, which became widely known as the Leeser Bible.[74]

Leeser maintained that he actually began his translation of the Pentateuch in 1838. Three factors contributed to his decision to begin systematic work at that time. First, he had recently completed his six-volume rendition of *The Form of Prayer According to the Custom of the Spanish and Portuguese Jews* (1838) and felt encouraged by his English version of the Psalms in the Sephardic liturgy. Second, Rebecca Gratz's Sunday school met for the first time in March 1838 in Philadelphia, and desperately needed appropriate study material. Third, the Zunz Bible, the most popular German Jewish translation of Hebrew Scriptures during the nineteenth century, was published in 1837–38. Leeser was particularly satisfied with Zunz's choice of Heymann Arnheim's (1796–1869) translation of the Five Books of Moses, and adopted it as the prototype for his own work. The achievements of the broader world of Jewish scholarship and his own personal agenda for American Jewry seemed perfectly synchronized.[75]

The success of *The Law of God* surprised Leeser. Because the work was primarily arranged for liturgical use in the synagogue, he doubted that the books would have much appeal in the general community. He was also less than sanguine about the response of American Jews to the project, since their support of Jewish literature had consistently been lackluster. (However, not only did *The Law of God* prove popular in America but a pirated edition soon appeared in Europe."[76]

Leeser faced two significant problems in trying to distribute his book. First, it was difficult and often impossible to find a commercial publisher for Jewish religious works. Second, Jews, unlike Christians during the Antebellum Period, had no organized societies that sought to disseminate religious literature. Christian tract and Bible societies were able to subsidize the cost of publishing books and distribute literature to the general public. Unfortunately, much of their missionary efforts were aimed at Jews.

In January 1845, following "some flagrant violations against our sacred faith," Leeser organized a "provisional publication committee" in Philadelphia to counter hostile missionary activity and promote Jewish literature in America. Abraham Hart, president of Mickveh Israel, supported the group locally, and Gershom Kursheedt of New Orleans, a close friend of Leeser, offered to look for supporters in the South. A prospectus for an American Jewish Publication Society was printed in the *Occident*, and *Caleb Asher*, a tale that had recently been published by a parallel British operation, the Cheap Jewish Library, was republished under the name *The Jewish Miscellany, No. 1*. Leeser further publicized the idea by writing a lead editorial, "Cheap Religious Publications," in the February issue of his periodical, and included a "Plan of a Jewish Publication Society."[77]

An "auxiliary society" was formed immediately in Richmond, but progress slowed in Philadelphia. Apparently, Abraham Hart was unable to work on the project until after the High Holy Days. At a large meeting held at Mickveh Israel on November 9, 1845, a committee was appointed to draft a constitution for the organization, and a slate of officers was elected. The core group of the new organization was very impressive: Hart was appointed president; Alfred T. Jones, recording secretary; and, among others, Solomon Solis and Louis Bomeisler, managers. Leeser, the driving force behind the organization, was named corresponding secretary.[78]

The corresponding secretary "was ordered to write to all the congregations in America," and on December 10, 1845, he mailed a circular. Hopes were running very high. Leeser proposed that "if twelve to fifteen hundred subscribers can be obtained, at but ONE DOLLAR per annum, we shall be enabled to issue eight numbers of the Miscellany every year." The response by the American Jewish public to the circular, however, was less than enthusiastic. Membership in the Society peaked at 450 people several years later.[79]

Nevertheless, the first American Jewish Publication Society produced an impressive array of publications. It distributed a total of fourteen works under the name of the *Jewish Miscellany*, each approximately 125 pages in length. The three most serious works included Leeser's *The Jews and Their Religion* (1847), Aguilar's *The Spirit of Judaism* (1849), and Moses Samuels' *Moses Mendelssohn* (1846). The other booklets were primarily either embellished biblical and midrashic stories or moralistic tales, written in a heavy Victorian style.[80]

On the night of December 27, 1851, after just six years of the Jewish Publication Society's existence, disaster struck. Its entire stock was destroyed in a fire that ravaged the Hart Building. The end, however, had already been in sight before the conflagration: the membership campaign had gone flat, the policy of automatically distributing each new publication to every subscriber had taxed the budget, and little interest was generated in the vast pool of immigrants. Moreover, Leeser was unable to devote much time or energy to the Publication Society in 1851, having recently resigned from Mickveh Israel in a storm of controversy. Subsequently, he traveled extensively to find new subscribers to the *Occident* (which became an important source of personal income), and he was also hard at work translating a lengthy geographical work and the Bible.[81]

But did the first American Jewish Publication Society really fail? Compared to parallel Christian organizations or to commercial publishing firms, it was small and shortlived. Moreover, it had not succeeded in accomplishing all of its goals. Yet from a broader, historical perspective, the society had set a new precedent for American Jews. The American Jewish Publication Society was the first national Jewish organization in the United States dedicated to the advancement of Jewish culture and religion. It had succeeded in creating a small Jewish library, and thus helped advance the still-new notion that modern Judaism could be expressed in contemporary literary forms and yet be faithful to the religious heritage of the Jewish people. America was a frontier of Jewish issues during the 1840s, and the short life of the American Jewish Publication Society was, in essence, a story of a Jewish cultural pioneer. The original society died, but a new trail had been blazed.

Leeser captured the spirit of the society in an 1845 editorial in the *Occident*. He wrote:

It is almost impossible to foretell what such a Society might be able to accomplish, how it might aid to awaken many, now inattentive to religious duties, to a sense of their delinquency; how it might unite distant congregations, seeing that they were all interested in an enterprise which is theirs in common; how it might aid to dispel ignorance among ourselves, and enable the Israelite to put many a work in the hand of his Christian neighbour to dispossess him of any prejudice he may entertain

7

THE FINAL BREAK WITH
MICKVEH ISRAEL, 1846–1850

We regret at not being able to announce that some
wholesome legislation with respect to the office of
Hazan, and the commutation of the money
offerings has not taken place; both the by-laws
affecting the subjects not having met with the
approbation of the members. They seem to be
affected with a sort of nervousness whenever any
measure somewhat new in its tendency is proposed; they
go into meeting with the resolve of the English iron-clad
barons, "not to change the laws" of their order.
—Isaac Leeser, *Occident*, October 1849

THOUGH ISAAC LEESER'S PUBLISHING career was going strong, his position as hazzan at Mickveh Israel was becoming an increasingly difficult one. Leeser's stormy relationship with Mickveh Israel typified tensions within the American synagogue of the period. Infighting, name calling, and threats and counterthreats—between religious functionaries and synagogue boards and among laymen—took place in city after city. The fact that Leeser remained at his pulpit for twenty-one years was unusual; so, too, was the important role he played in Jewish affairs beyond the confines of Mickveh Israel and the Philadelphia Jewish community. The particular circumstances that led to Leeser's final break with Mickveh Israel were also unique. But the end result, the hostile departure of a hazzan from a congregational post, was not.

To a large extent, the tumultuous state of affairs in the American synagogue of the 1840s and 1850s reflected the increasingly unsettled nature of life in the United States during the Antebellum Period. Schisms and realignments in church bodies were commonplace. Social reform movements increasingly challenged the status quo and redefined the meaning of charity and benevolence in American society. Life on the frontier was rough and unruly, as was daily existence in the urban immigrant enclaves. Most importantly, the people ruled. In

155

many Christian denominations, "trusteeism" circumscribed the role and authority of the clergy.[1]

The American synagogue was further destabilized during the 1840s and 1850s by the great historical changes that were then transforming the United States. An expansionist war against Mexico (1846–48) netted the country, at a relatively low cost, a tremendous amount of new land, including the entire Pacific Coast from San Diego to the forty-ninth parallel, and all the land between the coast and the Continental Divide. For potential immigrants, the new territories meant economic opportunities, both on the frontiers and in the cities that serviced the vast interiors.[2]

Moreover, the discovery of gold in California just months after the fall of Mexico City to American troops attracted tens of thousands to the West Coast. In 1849, more than 55,000 individuals crossed the continent by land, and 25,000 more traveled by ship. Thirteen thousand Mexicans and South Americans moved north to join the Gold Rush. Jews were disproportionately represented. By 1860, historian Lloyd Gartner suggests, "perhaps 10,000 Jews lived in the boom city of San Francisco and scattered among the mining camps." Tens of thousands of other Jews, mainly recent Central European immigrants, poured into the Midwest, upper Midwest, and Mohawk Valley, New York.[3]

The political ramifications of the influx of immigrants and the rapid settlement of California were tremendous. President Zachary Taylor, a hero of the Mexican War, suggested that the Californians should immediately apply for statehood and decide the critical slavery issue for themselves. A heated debate swept the country, as the control of the Senate was at stake. A complex formula designed by Henry Clay called the Compromise of 1850 preserved the Union, but it failed to solve the underlying problems, which would ultimately plunge the nation into bloody internecine warfare. Temporarily at least, peace was maintained and the United States remained an attractive location for new immigrants.[4]

Political and economic conditions in Europe not only were as complex and volatile as in the United States but also helped propel the great transatlantic migration of the 1840s and 1850s. In 1848 a revolutionary movement of a democratic and nationalistic character swept the Continent. Insurrections broke out in Austria, Bohemia, France, Hungary, Italy, and Prussia. Initially scoring impressive victories, various national assemblies were convened to write liberal constitutions to guarantee universal suffrage and the disestablishment of religion. In many countries, Jews were promised complete emancipation.[5]

Hopes were dashed, however, with the restoration of the ancien régime the following year. Disillusioned with their prospects in Europe, the movement among Jews to move to America continued to gain momentum until 1853, especially among the common people. Intellectuals, rabbis, and professionals were initially less willing to leave Europe for "uncultured" America. But as the reaction to the revolutions intensified and personal prospects dimmed, many of the educated "liberals" also found the dynamics of immigration irresistible and were pushed and pulled to the United States.[6]

The surge in immigration and the rapid expansion of the American frontier combined dramatically to affect the nature and scope of the organized American Jewish community. The number of synagogues in the United States tripled during the 1840s. In 1850, Leeser estimated that "there are at least full sixty congregations of various sizes now in the country." Two years later, he suggested that the total number of congregations had soared to eighty.[7] Scores of benevolent societies, educational organizations, and fraternal orders, most importantly B'nai B'rith (1843), were also organized. Thus, while the total number of synagogues continued to grow, the traditional house of worship began to represent only one of a number of options for American Jews who chose to participate in organized Jewish life.[8]

Immigration also profoundly affected the internal social structures of many American synagogues. Restrictive residency rules were employed by many of the older synagogues to prevent Jews recently arrived from overseas from becoming enfranchised members of their congregations. On the other hand, *landsleit* (compatriot) synagogues, especially in the larger communities, developed in response to chain migrations from Europe. Moreover, the rising tide of immigrants contributed to the strength of both traditional and reform-minded congregations and further aggravated the ideological tensions that were already dividing the religious community.[9]

Despite all the factors fueling the fires of chaos among American Jews during the late 1840s, Leeser continued to promote the idea of unity in American Jewish life. In fact, most of his achievements outside the pulpit during this period were designed toward that end. He advanced the work of the American Jewish Publication Society and helped organize Philadelphia's communal Hebrew Education Society in 1847. (The society's school, however, did not open until 1851.) Leeser also published both a *Daily Prayerbook* for Ashkenazic Jews and the first *Biblia Hebraica* with vowels in America.

157

Leeser's last years at Mickveh Israel also witnessed a renewed interest in creating new pancommunal and national Jewish organizations. In 1848, together with Isaac Mayer Wise, who had arrived in America only two years earlier, Leeser promoted a national convention of American Jewish religious leaders. The project failed to materialize, but both Wise and Leeser learned important lessons from their temporary setback. At the beginning of 1849, Leeser made the farsighted suggestion that Philadelphia's Jewish charities be centralized. The proposal was partially adopted in 1856 and, in any event, adumbrated the federation movement that fundamentally reshaped every major Jewish community in the United States during the twentieth century.

In the late 1840s, however, it was Leeser's literary work that proved to be of true enduring value, while his plans for communal reorganization largely remained on the drawing board. Among the projects Leeser undertook during his final years at Mickveh Israel were the publication of both a Hebrew-English version of the traditional Ashkenazic *siddur* (prayer book) and a complete, pointed Hebrew Bible. After some persuasion by an unknown party, Leeser agreed that the religious chaos among the growing ranks of Ashkenazic Jews in America could be remedied, in part, if a standard liturgy were developed. "I found myself induced to undertake the present labor," Leeser wrote about his *Divrei Tzadikkim* ("Words of the Righteous") in the spring of 1848, "from the entire absence of anything like a standard Prayer Book, furnished with an English translation, for the use of those who follow the German MINHAG [tradition]. . . . I thought I could not render a more acceptable service to the many communities of the German denomination lately sprung up in this country, than by furnishing them with a Daily Prayer Book."[10]

Leeser probably had second thoughts about working on an Ashkenazic prayer book, because he hoped that the Sephardic liturgy would ultimately be restored as dominant in the American synagogue. Moreover, although the immigrant population was large and still rapidly expanding, most of the newly arrived Central European Jews were poor and probably would have been satisfied simply to continue using the *siddurim* they brought with them from Europe. On the other hand, Leeser reasoned, any religious unity along traditional lines was better than the current state of affairs, and a common prayer book certainly would help create an atmosphere of consensus. He also hoped that his translation of the prayers into English might help speed up the Americanization of the new immigrants. Besides, he personally formed a natural bridge between the established American Jewish community and the newcomers. He decided to proceed with the project.

Leeser used Rabbi Wolf Heidenheim's (1757–1832) well-known and highly respected *Safah Berurah* or *clear Language* (1825) for his Hebrew text. Heidenheim, a resident of Offenbach, was a modernizing traditionalist. His work was approved of by many of the great rabbinic leaders of Germany early in the nineteenth century, although his lenient attitude toward reform raised the ire of many Orthodox religious leaders. His most important work was a nine-volume High Holy Day prayer book (Rödelheim, 1802).[11] "The translation, in many places entirely new," Leeser writes in the preface to his Ashkenazic prayer book, "has been prepared with great care, either according to received authorities, chiefly of our modern German translators, generally Arhneim of Glogau, David Friedlander, and Mendelssohn, or from my own studies and previous version of the Portuguese *Tephilla*, in which I had generally followed David Levi."[12] *Safah Berurah*, Heidenheim's work, also included a German translation printed in Hebrew letters.

As Leeser had feared, the Ashkenazic prayer book was not a commercial success. Moreover, a proposed second volume, a manual of supplementary materials primarily related to life cycle events and select festival celebrations, was neither compiled nor published. The importance of the prayer book, therefore, was not its popular acceptance. Rather, it served as a benchmark of Leeser's growing awareness of the German Jew in America, as well as his willingness to help his *landsleit* in the United States.[13]

A few months after the prayer book appeared, Leeser published a *Biblia Hebraica* (1848) with a scholarly Episcopalian minister, Dr. Joseph Jacquett of Philadelphia. The book was the first of its kind in the history of printing in North America because it included both vowels and the musical notations for chanting. Unlike the prayer book, which was primarily directed at just one segment of American Jewry, the *Biblia Hebraica* was universal in its appeal for scholarly Jews and gentiles alike.[14]

Leeser had been interested in publishing a *Biblia Hebraica* since the late 1830s. On July 11, 1839, he wrote to Rev. Nathaniel Hewitt in Bridgeport, Connecticut, to explore the possibility of printing a vocalized Hebrew Bible. Leeser had obtained a van der Hooght Bible and came to the conclusion that "if there is a demand for 1,000 copies I see no reason why Americans should depend upon Europe for a supply of the holy word, which they can ought to have in their own hands." Apparently, Hewitt declined.[15] Leeser then turned to Dr. Jacquett for assistance. Jacquett's role was to compare several polyglot Bibles to help determine the best Hebrew text. Leeser handled all the other aspects of the project.

The Leeser-Jacquett partnership was significant. Whereas no translation of the Bible, by definition, can meet the needs of all biblically based religious tradition, Leeser and his associate did, in fact, issue an interfaith Hebrew Bible by leaving the text in the original language. The Leeser-Jacquett *Biblia Hebraica* was first published in September 1848 and, as one scholar observes, "is a fine piece of printing as well as a careful edition of the text." It quickly superseded an earlier ecumenical effort—an unvocalized Hebrew Bible published in Philadelphia in 1814 by Thomas Dobson, with the assistance of Jonathan Horwitz, a Jewish medical student at the University of Pennsylvania.[16]

For all of its merits, the Leeser-Jacquett work was overshadowed by another, more controversial collaboration. In 1852, just four years later, the British and Foreign Bible Society (BFBS) issued a vocalized Hebrew Bible under the editorship of Hebrew poet and *maskil* (follower of the Jewish Enlightenment) Maier Letteris (1800–1871). Both Leeser and Letteris based their works on the Masoretic studies of Dutch Protestant scholar Everardus van der Hooght (who flourished around 1686). The Letteris Bible (1852), with the resources of the BFBS behind it, instantly became the standard Hebrew text of the Old Testament throughout much of the world and the BFBS continued to use it until 1922. However, Letteris's reputation among Jews suffered because of his association with a missionary group. (Ironically, early in the twentieth century, the Hebrew Publishing Company of New York produced a Hebrew-English Bible using Letteris's Hebrew text and Leeser's translation.)[17]

Unfortunately, Leeser's literary accomplishments and his success in creating new pancommunal organizations had little or no impact on his congregation. As typical American Jews of the period, they continued to see their hazzan as merely a religious functionary, and felt they indulged him by allowing him to engage in his extensive extracurricular activities. So far as they were concerned, his reading of the service and participation at life cycle events were his primary responsibilities.

Viewed broadly, the circumstances leading to Leeser's departure from Mickveh Israel's pulpit in the fall of 1850 exemplified many of the problems in the American Jewish ministry during the Antebellum Period, not just Leeser's private situation in Philadelphia. The crisis in the American Jewish ministry in the late 1840s had roots deep in the history of the American synagogue. Basically satisfied with the services provided by the hazzan-shochets in their synagogues, American Jews resisted any attempt to upgrade the profession of the Jewish minister. By 1846, however, scores of immigrant rabbis and hazzanim began arriving in America. Within their ranks were several educated, articulate, and ambitious religious leaders, some of whom had already gained considerable pulpit experience on the Continent and in England. Slowly, they began to lay the foundations of both the modern American rabbinate and the contemporary organized Jewish community in the United States.[18]

The most famous of the new American Jewish religious leaders to arrive in the late 1840s were Isaac Mayer Wise, Max Lilienthal, and Morris J. Raphall. The first significant Jewish religious leader to settle in Canada, young Abraham de Sola, who became a friend and confidant of Isaac Leeser, also arrived during this period.[19] Others too numerous to mention swelled the ranks of the American Jewish ministry, so that in the course of just a few short years the American rabbinate was transformed from a random collection of individuals into a nascent profession. Through his personal struggles at Mickveh Israel and in the pages of the *Occident*, Leeser worked indefatigably to redefine and upgrade the American ministry and in so doing helped to develop the basic contours of the contemporary American rabbinate.

In contrast, the congregations, with only one or two exceptions, were strongly opposed to upgrading the professional status of their hazzanim and rabbis and resisted almost every attempt by different religious leaders to improve their office. In fact, nearly every Jewish religious leader who sought to professionalize his relationship with his congregation during the late 1840s found himself summarily dismissed from his job. Leeser, Samuel M. Isaacs, Max Lilienthal, and Isaac Mayer Wise had all lost their original positions by the end of the decade. By 1850, the struggle between the clergy and laity for the control of the American synagogue had reached its climax, and in democratic America, "the people" clearly maintained the upper hand.[20] There were exceptions, such as Morris J. Raphall at B'nai Jeshurun in New York, but even his success was more a matter of providing the laity with what they wanted than establishing clerical control over a large and prestigious congregation.[21]

The expansion of the American Jewish ministry in the 1840s and the even more powerful response by lay leaders to retain control over their synagogues had profound consequences for Isaac Leeser. He was no longer a lonely voice crying out in a wilderness. Now, there were better, more polished, more effective speakers in American pulpits. The cause of union found other champions with increasingly refined organizational skills. A second newspaper was launched in 1849, and

161

several successful Jewish day schools and boarding schools were established. Although still primitive and chaotic, organized Jewish life was clearly taking shape during the 1840s, and Leeser had to strain to be heard not only by an indifferent laity but by his own growing professional peer group.[22]

The broadening spectrum of Jewish religious life in America also complicated Leeser's role as a national Jewish leader. He had no patience whatsoever for the reformers and was increasingly frustrated by the traditionalists, especially those who were unwilling to change any aspect of their synagogues but failed to live within the borders of the *Halachah* outside of their houses of worship. "One party," Leeser wrote in May 1850, "called out, 'Touch not the sacred edifice!' The other exclaimed, 'Pull down the rotten fabric.' " "We honestly dissent from both opinions," he added. If Judaism were truly "reformed," Leeser believed, it would become a decorous, modern, unified, and vibrant Orthodoxy.[23]

If Leeser had been a person of less determination, he might have become lost in the shuffle of American Jewish life after 1845. Frequently snubbed or ignored by "doctors and licentiate" rabbis, he remained persistent in his support of the cause of Judaism. Through hard work he managed to maintain his position as the "American Jewish advocate" par excellence until his death in 1868.

Several factors helped bolster Leeser's position. Although he lacked academic credentials, even before his fortieth birthday he was, by reason of experience, the senior American Jewish religious leader of his day. The *Occident* provided him with a unique forum in which to express himself and through which to maintain his role as a national clearinghouse for Jewish news and information. Nearly all the new rabbis and hazzanim who arrived during the 1840s published articles in Leeser's journal, and some, like Isaac Mayer Wise, openly used it as a springboard to further their own careers. "Leeser," Wise reflected about some of his early articles in the *Occident*, "introduced me to the American Jewish public. Every reader knew where and how to find me."[24]

Leeser closely monitored the activities of his peers and reported on their progress and problems in the *Occident*. Although he hoped that the immigrant hazzanim and rabbis would seek to strengthen Jewish traditionalism in America, he recognized that an ever broader spectrum of opinions was being represented in the American Jewish ministry. Some newcomers, such as Leo Merzbacher, quickly revealed themselves as reformers. Others, including James Gutheim, Max Lilienthal, and Isaac Mayer Wise, slowly gravitated to the cause of

Reform at varying rates. Finally, a handful of the new ministers remained strongly committed to Orthodoxy, most notably Abraham de Sola and Morris J. Raphall. The majority of hazzan-shochets serving smaller congregations also conformed to Jewish traditional practice and upheld orthodox theologies, but only a handful were able to articulate their beliefs fully in either English or their native languages.[25]

In January 1845, Leeser announced that Leo Merzbacher (1810–56) had been elected preacher of the Mendelssohnian Society, later known as Temple Emanuel in New York. "We cannot say we wish them success," the editor added, "if they mean to go upon the destructive plan." He later politely refused to attend the consecration of their "new Synagogue" in 1848. In his effort to check the influence of the New York congregation, Leeser maintained in vain that Merzbacher, whose claims to both the ordination and a doctorate remain unsubstantiated, "had little impact on his own congregation or on the New York Jewish community." Temple Emanuel, however, rapidly developed into one of the premier American congregations and, by example, set religious and social standards for many of the newly arriving German Jewish immigrants.[26]

Leeser was more pleased to announce the arrival of James K. Gutheim, a fellow *landsman* from Münster, Westphalia, in 1843. Trained at the Hainsdorf Institute, Gutheim was engaged in various mercantile pursuits and served as a correspondent for the *Occident* for several years before becoming the rabbi of Congregation B'nai Jeshurun in Cincinnati in 1846. He quickly learned to speak English, and became a popular lecturer who defended the doctrinal orthodoxy of Judaism. Many of his early addresses were published by Leeser, who saw in him a valuable comrade.

Later, Gutheim became "an ardent adherent of the Confederacy" and, to Leeser's dismay, gradually grew to be a supporter of Reform Judaism. For four years (1868–72), he even occupied the pulpit of Temple Emanuel in New York. However, like his predecessor, Merzbacher, Gutheim's contribution to the development of American Judaism, especially before the Civil War, was limited.[27]

The first of the new rabbis who held truly great promise was Max (Menahem) Lilienthal (1815–82). Lilienthal had excellent academic credentials. "He received his Hebrew education," his biographer and associate David Philipson wrote, "from Rabbi Moses Wittelsbacher and attended also the famous *yeshivah* of Wolf Hamburger in Fürth, the academy for higher Jewish learning, among whose pupils were other young men who also became famous reform rabbis, such as David Einhorn, Isaac Loewi, of Fürth, Leopold Stein, of Frankfort, Joseph

Aub of Berlin as well as that pillar of orthodoxy, Seligman Baer Bamberger." "He received the rabbinical degree," Philipson also reported, "from Hirsch Aub, rabbi of Munich."[28]

In 1837, Lilienthal received the degree of doctor of philosophy from the University of Munich. His thesis traced the roots of Alexandrian Jewish religious philosophy. He reportedly performed so brilliantly on his doctoral exams that he was immediately offered a position in the diplomatic service. Because accepting the offer would have required him to convert to Catholicism, he refused it. Meanwhile, Ludwig Philippson, his friend and the editor of the *Allgemeine Zeitung des Judentums*, recommended him to the Russian minister of education to help modernize Jewish schools in the czarist empire. Ludwig Philippson also published some of Lilienthal's subsequent research.[29]

On October 8, 1839, at the age of twenty-three, Lilienthal left Germany for Riga, Latvia, where he was appointed director of the Jewish school. In 1841, the czarist government invited him to participate in the establishment of modern state sponsored schools for Jews. Lilienthal immediately found himself in the unenviable position of having to work simultaneously with the government, various branches of Russian Jewish Orthodoxy, Hasidim, and *maskilim*. After a difficult start, he finally began making headway when he came to conclusion that the czar intended to exploit his work as an instrument for converting Jews to Christianity. He immediately left Russia and headed for the United States, where several members of his family had recently settled. Subsequently, he published several accounts of his travels in Russia in Leeser's *Occident*.[30]

Max Lilienthal's decision to come to America was made in such great haste that even Leeser was unaware of his arrival in New York late in 1845. "We were not apprised through the European papers before of the Doctor's intention of visiting this country," Leeser wrote in December 1845. "We were more even surprised," he continued, "because we thought that he was greatly in the Emperor's confidence, and was to be invested with a species of superintendence over Jewish affairs in Russia."[31]

In February 1846, Leeser again noted in the *Occident* that, without prior notification, the "Rev. Dr. Lilienthal has, since our last, been elected Chief Rabbi of the three German congregations in New York." Leeser's enthusiastic correspondent in New York, James K. Gutheim, attended Lilienthal's installation and reported that "indeed the appointment of a Chief Rabbi, may be considered a new era in our religious concerns." No longer would American Jews have to seek the counsel of British or German rabbis on fine points of Jewish law. Instead, they had a local authority whose rabbinic competence was beyond reproach. Leeser himself was equally pleased with Lilienthal's appointment and included the new chief rabbi's installation sermon, "The Vocation of the Minister," in the March 1846 *Occident*. (However, he was later upset when Lilienthal introduced the "Reform" practice of confirmation in the German congregations in New York.)[32]

As chief rabbi, Lilienthal immediately went about the business of trying to establish himself as the leading rabbinic figure in New York and, perhaps, the United States. In the fall of 1846 he organized the first *bet din* (rabbinic court) in America, and asked the newly arrived Isaac Mayer Wise as well as Dr. Hermann Felsenheld and a rabbinic student named Kohlmayer to join him as *dayanim* (judges). The purpose in establishing rabbinic authority over several synagogues was to prevent further fragmentation of the Jewish community in the face of uncontrolled growth. Standardizing Jewish practice and promoting greater decorum were also to be considered by the court.[33]

Because Leeser had publicly stated that he had no rabbinic training nor made any claims to the rabbinate, he was not invited to serve on the *bet din*. There was also a problem of ethnicity. Leeser was institutionally aligned with the Sephardim, and the court primarily intended to serve the Ashkenazic immigrant community. On the other hand, the *Occident* was still the only Jewish publication in the United States in the mid-1840s and, although Lilienthal published information about the *bet din* mainly in Philippson's *Allgemeine Zeitung des Judentums*, he also needed Leeser's journal to publicize the court's projected activities in the Jewish community nationally. However, the *Occident*'s main source of information about the *bet din* was not Lilienthal but his subordinate, Isaac Mayer Wise.

The adroit Wise immediately grasped the broadest implications of convening a *bet din*, both for his own career and for the possible unification of American Jewry. He also understood the value of the *Occident* to the rabbinic court. At the first and only meeting of the *bet din*, Wise proposed a new rite, a "*Minhag America* for divine service," to be based upon the "three pillars" of "the *din*, . . . scientific principles, and the demands of the times" and promptly announced his intentions in Leeser's journal.[34]

Committed to the idea of a free press, Leeser published Wise's articles but was furious with him for promoting what appeared to be unwarranted liturgical reforms. "We most emphatically object," Leeser wrote in June 1847, "to any such form of prayer, which, as proposed by Dr. Wise, should exclude the petitions for the rebuilding of the temple, and the reestablishment of the sacrifices. We believe in common with all orthodox Jews in the literal fulfillment of Scriptures." Furthermore, he added, "especially do we think that the Sephardim congregations will be averse to change their form of prayer, which already contains all the elements required, and they will scarcely take in its stead the perhaps crude and ill-digested system which can be elicited by the few Rabbis now in America."[35] (Undaunted by either Leeser's remarks or the failure of the *bet din* to establish itself on a permanent basis, Wise continued to promote the idea of a *Minhag America* until, in 1857, he edited and published a prayer book under that title.)[36]

The failure of Lilienthal's *bet din* came as no surprise. Ethnic rivalries, Reform-Orthodox animosities, indifference, anticlericalism, congregationalism, and the general condition of communal anarchy all contributed to its downfall. The coalition of German congregations that had banded together to name Lilienthal chief rabbi disbanded for many of the same reasons. It could also be maintained that Lilienthal was the wrong man to rally and unify a complex, problematic Jewish community. He certainly was not a builder of great institutions. In 1855, he was elected rabbi of Bene Israel congregation in Cincinnati, where he remained until his death in 1882. He primarily concerned himself with local affairs and gradually came to endorse the cause of moderate reform, not unlike James K. Gutheim. At the national level, Lilienthal served as the head of the Rabbinical Literary Association in 1882, a precursor of the Central Conference of American Rabbis, the first permanent rabbinic organization in the United States.[37]

The man on the move in the American Jewish community of 1846 was Isaac Mayer Wise, still largely unknown but talented and aggressive. Leeser quickly refocused his attention on the young upstart from Bohemia and carefully kept track of his progress. Like Leeser, Wise wanted to unify American Jewry and build a great Jewish center in the United States by modifying Jewish religious practice and restructuring Jewish religious thought. Unlike Leeser, however, Wise was invigorated by "the spirit of the age" and not exclusively by the immutable truths revealed at Sinai. Although the two were initially able to work together, they ultimately clashed as they competed to win the elusive "center" of American Judaism to their respective viewpoints.[38]

The history of the stormy relations between Leeser and Wise is one of the most interesting chapters in nineteenth-century American Jewish history. Wise clearly had a more dynamic personality and was a better propagandist than Leeser. Leeser, however, represented the religious perspective of the majority of American Jews in the late 1840s and 1850s, and had a considerable body of personal and ideological supporters scattered throughout the country. However, once he had relocated to Cincinnati in 1854, Wise also developed a national network for himself, largely through his work as a religious journalist and through public speaking. His papers, the English-language *Israelite* and the German *Die Deborah*, quickly matched the circulation of the *Occident*, and helped make Wise Leeser's most important ideological adversary in the Jewish community for almost two decades.[39]

The personal relationship between Leeser and Wise was complex and uneven. The two never really became friends, nor did they come to admire each other as worthy opponents. The principal interest they shared was the quest to unify American Jews. Briefly, in 1848 and 1849, they worked together to promote and establish a union of American synagogues. In December 1849, Wise allegedly wrote to Leeser and called him "my best friend in this world of flattery and falsehood." In the long run, however, as the ideological differences between them widened, they drifted apart, even viewing one another with some degree of hostility and condescension.[40]

Thirteen years Leeser's junior, Wise had European roots considerably different from Leeser's. He briefly studied at a yeshiva and was considerably more adept at reading rabbinic texts than Leeser, a fact he did not let Leeser forget. Wise had served as a low-level religious functionary in Bohemia. Finally, he had already married while still in Europe, and had one child before coming to America. But the biggest difference between the two men was neither education nor family status, but temperament: as a person, Leeser was insecure, shy, and self-effacing; Wise, on the other hand, was self-confident, arrogant, and bold.

Together with his wife, Theresa Bloch, and their first child, Emily, Wise arrived in New York on July 23, 1846, after surviving an extremely dangerous trip across the Atlantic. Apparently, he did not have firm plans for himself and was grateful when Max Lilienthal sent him to consecrate a new synagogue in New Haven, Connecticut, in August 1846. Later that month, Lilienthal again sent him on a mission, this time to Syracuse, New York. En route, he stopped at Albany and preached at Beth-El, a vigorous and growing synagogue in the state's capital city. He was invited to return for the High Holy Days. Impressed with his sermons, the congregation invited him to remain and agreed, at his insistence, that he be named "rabbi of Albany." He served Beth-El for four years and subsequently served at Congregation Anshe Emet in the same city for four more years before moving to Cincinnati.[41]

Leeser carefully observed Wise's rapid progress in America, and reported on his activities in Albany and with the *bet din*. Although Leeser objected to both Wise's ideas about a *Minhag America* and his use of Solomon Sulzer's new music at Beth-El, he gave the newcomer credit for aiding the cause of Judaism in America. Late in 1847, Leeser traveled to Albany and met Wise for the first time.[42] In the *Occident*, Leeser happily reported:

> During our recent absence from our post, we also paid a short visit to Albany, to make the acquaintance of Dr. Wise, who presides over that congregation; and we were gratified to hear the desirable progress made by our brothers there, both in prosperity and religious improvement. Dr. Wise's school numbers eighty scholars, and the Israelites there amount to fully 1,000, if we understand our informant correctly. Owing also to the exertion of the eloquent preacher at the head of this *kahal*, we are told that Sabbath is universally observed, with but few exceptions, a gratifying contrast to the formerly reported state of indifference.[43]

In his *Reminiscences* (written 1874–75), Wise also recalled his first encounter with Leeser in flattering terms.

> One morning late in the autumn of the year 1847, a lean pock-marked, clean-shaven little man, clad in black, stepped into my study. The sparkling eye and the black hair betrayed the Jew, the rapid enunciation designated the foreigner, and the readiness and unrestraint noted the man of intellect.

After a formal introduction, Wise recalled, the two conversed at length. By the end of the session, the "rabbi of Albany" was favorably impressed:

> Explanations followed, and in one-half hour we understood each other thoroughly, for there was nothing to conceal on either side. Leeser seemed to me a man worthy of respect, because he had espoused the cause of Judaism earnestly and zealously when it had no representative on the press. He appeared to me honest and well-meaning in his orthodoxy. He had conceived Judaism from this standpoint, and had not advanced beyond it. A man who strives for ideals is always superior to him who works only for material sustenance, honor, and wealth. . . . These idealists are the true nobility of the human race, however morbid they may be at times. They recognize, they long for something higher, for something foreign to the animal nature.[44]

"In a few hours," Wise reported, "we were very friendly." "I treated Leeser very respectfully," he added. "He seemed to appreciate being treated thus by an opponent."[45]

The most important collaboration between Leeser and Wise occurred late in 1848, just one year after their first meeting. Prompted by Wise, Leeser published an editorial article, "On Association," in the October issue of the *Occident*. Eager to revive his idea of a congregational union among American Jews, the editor urged his readers to "look at the Christian churches, who have all the advantages of numbers, wealth, organization, bishops, conventions, and whatever else tends to consolidate power and to encourage to popular creeds."[46] Two months later, in large type, Leeser printed a circular written by Wise entitled "To the Ministers and Other Israelites," in which the Albany leader challenged "all my honoured friends, both ministers and laymen, and all who have an interest in the promulgation of God's law— come, let us be assembled in order to become united!" The meeting, Wise and Leeser suggested, should take place in Philadelphia in May 1849.[47]

Leeser continued to publicize the proposed assembly with great vigor in the *Occident* for several months. In March, he widened the campaign by distributing a printed circular that he also included in his journal. Besides changing the location of the meeting to New York, undoubtedly because of pressure from what was now the nation's largest Jewish community, he also succinctly listed the goals of the proposed assembly:

1st. A union of all the congregations by delegation, and stated meetings.
2nd. Education of youth.
3rd. Instruction of all classes by the establishment of schools and publications of books, informing our people of their destiny, their religion, their duties, and their history.[48]

The limited agenda of the assembly reflected the total lack of consensus among American Jews on religious issues during the middle of the nineteenth century. Other goals, such as "the establishment of a respectable and respected ecclesiastical authority [and] the institution of hospitals," had to be dropped from the agenda, or at least held in abeyance.[49]

In discussing the difficulties the project was encountering, Leeser admitted, "There are the sectional feelings of the Portuguese and Germans; [and] a difference of views between natives and foreigners."[50] Many Orthodox Jews, either wary of any association with Reform Judaism or simply skeptical about Wise's real intentions, balked at the idea. On December 15, Rabbi Abraham Rice, Leeser's ultraorthodox friend in Baltimore, wrote to Leeser in broken English:

I think, we are acquainted enough to talk with you freely, what my humble opinion is, about the convention of Rabbis, spoken of in your last Periodical. I know that very much, that you are sincere in religious matters and that you are the last who would make any innovation, but let me tell you as a friend you have to consider also, that in your early times you were mingled with the amerikan life; many of your ideas will not do for true Judaismen [sic], though you may think it is no harm in it.[51]

Moreover, Rice asked Leeser to reconsider his planned assembly in light of recent Jewish history. "Is the convention of the German Rabbis lost from your memory?" Rice queried. "Are our Rabbis better men? Have we not some wolves clothed in sheep's cover?"[52]

Wise, too, encountered significant resistance to the idea of a meeting to organize a national Jewish religious body in America. While visiting in New York, he discovered that Lilienthal and his three Orthodox congregations opposed the plan. The radical reformers at Temple Emanuel even refused to attend an informational meeting about it.[53]

By May 1849, the original target date, only six congregations had announced their willingness to attend, and by the following month, only two more synagogues had signed up, fewer than half of the twenty institutions Leeser and Wise hoped to attract. At year's end, not only did the two leaders realize that their appeal had fallen on deaf ears, but they also began bickering with one another in the pages of both the *Occident* and Robert Lyons' new *Asmonean* about who originated the idea of a national assembly, and who was to blame for its premature demise. Wise's position was briefly strengthened after Lyons temporarily appointed him co-editor of the *Asmonean*.[54]

Perhaps in an effort to distance himself from Wise, Leeser published a notarized letter in August 1850 from Shearith Israel, the Orthodox congregation in Charleston, about Wise's publicly embracing heterodox views there during "a public controversy held in this city between the Rev. Dr. Raphall and the Rev. Mr. Poznanski."[55] The officers of the synagogue claimed that Wise, then in the city to interview for the position at Beth Elohim, emphatically remarked that he rejected both the doctrine of the coming of the Messiah and the belief in the resurrection of the dead.[56] In Wise's eyes, the event had been anything but scandalous. In his *Reminiscences* he later recalled the original incident of February 3, 1850: "Raphall seized his books, rushed angrily out of the hall, followed by his whole party. He had apparently given up the fight. The reform party was satisfied with the result; the whole affair appeared ridiculous to me."[57] The Charleston debate, however, did have serious consequences for Wise. Some members of his congregation in Albany, Beth-El, resented their rabbi's theological nonconformity. The new president of the synagogue, Louis Spanier, was especially outraged. The congregation split into pro- and anti-Wise factions. "Excitement," Wise recalled, "ruled the hour."[58]

The morning of Rosh Hashanah, 1850, witnessed one of the most notorious scenes in American synagogue history. The drama of the moment was not lost on Wise, who later described the scene in great detail:

> I went to the synagogue on New Year's morning, appeared in my official garb, but found one of Spanier's creatures . . . sitting in my chair. I took another seat. . . . Finally the choir sings Sulzer's great *Ein Komokho*. At the conclusion of the song I step up before the ark in order to take out the scrolls of the law as usual, and to offer prayer. Spanier steps in my way, and, without saying a word, smites me with his fist so that my cap falls from my head. This was the terrible sign for an uproar the like of which I have never experienced. The people acted like furies. It was as though the synagogue had suddenly burst forth into a flaming conflagration. The Poles and Hungarians, who thought only of me, struck out like wild men. The young people jumped down from the choir-gallery to protect me, and to fight their way through the surging crowd. Within two minutes the whole assembly was a struggling mass. The sheriff and his posse, who were summoned, were belabored and forced out until finally the whole assembly surged out of the house into Herkimer Street.[59]

Leeser was mortified by the news. Just days before the melee, the editor had urged Wise's congregation "'to be to his faults a little blind,' if even they cannot extend kindness to his good qualities."[60] Two months later, after investigating the incident at Beth-El, Leeser concluded that Wise had provoked Spanier and others at various times by exceeding his authority as a religious leader and by making extreme remarks. "Still," he noted, "it must strike every one that, let us blame Dr. Wise as we must, things would not have proceeded to the length they did, if there had been a *central board of reference* for all congregations."[61] The rights of the rabbi as a professional, Leeser believed, superseded even fundamental issues of religious doctrine.

Leeser had deep problems of his own at Mickveh Israel, and he probably knew that his days in the pulpit were limited. In his mind, the violence directed against Wise was symptomatic of a general problem in the antebellum synagogue. Leeser, too, was a victim, and, therefore, Wise deserved his support. Although never physically assaulted, Leeser believed he had been continually abused by his congregation, which from his vantage point had refused to treat him or his office with proper respect. Leeser strongly believed that no matter what the shortcomings of the individual hazzanim were, the system under which American Jewish religious leaders labored was both demeaning and unjust.

At the same time that Wise was literally fighting with his congregation in Albany, Leeser was involved in a disastrous round of negotiations with Mickveh Israel. His old contract was due to expire at the end of September 1850. Leeser used the negotiations to raise a number of general issues. His initial proposals found uneven support. Earlier, the congregation had voted to support the hazzan's call for a national meeting at its April 1, 1849, meeting. However, for unspecified reasons, it rejected a special committee's recommendation to abandon the "voluntary offering" system of raising synagogue revenues in favor of annual or triennial dues, one of Leeser's pet ideas.

Several weeks later, the congregation met again. At this meeting, the parnass, Abraham Hart, read a lengthy document drawn up by Leeser in which he suggested emending bylaw 27 of the synagogue's constitution.[62] Subsequently published in a modified form in the *Occident*, Leeser's "Law Respecting the Hazan" called for the election of a hazzan "for an indefinite time, or during good behavior" after a two-year probationary period. It also allowed for an impeachment of the hazzan by a two-thirds vote of the congregation. Finally, Leeser proposed that the hazzan "be empowered at all times to exhort the congregation and to address them on the subject of religion" without the prior approval of the president.[63] The board not only summarily dismissed Leeser's proposal, they mocked it. "One of the adjunta," Leeser reported later, "although all discussion is out of order when a paper is read, as it has to lie over for action till a subsequent meeting, moved *that the office of Parnass be abolished.*" "Of course," he continued, "this was merely a jest . . . but it shows how a fair and honourable proposition of a highly respectable member was regarded by the men in authority."[64]

With the reelection of "the gentlemen composing last year's Board . . . Mr. A. Hart as Parnass, and Messrs. J. A. Phillips, M. Arnold, A. S. Wolf, and I. J. Phillips, as Adjuntas; Mr. H. Gratz . . . Treasurer, and Simeon W. Arnold elected Secretary," Leeser realized that the congregation would not meet his terms for reappointment. "I despaired of sustaining my position," he later wrote in May 1851, "and that when the by-law came up *in order* in the meeting before Rosh Hashanah 5610 [September 1850], it was withdrawn by my friend, as a motion had been made already to reject it."[65]

The unwillingness of the board to consider Leeser's proposal infu-

172

riated him. With great anger, he recalled his outrage and disappointment.

> Had it [the proposed bylaw] been respectfully taken up, discussed, and rejected, or referred to the proper committee of which the proposer had been chairman or at least a member, for amendment, with whatever instructions the meeting might have thought proper to accompany it, I should have found no fault, deeply grieved and mortified though I might have been; as I have no right to force my views on any one, little as he has the right to force me. I am republican enough for that. But such an unceremonious act of tyranny, that will listen to no reason, but demands absolute submission, roused my indignation.[66]

In what he acknowledged to be an "imprudent" act, Leeser decided "to appeal to the public judgement for our own justification" by publishing a blistering attack against the officers and board of his congregation in the *Occident*. In the October 1849 issue, under the heading "News Items," he published the following statement:

> We regret at not being able to announce that some wholesome legislation with respect to the office of Hazan, and the commutation of the money offerings has not taken place; both the by-laws affecting the subjects not having met with the approbation of the members. They seem to be affected with a sort of nervousness whenever any measure somewhat new in its tendency is proposed; they go into meeting with the resolve of the English iron-clad barons, "not to change the laws" of their order, however useful, expedient, or even necessary the old rule may have proved in practice.[67]

"It is not to be supposed," the anonymous author of an 1850 anti-Leeser tract wrote, "that the constituted authorities of the congregation would pass over in silence an article like this."[68] On October 21, 1849, the whole board met to consider the matter. Leeser's old enemies joined forces to attack him. "The vote of censure on a few lines of the *Occident*," the editor recollected with bitterness, "must serve as a case in point to exhibit the malice of one at least of my original opponents, who never forgave me my being elected, notwithstanding he had exhausted all his legal skill and parliamentary tactics to defeat my choice."[69]

A sharply worded motion was introduced by Jonas Altamont Phillips (1806–1862), a respected attorney and a son of Leeser's late archenemy, Zalegman Phillips. The motion included a preamble and three resolutions:

173

WHEREAS, There appeared in the last number of the *Occident*—a periodical published here by the Hazan of this congregation—an editorial article, reviewing in terms of censure, the business proceedings of the congregation, and containing a threat to appeal to the public, unless certain things were done which the editor wishes done: And whereas, such misconduct on the part of an officer of the congregation, deserves the severest animadversion and reproof. Therefore—

RESOLVED, That in the opinion of the Board, that the conduct of Rev. Isaac Leeser in the premises, is highly censurable, as tending to provoke irritation, create bad feeling, and as interfering in matters with which he hath no rightful concern.

RESOLVED, That his threat to appeal to the public, shews an absence of the good feeling that should exist on the part of the Reader towards his congregation.

RESOLVED, That the Parnas transmit a copy of this preamble and these resolutions to Mr. Leeser, and also report the same to the congregation at their next meeting.[70]

Apparently, Leeser never "offered any explanation, palliation, or apology" to the congregation. For his part, he believed that he was well within his rights to publish whatever he pleased in the *Occident*, and he chose to remain silent about the article. His friends, on the other hand, vehemently argued the case for "liberty of the press" in his behalf. "This Philadelphia Adjunta," one unidentified supporter wrote in Leeser's defense, "riding above the spirit of the age, would trammel the press, and entrenching themselves behind the dignity of office, would punish by votes of censure any one who would differ from them, or animadvert upon their conduct."[71]

Leeser had done immense damage to himself, but he was also unprepared to take a conciliatory posture. When, on March 22, 1850, he met with the parnass to discuss the terms for reelection, it was clear to both parties that the hazzan would not stand for reelection, to protest the congregation's refusal to grant him life tenure. Two days later, the congregation voted on the terms it was willing to offer, and they were, predictably, not favorable ones.[72]

The congregational meeting of March 24, 1850, was a riotous affair. First, the board's October resolution censuring Leeser was read to the assembled congregants. During the subsequent discussion, "an onslaught on the Board, made by one or two of the Hazan's indiscreet friends . . . brought the members to their feet." The action of the board was then approved by a twenty-to-seven margin with only two abstaining. Second, the terms of the office of hazzan were discussed. The final wording of the resolution contained a terrible surprise for Leeser. His adherence to the practices and beliefs of traditional Judaism were publicly called into question.[73]

In addition to setting the date of the election for the third Sunday of June 1850 and fixing his salary at $1,300 per annum for ten years, the resolution required that Leeser *shall in all things conform to the Jewish law.* The exact intent of the clause in unknown. Most likely, it referred to the previous complaint that the hazzan, who rented an apartment in the home of a gentile widow, Delia Cozens, did not faithfully adhere to Jewish dietary laws. It is also possible that Leeser's association with Wise had aroused some suspicions that his Orthodoxy was "lukewarm." Leeser boldly advocated such unorthodox measures as the modernization of Jewish education and the reintroduction of preaching into the synagogue, and he campaigned for the reform of synagogue finances. On many occasions he was strongly critical of nonobservant Orthodox and did not desist from calling them hypocrites. Whatever the authors had in mind as the alleged basis for the ugly addendum, Leeser got the message. "Evidently," he wrote, it was "to be viewed as an insult to me personally."[74]

Ironically, the crisis that supposedly began because Leeser sought outside support in an affair internal to Mickveh Israel again ended up in the public domain. On April 9, 1850, an anonymous pamphlet was printed in Philadelphia entitled *A Review of the Late Controversies Between the Rev. Isaac Leeser and the Congregation Mikveh Israel.* "His best friends are always obliged to admit," the pamphleteer charged, "that [Leeser] is an indiscreet, imprudent man. It is certain that he never loved his congregation, and in turn they could not love him." On April 11, an insulted Leeser petitioned the board to give him "a chance of offering a word of explanation, or of justifying myself completely in the eyes of the people." The request was denied. The board was no longer interested in making amends with Leeser. However, it did agree to entertain a motion to disavow the pamphlet as an official publication of the congregation. Later that year, a pro-Leeser *Review of "The Review"* was published in New York, again by an unknown author.[75]

The publication of the anti-Leeser *Review* backfired and galvanized support for him. After reassessing the situation, Leeser's opponents concluded that if the election for the office of hazzan were held, as planned, on June 16, 1850, the incumbent stood a good chance of being restored to office as a write-in candidate. "A private threat was held out," it was reported in the *Occident*, "that if Mr. Leeser were elected it would lead to a separation from the Kahal of several of those opposed to him."[76] Unwilling to split the congregation, the board decided to move the election to April 13, 1851, a date more than six months after Leeser's fifth contract expired. The hazzan had to leave office. At best, he could win a Pyrrhic victory, and then would have to continue serving a number of people who had publicly proclaimed their total disdain for him.[77]

Undoubtedly, there were some mixed emotions. Not everyone in the congregation wanted to oust Leeser: he had been at Mickveh Israel for twenty-one years, and many ties were stronger than anyone wanted to admit. For Leeser, the separation from Mickveh Israel was a bitter-sweet occasion. While he was relieved to be rid of the burden Mickveh Israel had become to him, he became increasingly physically ill as the final day approached. Beneath his cool exterior, he was inwardly filled with a sense of loss and failure.

During the summer of 1850, Leeser kept his mind off his problems with the congregation by completing and publishing his translation of Rabbi Joseph Schwarz's *Descriptive Geography and Brief Historical Sketch of Palestine*, based, in Leeser's own words, on "a printed Hebrew copy and a German translation in manuscript." Schwarz had visited his brother, Abraham, in New York early in the fall the previous year and arranged for Leeser to introduce the work to the English-reading public. Leeser understood that the *Geography* was to be "viewed as a commentary on the geographical passages of the Bible, and by no means as a description of a journey of three or four months duration."[78]

Unfortunately, neither the work on the book nor the critical acclaim it later received helped resolve any of Leeser's personal or professional problems. In an almost pathetic memoir written in 1858, Leeser remembers that on his last day at Mickveh Israel, September 27, 1850 (Hoshannah Rabbah 5611), "I was too ill to walk to synagogue; but as it was *Chol Hammoed* I rode to and from the sacred edifice, to perform there, for the last time, the service which had been received acceptably for so many years by a people, who, at one time, appeared so attached to me." The parnass, Abraham Hart, approached the hazzan at the end of the service and asked him to continue leading services "for the concluding holy-days." "I would not do it for a million dollars," Leeser replied. He also declined to sit either on the *tebah* or in the front row. "In addition to this," he remembered, "I was confined in my house on [Yom] Kippur, and some days before and after, with a most painful if not dangerous disease, which the physicians . . . ascribed to intense mental excitement and anguish."[79]

With Leeser officially no longer in the pulpit, the congregation turned to Abraham Finzi, "a native of England, and a gentleman of character, mental attainments, and piety," to temporarily conduct services. Finzi was a member of Mickveh Israel and was active in a number of Jewish causes. Early in 1851, Mickveh Israel began looking for candidates, and four individuals applied. Two, Sabato Morais, a native of Leghorn, Italy, and Joseph Rosenfeld, a hazzan from Charleston, South Carolina, emerged as the front-runners. A group of die-hard Leeser supporters also succeeded in getting the retired hazzan's name on the ballot without his formal consent.[80]

The elections were held on April 13, 1851, and the thirty-seven eligible voters required six ballots to elect a new hazzan. Eleven individuals persisted in voting for Leeser until the end. In the fourth ballot, the Morais supporters managed to gather fifteen votes. Rosenfeld's bloc then lost heart, and the election went to Morais. It was a brilliant choice and a perfect match. Morais quickly endeared himself to the congregation and remained in its pulpit for the rest of his life. During the second half of the nineteenth century, he emerged as one of the principal spokesmen for modern Orthodoxy in the United States, and served as the first president of the faculty of the original Jewish Theological Seminary, organized in New York in 1886.[81]

The long, drawn-out war between Leeser and Mickveh Israel was over. Leeser maintained that "the causeless breach which has been brought about between me and the congregation" never fully healed. For six years, he boycotted the Sephardic synagogue "and went mostly to the German, where I was politely received; and occasionally I preached in all the houses of prayer in the city."[82]

Late in 1853, Solomon Solis, a member of Mickveh Israel and a close friend of Leeser's, made a motion at a congregational meeting to repeal the March 24, 1850, vote of censure against the hazzan. The motion was tabled for over a year, and then was defeated by a vote of twenty-one to twenty on April 30, 1854.[83] Solis's premature death two months later at age thirty-five and the unrelenting opposition to Leeser kept the motion in limbo until Joseph Newhouse (1812–92), a successful entrepreneur in the oil business and subsequently the first president of Philadelphia's Congregation Beth El Emeth (established 1857), secured the necessary votes to have Leeser exonerated on November 19, 1856.[84]

The termination of Leeser's position at Mickveh Israel marked another critical turning point in his life and career. Ambivalent about his initial calling to the congregation in 1829, he had made the hazzanate his life's work. His failure to win the hearts and minds of his congregants and to convince them of the nobility of the ministry and his own worth as a human being was devastating. Now he needed to reorder his life, seek new sources of income, and redefine his role in the Amer-

8

On His Own, 1850–1857

*We set out on the 9th of November, and returned on
the 27th of February, after an absence of nearly
sixteen weeks during which we travelled upwards
of five thousand two hundred miles, and visited
at least twenty-five settlements or congregations of
Israelites, from the shores of Lake Erie to the
Gulf of Mexico, and were about forty-one entire or
parts of days actually in motion.*
—Isaac Leeser, *Occident*, April 1852

THE 1850s WERE A PERIOD of tremendous change both for American society in general and for the Jewish community in the United States. A population explosion, fueled by immigration, urbanization, industrialization, nativism, and sectionalism, and the volatile slavery issue were rapidly changing the map and the politics of the country. Of the numerous political problems facing the growing nation, the most important and vexing was the future of the "peculiar institution" of Southern slavery. Throughout the 1850s, politicians often deliberately stirred up patriotism and ultranationalism as a ploy to help preserve the Union, but jingoism could not transcend the issues that were tearing the country apart, and many of these efforts quickly degenerated into undisguised xenophobia.[1]

Jews participated in the great debates of the period as individuals, but they generally refrained from introducing these issues into their own communal politics. Instead, the Jewish community focused its internal debates on ideological questions of religious reform and communal unity. Although philanthropic and social welfare activities were a high priority, the number of new Jewish immigrants from Central Europe was overwhelming, and the majority of the newcomers were simply left to fend for themselves in their vast new country.[2]

179

During the 1850s, the population of America and of many of its ethnic groups soared. Proportionately, the years between 1850 and 1860 witnessed the heaviest immigration in American history, with more than 2.5 million people arriving from Europe and Asia. In 1850, the total American population had surpassed 23 million, of whom about 3.2 million were slaves and approximately 1.7 million were immigrants. Ten years later, the total population had grown to nearly 30 million, with immigration the single most significant factor contributing to the increase. The growth of the Jewish population was even more dramatic. Approximately 50,000 in 1850, it tripled during the next ten years. By contrast, in 1860 Great Britain had a total population of 23 million and a Jewish population of less than 50,000.[3]

Organized Jewish activity in America during the 1850s expanded in many directions but for the most part was still limited and ineffective in reaching the masses of new immigrants, many of whom settled in the interior of the country. The majority of American Jews concentrated on making a living and adapting themselves to the American cultural milieu, and had little time for or interest in Jewish activities. The two primary consensus issues in the Jewish community were self-defense and philanthropy. The former included random monitoring of various governmental agencies and missionary organizations. The formation of the Board of Delegates of American Israelites in 1859 enabled American Jews to survey the situation in a more sophisticated manner and proved somewhat effective in representing Jewish interests in the Union during the Civil War. Philanthropic and cultural activities involved a wide range of organizations, from small immigrant mutual aid groups to New York's prestigious Hebrew Benevolent Society. The 1850s witnessed the establishment of Jewish hospitals, primarily for the indigent, and the continued expansion of the Sunday school movement, which combined catechetical education with elements of a social uplift program. The Jewish press expanded rapidly during this period. Leeser's *Occident* remained a leading publication, although it became increasingly identified with the cause of modernizing Orthodoxy, and no longer primarily functioned as a pancommunal organ.[4]

Unfortunately, coordinating community activities at the national level proved to be an impossible task. The principal activists promoting Jewish unity were religious leaders, and religion was among the most divisive issues in the community. Moreover, the spectrum of religious activity continued to widen to the left and to the right. With the arrival of David Einhorn in the United States in 1855, radical reformers acquired a brilliant and combative spokesman. On the Orthodox side,

180

America's first East European–style *bet ha-midrash*, complete with daily Talmudic studies, was organized in New York City in 1852.[5]

As late as 1855, several religious leaders, most notably Isaac Leeser and Isaac Mayer Wise, still believed that religion could be employed to bring about greater unity in American Jewish life. However, when Wise organized the Cleveland Conference that year, he was sharply attacked by David Einhorn for capitulating to the Orthodox. Leeser, who reluctantly attended the initial meetings, was castigated by the traditionalists for associating with reformers. For the time being, a middle ground in American Judaism did not exist.[6]

Although a bachelor and modest in his lifestyle, Leeser did not accumulate much wealth during his twenty-one years at Mickveh Israel. His income was fixed, and he generally financed his various projects from his own savings, often losing money in the process. He also sent funds to his sister in Europe. The loss of his position at the synagogue, therefore, had dire financial consequences for him. In October 1850, he resolved to support himself as a freelance writer. He announced in the *Occident* his intention to start a weekly paper, issue a new edition of the *Form of Prayers for Portuguese Jews*, and publish "a new translation of the Holy Scriptures having accomplished nearly one-third of the whole."[7] He was committed to remaining in Philadelphia and refused job offers from both Shearith Israel in Charleston and, at the invitation of the chief rabbi of England, the Jewish community of Sydney, Australia.[8]

Across the country, Leeser's friends rallied to support him. In addition to sending him letters of encouragement, some of his backers also offered a few words of advice. On March 10, 1851, Abraham Kohn (1819–71), a native of Bavaria who came to America in 1842 and quickly rose from a peddler to a successful Chicago merchant, wrote to Leeser and suggested that if he wanted to make a living from the *Occident*, he would have to be much more aggressive in marketing the journal. "If you wish more subscribers for your Occident or weekly paper about to be published," Kohn urged his friend, "do come out on an Editor's tour to the West, and by personally soliciting subscribers . . . you will get ten subscribers to one you might get without it." Leeser immediately liked the idea and began to make preparations. Travel would also allow the wounds from his fight with Mickveh Israel to heal.[9]

Leeser was not a novice at traveling, and he especially enjoyed riding on the railroads and on the steamships of the great rivers of the American interior. "Like the great Protestant and Roman Catholic missionaries of America," asserts Jacob R. Marcus, "Leeser, too, traveled almost everywhere, particularly in the old South and in the old West: this side of the Mississippi. With the exception of San Francisco and other far-western towns, there was hardly a city which he did not visit, where he did not preach, or where he did not dedicate a synagogue."[10] Wherever he went, he encouraged the development of synagogues and took great pains to collect demographic and historical information about the scattered communities, which he promptly reported in his journal.

Even before his great trip to promote the *Occident* and his Bible translation, Leeser had traveled extensively. For example, early in the spring of 1850, in the middle of his fight with Mickveh Israel, he went to New Orleans to participate in the dedication of Nefutzoth Yehudah Congregation's new synagogue, named after its chief benefactor, Judah Touro. The event had a profound effect on the wealthy, reclusive philanthropist, and upon his death four years later, he bequeathed thousands of dollars to dozens of Jewish organizations around the country at the suggestion of Leeser's New Orleans agent, Gershom Kursheedt. He also left Leeser $3,000 in his will. On June 6, 1854, Leeser was one of the ministers who gave a graveside address at Touro's funeral in Newport, Rhode Island.[11]

Again in the fall of 1851, just weeks before his great trip to the South and West, Leeser made a "hasty tour" through Connecticut, Massachusetts, and upstate New York, revisiting a number of communities in which he had stopped on his 1844 trip to Montreal, and also visited several new places. "Upon the whole," he reported to the readers of the *Occident*, "it will be seen that the field of Judaism is extending, and this very rapidly in the Northern States, where not long since the face of an Israelite was but seldom seen, and where our mode of worship was entirely unknown."[12]

Leeser's grand tour, however, was of a different order. "We set out on the 9th of November [1851], and returned on the 27th of February [1852], after an absence of nearly sixteen weeks during which we travelled upwards of five thousand two hundred miles, and visited at least twenty-five settlements or congregations of Israelites, from the shores of Lake Erie to the Gulf of Mexico, and were about forty-one entire or parts of days actually in motion."[13] Via Pittsburgh and Wheeling, Pennsylvania, he headed west to Ohio, where he visited several communities, including those of Columbus, Zanesville, and Cleveland. In Cleveland, he gave the first talk of his tour at Rev. Isidore Kalisch's synagogue on the evening of November 19, 1851. Two days later, he reached Cincinnati, where he found four synagogues, two German and two Polish. Bene Israel, the first synagogue organized west of the Appalachian Mountains, invited Leeser to speak. Still nominally Orthodox in 1851, the congregation was apparently drifting toward Reform. To combat the trend, Leeser finished his sermon "with an exhortation to the people to remain faithful as their forefathers had been."[14]

On December 1, Leeser left Cincinnati and headed west to Indianapolis, Indiana, where he "found but one Jewish family." En route to Louisville, Kentucky, he briefly stopped at Madison, Indiana, a river town, where he "became acquainted with several Israelites," including a shochet. "Other towns on the Ohio, both above and below Cincinnati," Leeser enthusiastically reported, "have Jewish inhabitants; and we should not wonder if, should the immigration from Europe continue in the ratio lately prevalent, in the course of ten years twenty new communities would spring up."[15]

Leeser arrived in Louisville on December 4 and spoke at Congregation Adath Israel's newly dedicated building with its "pretty portico, and a convenient arrangement within. . . . We think that there are about one hundred and twenty members; but the day we were there, the number present exceeded this greatly in the men's department, and the ladies' gallery was also well filled." "A school for religious instruction is much wanted at Louisville," he observed, "and we have no doubt but due efforts will be made before long to establish one on a permanent footing."[16]

Leeser's next stop was St. Louis, where he arrived on December 12. To his great surprise, he "found a remarkable degree of comfort among the Israelites of the place, as we understood that among a population of about a thousand souls or more, there is but one old man, afflicted with disease, who is dependent on charity." The vocational profile of the community typified German Jewish activity at mid-century:

> They are chiefly engaged in commerce, dry goods, clothing, millinery, cap-making, jewelry, and grocery business, and but few are mechanics, as far as we could learn. Some are professional men, lawyers and doctors, and a full average of intelligence is discoverable among them.[17]

To his great displeasure, Leeser learned that the St. Louis community was deeply divided along subethnic lines. On Sunday, December 14, he spoke at the Fifth Street Synagogue to over a hundred people, and urged them to unite the city's three synagogues. "We only placed before the people the absurdity of keeping up three organizations, when the Polish, German, and Bohemian customs hardly differ." He also noted "that the Israelites of this flourishing city" were lax in offering their children a religious education, "except teaching a little Hebrew by the Rev. Edward Miers."[18]

Inclement weather forced Leeser to remain in St. Louis longer than he expected. He was unable to begin his trip down the Mississippi until early in January 1852. At Memphis, Tennessee, he found "about twenty families and many single men" and urged them to form a congregation. On January 10 he arrived at New Orleans, where he noted, "Jewish affairs have progressed somewhat since our first visit, two years ago." He "found that both the Portuguese and German congregations had established Hebrew schools, for gratuitous instruction of all classes . . . and felt an inward sensation of gratitude that two of the best buildings in that city should be devoted to the God of Israel."[19]

Leeser then headed east and visited several communities in Alabama and Georgia. He quickly discovered that Judaism was still very weak in the deep South. Neither the congregation at Mobile nor the one at Montgomery had a hazzan. In northern and central Georgia, the Jewish population was too scattered and small to support any form of religious organization. In Atlanta, there was neither a synagogue nor a kosher butcher. Kahal B'nai Israel in Augusta had recently arranged to rent a Unitarian church but did not have a hazzan. Nevertheless, Leeser, who personally felt comfortable in the South, concluded that these areas were potentially good locations for intensive Jewish settlement. "Healthy country towns in the South and West," he told the readers of the *Occident*, "afford a much better field for industrial pursuits of every kind, than old and populous cities, where it requires wealth to commence any respectable pursuit."[20]

The state of Jewish affairs was somewhat better in South Carolina. At Columbia, where he arrived on February 4, 1852, Leeser was "pleased to see so neat a building as that owned by the charitable society of that place, and which is used as the Sunday School and Synagogue." He spent the next two weeks at Charleston but "came little in contact with gentlemen of the reform Synagogue," and he was quick to add, "the attendance there has greatly diminished, a result which was long anticipated." In contrast, the Orthodox congregation, Shearith Israel, "was in a prosperous condition and . . . public worship was well attended the two Sabbaths we spent there."[21]

The biggest disappointment of the trip was his return to Virginia. At Richmond, he reported, "much to our sorrow, we found the Portuguese and German congregations at variance about the possession of the burying-ground. . . . A weary law-suit has been commenced to settle the question; and we deeply regret to state that both parties seem averse to a compromise." At Petersburg, he reported, "we regret that we cannot say that the numerous Israelites of this place have formed a congregational union," although "a Kahal has been formally constituted" in Norfolk.[22]

On February 27, 1852, Leeser returned to Philadelphia with a new appreciation of the condition of American Judaism. Scattered geographically, and divided by subethnic politics as well as by competing religious ideologies, American Jews nevertheless were slowly creating an institutional infrastructure to perpetuate their heritage in the United States. Having visited every major and almost every minor Jewish community in the course of the previous two years, Leeser was convinced more than ever of the merits of the case for national Jewish unity, the development of a school to recruit and train hazzanim, and the publication of Jewish religious literature. Renewed in spirit, he again applied himself to the task of building up Judaism in America.

The trip had also been a commercial success. Through his personal appeals, Leeser had increased the readership of the *Occident* and found a sufficient number of subscribers to proceed with his translation of the Bible. He did, however, have to temporarily abandon the idea of a weekly paper for lack of support. Free of the pastoral responsibilities of the pulpit, he now turned with great vigor to the various literary projects by which he hoped to earn a living and upgrade Jewish cultural life in the United States.

Having been out of town for almost four months, Leeser had suspended publication of the *Occident* in December 1851. To reward his subscribers for their patience, he published his original translation of Moses Mendelssohn's *Jerusalem* in March 1852 as a supplement to the ninth volume of the journal. Originally prepared in 1838, the translation was preceded by a fresh introduction explicitly linking the publication of the treatise with Leeser's battle with religious reformers. "Our philosopher is often invoked in defence of *reform*, so-called, and at times, of absolute infidelity," Leeser contended, "when, in point of fact, nothing can be farther than the truth, than that he coincided with the wild schemes of our moderns, who reject rabbinical authority and *tradition*, not to mention that he had the fullest faith in the absolute inspiration of Scriptures."[23]

Leeser viewed Mendelssohn (1729–86) primarily as a symbol: the prototype of the modern Jew who remained loyal to Jewish tradition. Leeser's commitment to Americanizing Jews and Judaism, use of the vernacular, and interest in preparing a translation of the Bible all reflected his admiration for Mendelssohn. Leeser wrote enthusiastically in 1829, "Moses Mendelssohn has done more than any other individual who has lived since the days of Maimonides and Yarchi [Rashi], for the improvement of his fellow believers." However, in his zeal to defend Mendelssohn, Leeser often failed to understand him. "He only wanted to advance the idea," Leeser wrongly concluded, "which, for one at least, I also share, that the whole Bible is fundamental." Mendelssohn, the philosopher, strove to reconcile "reason" with revelation. Leeser, the preacher and biblical literalist, based his entire theology on the self-disclosure of God to Moses and the prophets as depicted in the Hebrew Scriptures.[24]

When Leeser began working on his translation of the Hebrew Bible in April 1852, he naturally turned to Mendelssohn's Bible (1783–91) and its commentaries (*biur*) for a model. To his surprise, he discovered that the rendition did not suit him because it sought "to avoid difficulties and improve the style" at the expense of "a close, literal rendering." Of course, Leeser understood the magnitude of Mendelssohn's contribution to the field of modern Bible translation. He observed, "Mendelssohn, though he has since been excelled by others, who have built on his foundation, paved the way which has been made comparatively easy by his pious labours. So, no one will be apt to pay more homage to his genius than myself; but, as a rule of faith, he cannot be regarded."[25]

In lieu of the Mendelssohn Bible, Leeser used *Der vier und zwanzig Bücher der Heiligen Schrift*, edited by Leopold Zunz and published in 1838, as a model for his own work. He even used the English equivalent, *The Twenty-four Books of the Holy Scripture*, for his Bible's title. "As respects the translation," Leeser wrote in the postscript to his Pentateuch, the author "feels it is his duty to acknowledge that he has received the greatest aid from the Pentateuch of Arnheim, and the Bible of Zunz, even to a greater degree than from the works of Mendelssohn, Hochstatter, Johlson, Heineman, and several anonymous contributors to our biblical literature." Where Leeser did not follow the Zunz Bible, he frequently cited the Zunz rendition in his notes.[26]

With regard to style, Leeser endeavored "to adhere closely to the ordinary English version [the King James], which for simplicity cannot be surpassed." "Though the slight verbal changes grated upon the ears of us the older generation," a sympathetic Rosa Mordecai recollected in 1901, "the constant reading and reciting from it in Sunday Schools made it familiar to the young." Some changes were easily accepted, such as his version of Psalm 90:3, "Thou turnest man to contrition," instead of the Authorized Version's "Thou turnest man to destruction." However, his modification of other familiar passages (for example,

Psalm 23:2, "In pastures of tender grass he causeth me to lie down: beside still waters he leadeth me") proved less than successful.[27]

To allay suspicions that his work was not original, Leeser reported that he had "not looked at a single work issued by the English Jews" and hence had "not borrowed a single idea or suggestion from any of them, living or dead." Actually, there was little material to consult. David Levi's Pentateuch with *haftarot*, published in London in 1787, was the best known Anglo-Jewish translation, but it closely followed the King James version. In 1844, David de Sola and Morris J. Raphall, then headmaster of the Hebrew National School at Birmingham, England, published a new translation of Genesis with extensive annotations. Finally, Leeser probably did not have immediate access to the *Jewish School and Family Bible* (1851–61) prepared by Dr. Abraham Benisch and officially approved by the chief rabbi of the United Congregations of the British Empire. In any event, Leeser finished a significant amount of his own work before the Benisch Bible appeared.[28]

In general, it appears that Leeser was better versed in Christian biblical translations and exegetical literature than he cared to acknowledge in public. He was familiar with the Vulgate and Luther's Bible. On occasion, he also referred to the Biblical commentaries of the English Nonconformist Matthew Henry. From the British firm of Samuel Bagster and Sons, he obtained Hebrew Bibles, polyglots, and various reprints of the King James Bible. In one instance, he even incorporated "a few notes" from an uncited Bagster Bible into his own commentary.[29]

Leeser also acknowledged that he made extensive use of the translation and commentary of the moderate German reformer Ludwig Philippson (1811–89). Isaac Mayer Wise later claimed credit for persuading Leeser to look at the Philippson Bible. "The year before he published his translation of the Bible," Wise recalled at the time of Leeser's death, "we saw him in his house. He informed us of his enterprise and of the German translations which he consulted. . . . Why do you not use Philippson's? we asked; because he is a reformer, was his reply. We convinced him, however, to the contrary in regard to that Bible and he bought a copy. With admirable skill, he used Philippson without betraying one word that this was his main authority."[30] Wise, however, greatly overstated his case. Leeser openly acknowledged his use of Philippson both in the preface to his Bible and throughout his notes. In the *Occident* Leeser also acknowledged his indebtedness to "the Rabbi of Magdeburg, in Prussia, whose work I only for the first time read last summer [1852], and it is up to this date, not quite finished." Moreover, Leeser and Philippson corresponded. Philippson wrote a favorable review of Leeser's *Discourses* and *Jews and the Mosaic*

Law in his newspaper, *Allgemeine Zeitung des Judentums*, in 1839. Leeser, in turn, announced his plans to publish the *Occident* in Philippson's journal in October 1842. As late as 1866, Leeser arranged for the private publication of M. Meyer's English translation of Philippson's *The Crucifixion and the Jews*.[31]

Leeser studied "the ancient versions, also, of Onkelos, Jonathan, and the Jerusalem Targumist . . . and wherever accessible, the comments of the great expounders," especially Rashi. Leeser also occasionally consulted commentaries by Redak (Rabbi David Kimchi), Ibn Ezra (Rabbi Abraham ben Meir ben Ezra), Rashbam (Rabbi Shelomoh ben Meir, the grandson of Rashi), Ralbag (Rabbi Levi ben Gershom), and Saadia Gaon. A lengthy and somewhat heated discussion in the *Occident* on the value of a literal translation of Exodus 3:14 suggests that Leeser did, in fact, consult a wide spectrum of rabbinic literature in connection with his Bible translation. "The commentary of Rashi has been of the utmost service in this work, as it has been to all previous ones," Leeser wrote of his *Law of God*, "and the authority of the Neginoth [musical accents] were also adhered to wherever practicable, it being the oldest and best among us." However, with the exception of Rashi, Leeser's knowledge of medieval commentaries was largely based on secondary sources.[32]

Rashi, in the words of Jakob Petuchowski, was Leeser's "link to the event at Sinai."[33] Not only did Leeser translate many of Rashi's comments and include them, or parts of them, in his own short explanatory notes, but he would frequently use Rashi's perspective as a guide to a revised rendering of a given text. Thus, Leeser interprets Ezekiel 20:25 as "And also I let them follow statutes that were not good," instead of the King James's more literal "Wherefore I gave them also statutes that were not good." In this manner he solved theological problems in a traditional Jewish fashion, but at the expense of an accurate translation. In other cases, the Rashi-based Leeser version corrects nonliteral interpolations of the Authorized Version. For example, Leeser renders Exodus 25:17 as "And thou shalt make a mercy seat." Most often, however, he would simply use Rashi to give a traditional Jewish perspective on a selected verse. The Authorized Version renders the end of Jeremiah 52:13 as "And all the houses of the great *men* burned he with fire." Leeser retains the translation, drops the emphasis on "men," and adds a comment after the word "great": "The Rabbins [i.e., Rashi] take this to mean either the synagogues where the prayers were offered, or the schools where the law was taught."[34]

The early editions of the Leeser Bible included a modest commentary. Most of the notes simply reported variant translations that he did not use in his version but still considered significant. In later versions of the work, the number of notes containing translations from Zunz, Philippson, and others were reduced, leaving mainly his substantive comments. The decision to abbreviate the commentary was made both for economic reasons (to hold down the production costs of his Bible) and to conform to widespread Protestant practice in America of emphasizing the "Word" itself and not subsequent cumulative traditions in popular versions of Scripture.[35]

A close reading of Leeser's notes confirms that his Bible was meant to be, above all, an *apologia Judaica*. Leeser frequently explained biblical passages that might have appeared objectionable to a modern person in a way that made them more acceptable. Likewise, he defended the actions of ancient Israelites whenever their honor was at stake. "The Law knows of no distinction between the Israelite and the foreigner," Leeser says of Deuteronomy 1:16, "All are alike before the Supreme Judge of the world." Concerning Deuteronomy 14:21, "Ye shall not eat anything that dieth of itself: unto the stranger that is in thy gates canst thou give it, that he may eat it," Leeser maintained that "these things [were] not being interdicted for their unhealthiness, but because God chose to forbid them to Israel, they may be eaten by others if they will."

Apologetics and polemics are, of course, different sides of the same coin. Just as the Leeser Bible sought to give an authentic Jewish rendition of Scripture in English, so it actively refuted Christian exegetical traditions. A well-known Christological reference in Scripture, "until Shiloh come" (Genesis 49:10), received perhaps the longest comment in Leeser's notes, in which he equates "Shiloh" with "the King Messiah, [who] shall come." In some cases, he even admits to giving a nonliteral translation of a verse to distance the text from Christian interpretation.

Leeser also sought to distinguish between what he considered a legitimate explanation of biblical miracles and Christianity's misunderstanding of the same. In a comment on false prophets (Deuteronomy 13:2–4), he wrote, "The Divine legislation is the standard of truth; consequently no miracle should such be sought, can be considered as an evidence of Divine mission if it contradict the law. The will of God is expressed in his revelation, and he is no man, that he should change [it]." In other places, however, Leeser was content to give a naturalistic explanation of miracles. Similarly, he frequently referred to reports of ancient and contemporary travelers in the Middle East to confirm the accuracy of Scriptures.[36]

In conformity with his brand of modern Orthodoxy, Leeser offered only a few notes on Jewish practice. In a note to Esther 9:22, he pointed out that "the poor should of right therefore be remembered on this day [Purim] especially by their more wealthy neighbors, so that they too may bless the Lord in joy and plenty—perhaps as a criticism of the extravagant Purim balls that were becoming popular in his day. The most poignant remark, however, was directed at Reform Judaism. In a detailed discussion of a special dispensation given to princes so that they could individually offer incense at the consecration of the Tabernacle during the exodus from Egypt (Numbers 7:86), Leeser concluded, "It will always be seen that there were weighty reasons for the suspensions—that they were sanctioned or ordained by the Holy Spirit; and that consequently we are from such premises not authorized to suspend any precept by our own authority, except that there be an absolute necessity which compels us to disobey."

To Leeser, the only correct understanding of Scripture was an Orthodox Jewish one. He openly declared in the preface to his Bible that "he always studied the Scripture to find a confirmation for his faith and hope . . . [and] no perversion or forced rendering of any text was needed to bear out his opinions or those of other Israelites." Like other literalists, Leeser was basically concerned with theological correctness. "Most often," writes one historian, "calls for 'literalism,' or movements 'back to the Bible,' really seek to cloak with legitimacy efforts aimed at replacing one mode of interpretation with another." So Isaac Leeser in his translation of the Bible sought to provide American Jews with an authentic Jewish version of Scripture and free them from their reliance on the Authorized Version.[37]

Under the guise of literalism, Leeser used different methods to introduce rabbinic exegesis into his translation. For example, he used parentheses to indicate words he added to elliptical verses "to make the sense clear." Instead of having Samuel "lying down in the temple of the Lord," he had him "sleep in (the hall of) the temple" (I Samuel 3:3), a correction that brought the translation into agreement with a rabbinic understanding of priestly protocol but nevertheless was a nonliteral addendum.[38]

In some instances, Leeser significantly surpassed literalism and actually sought to harmonize conflicting passages. Such bold emendations of the text are not without precedent in the history of Bible translations. Even in a recent Orthodox English-language version of the Pentateuch, the translator forthrightly states, "We have consistently translated passages so that they reflect the final decision in Jewish law." Leeser translated the end of Exodus 21:6 as "He [the servant] shall serve him till the Jubilee," although the Hebrew reads "forever," in order to have the verse agree with Leviticus 25:10. In modifying Exodus 21:6 in his Bible, Leeser was also influenced by the Antebellum debate over slavery. Although discreetly pro-South, he believed that ancient Hebrew slavery differed from its practice in the United States. Like other hazzanim of the period, Leeser believed that Biblical legislation mandated the humane treatment of slaves and provided liberal terms for manumission, whereas the American system of slavery was harsh by comparison.[39]

Leeser strongly believed that his work as a Bible translator was carefully guarded over by Heaven. In the preface to his Pentateuch he wrote, "together with the little knowledge I have myself of the Sacred Tongue, I thought, in all due humility, that I might safely do the task, confidently relying upon that superior aid which is never withheld from the inquirer after truth." To the unphilosophical, theologically oriented Leeser, "superior aid" meant "inspiration," which he defined as "the endowment of superior knowledge from God as a special gift." The God who had revealed himself to Moses, he was convinced, also watched over his own work of translating the Holy Scriptures.[40]

Completing the translation and overseeing the printing of the Bible was arduous work that required more than a year and a half of Leeser's time. From April 1852 to September 1853, he worked methodically on the project with a minimum of interruptions. He began by carefully editing his earlier work on the Pentateuch, *haftarot*, and Psalms. Abstruse passages were subjected to substantial revisions, and the explanatory notes were greatly expanded. Finally, in September 1853, Leeser wrote with satisfaction, "The translator surrenders a labour in which he has been engaged, occasionally, for more than fifteen years," and sent his finished manuscript to the printer. The January issue of the *Occident* included a literary notice that *The Twenty-four Books of Holy Scriptures*, "which has been so long announced, is at length completed . . . [and] we may be permitted to state, that as far as a mechanical execution is concerned, it may freely challenge comparison with any work of the kind ever issued in America."[41]

The original quarto edition of the Leeser Bible, although it probably made a handsome pulpit Bible, was basically "intended to supply families with a plain version of the Word of God" for home study. It also included "four pages of FAMILY RECORD, printed in a neat manner on very strong paper . . . at the end of the canon, in which marriages, births, and deaths can be recorded."[42]

Both Leeser and his opponents knew that the success of his Bible depended primarily on its acceptance among Jews, although he warmly welcomed praise from Christian scholars. Several Reform rabbis attempted to discredit the Leeser Bible. Writing in Wise's newly founded *Israelite* in 1854, Isidore Kalisch concluded that he would have to "write a book as thick as Mr. Leeser's biblical translation is, if I should point out all the gross errors and mistakes." Leeser, however, was not easily intimidated. "The best of this transaction," he replied in the *Occident*, "is that Mr. Kalisch pretends to judge the English style of the work, when he is confessedly unable to write his own thoughts in this language." Furthermore, Leeser invited Rev. Dr. Isaac Mayer Wise of Cincinnati to refute Kalisch's "groundless and illogical censures" point by point.[43]

Fortunately, Wise decided not to sustain the controversy, although he might have wanted to do so. Leeser's Bible and Wise's *History of the Israelitish Nation* (1854) were published simultaneously. After promoting Wise's book in the *Occident*, Leeser found the finished work unacceptable. Shocked at the unorthodox character of Wise's *History*, Leeser immediately warned his *Occident* readers of its heterodoxy: "Dr. W[ise] has spoken out so plainly against the inspiration of the Bible and the truth of the miracles, or even the facts as there plainly recorded, that no one who believes in the ancient method can be deceived."[44]

By contrast, the Leeser Bible drew high praise from scholars and clergymen in the broader American community. Rev. Charles Hodge, a leading "old" school Presbyterian theologian at Princeton Theological Seminary, applauded Leeser's Bible in his *Biblical Repertory and Princeton Review* (July 1854) and called for "a work on a similar plan, from a competent Christian scholar." Similarly, Dr. Silas Weir Mitchell (1829–1914), a physician and author of *Hugh Wynne, Free Quaker* (1898), is reported to have stated, "When I want to get to the true meaning of the Psalms and Prophets—I go to my friend Rev'd Isaac Leeser's translation as the most satisfying."[45]

Two years after the Bible first appeared, Leeser admitted, "The translator cannot flatter himself that it has met with such a reception as would have gratified his ambition." He decided to work on a revised edition, which he completed in 1856, incorporating several changes. He decided to use a smaller format, because the quarto proved too expensive for mass distribution. The new size in turn required an abridgment of his notes and their reproduction at the end of the book instead of at the bottom of each page. Last and most importantly, he explicitly promoted the Leeser Bible as the Jewish successor to the King James version.[46]

The new preface sounded the battle cry. "It would be a species of mental slavery," Leeser told his readers, "to rely for ever upon the arbitrary decree of a deceased King of England, who certainly was no prophet for the correct understanding of Scriptures." He also noted that "although those who assisted in furnishing the common version may have been as honest as men writing for their sect are likely to be," they still colored the work to "confirm their peculiar views." Worse, "most of the editions in use are disfigured by chapter and page headings . . . and the merest inspection will at once show that these expositions are perfectly arbitrary." Finally, Leeser observed that "since the time of King James the world has progressed in biblical knowledge no less than in all other branches of science." In an advertisement for the London edition of his Bible, he even maintained that the need for a new English translation "has long been recognized by the highest dignitaries and most accomplished scholars in the Anglican Church itself."[47]

By the time Leeser died (in 1868), his Bible had won wide acceptance among American Jews. Ironically, for more than a quarter-century beginning in 1874, his Bible was promoted by the Union of American Hebrew Congregations, the national umbrella organization of the Reform movement. After the appearance of the Jewish Publication Society's own Bible in 1917, the Hebrew Publishing Company began printing and distributing the Leeser Bible at a greatly reduced cost, particularly among the East European Jews who had begun immigrating to America in large numbers after 1881.[48]

The ultimate success of the Leeser Bible was not just a matter of good advance work and marketing. "Throughout the millennia," writes Matitiahu Tsevat, "prominent versions of the Bible have often been distinguished or properly appraised not by the linguistic accuracy with which they rendered difficult passages, but by their achievement of a specific synthesis between the ancient book and the genius of their times." In many ways, Leeser, and by extension his Bible, represented the "specific synthesis" of the American Jewish experience during the middle decades of the nineteenth century. He was at once an American, Sephardic, and German Jew. The Bible was the centerpiece of his religion, an orientation few people of his time and place would have contested. His Orthodoxy was also an asset. Reform was still in its infancy, and in any event, it might be assumed that most American Jews would have wanted the translation of the Bible to be entrusted to a staunch guardian of tradition.[49]

In addition to his traveling and his translating, Leeser's efforts to prevent a schism between the Reform and Orthodox parties in American Judaism constituted a third major area of activity from 1850 to 1857. As the spectrum of organized Jewish religious life broadened during these years, the debate became increasingly vitriolic and the possibility of forging a central position more and more remote. To complicate matters, the personality conflict intensified between Leeser and Wise, who respectively represented traditionalism and Reform to the "middle" of American Judaism. By 1857, despite the efforts of the two leaders, the distance between the two camps had grown irremediable.

The disputation over eschatological doctrines held in Charleston in April 1850 between the Orthodox Morris J. Raphall and two reformers, Gustavus Poznanski and Isaac Mayer Wise, moved Leeser to consider the origins of the Reform movement. The following month, he wrote an editorial piece for the *Occident* entitled "Reforming and Deforming." Rejecting both the obscurantism of traditionalists, who "regard everything ancient as sacred," and the radicalism of reformers, who "only saw before them abuses," Leeser suggested that Judaism could be "*reform*[ed] . . . upon *correct* principles." More decorum during worship and ministers who could speak "words of truth and life" were the only reforms Jewish worship really needed. But, Leeser pointed out in a second article by the same title in the July issue, the sins of the Orthodox and those of the reformers were qualitatively different. Some traditionalists were hypocrites, others too zealous; as a group, however, they embraced the ancient, divinely based teachings and practices of Judaism. Reformers, on the other hand, had placed themselves outside the pale of historical Judaism and created a new "ism" of their own. The responsibility of maintaining religious unity in Israel, according to Leeser, thus rested on the reformers. Rejecting the invitation of some reformers to meet them in their place of worship, he concluded that "our ancient Synagogue . . . is the only place where all can unite in one assembly."[50]

A sermon, "The Mission of Reform," preached by Rabbi Maurice Mayer at Beth Elohim in Charleston on March 25, 1854, was the occasion for a second and more sustained attack on Reform by Leeser. From June 1854 through March 1855, Leeser published a total of eight editorials in the *Occident* under the banner "Progressive Reforms." Viewing himself as a latter-day Elijah, and Mayer, by implication, as a priest of Baal, Leeser attempted to dismember Mayer's arguments concerning the historical necessity, religious legitimacy, and means of "reform" in Judaism. The release of Isaac Mayer Wise's controversial *History of the Israelitish Nation* and the initial success of the Cincinnati rabbi's new newspaper, *The Israelite*, further provoked Leeser's wrath.[51]

Long-winded and unstructured, Leeser's critique of Reform revolved around a few basic ideas. Leeser attacked Reform on three fronts: its legitimacy as an interpretation of "historical" Judaism, its philosophical underpinnings, and finally, the utility of Reform as an instrument of improving modern Jewish religious life. In all three areas, he found Reform in general and Mayer's sermon in particular to be not only deficient but fraudulent.

Leeser rejected the idea that the Reform movement was essentially the latter-day expression of an ancient process of internal reforms in Judaism. Instead, he characterized Reform as an aberration that denied both eternal Biblical teachings and the authority of the ancient rabbis. He also attacked the idea of the "historical necessity" of Reform. Judaism, especially in Central Europe during the eighteenth century, simply was not as wretched and anachronistic as reformers depicted it. The shortcomings of traditional Judaism, he insisted, could be corrected without violating either the *Halachah* or the principal tenets of the Jewish faith.[52]

Moreover, he both attacked the subjective basis of Reform and questioned the effectiveness of the movement. Wise's characterization of religion as "a matter of the heart" was totally unacceptable to Leeser. He believed that Judaism had an objective, historical basis in the theophany at Sinai. Anything less than that, he suggested, reduced Judaism to a whim or fad with no basis in reality. Finally, Leeser observed that Reform was an institutional failure. Its adherents had not returned to the synagogue, did not observe the Sabbath, and did not live deeper, more spiritual existences. In short, Reform was nothing more than an eloquent excuse for religious nihilism.[53]

The high point of Leeser's battle with Reform occurred not in reasoned arguments in the *Occident* but rather during the course of a second great trip to the Midwest and South. On April 28, 1855, he spoke at the Broadway Synagogue (Congregation Bene Israel) in Cincinnati. "I ventured in the lion's den," he remembered twelve years later, and attacked "them [the Reformers] where they are all-powerful, and I equally powerless." "There were," he speculated with some pride, "eight hundred, or perhaps near a thousand persons in the synagogue to listen to me."[54]

Leeser's talk, "The False Prophets," was both an anti-Reform harangue and an attempt to thwart the efforts of Isaac Mayer Wise, who had moved to the city a year earlier. Wise's quick success in establishing himself in Cincinnati and founding his own paper, and his increasing boldness as a reformer, were all matters of grave concern to Leeser. In the first issue of *The Israelite*, Wise listed five principles of Reform, one stating, "All forms to which no meaning is attached any longer are

195

an impediment to our religion, and must be done away with," and another asserting, "Whatever tends to the elevation of the divine service, to inspire the heart of the worshipper and attract him, should be done without any unnecessary delay." To make matters worse, in addition to Congregation Bene Jeshurun, which had originally invited Wise to come to Cincinnati, the other three synagogues in town, including the prestigious Bene Israel, had all asked Wise to serve as their rabbi.[55]

Leeser felt the urgency of the moment, and in an extraordinarily emotional appeal attempted to disabuse Cincinnati Jewry of their romance with Wise and Reform. Speaking on a well-chosen text, Jeremiah 23:23–27, Leeser began by proclaiming, "We have indeed fallen on evil times when men put their dreams in the place of the revelation of God, and endeavor to subvert the customs of our forefathers for idle fancies." "If you mean to follow those who call on you to accept their dreams as your guides through life," he thundered in conclusion, "*better burn the law*. Then let it stand here forsaken, and its precepts neglected."[56]

Though the speech was warmly received by the majority of those who heard it, Leeser did not turn the tide against Wise and Reform, nor was he able to restrain the Cincinnati rabbi from pursuing his goals. The two most important ideas Wise was promoting early in 1855 were his plans for Zion College, the forerunner of the Hebrew Union College, and for an assembly of rabbis, which, among other things, would develop a *Minhag America*, a standardized liturgy for the American synagogue. Leeser was able to counter the former by helping the Hebrew Education Society in Philadelphia secure a charter for a parallel college in his own city.

Wise's plan to convene a national body of religious leaders was more troublesome to Leeser. Both alone and with Wise's help, Leeser had been unable to create a national assembly of American rabbis. He knew that Wise had gained a following among many of the American hazzanim and that the long-awaited conference would probably take place in the near future. Leeser was caught in a no-win situation. If he boycotted the proposed meeting, he would appear to be abandoning his longstanding policy of union. If he attended the meeting, the wrath of the traditionalists would fall on his head for cooperating with Wise and his supporters, and thereby helping legitimize the Reform movement in the eyes of the Jewish masses in the United States.

Leeser decided to take the risk and urge traditional hazzanim to attend the proposed gathering. His plan was to try to attract enough Orthodox leaders to the conference in Cleveland to change its character from an assembly of Reform leaders to a general meeting of American rabbis that would endorse his original 1841 plan of union. To this end, he placed a notice in the advertising supplement to the April 1855 issue of the *Occident*. "I deem it my duty," he told his colleagues, "to request all Ministers and Congregations who belong to the orthodox section to inform me, at their first leisure, whether they will attend the above conference. . . . Many subjects besides *reform* can and ought to be discussed at such an assembly."[57]

The formal call for the assembly appeared in *The Israelite* on August 17, 1855. It requested "ministers and delegates of the Israelitish congregations . . . to assemble in a conference to take place the 17th day of October, 5616 [1855] in the city of Cleveland." The delegates were also asked to prepare to deliberate on five points:

1. The articles of Union of American Israel in theory and practice.
2. A plan to organize a regular synod . . .
3. To discuss and refer to a committee a plan for a *Minhag America*, to be reported to the synod at its first session.
4. A plan for scholastic education in the lower and higher branches of learning.
5. Other propositions . . .[58]

The notice was signed by nine rabbis, including three Orthodox leaders: two from Baltimore, Rabbi Hochheim and Dr. Gunzburg, and Dr. Illowy, rabbi of the United Hebrew Congregation at St. Louis.

Dr. Bernard Illowy was the most distinguished of the traditionalists. Born in Kolin, Bohemia, in 1812, he had been ordained by Rabbi Moses Schreiber of Pressburg, the leader of Hungarian Orthodoxy. He also was alleged to have received a Ph.D. at the University of Budapest. Illowy proved particularly effective in critiquing Wise's *History of the Israelitish Nation*, as well as in criticizing his proposed Zion College. To Leeser's great disappointment, however, Illowy, after signing the initial call for the Cleveland Conference, "refused to attend because he feared he would be in the minority and overwhelmed by the majority of Reformers who would be present." The two men from Baltimore, Hochheim and Gunzburg, also decided not to attend.[59]

The absence of the three Orthodox signatories proved critical. A total of thirteen ministers and congregational delegates met, as planned, at Cleveland's Medical College on Erie Street at 2 P.M. on October 17, 1855. According to Leeser, the Reformers had a clear majority of eight to five and immediately elected their leaders as the officers of the conference: president, Isaac Mayer Wise; vice-president, Dr. Elkan Cohn of Albany; secretary, Dr. Max Lilienthal. Along with Wise,

Benedict H. Gotthelf, rabbi of Congregation Adath Israel, Louisville, Kentucky, was appointed to translate the proceedings, conducted in German, into English.[60]

Realizing that he would be totally unable to influence the outcome of the conference, Leeser, the fourteenth member of the meeting, decided to distance himself from the proceedings. Having refused to participate in the vote for the meeting's officers, he was asked to clarify his status: was he a delegate or an observer? Although authorized to represent both Mickveh Israel and Beth Shalome (Richmond) as well as the *Occident*, Leeser, who probably planned to take an elusive course of action before arriving at Cleveland, begged the question by answering that he was "not yet certain what part I should take." Resentment was quickly growing toward him, and had Wise not taken control of the meeting, chaos might have ensued.[61]

Wise proved himself to be a truly clever leader. Prepared for the probability of a deadlock early in the meeting, he decided it prudent to let the issue of Leeser's status pass unresolved, and launched directly into his lengthy opening speech. To Leeser's great surprise, Wise was ready to compromise with Orthodoxy. He moved that the conference organize a synod "to preserve the Union of Israel." The synod, Wise suggested, would be guided by four "leading principles" affirming the value and legitimacy of tradition. The final, approved wording of the principles stated:

1. The Bible as delivered to us by our fathers and as now in our possession, is of immediate divine origin, and the standard of our religion.
2. The Talmud contains the traditional, legal, and logical exposition of the biblical laws which must be expounded and practiced according to the comments of the Talmud.
3. The resolutions of the synod, in accordance with the above principles, are legally valid.
4. Statutes and ordinances, contrary to the laws of the land, are invalid.[62]

Delighted, Leeser asked to speak in favor of Wise's proposals. "Had the orthodox ministers and congregations known on what principles those who had called the conference meant to act," he began, "no doubt many more would have been present. . . . For my part, I would consider the 17th day of October as a day of joy for Israel." After some debate, the first session of the meeting was adjourned, and "Rev. Dr. Cohn thereupon read the Minchah [afternoon] and evening service" from a traditional prayer book, "as the day was the anniversary of the death of one of his parents." Overly enthusiastic, Leeser misinterpreted

Wise's devotions as a symbol of the unity the conference's initial work had produced.[63]

The next day, October 18, 1855, the delegates reconvened to debate and refine the wording of Wise's principles. Leeser unsuccessfully attempted to strengthen the second principle by suggesting the following alternative: "That it is the opinion and conviction of this conference, that the Talmud contains the divine tradition given to Moses, and that all Israelites must decide all questions according to its decisions." Curiously, he did not request the conference to consider the authority of the *Shulchan Aruch*, an authoritative sixteenth-century code of Jewish law broadly employed by Orthodoxy in determining the *Halachah*. Instead, satisfied that the word "traditional" in the second principle of Wise's platform "necessarily embraces a divine communication," Leeser agreed to cease debating the issue, and Wise's platform was adopted by the conference.[64]

Immediately after the measure passed, Leeser announced his intention to return to Philadelphia that evening, and he advised the others to return to their homes. He believed that the conference had done its work. In his opinion, it had created an ideological basis for union in American Judaism. Leeser felt to proceed any further and begin considering specific programs was premature and might prove counterproductive. His advice fell on deaf ears. The conference continued its work unabated and even held a night session on the evening of October 18. For unknown reasons, Leeser did not change his plans and left Cleveland with the full knowledge that the conference would carry on without him.[65]

Leeser's decision to leave the meeting before it had finished its business was a tactical error. The conference had only considered the first of three issues listed on its published agenda. The remaining two issues, liturgy and education, were both extremely sensitive. With the vigilant leader of the Orthodox out of the picture, Wise sensed an opportunity to consolidate his gains and proceed with his program for moderate reform. He quickly reorganized the conference and relegated the unfinished business to committees. Three or more working groups were organized. They conducted their business in situ until at least Monday, October 23. Two committees were assigned the complex job of preparing the groundwork for a standardized American Jewish liturgy, the original desideratum on Wise's wish list of "reforms." Another committee began to prepare for the first meeting of the full, upgraded synod. "Zion College Association No. 3" was also formed, the first two associations having already been established in Cincinnati and New York. Finally, the conference passed a resolution endorsing public school education.[66]

"I doubt very much," Leeser wrote angrily in Philadelphia on October 25, after learning of the conference's activities following his departure from Cleveland, "whether I should have assented to a single one of all these propositions." For all intents and purposes, the work of the first two days of the meeting had been overturned. Leeser had been duped into believing that Wise had shifted his theological position in the direction of tradition.[67]

Reaction to the Cleveland Conference poured into the offices of *The Israelite* and the *Occident* from around the country and the world. It ran the gamut from high praise to hostile condemnation. In *Lien d'Israel*, published in Mulhouse, France, Rabbi S. Dreyfuss wrote glowingly of the "American Provisional Sanhedrin" and expressed the hope that it would "be the first link of that universal authority which will, sooner or later, prevail in the Jewish world."[68] In a two-part Hebrew letter in the *Occident*, Rabbi Illowy gently praised the members of the conference as the "shepherds of Israel," but admonished Wise to practice what he preached. Leeser, on the other hand, was censured by Morris J. Raphall of New York, "who objected to his compromise with reformers." His other critics, Leon Jick points out, "took even greater offense at the claims to leadership put forward by the representative of midwestern 'yokeldom.' "[69]

The most stinging indictment of the Cleveland Conference, however, came not from the ranks of the Orthodox but from the newly arrived radical reformer David Einhorn (1809–1879). Born in Dispeck, Bavaria, he received his rabbinical training at nearby Fürth and then studied philosophy at Erlangen, Würzburg, and Munich. Attracted as a young man to Reform Judaism, he attended several of the German rabbinical conferences of the 1840s and publicly rejected both the divine authority of the Talmud and many ceremonial laws. A political radical as well, Einhorn openly sided with a number of revolutionary struggles in 1848. Finding himself in constant trouble with either his congregation or a government, he concluded that he had no future in Europe and accepted the invitation of Congregation Har Sinai in Baltimore to become its rabbi in 1855.[70]

Einhorn's arrival in America coincided with the convening of the Cleveland Conference. He was outraged when he learned that Wise had taken a conciliatory posture toward Orthodoxy. On November 6, 1855, he issued a formal protest in the form of a printed petition signed by numerous members of his congregation. Although he had "a profound regard for the Talmudic writings, on account of their rich exuberance of contributions to a religious progress, and the excellent formations which Judaism had engendered during this stage of its development," he could "not consider the Talmudic exegesis of the Bible . . . as legal and obligatory." Einhorn continued, "With the Talmud in hand, it is no longer possible to obtain the honorable and efficient means of healing the gaping wound in the heart of Israel." "Reforms bearing on public worship," he lamented, ". . . can at best be only smuggled in by a disregard of the law, and a resort to juridical trick and chicanery." He concluded, "A peace which necessarily degrades Judaism appears to us to be too dearly bought." The ranks of the Reform movement were now hopelessly split, and Wise, accustomed to defending himself to traditionalists, was put on the defensive by the more radical members of his own party.[71]

The Cleveland Conference, originally intended to unify American Judaism, ironically marked the beginning of a new era of religious divisions among American Jews. Leeser strenuously disavowed his role at the 1855 meeting. No one, he maintained in an editorial in the February 1857 issue of the *Occident*, was bound by any of its resolutions. "There is still no authority," a strident Leeser maintained, other than "the *Talmud, Shulchan Aruch,* and *Possekim;* and if these do not suffice to teach us, or guide us to elucidate questions not yet decided by them, we shall seek in vain for help in the light-obscure of modern theorists."[72]

Symptomatic of the polarization of American Judaism and Leeser's move to the right after 1855 was a lengthy exchange of published letters, beginning in 1856, between Leeser and Max Lilienthal, the new rabbi of Congregation Bene Israel in Cincinnati and a co-editor of *The Israelite.* Lilienthal had been strongly inclined toward modernizing Judaism while he was still in Europe, and had taken the modest step of introducing "confirmation" in his New York congregations. His connection to Orthodoxy was further weakened by his disappointing experience as chief rabbi of the three immigrant German synagogues and by the failure of his *bet din.* After arriving in Cincinnati, Wise completely and easily won him over to the side of moderate reform. At Cleveland, Lilienthal proved to be loyal to his new cause.[73]

With the zeal of a new convert, Lilienthal attempted to demonstrate to Leeser that the "spirit of the age" demanded religious reform. "Not surprisingly," writes Naomi Cohen in her important study *Encounter with Emancipation: The German Jews in the United States, 1830–1914,* "Leeser remained unmoved" and repeated many of his stock arguments. According to the editor of the *Occident,* the "spirit of the age" was a vacuous concept predicated on whims and a problematic understanding of the meaning of "the present." Similarly, he insisted that Reform was a self-indulgent, sectarian impulse. True Judaism, on the other hand, rested on eternal principles and, at various periods of history, was actually a rebellion against the spirit of the age.[74]

However, Leeser did agree with Lilienthal on one fundamental point: America presented Judaism with a challenge. In the United States, Jews were essentially free to preserve or abandon their traditions as they saw fit. The government took no interest in controlling the internal affairs of the community. A few legal restrictions on Jews, such as test oaths and Sunday Laws, still existed, but these were more of an annoyance than a threat to the community's security. Nor was anti-Semitism a significant social force in antebellum society. In America, Judaism had to be preserved on a voluntary basis. By mid-career, Lilienthal had come to the conclusion that American Judaism would be best served if it redefined itself according to the zeitgeist. Leeser, on the other hand, believed that Judaism was divinely revealed and, except for a few externals, immutable. To preserve itself in America, Leeser maintained, Judaism had to remain true to the ancient divine commands, which had guided it through the ages, and simultaneously improve its educational methods and institutional infrastructure.

Leeser's efforts to develop and improve Jewish communal institutions, like his work promoting the cause of modern Orthodoxy in America, were largely unencumbered by the restraints of religious law and doctrine. Between 1850 and 1857, when he also was free of the heavy responsibilities of a pulpit, Leeser actively assisted a number of new Jewish institutions and organizations. He naturally focused most of his efforts in Philadelphia, but he also found time to dedicate synagogues in different areas of the country and to campaign vigorously on behalf of the Jewish community of Ottoman Palestine in the pages of the *Occident*.

In general, the 1850s witnessed a dramatic increase in Jewish institutional activity in the United States, largely in response to the rising rate of Jewish immigration to America and the increasing sophistication of the established community. Jacques J. Lyons and Abraham de Sola's 1854 book, *A Jewish Calendar for Fifty Years*, included listings for five synagogues, five Jewish cemeteries, and seventeen Jewish societies in Philadelphia alone. The city's B'nai B'rith organization consisted of three lodges with "nearly 300 members" total. The same year, scores of Jewish institutions throughout the country were named as beneficiaries in the will of Judah Touro, including a one-time gift of $20,000 to Philadelphia's Hebrew Education Society. The city's Female Hebrew Benevolent Society and United Hebrew Benevolent Society received $3,000 apiece.[75]

One of Leeser's most important goals after 1850 was to bring order to the complex and chaotic world of Jewish relief work. As early as 1844, Jewish benevolent societies in Philadelphia sponsored charity balls to raise funds for their respective operations. The ball of the Hebrew Education Society (established in 1847) was particularly successful. The guest of honor at their second annual School Fund Ball was Henry Clay, the distinguished senator from Kentucky. The event netted the society the sum of $427.15.[76]

While praising the philanthropic efforts of the Jews, Leeser also urged them to consider the benefits of centralizing some of their activities, especially in the area of distribution. On numerous occasions, he also suggested developing vocational training schools to provide a long-term solution to the problem of poverty among Jewish immigrants. Fearful that they would either lose their autonomy or have their areas of operation restricted, the various groups ignored Leeser's suggestion to restructure Jewish charity work in America along "federal" lines.

Ironically, the first effort to coordinate fund-raising activities happened unintentionally at a board meeting of the Hebrew Education Society early in 1853. Several of the trustees of the Education Society also belonged to the board of the Hebrew Fuel Society, so they decided to create a joint Hebrew Charity Fund and sponsor a dinner on February 23. The event was a smashing success. Held at the prestigious Sansom Street Hall, the affair's guests of honor included George M. Dallas, vice-president of the United States under James K. Polk (1844–48); Charles Gilpin, mayor of Philadelphia; and numerous distinguished Jewish ministers. Leeser responded to the "fourth toast" of the evening. Proceeds for the event exceeded $4,200.[77]

His belief in the value of union vindicated, Leeser pressed for even greater interagency cooperation. On June 1, 1856, a general conference of Jewish organizations convened in Philadelphia. Four synagogues and seven agencies sent delegates, and Leeser was selected as the chairman. He reconvened the council on June 15 and presented a lengthy, detailed draft of a plan for union. In some ways, Leeser's plan adumbrated the development of the American Jewish Federations of the twentieth century. He called for the establishment of a general committee with delegates from every Jewish organization in the city. Each organization would donate its excess resources to a central fund to be administered by the general committee. Furthermore, the committee would arrange for visiting committees to monitor Jewish relief activities in six districts in the city and the distribution of matzah to the poor during Passover. Finally, he called for the establishment of "a house of refuge for the aged, the infirm, and minors."[78]

At two subsequent meetings, on October 5 and November 16, interest in the plan waned. A saddened Leeser reported in the December 1856 *Occident* that "the greater part of the people think the present system of raising and distributing charity funds the only proper and the best mode." "Gladly as we should have seen the work at once commenced," he lamented, "we are willing to wait, satisfied that the seed has been sown; and that the project has attracted the attention of the thinking in all parts of this country and Europe."[79] Almost one year to the day after Leeser's death, Edward H. Weil, one of the original supporters of the consolidation movement in 1856, was to succeed in establishing the Society of United Hebrew Charities on February 15, 1869, in Philadelphia.[80]

Leeser's disappointment over the failure of the plan to federate the Jewish charities of Philadelphia was in part offset by the progress of the Hebrew Education Society. Organized in 1847 at his urging, the society quickly made progress toward organizing a day school. The plan was supported by a broad spectrum of Jewish leaders in Philadelphia, including Solomon Solis (who served as the first president of the organization), Abraham Hart, the young Moses Dropsie, Julius Stern, and Alfred T. Jones.[81]

Early in April 1849, the Pennsylvania state legislature passed a bill incorporating the society, allowing it not only to offer instruction "in the elementary branches of education" but to establish "a superior seminary of learning . . . which shall have the power to furnish its graduates and others the usual degrees of bachelor of arts, master of arts, and doctor of law and divinity, as the same is exercised by other colleges in this commonwealth."[82] Subsequently, both Maimonides College and Gratz College were organized in part under the auspices of the Hebrew Education Society.

Mindful of the success of Max Lilienthal's Hebrew Boarding School in New York, the members of the Philadelphia Society worked diligently to lay the fiscal and organizational foundations of a school in Philadelphia. On Sunday, April 6, 1851, Leeser delivered an address, "The Testimony," at the Hebrew Education Society's opening ceremonies. Unfortunately, because of the tense situation at Mickveh Israel, "many were absent who should have taken an interest in the matter." Nevertheless, when the school commenced its operation the next day, 22 students were enrolled. A month later, the student body had grown to 63 and subsequently peaked at 170. Its operation was combined with that of the Hebrew Sunday School, a link which certainly pleased Leeser. Judah Touro's legacy allowed the society to buy a large building on Seventh Street below Callowhill Street, and on November 12, 1854, the Hebrew Education Society moved into its permanent home with great fanfare. Again, Leeser was invited to give the keynote address in which he reviewed, in great detail, the history of the school and its goals.[83]

Leeser was also instrumental in developing the Hebrew Education Society's curriculum. Entering students would learn both English and Hebrew. More advanced pupils received instruction in geometry, natural history, natural philosophy, rabbinic literature, German, French, Latin, Greek, botany, and chemistry. Sessions were held five days a week. Graduates were able to continue in boys' and girls' high schools without any supplemental work. The Hebrew Department proved the weakest link in the program: in 1878, ten years after Leeser's death, the Hebrew studies were reduced to supplemental programs.[84]

At the prompting and under the guidance of Isaac Leeser, a second Jewish communal institution, a Jewish Foster Home, was also organized, and it flourished during the 1850s. The idea for a Jewish orphanage in Philadelphia was originally raised by Rebecca Gratz in 1847 in her twenty-eighth annual report of the managers of the Female Hebrew Benevolent Society. Leeser, having been orphaned at an early age himself, gave the proposal his unqualified support and publicized it broadly in the *Occident*. The community, however, did not respond immediately to the idea.[85]

Hoping to overcome the indifference that initially greeted the idea of a foster home, Leeser published a brief appeal written by Gratz as the cover story of volume 8 of his journal in April 1850. To it he appended a note of his own, which included a personal experience reminiscent of Dickens's *Oliver Twist*:

> We recollect, we were in the Philadelphia House of Refuge, to look after some Jewish boys imprisoned there; it was a beautiful spring day; the sun shining bright and warm, and it was the first day of the week, the usual labours were suspended, and the boys were, according to the humane rules of the institution, allowed to play about in groups in the prison-yard under the inspection of the keepers. We noticed one boy, about twelve years old, sitting apart from the others, basking in the sunshine near the door at which we were standing speaking to the superintendent. He appeared wan and dejected, his youthful cheeks hollowed by the insidious hand of a consumptive disease. He did not appear to our view one reared to crime; his countenance did not betoken him hardened in sin,

and upon inquiring, we found our opinion correct. He was an orphan boy, was neglected and cast on the world, committed some little offence, perhaps vagrancy, which the good of society was bound to punish, and jail became his home for a while, but, the superintendent thought that he could not long survive, death having marked him his own by the unmistakable traces of inward decay. We pitied the poor child; but what could we do?[86]

Unfortunately, the joint appeal was weakened by Leeser's dispute with the board of Mickveh Israel. Gratz was placed in the awkward position of working publicly with Leeser and dealing privately with the leaders of her congregation. Five years after Leeser left Mickveh Israel, feelings were still so raw that Gratz had to gamble and go ahead with the foster home project without Leeser's direct participation in the preliminary organizational work. On February 4, 1855, a meeting was held at the Cherry Street synagogue to organize the children's home. Unable to attend the session, Leeser nevertheless reported on it favorably in the *Occident*. However, his relationship with the official organization promoting the home remained problematic. On February 22, Leeser spoke to the Young Men's Literary Association, at their request, on the topic "Our Charities" and urged them to support the foster home. "It has been asserted by some not ever-wise people," he wrote later, "that it was insulting to the ladies of the Foster Home, [but] it surpasses my ingenuity to discover how this could be."[87]

Subsequently, Leeser was not invited to the dedication of the foster home in May 1855. To Rebecca Gratz's great surprise and embarrassment, the president of Mickveh Israel refused to invite Leeser to the home's first annual meeting, which took place at his synagogue in 1856. The following year, the meeting was held at the Hebrew Education Society's school, a neutral location, and Leeser was invited to speak at the occasion. In a hostile article in the *Asmonean* signed by "Franklin," a nom de plume, it was reported that Leeser "spoke very disrespectfully both of the Institution and its managers, and displayed much temper."[88] The politics of the foster home became even nastier after Leeser's supporters formed Congregation Beth El Emeth in 1857. They threatened to withdraw their financial support for the home unless Leeser was treated more respectfully by its directors.[89]

Despite its early political problems, the Jewish Foster Home flourished. The growing number of orphans necessitated moving the institution several times between 1855 and 1881, when, with the assistance of Isidore Binswanger, "the large and attractive Chew Mansion and grounds on Mill Street, Germantown, were purchased." According to

Henry S. Morais, an early historian of the Philadelphia Jewish community, "In 1894, there were then 99 children—55 boys and 44 girls—in the Home, and 24 [more] were either indentured or in situations." As Leeser had hoped, the foster home became an important Jewish communal and relief agency in Philadelphia.[90]

Leeser's interest in Jewish institutions was not confined to either Philadelphia or the United States. During the 1850s he also continued to pay close attention to developments in the Jewish community of Ottoman Palestine and promoted various modernization and agricultural programs there through the pages of the *Occident*. His concerns in this area were heightened by the return of his old acquaintance Warder Cresson (1798–1860), an eccentric convert to Judaism, to Philadelphia from Jerusalem in 1848 after living for four years in the Holy City. On May 15, 1849, Cresson's family, members of Philadelphia's Quaker elite, motivated by both greed and prejudice, obtained an "inquisition of lunacy" against him. Declared insane at a jury trial, Cresson was quickly granted a traverse and was subsequently vindicated at a retrial in May 1851. "This decision is of vital importance," the Philadelphia *Public Ledger* editorialized on May 22, "as settling forever . . . the principle, that a man's 'religious opinions' never can be made the test of his sanity."[91]

Leeser closely followed the Cresson case and the "Quaker rabbi's" subsequent return to Jerusalem in the fall of 1852. Cresson's interest in agriculture stimulated Leeser's own thinking about modernizing and expanding Jewish life in the Land of Israel. Beginning in December 1853, he ran three consecutive editorials in the *Occident* on Palestine. With great enthusiasm, he painted a picture of an ideal, highly productive modern Jewish society in Palestine. Moreover, he wrote, the Jewish community there would serve as a safe haven for Jews fleeing from oppression, and could provide work for "the surplus of unemployed Israelites of Poland, Russia, Galicia, Hungary, and Turkey."[92] He even suggested that the Jews of the Land of Israel "obtain permission from the Sultan to form themselves into regular companies of national guards, for the defence of their own firesides and homesteads."[93]

The boldness of Leeser's proto-Zionist vision, his success in establishing new and important Jewish institutions, and his continued literary productivity impressed his friends and supporters. Early in 1857, a small group of pro-Leeser members of Mickveh Israel met and decided to organize a second Sephardic synagogue in Philadelphia for the sole purpose of providing the "retired" hazzan with a pulpit and a steady source of income. They concluded that the Philadelphia Jewish community dishonored itself by failing to support his indefatigable efforts. Thus, Congregation Beth El Emeth became Leeser's new spiritual home. He served as its hazzan for the rest of his life. From its pulpit he observed America's rapid descent into internecine war and later helped the American Jewish community, particularly in the South, rebuild itself after four years of bloody fighting. In its wake, the Civil War also brought a new sophistication to institution building among American Jews. Leeser ably placed himself at the vanguard of the development that he had been fostering since he first arrived in Philadelphia in 1829.

9
Triumphs and Tragedies, 1857–1865

*We are not going to discuss any political theme, it being foreign
to our purpose, but simply matters belonging to us as a
religious community.*

—Isaac Leeser, *Occident,* July 1861

LEESER'S RETURN TO THE active hazzanate early in 1857 marked
yet another turning point in his career. Congregation Beth El Emeth
gave the fifty-one-year-old Leeser the respectability in the community
and the personal security that he had not enjoyed since leaving Mickveh Israel seven years earlier. Once again he could function as a peer
in America's growing community of Jewish ministers and as the representative of a local religious institution in Philadelphia society. Although his friends' decision to give him both personal and institutional
support was very reassuring, he certainly realized that the favorable
terms he received from the new congregation did not represent a victory of the principles for which he had been fighting. His friends were
doing him a favor and nothing more. Nevertheless, Leeser's personal
and professional situation was greatly improved by his appointment to
Beth El Emeth, and he did not waste any time in making the best of
his new situation.

During his first eight years as hazzan at Beth El Emeth, Leeser
became involved in a number of causes and issues. Naturally, his first
priority was to help his new congregation grow and make its presence
felt in the Philadelphia Jewish community. He also continued editing
the *Occident,* arranged for the publication of M. Mocatta's *The Inquisi-*

tion and Judaism (1860) and Hester Rothschild's *Meditations and Prayers* (1864), and again sounded the rallying cry for union in American Jewish life.[1] Locally, Leeser organized a Board of Jewish Ministers in 1858. Nationally, he played an important role in the formation of the Board of Delegates of American Israelites the following year. Finally, like the rest of the country, he found himself confronted with the vagaries and tragedies of war from 1861 to 1865 and worked diligently to bring comfort to the wounded, the bereaved, and the displaced.

The individual most responsible for the formation of Beth El Emeth was Joseph Newhouse. On March 11, 1857, he organized a small committee that presented Leeser with a "testimonial." Newhouse's committee praised the former hazzan as "the pioneer of Jewish literature in this country," and for his "sufficient strength of character and energy of purpose to turn aside from the struggle after wealth and power to devote [himself] to the cause of truth." Subsequently, it was announced in the *Occident* that on March 22 the new congregation was founded, and "on the 5th of April . . . duly organized by electing a full board of officers." The elections resulted in no surprises. Newhouse was chosen the parnass and Leeser the hazzan. Philip Honsberg was named shamas (sexton).[2]

"Soon after organizing," Leeser reported in September 1857, "the congregation purchased a church building situated in Franklin Street above Green, in that part of the Consolidated City known as the district of Spring Garden." Alfred T. Jones, a native Bostonian and a Jewish community activist, served as the building chairman. The Franklin Street Synagogue, "built in the old simple style," had 230 seats downstairs in the men's section and approximately 180 seats in the women's gallery. Fund-raising for the building was generally limited to Philadelphia; however, Benjamin Nathan, a former parnass of Congregation Shearith Israel of New York, donated a *Torah scroll*, and Asher Kursheedt, Gershom Kursheedt's brother, indefinitely loaned the new congregation a second scroll.[3]

On September 3, 1857, Beth El Emeth was formally dedicated. A small crowd, representative of the Philadelphia Jewish community, gathered to witness the congregational officers carrying the sacred scrolls into the synagogue and listened as Leeser delivered a modest address, at the end of which he reaffirmed his commitment to Jewish unity.[4] Leeser chanted the brief evening service, and both a band and a choir provided some entertainment. Rev. Solomon Jacobs, the preacher of the Polish synagogue (Crown Street), was invited to give the sermon at the first Sabbath morning service to help give the new congregation legitimacy in the community and to symbolize Leeser's belief in Jewish communal unity.[5]

The high degree of internal harmony enjoyed by Congregation Beth El Emeth was predictable. Formed to honor and support Leeser, the congregation was, by definition, a community of consensus. Still, some internal conflicts developed. Among the most serious problems the synagogue faced was the resignation of David H. Solis on September 22, 1863. Solis had become livid after learning that Leeser not only lived with a non-Jewish family but also ate some of his meals with them. He believed that the hazzan was setting a terrible example for his congregants, and possibly was less than meticulous in his observance of some dietary laws.[6] The majority of the synagogue's members, however, were willing to overlook the problematic aspects of Leeser's living arrangements. In the October 1858 issue of the *Occident*, Leeser cheerfully announced the synagogue's first anniversary. "The members act in unison," he reported, "and thus far they have expressed perfect satisfaction with the work in which they have been engaged."[7]

More serious problems developed between Beth El Emeth and Mickveh Israel. Tension between the two Sephardic synagogues often rose to an uncomfortable level while Leeser was in office and the rift between the two congregations even affected the American Jewish community as a whole. Most of the intercongregation problems, however, were local and generally petty. Ten of the newly formed congregation's charter members had formerly belonged to Mickveh Israel. Two of them completely broke with the older institution; the others maintained a dual membership. Joseph Newhouse, who had been a board member at Mickveh Israel, was officially invited to resign his position by their trustees.[8]

Except for Mickveh Israel, the new congregation's relations with Philadelphia Jewish institutions were generally good. The most serious problem developed in the wake of a joint call by Leeser and Jacobs at a meeting at Beth El Emeth in March 1858 to establish a Jewish home for the indigent. Loud and angry protests were lodged by a variety of local Jewish benevolent associations, whose members believed that implicit in the Leeser-Jacobs proposal was an unfair indictment of their welfare operations.[9] The fact that many of the leaders of these charities were members of Mickveh Israel further politicized the situation.

The abduction of a six-year-old Italian Jewish boy, Edgardo Mortara, in Bologna on the night of June 23–24, 1858 by officials of the Catholic Church and the subsequent need to mount a unified, international Jewish protest revealed the depth of the hard feelings between

Mickveh Israel and Beth El Emeth. Unwilling to work with Beth El Emeth to help resolve the international crisis, Leeser's old congregation decided to take unilateral action. Leeser, on the other hand, saw yet another opportunity to try to foster unity in the local Jewish community and used the occasion to form an ad hoc committee representing several Philadelphia synagogues. Remarkably, the committee's delegates pursued the matter all the way to the Buchanan White House. Although America's foreign policy and domestic political situation prohibited the president from taking any direct action in support of Mortara, the crisis helped weld a permanent coalition of different interests in the American Jewish community, which would fight to protect Jewish rights at home and abroad for several decades. Mickveh Israel, because of its elitist Sephardic attitudes and its dispute with Leeser, remained outside the emerging consensus in American Jewish life.[10]

The dramatic, widespread response of American Jews to the Mortara Affair culminated in the organization of the Board of Delegates of American Israelites in 1859. By contrast, the protests mounted by the Jewish community in opposition to the Swiss-American Treaty of Friendship, Commerce, and Extradition, endorsed by President Millard Fillmore on March 12, 1851, and ratified by President Franklin Pierce on November 6, 1854, failed to strengthen the cause of Jewish unity in America. The debate over the Swiss treaty dragged on for years, but reached its peak during the fall months of 1857, just prior to the abduction of Edgardo Mortara.[11]

The controversy over the Treaty of Friendship resulted from the failure of the original American negotiator to challenge a provision, requested by the Swiss, that stated that "Christians alone are entitled to the enjoyment of the privileges guaranteed by the present article." American Jews quickly pointed out that this clause was a violation of the First Amendment of the United States Constitution, and was tantamount to the "establishment of religion." On the practical side, American Jews would also be excluded from transacting any business deals in Switzerland under the terms of the treaty. In defense of the treaty, the Swiss responded that their government was a confederation of cantons and had to respect the laws of the cantons in regard to religion just as the federal government in the United States could not interfere with the "peculiar institution" of slavery in the Southern states.[12]

The Swiss treaty affair had become entangled in American sectional politics. The fundamental constitutional issues and the rights of Jews abroad were now obscured by political and economic considerations. A politically astute Leeser told his readers in the *Occident* in September 1857, "We [American Jews] are not important enough to have any serious influence on the political complexion of the country. Perhaps . . . a sense of justice may prevail, and . . . the treaty may thus be abolished." However, in the last analysis, Leeser was less than sanguine, and concluded that "all expression of wrath and indignation will just avail *nothing*, and be merely the exhibition of impotent rage."[13]

The Mortara Affair, on the other hand, which also involved American domestic politics, proved effective as a consensus-building issue. First, it linked American Jews with a broad range of nativists who saw in the matter a clear-cut example of Catholic treachery. For the most part, American Jews stood alone in their protests against the Swiss treaty. Second, the Mortara Affair involved an innocent victim, not merely an abstract principle. Finally, frustrated over their inability during the fights over the Swiss treaty to move four different administrations—Taylor, Fillmore, Pierce, and Buchanan—American Jews were ready for what they initially perceived as a fight they could win.

The Mortara Affair actually had its roots late in the summer of 1851, when Edgardo, then only a baby, became very sick. Anna Morisi, a young domestic servant in the Mortara household, secretly took it upon herself to baptize the Jewish infant to save him from damnation. Seven years later, another Mortara child became ill and died before the maid could take any action. Tormented by guilt, Morisi talked openly to her friends about the situation. The matter was quickly brought before the archbishop of Bologna, and a decision was reached to send some of the pope's gendarmes to forcibly take the baptized child away from his parents.[14]

The Church was able to quickly develop a legal fiction to justify the kidnapping of the boy. According to Church law, it actually was illegal for a Christian domestic to work in a Jewish home. In this situation, it was further determined that Momola Mortara, Edgardo's father, was "responsible for the deed of the menial whose services he utilized against the law."[15] Thus, the Church concluded that the family had technically sanctioned the conversion of their child to Catholicism and also was now unfit to raise the boy. To protect the child, the Church decided it best to take him into its custody and hold him at the House of Catechumens in Rome. A similar procedure had been used in Ancona in 1826.[16]

"Neither Archbishop Viale-Prela of Bologne nor Pope Pius IX," writes Bertram W. Korn in *The American Reaction to the Mortara Case:*

1858–1859, "could have possibly imagined the storm of protest which was to break upon their heads as a result of the, to them, quite natural and perfunctory 'separation' of Edgar Mortara from his family." Napoleon II remonstrated against the infringement of the child's freedom of religion and parental rights, and Sir Moses Montefiore, the leading British Jew of the age, went directly to Rome and unsuccessfully lobbied for the boy's release.[17]

By mid-September, stories about the Mortara Affair were appearing regularly in the American press, becoming a potent source of anti-Catholic propaganda in nativist political circles as well as a cause célèbre among American Jews. Leeser was particularly energetic in his attempts to aid the Mortara boy. First, in November 1858 he urged all American and European Jews "to form a central council, which is to watch over our affairs in all parts of the world."[18] Second, he quickly began organizing a mass rally to express the outrage of the local Philadelphia Jewish community, and he published notices and accounts of parallel meetings in other cities. As many as twenty similar demonstrations of indignation were planned and held throughout the country without any coordination at the national level. The largest took place at New York's Mozart Hall, which attracted over two thousand people on December 7, 1858, and in San Francisco on January 27, 1859, with three thousand people in attendance. Finally, like many other American Jews, Leeser debated the Mortara case in the columns of the secular press. He published four lengthy letters in the *Public Ledger*, a Philadelphia newspaper, beginning on November 25, 1858, urging the American government to support the ideal of freedom of conscience. An anonymous priest responded in the *Public Ledger* in defense of the Church.[19]

The Philadelphia protest meeting was held at Beth El Emeth on November 18. Five of the six local congregations responded positively to Leeser's call. Only Mickveh Israel, unwilling to work with their former hazzan, refused to participate. Leeser wrote and presented a preamble and resolutions to the large, mixed crowd at his synagogue. Most importantly, he called upon the president of the United States to intervene directly in the case in the name of liberty. Leeser also made a motion that a special committee of community leaders be formed and "proceed to Washington, and represent the matter personally to the Government."[20]

Unknown to Leeser and his supporters, several letters calling on the United States to protest the Church's abduction of Edgardo Mortara, including one from Abraham Hart, the president of Mickveh Israel, had already been sent to Secretary of State Lewis Cass before the

Philadelphia rally was held. Cass responded to Hart in a formal and terse fashion. He maintained that the United States had no intention of interfering in the internal affairs of a foreign country. Dissatisfied with the reply and not ready to disengage himself from the effort to rescue the Mortara child, Hart again sent a private note to the secretary on December 1. Angered by Hart's persistence, Cass decided to put an end to the matter. He consulted with the president, and then wrote a full explanation of why the United States would not take any action in the case. Noninterference, even in a worthy cause, the secretary again insisted, was the only option available to the United States. On January 4, 1859, President Buchanan wrote to Benjamin Hart, a delegated representative of the New York Jewish community, refusing "to express a moral censorship over the conduct of other independent governments and to rebuke them for acts we may deem arbitrary and unjust towards their own citizens or subjects."[21]

After learning of the Cass-Hart correspondence, but not yet aware of the Buchanan letter, Leeser, along with the other members of the Philadelphia Committee organized in compliance with the resolutions of the November 18 mass rally, went to work "to mitigate the effect not only of Hart's letters, but also of Cass' answers to them." A letter was sent to Cass to explain that Hart's correspondence represented "the mere act of an individual." Furthermore, the committee suggested that it also disapproved of the idea of direct interference, and only sought a "kind expression of solicitude to remedy the evil."[22]

Authorized to lobby for their cause in Washington, the Philadelphia Committee wasted no time in taking their case directly to the capital. A delegation, composed of Leeser, Alfred T. Jones (president of Beth El Emeth), and Jacob Mayer, left Philadelphia on Saturday evening, January 8, 1859, and arrived in the District of Columbia early the next day. During the early afternoon of January 9, they visited two Pennsylvania congressmen, Thomas B. Florence and Henry M. Phillips, the latter a Jew from Philadelphia and a relative of Leeser's old nemesis, Zalegman Phillips. The next morning they were "cordially received" by Cass, who then escorted them to the White House.[23]

President Buchanan received the Philadelphia Committee in a "kindly" manner. Although he insisted that his letter to Benjamin Hart of New York was his final reply, he was still willing to discuss, at least briefly, his understanding of the United States' role in the Mortara Affair. He began by restating the policy of noninterference adopted by his administration. One of the delegates, probably Jones, then mentioned that President Martin Van Buren had taken a different course during the Damascus Affair of 1840. "To this," Leeser subsequently reported, "the President smilingly replied, 'It happened when I was not the President.' "[24]

Buchanan then allowed the Philadelphia Committee to make a few additional arguments. "We need the moral weight of a free people," they insisted, "to help those of our nation who live in countries not so happily governed as this, and this we thought could be best secured by the intervention of the President in the present case." The president was unpersuaded. "Finding that it would be useless to urge our request any further," the *Occident* reported later, "we took our leave, and only asked him in parting to read our memorial with the care it deserved."[25] In a statement prepared on January 16, the delegation publicly acknowledged that its mission had failed. However, it also refused to accept the blame: "Had our memorial been the first to reach the Executive, he might perchance have complied with its terms, which are, we are certain, such as would not have been offensive to the papal government."[26]

Although Leeser had been convinced that it was fruitless to continue to lobby the American government, he still intended to apply as much pressure to the Catholic Church as he could, especially through the press. In an editorial in the March 1859 *Occident*, he claimed that the Mortara case was

> a reassertion of the ancient power claimed by the Church of Rome to coerce all mankind to enter its communion. This it was which authorized it to arm monks and other ecclesiastics with the terrors of the inquisition. . . . And we deem it self-evident to any one who will take the trouble to think, that grant once the Church the right to take a child which has been sprinkled with water, according to its ordinances, when the consent of the pretended convert was not voluntarily given, and you yield to it the whole power which it has ever claimed.[27]

Curiously, Leeser did not follow through on his early call to develop a "central council" to defend Jews' rights at home and abroad. Nor did he attempt to transform the committee that had visited President Buchanan into a permanent body. He was even skeptical of a proposal made by Samuel M. Isaacs, hazzan of Congregation Shaarey Tefillah of New York and editor of the *Jewish Messenger*, to organize a board of representatives of American Jews.[28] Immigration, the development of a Reform movement, and intrasynagogue conflicts had resulted in even greater divisions in American Jewish life than had existed in 1841, when Leeser first suggested a "Jewish consistory" in America.

This time, however, the idea of developing a national Jewish body took root among a coterie of Jewish lay leaders. In New York, twelve synagogues had cooperated in organizing a meeting to protest the Church's abduction of Edgardo Mortara. Meeting in the home of Rabbi Morris J. Raphall of B'nai Jeshurun Congregation on December 4, a permanent committee was created, named the Executive Committee of the Representatives of the United Congregations of Israelites of the City of New York. Four months later, with the aftershocks of the Mortara Affair still being felt in the Jewish community, Samuel M. Isaacs convinced his congregation of the necessity of sponsoring the creation of a national board. At least two preliminary meetings were held to explore the proposal. The idea of national Jewish defense organization was endorsed by nine New York congregations. A steering committee was organized, and a date, November 27, 1859, was set for a general meeting. Every synagogue in the country was invited to send two delegates.[29]

Leeser, of course, could not resist. "When the meeting was called to order," Hyman B. Grinstein observed, "the old leader of American Jewry was in his place. How could he have stayed away when the project of a union was so dear to him, something for which he had planned and fought for so many years."[30] The leading Reform rabbis, including Wise and Einhorn, declared that the planned organization was being formed to crush their branch of Judaism, and refused to attend. The two oldest Sephardic synagogues, New York's Shearith Israel and Philadelphia's Mickveh Israel, also refused to join the board for elitist reasons and, in the case of the latter, to distance themselves yet again from their former hazzan. In the end, a total of only twenty-four congregations, less than 20 percent of all the synagogues in the United States, sent representatives to the meeting at New York's Cooper Institute. Almost half of the synagogues who sent delegates were in New York City.[31]

In Article I of its constitution, adopted on November 29, 1859, it was declared that "the union herewith formed shall bear the name and title of THE BOARD OF DELEGATES OF AMERICAN ISRAELITES." Leeser was elected as one of the organization's two original vice-presidents, a position he held until his death. He also frequently served as its leading spokesman and correspondent. However, he played only a limited role in shaping the board's basic objectives and policies.[32]

As in the past, Leeser argued for the creation of a powerful central Jewish body to closely monitor the communal and religious life of the American Jewish community, patterned on the Board of Deputies of British Jews. He suggested that the board adopt seven principal objectives. They included many of his old pet ideas: a congregational board of arbitration, an ecclesiastical board, a Jewish publication society, a school to train Jewish ministers, a centralized charity campaign, and a national conference of Jewish ministers.[33]

The Board of Delegates, aware that it was not broadly representative of American Jewry, approved only three limited objectives, all of which were acceptable to Leeser: first, the collection and publication of statistical data on American Jews; second, the promotion of Jewish religious education; and third, the protection of Jewish civil and religious rights at home and abroad.[34]

Even these moderate goals were met with a great deal of suspicion and hostility, especially among Reform rabbis, who feared the board would seek to stifle them. In 1860, some of the board's enemies organized chapters of the Alliance Israélite Universelle, a French Jewish organization that also developed in the wake of the Mortara Case, to weaken the board's claims to national leadership. "To still the clamor of opposition," Allan Tarshish states, "Leeser offered to travel through the country to champion the Board, but was told that the time was not propitious."[35]

Compared to contemporary Jewish defense organizations such as the American Jewish Committee, the American Jewish Congress, or the Anti-Defamation League of B'nai B'rith, the Board of Delegates of American Israelites was a weak, limited organization. Its chief significance was that it was the first of its kind in American Jewish history. During the course of the Civil War, however, it did not shrink from fighting anti-Jewish discrimination on a number of fronts. Yet, as Bertram W. Korn correctly observes, "Its leaders were moderates who would not for an instant have injected politics into its proceedings."[36] Certainly, Leeser was in complete agreement with the board's policy of silence on the issues of slavery and union. He adopted the identical position for himself, both as editor of the *Occident* and as hazzan of Beth El Emeth, probably to the great relief of the majority of American Jews and Jewish institutions, who remained strangely but almost universally uninvolved in the great American debates of the 1850s.[37]

During the course of his long career, Leeser, like Isaac Mayer Wise and others, consistently refrained from making public his opinions about politics and current events outside of the Jewish community. Not only did he refrain from the debates prior to the outbreak of the Civil War, he rarely commented on the war itself. Instead, he strictly confined his public comments to Jewish issues such as the "chaplaincy controversy," humanitarian causes, and casualty reports. "We are not going to discuss any political theme, it being foreign to our purpose," he wrote in the *Occident* in July 1861, several months after the opening shots at Fort Sumter were fired, "but simply matters belonging to us as a religious community." In November 1862, he even admonished editors of other religious papers for failing to stay clear of the conflict. Writing in the *Occident*, Leeser observed that "papers edited professedly in the cause of religion, teem with war articles and accounts of battles; so that it almost appears that for the time all matters are subordinate to the one absorbing thought which sways all the inhabitants of the country alike, while the service of the Most High is regarded as of inferior moment to the political questions of the day."[38]

The debate over slavery had consequences in nearly every part of society. Many mainstream Protestant organizations, most notably the Baptists and the Methodists, split over the slavery issue. By contrast, American Jews generally steered clear of the debate and carefully maintained an unofficial communal policy of silence on the question, to the great displeasure of the abolitionists. The close ties of many antislavery activists to evangelical and missionary causes, ethnic and immigrant insecurities, and the priority of preserving the union all combined to shape Jewish attitudes during the antebellum period. As war approached, however, Jews in the South and even a few in the North became public apologists for slavery. In a famous address given on January 4, 1861, Morris J. Raphall, preacher at New York's B'nai Jeshurun, presented a proslavery biblical view of the issue before his congregation.[39]

Several other factors also may have contributed to Leeser's silence about the war and slavery. First, his personal insecurities and anxieties might have prevented him, to some extent, from being more outspoken. Second, he did not believe that war was really necessary, and he felt that leaders truly interested in peace could have averted the outbreak of hostilities. Third, he abhorred war in general and was particularly horrified by the prospect of Jews from the North and South killing one another on the field of battle. Finally, he probably was more sympathetic toward the South than the North, an uncomfortable situation for a man who lived in Philadelphia. "Five years of young manhood spent in Richmond and close ties of blood and friendship with many people throughout the Southland," writes Bertram W. Korn in *American Jewry and the Civil War*, "could not be erased by thirty years of devoted ministry in the North."[40] Korn also calculates that there were more subscribers to the *Occident* in the South than in the North.[41]

Only once did Leeser clearly state that he principally blamed Northern radicals for leading the nation into war. In an editorial enti-

219

tled "The Prospect," which appeared in the *Occident* on January 17, 1861, he began by apologizing for discussing a political matter even briefly. Clearly anguished by the country's rapid descent toward armed conflict, he wrote, "Whether one wishes it or not, the state of the country demands of all who habitually employ the pen or speech to touch on the momentous events which are passing before our eyes." "It appears," Leeser continued, "that the ruthless spirit of intermeddling in matters which concern them not on the part of the inhabitants of the North, has unduly excited the partisan leaders of the opposite section, so that men who formerly were ready to meet death in defence of each other, now are only waiting for the signal to imbrue their hands in their brothers' blood."[42] True to his word, Leeser made no further comment about either the long-term or proximate causes of the Civil War.

Whatever the reason for it, Leeser's official silence was certainly welcomed by synagogue boards across the country, which wanted to keep politics out of their congregations. They preferred institutional Judaism to remain narrowly defined as ritualistic. Not all of the rabbis, however, were so reticent. Sabato Morais, Leeser's successor at Mickveh Israel, and Samuel M. Isaacs strongly supported the Union cause. Bernhard Felsenthal and David Einhorn were staunch abolitionists. Leeser's *landsman* James K. Gutheim not only aligned himself with the Confederacy but after the war continued to involve himself in various activities to preserve the memory of the "lost cause." Rev. George Jacobs of Richmond employed slaves in his home, and his colleague Rev. J. M. Michelbacher preached that slavery was ordained by God. Isaac Mayer Wise sided with the Copperhead Democrats and maintained that peace was more important than union.[43]

Some of the rabbis paid a heavy price for taking public positions on slavery and the war. Einhorn had to flee from Baltimore in the spring of 1861, to escape the wrath of rioting antiabolitionist mobs. In May 1863, Gutheim was ordered to leave New Orleans after it had been captured by federal troops and he refused to take an oath of allegiance to the United States. Besides losing its Southern readers because of the exigencies of war, Wise's paper also lost Northern readers who boycotted it for failing to take a stronger stand against secession.[44]

Leeser's neutrality was also challenged early in 1861, when war fever was running high. On May 7, 1861, a pro-North demonstration was held at the Hebrew Education Society's school. Moses A. Dropsie, a pro-Republican Jewish lawyer associated with the society, raised the American flag and gave an impassioned patriotic address. In the *Occident*, Leeser tried to place the incident in perspective and criticized

Dropsie for fueling the war fever then sweeping the country: "At present, we sicken at the thought of the fratricidal strife in which parties are about to plunge. Let us hope that the contest will be brief, and peace and plenty smile again with renewed industry and strengthened commerce over this land, which only can flourish when the arts of peace are cultivated."[45]

Dropsie sought Leeser out and accused him of endorsing secession. "You better take care what you say," the hotheaded attorney threatened. "You are already on the suspected list, and you may be compelled to quit the city before long." Totally unnerved, Leeser wrote to the mayor of Philadelphia, Alexander Henry, to ascertain if, indeed, he had been labeled a fifth columnist by the local authorities. Unwilling to modify his neutral position, Leeser volunteered to exile himself and return to Germany. "You will therefore greatly oblige an old resident who knew your grandfather thirty years ago," Leeser wrote, "whether such a suspected list is in existence, and if so, for what cause my name was placed thereon; and if so whether I shall be liable to a summary expulsion from this place; so that I may make the necessary preparations."[46]

On June 3, the mayor received Leeser's note and immediately responded:

> The contents of your note of this morning greatly astonish me. I do not know why the language of which you complain should have been used by Mr. M. A. Dropsie. I can with pleasure assure you that your loyalty has never been impugned, so far as I am aware—and I have no knowledge of the existence of a "suspected list."[47]

If Leeser's innermost loyalties to either the North or South were a matter of public conjecture, his position on slavery was no secret, although he characteristically declined to speak or write at length on the explosive issue. He first stated his position in a brief article commenting on Morris J. Raphall's controversial discourse "The Bible View of Slavery." Delivered at the peak of the secession crisis, on January 4, 1861, a day President Buchanan declared a National Fast Day, the talk was widely circulated in the United States and Europe. Raphall attempted to prove that the Bible, including the Ten Commandments, sanctioned slavery. To soften his message, he introduced the idea that biblical and Southern slavery were not identical, and that, as Leeser wrote of Raphall, "he himself was not an adherent of slavery, but that an objective consideration of the text of the Bible forced him to assume this position."[48]

221

After securing a copy of Raphall's text and carefully examining it, Leeser wrote in the *Occident* in February 1861 that "we share nearly all that the eloquent divine says on his subject. . . . It is, to our mind, proof enough in favor of the legality of human involuntary bondage, that our forefathers were permitted to acquire perpetual servants." Like Raphall, Leeser emphasized that "the condition of the Canaanite servant among the Hebrews was entirely different from that of the Africans in America." Leeser, however, disagreed with Raphall's assertion that the "negro race [was consigned] to bondage through Noah's cursing Canaan." Leeser's qualification is important because, at least in theory, it means that he rejected racism as the basis for slavery and instead viewed "involuntary bondage" solely as an economic and legal institution.[49]

True to his policy of keeping politics and religion separate, Leeser strongly criticized Raphall for delivering his controversial lecture from a pulpit. "Though the sermon is well put together," Leeser wrote, ". . . we must again express our regret that it was preached in one of our Synagogues; they are no places for political discussions, though they may be founded on the Bible; the public lecture rooms are far more suited to this purpose."[50] According to Leeser, only public issues that directly affected the Jewish community were legitimate topics of discussion in the Jewish press and in American synagogues.

Maintaining the Jewish press in wartime, however, was not an easy undertaking. Once the fighting began, Leeser found it difficult either to collect from his Southern readers or to have the *Occident* delivered to them. Matters were scarcely better in the North. Moreover, Leeser had injured himself in a severe fall in Pottsville, Pennsylvania, on July 12, 1860, and there were indications that he was beginning to suffer from respiratory problems. As a result, in October 1862, he invited Jonas Bondi (1804–1874), a former student of Rabbi Nathan Adler, to serve as the assistant editor of the *Occident*. Bondi continued to work with Leeser until the fall of 1865, when he started his own paper, the *Hebrew Leader* (1865–74) in New York.[51]

Leeser felt that it was critical to keep publishing the *Occident* at all costs during the war years. Military conflicts inevitably lead to the curtailing of civilian rights and an increase in social animus, and the Civil War was no exception. In fact, the years from 1861 to 1865 witnessed a rise in anti-Jewish prejudice in both the North and the South. The legal consequences of the increase in anti-Jewish prejudice might have been much greater had it not been for the defense work of the *Occident* and other contemporary American Jewish papers. As a defender of his people, Leeser was at the forefront of nearly all the major campaigns involving the protection of Jewish rights in the United States during the Civil War.[52]

The first important "Jewish" issue that emerged during the war was the legal disability preventing the commissioning of Jewish chaplains in the Union army. On July 12, 1861, Congressman Clement J. Vallandigham, a Democrat from Ohio, raised an objection to the Volunteer Bill. The legislation stipulated that a regimental chaplain be a "regularly ordained minister of some Christian denomination." Vallandigham moved that the phrase "religious society" be substituted for "Christian denomination." "There is a large body of men in this country, and one growing continually, of the Hebrew faith," the congressman told his colleagues, "whose rabbis and priests are men of great learning and piety, and whose adherents are a good citizens and as true patriots as any in this country." His peers—some of whom considered Vallandigham a near traitor—were unpersuaded, and the original language became law. By contrast, there was no legal obstacle to the appointment of Jewish chaplains in the South, nor was there any attempt to commission a Jewish chaplain in the Confederate army.[53]

Less than three months elapsed before the law was tested. A YMCA worker who happened to be visiting a Union army camp in Virginia contested the fact that Michael Allen, a Jew, was serving as the chaplain of the Sixty-fifth Regiment of the Fifth Pennsylvania Cavalry, popularly known as "Cameron's dragoons." He had been appointed by the commanding officer, Col. Max Friedman, who also was Jewish, as was a large portion of the 1,200-man outfit.

The affair touched Leeser directly. Allen was born in Philadelphia, and from childhood on he had studied regularly with Leeser, even preparing for the Jewish ministry under his guidance. Later, he taught at the Hebrew Education Society's school and regularly substituted for Leeser at services at Mickveh Israel when the hazzan was out of town. However, Allen was not ordained, nor did he work full time as a "minister." He made a respectable income as a liquor salesman. The army, therefore, had two reasons to dismiss him, although he had already proven himself effective as a chaplain: he was not a minister, and he was not a Christian. Under protest, he resigned his commission.[54]

The Board of Delegates of American Israelites decided to pursue the matter and appointed Dr. Arnold Fischel, formerly the "preacher" at Shearith Israel, to represent them in Washington, D.C. En route to the capital from New York, Fischel met with Leeser in Philadelphia, who helped him prepare for his mission. Fischel ably represented the situation before President Abraham Lincoln and numerous congressional committees. Meanwhile, the board organized a petition drive to bring public pressure to bear on the issue. One of the principal opponents of the board's campaign for a Jewish chaplain was a group of Reform rabbis who objected to the Board of Delegates' claim to be the representative body speaking for American Jewry. Nevertheless, on July 12, 1862, bowing to public pressure, Congress reversed itself and changed the law to allow non-Christian clergy to be appointed as military chaplains.[55]

Leeser was anxious to test the new law. As secretary and founder of Philadelphia's Board of (Jewish) Ministers, the first of its kind in the United States, he wrote a letter on August 21 to President Lincoln requesting the appointment of a Jewish hospital chaplain for all of southeastern Pennsylvania. Philadelphia, in particular, Leeser noted, was becoming "a central depository for sick and wounded soldiers," and he had already heard of two Jewish servicemen who had died in local hospitals without the comfort of a Jewish chaplain. The president was sympathetic to the proposal and through his personal secretary, John Hays, asked the Board of Ministers to "designate a proper person for the position."[56]

The Board of Ministers chose Jacob Frankel (1808–1888), the fifty-four-year-old minister of Congregation Rodeph Sholom in Philadelphia. Born in Grünstadt, Bavaria, Frankel had an excellent singing voice and a cheerful disposition. "A small fund was placed at his disposal for purchasing inexpensive gifts and necessities for the men he visited," Korn reported, "but the men were most grateful for the gift of his voice."[57] Frankel continued to serve as a chaplain until July 1, 1865, and took his work very seriously. After Frankel left the service, Leeser observed in a quasi-military style that Chaplain Frankel "faithfully discharged the duties incident to the office, and the Jewish soldiers in the hospitals in this vicinity were properly cared for under his supervision."[58]

Leeser himself neither sought nor received an appointment as a chaplain. On March 30, 1864, however, the Medical Director's Office of the Department of the Susquehanna issued him a pass "for the purpose of administering to the spiritual wants of the sick of his persuasion." To his great disappointment, not all of the infirm Jewish soldiers were glad to see him. He wrote about his experiences in the *Occident*:

> To some soldiers we were welcome, while others would scarcely confess their Jewish origin. Some even refused prayer-books when tendered to them, and all had to partake of the hospital foods, and only on holy days could we get permits for them to leave when one or more again refused to come out. There was, on the whole, a hesitancy to confess our religion,

in fear of taint or shame, false indeed, yet powerful enough to act as a check on them. . . .[59]

The debilitating effects of anti-Semitism on Jewish soldiers infuriated Leeser. As a defender of the faith, he was always prepared to fight against anti-Jewish bigotry and for the civil rights of American Jews. Thus, when news reached Philadelphia that Gen. Ulysses S. Grant had issued General Order No. 11, expelling all the Jews from the Department of Tennessee, which included northern Mississippi and the parts of Kentucky and Tennessee west of the Tennessee River, Leeser immediately went into action to have the order revoked. Although he failed to persuade the *Philadelphia Enquirer* to either cover the story or editorialize against the action, he censured Grant's act in the *Occident* and used its pages to encourage both mass protest meetings and private lobbying efforts in Washington.[60]

At the same time, Leeser was not unmindful of the activities of opportunistic Jewish entrepreneurs in the Department of Tennessee and blasted them for jeopardizing the civil rights of their coreligionists. There was a shameless "crowd of needy [Jewish] adventurers," he wrote, "who travel or glide rather through the highways and byways of the land in quest of gain, often we fear unlawful[ly], who in their material labors are perfectly indifferent to the duties of their religion, and not rarely conceal it by a pretended conformity."[61] Such activities had long been noted by Grant, other officers, and officials from the Treasury Department, who feared they were disruptive to the normal course of military operations. The majority of the offenders, however, were gentiles.

As the result of private lobbying, an internal review of the matter by army officials, and a presidential order, General Order No. 11 was revoked. Grant was not censured by Congress for his action, even though many Democratic members of the House thought they could make "political hay" of the affair. (Later, as president, Grant even apologized to American Jews. "It never would have been issued," he reflected, "if it had not been telegraphed the moment it was penned, and without reflection."[62] This excuse, however, is not borne out by Grant's papers.)

No sooner had Grant's order been revoked than another, equally serious threat to Jewish civil rights in the Union developed in the Midwest. Thousands of American Protestants had understood the outbreak of the Civil War as divine punishment—not for the perpetuation of the institution of slavery but for the ratification of a "godless" Constitution in 1787. Ministers had been warning their congregations

225

since the 1790s that the Lord would ultimately "crush us to atoms" for the omission of his name in the nation's most essential document. With the outbreak of the Civil War, hundreds of sermons were preached and as many pamphlets written declaring that the divine wrath could no longer be contained.[63]

In the wake of a series of interdenominational meetings in the Midwest early in January 1863, a consensus developed among many Protestant groups in the Union that a National Reform Association (NRA) should be organized with the principal purpose of championing a "Christian nation" amendment to the Constitution. The NRA quickly received broad support from ministers, theologians, college professors, and a broad spectrum of politicians and judges. On September 20, 1864, the Presbytery of Cincinnati officially endorsed the NRA platform and petitioned Congress, stating that a "Christian nation with an atheistical Constitution is an anomaly," and that "now is the time to make this correction of fundamental error when God is baptizing the nation in blood, in order, as we trust, to purify it from destructive evils, so as to preserve our nationality and give us in the end peace and prosperity."[64]

Leeser immediately sounded the alarm. In the *Occident*, he asked, "ARE WE EQUALS IN THIS LAND?," and pressed for unified action to counter the proposed amendment. The Board of Delegates accepted his suggestion to send a strongly worded letter to both houses of Congress "to protest energetically against the amendments to the preamble of the Constitution as prayed for in the memorial of the Presbytery of Cincinnati." The board empowered Leeser to prepare the letter, which he completed and mailed on January 30, 1865. On February 11, Charles Sumner of Massachusetts submitted Leeser's memorial to the Senate, where it was referred to the Judiciary Committee.[65]

Leeser's argument was a familiar one, well hewn by his many years as an unrelenting defender of Jewish rights in America. He began by reviewing the contribution of American Jews during the Revolution and the many benefits liberty had afforded his fellow Jews in the United States. "But," he continued, "they observe with the deepest regret that they are threatened with a total withdrawal of their precious rights as citizens equal with any others, by introducing a Christian element into the Constitution."[66] "It is in vain," Leeser concluded, "to say that the absence of a national creed renders this an atheistical nation; for the deeds of the people prove the contrary." He boldly and perhaps recklessly pointed out, "It would be akin to blasphemy to assert that the offended Deity should be appeased by mere words . . .

226

and not accept of works, which are the true evidences of sincere conviction."[67]

Although the Senate Judiciary Committee tabled the NRA's proposed amendment because of its lack of merit or political support, Leeser's "memorial" was not without significance. It demonstrated that the American Jewish community was becoming increasingly capable of quickly organizing politically astute responses to Jewish and national crises. Leeser and at least a dozen others had learned to lobby effectively at the highest levels of government.

By February 1865, however, watchdog activities were not the only items on the agenda of Isaac Leeser and other responsible Jewish leaders around the country. The time had finally arrived to begin considering the tasks of the postwar period. The human cost of the war had been heavy: over 600,000 casualties. Much of the South had been totally devastated. The destruction was also keenly felt in the Jewish community. Of the ten thousand Jews who had served in the armies, five hundred, mainly recent immigrants, had been killed. Hundreds of Southern Jews were impoverished by the war, and some of their synagogues had been destroyed in the fighting. By the spring of 1865, the South was virtually without rabbinic leadership.[68]

"I well remember being with him Seder night, April 2, 1865 at the house of a mutual friend," Rosa Mordecai later recalled, "when the boys called through the streets the surrender of General Lee." "Mr. Leeser," she continued, "was so overcome that he had to stop the Service and walked home with me almost without speaking—the strongest possible sign of emotion."[69]

Leeser had barely had time to collect his thoughts when the news arrived that an assassin had shot and killed President Lincoln on the night of April 14, 1865. The Washington City Hebrew Congregation, which earlier had turned to Leeser to dedicate its new building in March 1863, again asked him to address them and interpret the meaning of the sad turn of events. On April 22, 1865, the Sabbath following the president's death, Leeser preached a sermon on "How to Mourn" in the nation's capital. He urged the congregation to accept the catastrophe in the spirit of the biblical figure Aaron, who quietly resigned himself to the death of two of his sons (Leviticus 10:3). "And if men therefore wish to honour the memory of Mr. Lincoln," he added, "let them and their new ruler [President Andrew Johnson] . . . imitate and follow up his merciful intention, and pour, as he had intended to do, the oil of kindness on the bleeding wounds of the land, to stifle the tumult of the feelings of the conquered, and induce them to again accept the control of the general government with cheerful acquiescence and unforced obedience."[70]

227

10
The Final Years, 1866–1868

*There have been greater Talmudists, there may
have been more eloquent orators and more graceful
writers; but among them all, there has been no
greater genius, no better Jew, and no
purer man than Isaac Leeser.*
—Mayer Sulzberger, *Occident*, March 1868

WITH THE WAR OVER, Leeser focused his attention on the plight of
Jewish communities in the defeated Confederacy and began working
to assist them both materially and spiritually. Along with the others of
the region, many Southern Jews had suffered terribly, especially
toward the end of the war. Leeser was extremely sympathetic to their
situation. In February 1865, the Jews of Savannah asked both Leeser
and Rev. Samuel M. Isaacs, editor of the *Jewish Messenger*, to help them
procure matzah for Passover. The two editors were able to secure five
thousand pounds of unleavened bread. Congregations throughout the
South also wrote to Leeser to seek his help in locating hazzanim to fill
their empty pulpits and, in many cases, for financial assistance as well.
In 1866, Leeser made a trip with his arch-rival, Isaac Mayer Wise, in
itself an act of reconciliation, to visit the Jews of Richmond, Virginia.
Both men were moved by the still-visible scenes of destruction and the
great hardships the people had to endure.[1]

The reconstruction of Jewish communities in the South was paralleled by an expansion of Jewish institutional life in the North. Relatively soon after the war ended, two important Jewish institutions that
Leeser had been promoting for almost two decades, a Jewish hospital
and a rabbinic seminary, were established in Philadelphia. Supported

by the two leading national Jewish organizations of the period, B'nai B'rith and the Board of Delegates of American Israelites, respectively, it seemed possible that the two new institutions would succeed and provide years of significant service to the Jewish community of Philadelphia and the United States as a whole. But they did not share the same destiny. The hospital quickly struck deep roots in the Philadelphia community, while the rabbinic school was crippled by a lack of students and slowly died of neglect. A practical, nonreligious communal institution proved more appealing to American Jewry than a narrowly defined theological institute.

The success of Philadelphia's Jewish hospital reflected both Jewish tradition and the growing ability of American Jews to organize community institutions. During the Middle Ages and the early modern period, European Jewish communities generally maintained a *hekdesh* (a hostel for the poor) that served the dual purpose of providing lodging for poor or sick travelers. During the eighteenth century, especially in Western Europe, the *hekdesh*, influenced by developments in hospital care in the Christian community, increasingly confined itself to dealing with the indigent sick. The prototype for the modern Jewish hospital was first developed in the 1740s by Sephardic Jews in London. Subsequently, Jewish *krankenhäuser* (hospitals) were established in Berlin, Breslau, and Vienna.[2]

Although American Jews did not maintain a *hekdesh* during the Revolutionary Period, they did begin to organize societies (*hevrot*, plural of *hevra*, or *hebra*) charged with a wide range of social responsibilities including mutual aid, visiting the sick, and burying the dead. These *hevrot* were especially important in immigrant communities, where individual families had not yet developed financial resources to deal with life's crises alone. Originally closely aligned with the synagogue, the *hevrot* slowly emerged as independent entities. "When the *Hebra Shel Bikur Holim Ugemilut Hasadim*, or Society for the Visitation of the Sick and Mutual Assistance, was organized in 1813," Maxwell Whiteman reports, "it was [one of] the first extra-synagogal Jewish organizations to appear on the Philadelphia scene."[3]

Members of the society "offered more in spiritual solace than in medical aid," according to Jacob R. Marcus. They called upon Jews in boardinghouses and wayside taverns convalescing from prolonged illnesses and brought comfort to those with terminal diseases. They also sought to remove indigent Jewish patients from Philadelphia's Blockley Almshouse. As their organization grew, they took the enlightened step of enlisting the services of Dr. Isaac Hays (1796–1879), a

229

native Philadelphia Jew who received his M.D. from the University of Pennsylvania in 1820.[4]

Leeser, who was a member of the *hebra*, had been urging American Jews to expand their communities' social welfare programs since the 1830s. He enthusiastically applauded the establishment of the first Jewish hospital in the United States in Cincinnati in 1850. Three years later, the opening of Jews' Hospital (now Mount Sinai Hospital) in New York also met with his strong approbation. During the course of the 1850s, he used the pages of the *Occident* to promote the development of a Jewish hospital in Philadelphia. The establishment of a Jewish Foster Home in 1855 gave him the opportunity to criticize the community for failing "to advance its medical program." Public support for the idea was also offered by Rev. Louis Naumberg of Philadelphia's Rodeph Sholom congregation. His plea, like Leeser's, fell on deaf ears.[5]

Two national disasters, of very different dimensions, finally convinced Philadelphia's Jews of the need for a local medical facility. First, the depression of 1857 spread misery among the city's thousands of poor Jewish immigrants. An ad hoc Hebrew Relief Association "engaged the services of two physicians to attend to poor on their list." Following the model of the *hebra*, the association's doctors visited patients at home and tried to give indigent Jews the option to go to the public poorhouse. The second crisis, the Civil War, was of much greater proportions. By 1864, the Jewish community was overwhelmed with medical and welfare emergencies. The need to serve the combined needs of its large poor population, as well as the wounded from the battlefront who were scattered in institutions throughout the city and in nearby towns, finally convinced a small group of German Jewish immigrants, headed by Leeser and Abraham Sulzberger (d. 1886), to develop a modern Jewish hospital in Philadelphia.[6]

Abraham Sulzberger, the father of Leeser's most important protégé, Mayer Sulzberger, came to the United States in 1849. Leeser was a frequent visitor in his home and spent long hours tutoring young Mayer in Hebrew, Bible, and Jewish thought. The Sulzberger family came from Heidelsheim, in Baden, Germany. Abraham Sulzberger had served as the hazzan of the local synagogue in Heidelsheim. Earlier, his father had been rabbi there for many years. Passionately interested in the welfare of his coreligionists, Abraham Sulzberger frequently accompanied Leeser to visit the wounded during the Civil War. According to Maxwell Whiteman, "It was on the occasion of one of their hospital visits, after the Battle of Gettysburg, that Leeser and Abraham Sulzberger talked at length of a plan for a hospital."[7] Later that year they privately organized a *hekdesh* on Powelton Avenue near Thirty-fourth Street.

Support for the institution was difficult to find. Mickveh Israel remained aloof, preferring not to work directly with Leeser. The new Reform congregation, Keneseth Israel, objected to the *hekdesh*'s strict adherence to *kashrut* (Jewish dietary laws) and also refused to support the new institution. Their opposition was surprising given the number of extant denominational hospitals in Philadelphia. St. Joseph's had been founded by the Catholic Church in 1849. Three years later the Protestant Episcopal Church opened a facility, Episcopal Hospital, to serve the needs of Philadelphia's large immigrant population from the British Isles. Finally, in 1860, the German Hospital, later renamed Lankenau, was organized to serve the German-speaking Christian immigrants in the city. The Jews alone had been unable to create a facility to provide their poor with on-site service.[8]

Realizing that the religious institutions were too severely factional to be of any service to them, Sulzberger and Leeser turned to the local B'nai B'rith lodge to salvage their plan. During the late 1850s, B'nai B'rith emerged as the largest and most important national Jewish organization in the United States. Founded in 1843 in New York by German Jewish immigrants who had allegedly been refused permission to join Odd Fellows Lodges "on account of their religion," B'nai B'rith quickly emerged as the premier Jewish men's lodge in the country. By 1856, membership in New York alone surpassed a thousand. During the course of the Civil War, national membership exceeded five thousand and by 1890 the order claimed 28,000 members.[9]

B'nai B'rith, in Deborah Dash Moore's phrase, was American Jewry's "secular synagogue." In the preamble to its constitution, the noble goals of the organization were set forth:

> B'nai B'rith has taken upon itself the mission of uniting Israelites in the work of promoting their highest interests and those of humanity; of developing the mental and moral character of the people of our faith; of inculcating the purest principles of philanthropy, honor, and patriotism; of supporting science and art; alleviating the wants of the poor and needy; visiting and attending the sick; coming to the rescue of victims of persecution; providing for, protecting, and assisting the widow and the orphan on the broadest principles of humanity.[10]

The key to the organization's success, however, was an inexpensive benefits program, which included life insurance. B'nai B'rith also offered its members a sense of community and held secret meetings complete with Masonic-type rituals and passwords.[11]

231

Initially, Leeser was wary of organizations such as B'nai B'rith. In November 1854, he published a note in the *Occident* stating that he would open the pages of his journal to the organization, although "we cannot say that we deem a secret society . . . as the best calculated to effect a religious revival." In fact, Leeser was justifiably suspicious that a hidden purpose of B'nai B'rith was to promote Reform Judaism. He also noted, "Nearly if not all the ministers of German extraction, and other prominent men, are members."[12] During the 1860s, his resistance to the order weakened while its secrecy declined. Its popularity, benevolence, and his realization that it was not a Reform organization finally attracted Leeser to the fraternal organization. After joining, he quickly rose through the ranks and gained entry to regional and national councils.[13]

According to Maxwell Whiteman, Sulzberger introduced the idea of a B'nai B'rith–sponsored Jewish hospital at a Grand District Lodge meeting on August 14, 1864. He was well received: he was a past president of District Lodge No. 3, and Leeser was then serving as a vice-president of the Elim Lodge. Four days later, a provisional committee of seven men met at Union Hall. Max Thalheimer, "segar-box" maker, was appointed chairman, and Leeser was named vice-chairman. Sulzberger became the group's secretary. After thoroughly discussing the issue, the committee resolved to print five thousand copies of a bilingual (German and English) circular promoting the idea of a "hospital for Israelites in Philadelphia."[14] The handbill succinctly reviewed the major reasons for the need for the hospital:

WHEREAS, A Jewish Hospital has been found to be a necessity in the cities of New York and Cincinnati, and in the large cities of Europe, and

WHEREAS, All the causes that make such an institution a necessity there, are in full operation here, and

WHEREAS, Within the last six months three Israelites have died in Christian hospitals, without having enjoyed the privilege of hearing the . . . watchword of their faith and nation, and

WHEREAS, It reflects the greatest discredit on so large a Jewish population as that of Philadelphia, to force friendless brothers to seek, in sickness and the prospect of death, the shelter of un-Jewish hospitals, eat forbidden food, to be dissected after death, and sometimes even to be buried with the stranger. Therefore be it

RESOLVED, That the District Grand Lodge No. 3, of the Independent order of the Benai Berith [sic], acting on that Benevolence and Brotherly Love, which are the motto of the Order, take immediate steps to secure the cooperation of all Jewish societies and individuals for the purpose of founding a Jewish hospital.[15]

Leeser must have been very pleased with the provisional commit-tee's wholehearted endorsement of Orthodox principles. Providing pa-tients with a Jewish environment, especially kosher food; comforting the dying and giving them their last rites; disallowing autopsy, a fla-grant violation of Jewish law; and guaranteeing a proper Jewish burial—these were all embraced by Thalheimer's committee. The same rationale for developing Jewish hospitals in the United States remained until the 1920s, when discrimination against Jewish physicians added a new dimension to the Jewish hospital movement.[16]

The Philadelphia Jewish community at large also responded posi-tively. At a large public meeting held on Sunday, February 19, 1865, the Jewish Hospital Association was formally organized. Alfred T. Jones, the parnass of Leeser's synagogue, Beth El Emeth, and an active member of B'nai B'rith, was elected president. Mayer Sulzberger re-placed his father as corresponding secretary, and Leeser, one of the principal speakers at the meeting, was elected as one of the twelve trustees. He formally requested that a Women's Auxiliary be organized. Eighty-four-year-old Rebecca Gratz immediately responded with a hundred-dollar contribution.[17]

The first issue facing the Jewish Hospital Association was finding a suitable location for the hospital. Bernhard Felsenthal, an important rabbi in Chicago, argued that it would be less costly and more efficient to share space with an existing hospital. After a brief investigation, a committee rejected the idea: the other hospitals in the area did not have adequate space to absorb the new operation, or would not grant the Jewish hospital total autonomy if it rented space. Late in April 1865, a site was located in West Philadelphia, at Fisher's Avenue and Haverford Road, near Beth El Emeth's cemetery.[18]

After a brief but successful fund-raising campaign, the hospital site was purchased on September 5, 1865. Renovating the large, old stone house took eleven months. On August 6, 1866, the hospital opened, with twenty-two beds and the best contemporary equipment. Dr. Adolph Feldstein, an 1864 graduate of the University of Prague, was named staff physician, and Lazarus W. Kronheimer was named super-intendent of the hospital. Mrs. Kronheimer worked in the women's ward.

The Jewish Hospital instantly proved a great success. Easy access by street-car and a liberal policy that allowed non-Jews to be admitted helped to establish the hospital's reputation in the city. At Mayer Sulz-berger's suggestion, the hospital posted that it was "dedicated to the relief of the sick and wounded without regard to creed, color, or na-tionality." Mary D. Brown, scion of a wealthy Quaker family, even made a $500 contribution to the hospital after learning that it had provided gratis eighteen months of care for a terminally ill, indigent non-Jewish woman, who had only been nineteen years old when she died.[19]

The formal dedication of the hospital did not take place until May 28, 1867, after ten full months of operation. Among the guests were the members of the Board of Delegates of American Israelites, which was holding its annual convention in Philadelphia. The principal speaker was Isaac Leeser. It was the last time that the ailing sixty-one-year-old would give a major speech in public. In his talk, he reviewed the reasons for organizing a Jewish hospital, gave a brief history of the institution, and thanked its sponsor, B'nai B'rith. He concluded by mentioning that two Passover Seders had already been conducted at the hospital, and he offered a final prayer asking for God's blessing and healing.[20]

The Board of Delegates of American Israelites did not hold its annual convention in Philadelphia merely to attend the ceremonial opening of the new Jewish Hospital. Other, serious business needed attention, including the ratification of a proposal to create a rabbinic school in Philadelphia. After a considerable debate, the Board was persuaded by Leeser to begin "the great fight against ignorance." A resolution empowering the Executive Board to take all necessary steps to establish a college in conjunction with Philadelphia's Hebrew Education Society passed unanimously on May 27, 1867. Five months later, in October, Maimonides College opened. Leeser was named provost as well as "professor of homiletics, belles lettres, and comparative theology." After more than a quarter of a century of continuous promotion, Leeser's dream of an American theological seminary was a reality. Unfortunately, he had only another four months to live.[21]

Leeser had been the first person to campaign specifically for a Jewish ministerial school in the United States. Others, including Mordecai Manuel Noah, preceded him in calling for the establishment of modern Jewish day schools. To these pleas, Leeser added his own for the training of American Jewish ministers. In his 1841 "Plan of Union" he had already proposed that a theological school be created in America.

A High School [i.e., a *Hochschule*] for education in the higher branches, is to be established in some central point whenever practicable . . . where young men are to be educated in such a manner, that they may be for the office of Hazan, lecturer, and teacher; and young women be educated for the high calling of female instructors.[22]

234

Isaac Leeser as a young preacher.
Oil portrait by Solomon N. Carvalho, c. 1840.
(Courtesy of the National Museum of American Jewish History,
Philadelphia.)

*First formal Mikveh Israel synagogue was dedicated in 1825.
(Courtesy of the American Jewish Archives, Hebrew Union
College-Jewish Institute of Religion, Cincinnati.)*

Zalegman Phillips. (Courtesy of the American Jewish Archives, Hebrew Union College-Jewish Institute of Religion, Cincinnati.)

Jacob Mordecai. (Courtesy of the American Jewish Archives, Hebrew Union College-Jewish Institute of Religion, Cincinnati.)

Rebecca Gratz. (Courtesy of the American Jewish Archives, Hebrew Union College-Jewish Institute of Religion, Cincinnati.)

Rev. Dr. Isaac M. Wise,
RABBI OF K.K. BENAI YESHURUN, CINCINNATI L.

*I. M. Wise, ca. 1854. (Courtesy of the American Jewish
Archives, Hebrew Union College-Jewish Institute of Religion,
Cincinnati.)*

Leeser's tomb. (Courtesy Stephen Hebden.)

THE REVEREND
ISAAC LEESER,
FIRST MINISTER OF THE
KAHAL KADOSH BETH EL EMETH
FOR FORTY YEARS A PREACHER OF
THE WORD OF GOD
BORN AT NEUENKIRCHEN PRUSSIA
DECEMBER 12TH 1805,
DIED AT PHILADELPHIA
FEBRUARY 1ST 1868.
MAY HIS SOUL REST IN PEACE

Leeser's tomb. (Courtesy Stephen Hebden.)

Isaac Leeser. (Courtesy of the Jewish Museum/Art Resource, New York.)

The idea for a Jewish theological seminary, however, did not originate with Leeser. In Europe, several seminaries were fully in operation by 1867. The first modern rabbinical seminary was founded by Isaac Samuel Reggio (1784–1855) in Padua in 1829. The Istituto Convitto Rabbinico, later called the Collegio Rabbinico Italiano, served as the model for all future seminaries. In contrast to the traditional yeshivas, the seminary curriculum demanded a mastery of the vernacular and a knowledge of a wide range of secular and extra-Talmudic Jewish studies. One year later, the École Centrale Rabbanique was established in Metz. The most famous of the early European seminaries was the Jüdisch-Theologisches Seminar, which was founded in Breslau in 1854 by Zecharias Frankel (1801–1875). In 1855, Jews' College was founded in London, and in 1862, Adolph Jellinek established the Israelitisch-Theologische Lehranstalt in Vienna.[23]

While Leeser was certainly aware of the European developments, he was probably more directly influenced by the rapid expansion of theological studies in the United States during the first half of the nineteenth century. Only a handful of the 516 American colleges founded prior to the Civil War were not church affiliated. "This half-century," reports Sydney E. Ahlstrom, "was the great age of the church-college, an age in fact when these church-related institutions virtually constituted American higher education. . . . About 90 percent of the pre–Civil War college presidents were clergymen."[24] "The dominant motive in the founding of colleges," adds Winthrop S. Hudson, "was to provide an educated ministry for the churches."[25]

"Specifically theological education, as distinguished from the classical education given aspiring ministers in the colleges," Hudson continues, "also evolved during this period. The founding of Andover Theological Seminary in 1808 is usually considered to be the beginning of specialized institutional training for American ministers. "In the next years," he adds, "the movement rapidly gained momentum in most denominations." In Philadelphia, two prestigious institutions, the Protestant Episcopal Divinity School (1862) and the Lutheran Theological Seminary (1864), were established just prior to the founding of Maimonides College. St. Vincent's Roman Catholic Theological Seminary opened in Philadelphia in 1868, a year after Leeser's death.[26]

Leeser clearly viewed the Protestant clergy as a model for the American Jewish ministry. In an article, "The Demands of the Times," published in the *Occident* in October 1844, he noted, "There is hardly any Christian society which does not strain every nerve to have an intelligent and virtuous ministry, composed of men who would honour any calling by their acquisition and general conduct." "Jews," he

235

wrote subsequently, "have hitherto been neglectful in the greatest duty they owe themselves, to rear up from among themselves persons to fill the important office of minister of religion."[27]

Leeser was aware that what he termed a "Jewish minister" was not a rabbi in the traditional sense of the word. In an editorial entitled "The Ministry" in August 1866, he openly acknowledged the novelty of his views.

> Perhaps it will be urged as making against us that by our present plans we shall be able to raise *Rabbins* in this country for . . . there will be no time for extensive Talmudical study. We confess that it is so. But for the present and years to come, we need ministers and teachers more than those thoroughly versed in all the casuistry of Judaism, and for this purpose we are perfectly willing to depend on Europe, or Asia, or Africa for some considerable time, till the period when Jewish literature and learning shall have pitched their tent on the western hemisphere.[28]

A number of American Jews, ranging from Orthodox to radical Reform, shared Leeser's view of the Jewish ministry and had unsuccessfully worked on developing institutions of higher Jewish learning before 1867. The earliest known plan was formulated in 1821 by Moses Elias Levy, one of the first Jews to settle in Florida. It called for a nationally funded Jewish trade institute but did not specifically call for the training of ministers. The Levy plan never left the drawing board. Thirty-one years later, the eccentric New York philanthropist Sampson Simson organized a Jewish Theological Seminary and Scientific Institute and even purchased a small parcel of land in Yonkers to build the institution. Unfortunately, he died in 1857 before being able to devote significant time or energy to the project.[29]

The most famous of the early attempts at creating a general American Jewish institution of higher learning was Isaac Mayer Wise's Zion College project (1855). Leeser supported the plan and frequently reported on its progress in the *Occident*. Wise had nearly succeeded in organizing a national system to finance the school when he unilaterally decided to start the school in Cincinatti without consulting his supporters on the East Coast. They resented Wise's high-handed move, withdrew their assistance, and forced the closing of Zion College sometime during 1856 or 1857. The school, however, did operate for one academic year and attracted fourteen young students. According to Michael A. Meyer, Wise learned two things from the debacle: "that a rabbinical seminary was the more necessary and feasible project, and that such a seminary could only be supported by a preexisting union of congregations brought into being specifically for that purpose." Leeser also took these lessons to heart.[30]

Not all American Jews agreed that a rabbinic school should be organized in the United States. Many German Jews in America believed that Europe was able to supply an adequate supply of "superior clergy." Intellectual elitism and resistance to Americanization were, in Leeser's opinion, self-defeating for American Jews. "We know well enough," he wrote in the *Occident*,

> that in so speaking we shall be charged with committing treason to our native land, as we are German ourself, and have, whatever information we have, brought it over with us when we crossed the Atlantic. . . . But after all is nothing due to the *native* population, who cannot speak German? or do our Germanists (to make a new word) expect to maintain the Teutonic tongue for more than two generations in large cities, unless it be done by excluding Israelites from a general intercourse with society.[31]

Through continual campaigning, Leeser slowly was able to sell his idea to an ever-widening circle of American Jews.

By 1865, three distinct efforts to create a national Jewish educational institution were simultaneously in progress, including the plans for Maimonides College. In New York City, two radical-reform rabbis, Samuel Adler of Temple Emanuel and David Einhorn of Temple Beth-El, created the Emanuel Theological Seminary Association. The organization received strong financial support. However, its purpose was ambiguous, and the association's members were unable to determine whether it should sponsor a school or merely provide scholarship money for prospective rabbinic students. By default, the latter became the usual policy of the association until its funds were consigned to the Hebrew Union College–Jewish Institute of Religion in 1953.[32]

The second effort to create a Jewish institution of higher learning attracted a much greater degree of attention in the general community but ultimately fared no better. In October 1866, at its annual convention, B'nai B'rith, which had grown to seven thousand members, voted to sponsor an "American Jewish university." A plan was drawn up to raise $70,000 and recruit 390 scholarship students. The "B. B. University" was the talk of the American Jewish community for several months, until the Constitution Grand Lodge, the supreme authority of B'nai B'rith, vetoed the plan in August 1867 as "fraught with danger and injury to the best interests of the Order."[33]

In part, the Grand Lodge may have decided to drop the plan for a B'nai B'rith–sponsored university because of promising reports from one of its most illustrious members, Isaac Leeser, about the imminent opening of Maimonides College in Philadelphia in October 1867. Plans for opening a rabbinic school in Philadelphia had first been discussed on November 6, 1864. With President Lincoln still preparing for a tough race for a second term and General Sherman's troops leaving a wide path of destruction between Atlanta and the port city of Savannah, it might have seemed an odd time to begin discussing plans for a rabbinic school. Perhaps the "chaplaincy conflict" had added to the prestige of the Jewish ministry by placing it on par with the clergy of other denominations. Certainly, the war effort provided a good model of interinstitutional cooperation. Moreover, the heartland of the North was untouched by the ravages of war, and the Union was enjoying economic prosperity.[34]

With Leeser urging them to take action, a group of prominent Philadelphia Jews met to discuss the establishment of a rabbinic seminary. The committee was headed by Abraham Hart, the president of both Mickveh Israel and the Board of Delegates of American Israelites, Moses A. Dropsie, then president of the Hebrew Education Society, and Isidore Binswanger, a successful businessman and Jewish community activist. They initially turned to the local congregations for support without much luck. Two years later, they "opened up a subscription book" and sought contributions from the Jewish elite of Philadelphia. The response was better than expected, and it was determined that a school was now financially possible.[35]

Philadelphia Jewry could not be expected to carry the burden alone, and ties were sought with the only national synagogue-supported institution in the country, the Board of Delegates. Hart provided the natural link. In August 1866, the executive committee of the board agreed to enter into partnership with Philadelphia's Hebrew Education Society to establish a seminary. At Leeser's urging, two years after it was organized in 1847, the society obtained a charter from the Pennsylvania legislature that allowed it "to furnish its graduates and others the usual degrees of bachelor of arts, master of arts, and doctor of law and divinity, as the same is exercised by other colleges established in this commonwealth."[36]

At the annual convention of the Board of Delegates, held in Philadelphia in May 1867, the seminary proposal was debated and put to a vote. Sabato Morais, hazzan of Mickveh Israel, cautioned the assembly against acting too hastily, and even clumsily suggested that the matter of a uniform liturgy needed to be considered before the establishment of an American seminary. Others were more positive. A. S. Cohen (Congregation Darech Amuno, New York), Samuel M. Isaacs (Congregation Shaarey Tefillah, New York, and editor of the *Jewish Messenger*), and Rabbi Marcus Jastrow (Congregation Rodeph Sholom, Philadelphia) all spoke in favor of the proposal, as did Leeser. The board then voted, and the measure passed without a single dissenting vote.[37]

Seven trustees were elected, including Hart, Binswanger, Dropsie, and Mayer Sulzberger, all from Philadelphia. The other three were from New York. They immediately went to work, appointing a faculty of five and designing a curriculum. Pledges totaling $6,635 were secured, as well as scholarship money for the students. Books were donated to the library from all over the country, and temporary quarters were found in the basement of the Hebrew Education Society's building on the east side of Seventh Street below Callowhill Street. On July 1, 1867, the trustees officially announced the forthcoming opening of the school.[38]

The faculty was surprisingly strong. Sabato Morais was named professor of Bible and biblical literature. Rabbi Marcus Jastrow (1829–1903), who had been rabbi of Rodeph Sholom for one year, was appointed professor of Talmud, Hebrew philosophy, and Jewish history and literature. A brilliant scholar, he had received his ordination from rabbis Feilchenfeld of his native Rogasen (Posen) and Wolf Landau of Dresden. In 1855 he took his doctorate at Halle with a thesis on medieval Spanish Jewish poet Abraham ibn Ezra. Before emigrating to the United States, he served congregations in Warsaw and Worms. Aaron Bettelheim (1830–90), who like Jastrow had only recently arrived in the United States, was appointed professor of *Mishnah* with commentaries *Shulchan Aruch* and *Yad He-Chazakah*. Born in Galgoc, Hungary, he was ordained by Rabbi Judah Loeb Rapoport at the age of eighteen and received his Ph.D. the same year from the University of Prague. Subsequently, he also studied to become a medical doctor. The only paid member of the faculty was Laemmlein Buttenwieser (1825–??). He served as professor of the Hebrew and Chaldaic languages and of the Talmud. In addition to his responsibilities at Maimonides College, he also was principal of the Hebrew Department of the Hebrew Education Society's school.[39]

As Leeser and Morais had warned the trustees, the biggest problem Maimonides College faced was attracting students. Of the original eight accepted by the college, only two registered on opening day at the end of October 1867. They were joined by three additional applicants. Only one of the five paid any tuition, and the original two students dropped out of the program after one year. "To say that this response to the opening of the first Jewish theological seminary in America was unenthusiastic," writes Bertram W. Korn, "would run the risk of inviting ridicule. Three students from the total American Jewish population of perhaps one hundred and seventy-five thousand souls!"[40]

Of the original students, only one, David Levy (1854–1930), entered the rabbinate. Ironically, he was attracted to the ideals of radical Reform Judaism. For eighteen years (1875–93) he served as rabbi of Beth Elohim in Charleston, South Carolina. Thereafter, he held pulpits in New Haven and Bridgeport, Connecticut, and Easton, Pennsylvania. He joined the Central Conference of American Rabbis and contributed a number of original hymns to the conference's first hymnal. Every summer, he vacationed in Bethlehem, New Hampshire, and was a guest preacher in the local Methodist church. A second student, Dutch-born Marcus Eliezer Lam (1854–1934), remained active in the Jewish community but made a living as a salesman. Finally, Samuel Mendelsohn (1850–1922), a scholarly Russian-born Jew who entered Maimonides College in 1870, also became a Reform rabbi. Both Mendelsohn and Levy were deeply influenced by Rabbi Marcus Jastrow, who was appointed provost after Leeser's death in February 1868. Mendelsohn married a niece of Rabbi Jastrow. The spirit of the age had worked to undermine Leeser's dream of what a Jewish seminary in America would accomplish.[41]

Had Leeser lived a few more years after the establishment of Maimonides College in 1867, the school might have had a very different destiny. He alone had the drive and commitment to nourish the young institution. The trustees made a mistake in selecting Jastrow as Leeser's successor. Although he had good scholarly credentials, he was a lackluster leader. Unlike Isaac Mayer Wise, he failed to actively recruit students, a need the school faced from the day it opened. Moreover, neither the Hebrew Education Society nor the Board of Delegates viewed the college as a high priority. They sponsored the school but were not fully committed to it. Finally, the college represented the ideals of the waning Sephardic community. German Jewry was in ascent in America in 1867, and within a few decades East European Jews were to reshape the American Jewish community once again.

Reflecting on the fate of Maimonides College, Bertram Korn suggests that "even failures have a kind of immortality." Leeser had blazed a narrow path in the wilderness that was still American Judaism of the late 1860s. Isaac Mayer Wise certainly followed it with great care and was able to avoid many of the obstacles that hindered Maimonides College. In 1875, Wise opened the Hebrew Union College in Cincinnati. Today, it is the oldest Jewish seminary in the world. Similarly, Sabato Morais was able to do the same for the original Jewish Theological Seminary. However, the real expansion of modern American rabbinic education did not occur until the early decades of the twentieth century.[42]

Leeser's health had begun to deteriorate seriously a year before Maimonides College opened. His doctors had already ordered him to spend the winter of 1866 in the South after detecting a serious lung infection. Weak and often uncomfortable, Leeser nevertheless felt the urge to continue his life's work. His final projects were strictly literary. He undertook to have several of his original works republished, and he actively promoted the publication of several Jewish classics, including a translation of Maimonides' major philosophical work, *A Guide to the Perplexed*, based on Solomon Munk's critical Arabic edition.[43]

Equally ambitious was Leeser's attempt to gather and publish the manuscripts of his scores of sermons. Over twenty-five years had passed since he had last published a volume of discourses, although he occasionally printed samples of his pulpit lectures in the *Occident*. After he left Mickveh Israel in 1850, he recalled, "I seldom committed my remarks to writing, and depended almost universally on extemporaneous speaking, even without any notes whatever, and it was but rarely that I wrote down afterwards what I delivered from the inspiration of the moment."[44]

On July 21, 1867, Leeser wrote the preface to volume 4 of his *Discourses* and explained his motivation for sharing his vast collection of sermons with the American Jewish public: "It is confidently hoped . . . that all the various sermons, addresses, and prayers may be found to have sufficient interest to make them somewhat valuable for future reference and use, and that they may be regarded hereafter as vehicles of information on many points, and be used for private devotion in the family circles of our people."[45] "If this wish should be realized," he concluded, "I shall be amply compensated for the thought, labour, and care expended in preparing them for the press, and presenting them to the public as my humble contribution to Jewish religious literature."[46]

Leeser continued to work on his *Discourses* until late in the month of December 1867. He had completed work on Volumes 4 through 8 and was nearly finished with the ninth book of the set. Cancer, however, was rapidly diminishing his strength. His illness had become so serious that he was unable to leave his bed after December 19. Aware that his time was limited, he stopped working on the *Discourses* on December 26, 1867, to prepare his will. Just two days later, Mayer Sulzberger sent him a partial copy of a sermon ("The 'Omer") that Leeser had preached at Beth El Emeth many years earlier to proofread and complete. Several more days passed before Leeser sent a note to the printer without the manuscript. "I tried yesterday to write," Leeser told the unidentified man, "and succeeded in jotting down about twenty lines, but I find I must wait a little longer. There shall be no useless delay. I feel easier, but suffer greatly."[47] He did manage to write something for the January edition of the *Occident*. Thereafter, Mayer Sulzberger wrote, "he gradually began to sink."[48]

Leeser's sufferings ended on Saturday, February 1, 1868, at 7:38 A.M. He died the death of a righteous man, in his sleep on the Sabbath. At the end, he was faithfully attended to by his friend and physician, Dr. Silas Weir Mitchell, an accomplished novelist and a great admirer of Leeser's literary work. A somber Mayer Sulzberger, who took it upon himself to complete the tenth volume of Leeser's *Discourses*, informed the general public of his mentor's death. "We can conceive of no tidings more painful to the Israelites of America," he wrote, "than the announcement of the death of Rev. Isaac Leeser."[49]

Leeser's funeral took place on Tuesday, February 4, at 10 A.M. It began at his residence at 1227 Walnut Street. "The attendance was extraordinarily large," Sulzberger reported. "Probably the majority of the Jewish male population of Philadelphia, and quite a number of Christians, clergymen, and others, were present."[50] Eleven friends were called upon to be pallbearers. His coffin was followed by five hundred members of B'nai B'rith and sixty carriages. "So lengthy was the cortege," it was reported, "that it was impossible for the eye to reach from one end to the other."[51]

Slowly and solemnly, the procession moved past the leading synagogues of Philadelphia, including Mickveh Israel, Beth Israel, and Rodeph Sholom. At Beth El Emeth, a large crowd had gathered, including "many of the ladies of his and other congregations." "A circuit was performed round the building with the corpse, and then . . . proceeded to the cemetery of the congregation Beth El Emeth." Along the way, the cortege passed the Jewish Hospital, "the inmates of which institution, who were well enough, followed the remains" to the nearby cemetery.[52]

The burial service was jointly conducted by Sabato Morais and the "Rev. Mr. Pereira," Leeser's interim replacement at Beth El Emeth. In attendance were "all the Jewish ministers" of Philadelphia, Rev. Jacques Judah Lyons (Shearith Israel, New York), and Rev. J. S. Jacobson (Washington, D.C.). A representation from the Board of Delegates of American Israelites and the various Philadelphia congregations also "attended as bodies." At Leeser's request, "there was no sermon or extra prayer, but ritual, as printed in the prayer-book, was strictly adhered to." "During the ceremony," Sulzberger observed, "the scene was truly affecting. Strong men wept like children, when they began to realize that they were about to lose forever their trusted and tried friend, and no panegyric could have expressed half so well the public sense of his worth as the involuntary tribute of the mourner's tears." Afternoon services were held at Beth El Emeth. Rev. Lyons officiated.[53]

Tributes and resolutions poured into the office of the *Occident* from all over the country. The most articulate, however, came from the pen of Mayer Sulzberger, who wrote movingly about his late friend and teacher in the March edition of the journal:

> More widely known than any other Jewish minister in the country, acquainted with more persons in different portions of the Union than probably any clergyman in the land, he had, by his speeches, his writings, and his presence, interwoven himself into the whole system of American Judaism. No intelligent Israelite could be found in this broad land, who had not read or used some of the works produced by his genius and enterprise, and the veriest dolt knew him by the reputation he had justly acquired. Nor was this confined to his co-religionists; for among our Christian fellow-citizens, his fame as an elegant writer, a deep thinker, a profound theologian, and a good man, was firmly established.[54]

Sulzberger ended his article with stirring words of high praise:

> We honestly believe, that since the great Mendelssohn, no one follower of the Law of Moses, either in Europe or America, has done so much and so successfully to vindicate Jacob's sacred inheritance when aspersed, to diffuse it when neglected, to promote its study when it had almost died out, as our lamented friend. There have been greater Talmudists, there may have been more eloquent orators and more graceful writers; but among them all, there has been no greater genius, no better Jew, and no purer man than Isaac Leeser.[55]

From Cincinnati, Isaac Mayer Wise reflected on the death of Isaac Leeser as a personal loss. "We can not write the biography of Isaac Leeser," Wise astutely observed, "without writing our own (a task which we do not like) because for the last twenty years we worked either with or against each other." "We had many a controversy publicly and privately, which did not sound very friendly," Wise continued, "nevertheless we never became so far estranged to each other, that we were not on speaking terms, or could not meet each other cordially on any occasion, because we never offered each other any personal insult, nor did we at any times disrespect each other."[56]

Wise pointed out that Leeser was "the banner-bearer" of traditional Judaism in America. "All the rest of their leaders are of local importance only," Wise wrote, "while he, by his literary efforts, his travels, his numerous acquaintances, his unfeigned attachment to his cause and his consistency, had a wide-spread influence. We know of no man in America who will replace Isaac Leeser in the Orthodox camp." Wise also praised Leeser for his honesty and tenacity: "He had a cause to plead, and he did it without fears or favors. He did not beg the favors of this or that order, this or that party, this or that man. He did not yield an inch to any body. He unfurled his true colors on every occasion."[57]

Leeser's will left no provision for a monument to be erected over his grave. Friends, however, wanted him to be properly memorialized, and on April 9, 1868, an ad hoc committee of five men circulated a broadside soliciting funds "in order to have the monument one that will be befitting the high and national standing of the deceased and which will redound to the credit of the Jewish people at large." The response was even better than expected, and plans were made for an impressive monument.[58]

On January 28, 1869, one year after Leeser's death, "a large concourse of friends" gathered in the cemetery of Beth El Emeth in West Philadelphia to dedicate "a handsome monument . . . on the remains of Rev. Isaac Leeser." Made of Italian marble and Pennsylvania bluestone, the monument "stands twenty-four feet high, and weighs nearly twelve tons." The inscription on the north side of the base is simple but elegant:

> Isaac Leeser; a Minister who devoted his whole life to the practice of the Religion which he taught: a Journalist, the vigor of whose pen was excelled only by the depth of his learning: an Author, who created a literature which spread his fame over two continents: a model Philanthropist: a sincere Jew.[59]

The executors of Leeser's estate quickly carried out his wishes. His books were given to the Hebrew Education Society. His personal effects were sold. Copyrights to his Bible were transferred to Abraham de Sola. Sulzberger also fulfilled his promise to continue the *Occident* through March 1869. Thereafter, the demands of his own career in law demanded that he stop working on the journal. After twenty-three years of continuous operation, the office of the *Occident* was closed for the last time, and with it an era in American Jewish history.[60]

CONCLUSION
The Living Legacy

*The history of American Judaism and that of
Isaac Leeser are one and the same.*
—Henry Samuel Morais,
Eminent Israelites of the Nineteenth Century, 1880

THE NATIONWIDE TRIBUTE PAID to Isaac Leeser after his death and the large gathering at his funeral clearly indicated the impact he had on his own generation. As we have seen with Isaac Mayer Wise, even several of his ideological opponents stepped forward to praise his sincerity as a Jew and his industriousness as a pioneer in building up American Judaism. As late as 1880, Henry Samuel Morais, son of Leeser's successor at Mickveh Israel, Sabato Morais, wrote in his *Eminent Israelites of the Nineteenth Century* that "there is probably no name so familiar to American Israelites, as that of Isaac Leeser; and none will ever say that the fame acquired was not justly earned." "In fact," Morais concluded, "the history of American Judaism and that of Isaac Leeser are one and the same."[1]

Isaac Leeser, it seemed, had gained a permanent place in the collective memory of American Jewry. His memory was invoked at the founding of Gratz (1897) and Dropsie (1909) colleges as well as at numerous commencement exercises at the Jewish Theological Seminary. A Sunday school in Philadelphia's Hebrew Education Society, a Jewish agricultural colony in Kansas, and even a child in the Solis-Cohen family were all named after him. The fiftieth anniversary of his death was a lead story in the American Jewish press in 1918, including,

245

remarkably, a monograph-length study by Henry Englander in *The Yearbook of the Central Conference of American Rabbis*, an important Reform publication.[2]

After 1920, however, awareness of the many contributions of Isaac Leeser to the cause of American Judaism began to diminish. Scholars paid scant attention to him for the next thirty years. Emily Solis-Cohen, a scion of a great Philadelphia Jewish family who was close to Leeser, twice unsuccessfully attempted to write his biography.[3] No great Jewish institutions were named after him. His Bible was widely replaced by the Jewish Publication Society's 1917 version, except for inexpensive editions that mainly circulated among East European immigrants. They knew very little about him and probably would not have been attracted to the highly Americanized mode of Orthodoxy he represented.[4] Religious and institutional continuity with the nineteenth-century American Jewish experience was primarily supplied by the growing Reform movement, which promoted memories of its own founders, especially Isaac Mayer Wise, about whom several books and many articles were written.[5]

The most active attempt to preserve the memory of Isaac Leeser was made by the elite of the Conservative movement. Several of Leeser's disciples, including Mayer Sulzberger, Solomon Solis-Cohen, and the young Cyrus Adler, were instrumental in the early development of the Jewish Theological Seminary. They frequently alluded to the profound effect Leeser had upon them as individuals. But it was not until after World War II that Conservative historians began to actively research their movement's claim that Leeser was a founder of the positive-historical school in America. Moshe Davis led the way in his brilliant 1951 study *The Shaping of American Judaism* (*Yahadut Amerika Be-Hitpathutah*) and his 1963 book *The Emergence of Conservative Judaism: The Historical School in 19th Century America*.[6] More recently, Orthodox scholars have also begun to assess, for the first time, the role of Leeser in the early history of Jewish traditionalism in American and have highlighted his struggle against Reform Judaism in the pre–Civil War era.[7]

Identifying Leeser with either the Conservative movement or contemporary Orthodoxy, however, is highly problematic. Although he sought a middle ground for American Judaism, Leeser was not a Conservative Jew. He firmly believed that an immutable Torah was revealed to the Jewish people on Sinai and that only an Orthodox approach to tradition was authentic, especially in the area of doctrine. To Leeser, the *Shulchan Aruch*, the great sixteenth-century code of Jewish law, was the unchallengeable standard for Jewish observance. On the other hand, his mode of Orthodoxy was very different from that of the East European Jews who began arriving in the United States in large numbers during the 1880s. Interested in the Americanization of Judaism, he downplayed traditional Talmudic study and instead emphasized the centrality of Bible-based homiletics as the intellectual basis for American Judaism. In sum, he represented an accomodationist mode of Orthodoxy that did not survive the nineteenth century. Thus, to associate Leeser with any one of contemporary American Judaism's major branches is to oversimplify the complex story of American Jewish denominationalism and to wrench Leeser out of his proper historical context.

Philadelphia-based scholars, on the other hand, have tended to stress the national role Leeser played in the historical development of American Jewry. Rabbi Bertram W. Korn, Maxine Schwartz Seller, and Maxwell Whiteman have consistently and correctly argued that Leeser was primarily concerned with broad issues affecting the American Jewish community although he did have strong local interests as well. Korn views Leeser as a great organizer of institutions (but also as a relatively unimportant and unoriginal religious thinker). Seller suggests that Leeser was the primary architect of the American Jewish community. Like Korn, she emphasizes Leeser's work as an institution builder as well as an early advocate of both interfaith cooperation and Zionism. Whiteman observes that Leeser helped create a class of national figures, mainly Philadelphians, who led American Jewry into the twentieth century. Abraham Hart, William B. Hackenburg, Moses Aaron Dropsie, Alfred T. Jones, Hyman Gratz, Mayer Sulzberger, and Solomon Solis-Cohen are but a few of the many in the "Philadelphia group" who were influenced by Leeser to work on behalf of the American Jewish community.[8]

The Philadelphia school is correct in viewing Leeser more as a national than as a local or denominational leader. He was the first person to fully appreciate the tremendous potential of the American Jewish community. In Leeser's opinion, the regenerative powers of America held special promise for Jews. American democracy afforded them an unprecedented claim to full civic equality. The rising cities and the expansive frontiers presented Jews with unrivaled economic opportunities. Disestablishment of religion allowed them the unparalleled opportunity to voluntarily create a great and unfettered Jewish community. Leeser fully expected that Judaism would enjoy a "great awakening" in America and become the most important diaspora community in the history of the Jewish people. To that end, he devoted his entire life's work.

247

When Leeser arrived in the United States in 1824, the American Jewish community was still a relatively unimportant outpost of Jewish life. Lay leaders in the community concentrated on local matters. The role of religious leaders was circumscribed and reduced to that of a mere functionary. Synagogues only promoted Jewish education for young children and attempts at original Jewish literature were rare and not encouraged by the American Jewish public. A permanent Jewish press had not yet developed, and communication among the various places of Jewish settlement was random. Finally, no sustained or coordinated effort was being made to protect and expand Jewish political rights in America. The community was small, weak, and basically uninterested in upgrading itself into a cohesive, dynamic center of Jewish life.

Unlike his contemporaries, Leeser did not view the condition of American Jews with indifference or limit his hopes for the American Jewish future. He believed that America was the place where Jews and Judaism could excel. Irreligion could be overcome. Apostasy would be eradicated, and an exciting modern Orthodoxy could be created on American soil. The Jewish future in Europe, Leeser maintained, was far less sanguine. Poverty, discrimination, obscurantism, and religious radicalism all blocked Jewish progress there. He was convinced that the future of Judaism was contingent on its development in the New World.

In many respects, Leeser anticipated the flowering of the American Jewish life of recent years. Immigration, especially at the beginning of the twentieth century, transformed the American Jewish community from a remote corner of the diaspora into the largest community in Jewish history. Jewish awakenings during the last quarter of the nineteenth century, the 1920s, and the post–World War II periods led to the development of a network of Jewish institutions and to a previously unimaginable degree of Jewish cultural creativity in the United States. As Leeser had hoped, America became a major center of Jewish life.

Leeser's contribution to the development of Jewish life in America was both deep and wide. Besides founding the Jewish press and providing the Jewish public with nearly all the basic books of Jewish life, he also sought to modernize Jewish religious leadership, education, and philanthropy. He believed that Jews needed to zealously protect and expand religious freedom in the United States and to work on behalf of Jews abroad. Cultural adaptation and modernization, Leeser repeat-

248

edly taught his generation, did not necessarily demand the reduction of Jewish life. Rather, social change could be harnessed and used to help create an exemplary Jewish community in the United States.

The key to Leeser's program for Judaism was to control acculturation and to use Americanization selectively to further Jewish communal interests. "Through the institutions and patterns he created," writes Maxine Schwartz Seller, "Leeser made it possible for the American Jews to affirm their Jewishness by participation in American cultural patterns and, conversely, to become Americanized through their participation in Jewish life."[9] American Jews, Leeser believed, could maintain their group identity, actively practice Judaism, and adopt the social customs of general American society.

Leeser found an appealing model for Jewish "church government" in the American political system. Beginning in the 1840s, he strongly and consistently advocated the idea that American synagogues should form a "federal" union while retaining their individual autonomy as congregations. The most important function of the proposed synagogue union would be to upgrade Jewish education in the United States and regulate Jewish religious life. A national *bet din*, in Leeser's opinion, also needed to be formed to handle all juridical matters yielded to it by the individual congregations. Furthermore, the court would be responsible for certifying the credentials of all religious leaders serving American synagogues.

Similarly, Leeser believed that the Americanist ideal of E *pluribus unum* ("Out of many, one") could specifically be applied to American Jewry. As Jews from throughout Central and Western Europe began arriving in the United States in soaring numbers between 1830 and 1953, the small, nearly homogeneous native American Jewish community was overwhelmed by ethnic diversity and conflict. Leeser, however, believed that from the complex mix of subethnic Jewish identities, a distinctively American Jew would emerge. The first step toward realizing that goal was the creation of a national Jewish ecclesiastical organization to regulate and upgrade Jewish religious life in the United States.

Although he failed to organize a national union of synagogues in 1841 or to persuade the founders of the Board of Delegates of American Israelites to become an ecclesiastical organization in 1859 and not limit itself to defense and informational functions, Leeser's dream of a national synagogue organization was ultimately realized in a modified form. Five years after he died, leaders of the Reform movement organized the Union of American Hebrew Congregations to help coordinate its activities and sponsor a rabbinic college. Subsequently, parallel

249

organizations were founded by the Conservative movement and modern Orthodox Jews. Today, the national synagogue organization is a distinctive feature of American Jewish life. While Leeser would have strenuously disagreed with organizing Jewish institutions along denominational lines, the basic idea for a national synagogue organization still must be traced back to him.[10]

In his own lifetime, Leeser was more successful in transforming the office of hazzan into a Jewish ministry than in uniting American synagogues. He believed that American Jews could never be adequately served either by inarticulate hazzan-schochetim or by traditional rabbis who were expert in Jewish law but unaccustomed to giving popular lectures on Judaism. American Jews, he felt, needed instruction on the doctrines and practices of Judaism. They needed inspirational words to sustain them in a society that was indifferent to Jewish corporate and religious needs. They needed to see exemplary Jews: modern, educated, and refined, but totally committed to the perpetuation of Judaism. A native Jewish ministry, trained at a Jewish seminary, Leeser believed, was essential to American Jewry's spiritual welfare.

The founding of Maimonides College in 1867 in Philadelphia capped Leeser's lifelong struggle to improve Jewish religious leadership in the United States. The school's premature collapse several years after his death does not, however, belittle its significance. Maimonides College established the basic model for rabbinic education in the United States. Its mere existence caused its ideological opponents, particularly in the Reform movement, to redouble their efforts to create a rabbinic school representative of their own view of Judaism. Furthermore, many of Maimonides College's supporters subsequently helped found the original Jewish Theological Seminary of America (1887) as well as the reorganized seminary (1902).

Modern rabbinic education was only one aspect of Leeser's plan for Jewish education in America. Perhaps his most cherished dream was to develop a Jewish day school system that would use modern pedagogical methods to provide its students with comprehensive Jewish and general educations both. The traditional heder and yeshiva were, in Leeser's opinion, totally out of place in America. On the other hand, public schools, which took root in American society during the course of Leeser's career, were, in his opinion, inimical to Jewish interests. He maintained that public schools weakened Jewish identity and undermined Jewish religious convictions. For Leeser, modern Jewish day schools were essential to the future of Judaism in America.

Leeser's philosophy of Jewish education, perhaps to a greater extent than any other area of his thought, exemplified his attitude toward both the advantages of modernization and the limits of Americaniza-tion. America provided Jews with a unique opportunity to improve Judaism without fear of governmental interference or social ostracism. Freedom of religion guaranteed the right of the American Jewish com-munity to educate its own children. He felt that Jews had an obligation to maximize the opportunity to create a generation of children who would be totally literate in Judaism and well prepared for life in a modern, democratic society.

Only a tiny fraction of Jewish parents, however, agreed with Leeser. An ever-growing majority of Jewish children were sent to pub-lic schools to receive their general education. Public education was widely viewed as the best agent for cultural adaptation and integration into the mainstream of American society. Thus, Jewish education was largely reduced to a supplementary activity. Not blind to the reality of his times, Leeser worked diligently to create a radically new way of transmitting tradition to the young.

The Jewish Sunday school movement began in Philadelphia in 1838 with the full support of Isaac Leeser. He maintained that it was better for a child to receive some, instead of no, Jewish education. He was convinced that by focusing its curriculum on Judaism's doctrines and the Bible, the Sunday school could provide a child with at least a satisfactory minimum of Jewish knowledge. He often went out of his way to defend the utility of the Sunday schools, especially to recently arrived German Jewish immigrants who viewed the Jewish Sunday school as an outrageous imitation of a Protestant tradition. By the time the Civil War ended, the majority of American Jews accepted the Sun-day school as the basic institution for elementary Jewish education in the United States. In the post–World War II era, however, a strong Jewish day school movement emerged in the United States, particularly among Orthodox Jews.[11]

Leeser's efforts to modernize Jewish philanthropic and welfare work also had a decided impact on American Jewish life. Living in an age of city building, he foresaw the development of a strong, voluntary Jewish polity in every great American urban center. He was one of the first to call for the centralization of both fund-raising and disburse-ments at the local level. He urged his contemporaries to build a wide array of Jewish social and welfare institutions including hospitals, or-phanages, and retirement homes. Like others of his generation, he strongly advocated training Jewish youth in various crafts to make them self-sufficient.

Moreover, he did not confine his program for the modernization of Jewish charity work to the United States. Relief work on behalf of the Jews of Palestine, he strongly believed, ought to be systematized, and a modern, self-supporting Jewish community needed to be developed in the Land of Israel. Although initially motivated by traditional Jewish restorationism, his practical and, later, nationalist approach to Jewish life in Palestine qualifies him as a leading American proto-Zionist. His 1866 prediction that America and Israel would emerge as the twin foci of Jewish life proved remarkably accurate.

The strength of the American Jewish community, Leeser correctly believed, rested on its ability to protect itself through legal and political channels. Although American Jews did not need to be emancipated like the Jews of Great Britain and Germany, they did have to fight to maintain and expand their rights. The majority of American Jews either assumed that the American legal system had a benign attitude toward Jews and Judaism or else were simply too frightened to protest any attempt to weaken the disestablishment of religion in the United States. Leeser, on the other hand, took on the role of watchdog over American Jewish rights. He believed that every attempt to enforce Sunday Laws, write Test Oaths, or pass "Christian nation" amendments could potentially undermine Jewish security in the United States. His basic position on church-state relations was that American Jews had a claim to a full equality of rights. Jews were not merely to be "tolerated" in the United States. They lived under the same laws and had the same privileges as everyone else.

Based on the same enlightened Mendelssohnian viewpoint, he also vigorously fought against Christian missionaries. Proselytizing Jews was, in his opinion, an action that fundamentally and flagrantly violated American egalitarianism. If all Americans are equal, he postulated, then no group has the right to constantly try to prove its superiority over another. However, this did not stop him from also positing theological challenges to Christianity. The Hebrew Bible carefully and correctly considered, he insisted, only upholds the veracity of Judaism.

Finally, Leeser held the conviction that American Jews had a special responsibility to protect the rights of Jews abroad and frequently appealed to the United States government to intervene on behalf of Jewish causes and individuals. "Liberty and justice for all" was a basic American belief, and Leeser wanted to make sure that it would be applied to Jews as well as other people. Despite the small size of the community and its lack of internal unity, he was able to mount several impressive campaigns during the course of his career. Today's sophisticated and effective Jewish political presence in Washington owes a great deal to the tenacity of Leeser in his pursuit of justice for Jews the world over.

The defense of Jewish rights at home and abroad provided Leeser with consensus issues within the Jewish community upon which he might have sought to unify American Jewry. As an Orthodox Jew, however, he could not separate his communal activities from his religious obligations. They were indivisible, and for Leeser religious duty was paramount. In his opinion, the only basis for Jewish unity was religion. Even in the face of widespread religious indifference and the development of a Reform movement, he continued to maintain that the "platform" of the Jewish people was the Maimonidean creed.

It is interesting to note that Leeser's primary objection to Reform Judaism was doctrinal and not practical in nature. The *Occident* was frequently filled with articles defending the traditional belief in the resurrection of the dead or the coming of a personal Messiah. By contrast, relatively little ink was spilled in discussions of mixed seating in the synagogue. Because liturgical reforms usually touched on deeper theological issues, they were dealt with at length. On the other hand, some nonessential reforms, especially the mode of fund-raising and even decorum, were acceptable if not desirable to Leeser. But as Orthodoxy continued to grow in the 1840s and 1850s and the polarization between reformers and traditionalists intensified, Leeser increasingly sided with tradition. Ultimately, the widening of the spectrum of American Jewish religious life made both religious conformity and communal unity impossible. His most cherished dream went unrealized.

Late in life, Leeser gravitated toward B'nai B'rith, then a secret Jewish fraternal organization. It was the first of America's many "secular synagogues." However, he did not view its program as the basis for a potential ideology for American Jews even though several of his pet projects greatly benefitted from B'nai B'rith funds. He was simply unwilling to accept the fact that religion was a divisive and not unifying force in American Jewish life.

Other factors that limited Leeser's impact on his own generation were more subjective. He was a difficult person. People were not naturally attracted to him. He was often defensive and argumentative. Similarly, his physical appearance worked against him. He was very short, nearly blind, and badly scarred by smallpox for most of his adult life. Finally, his literary style was far from felicitous and his argumentation often flawed by digression or lack of balance. He basically lived a hard, lonely life. His greatest comfort and his greatest source of tension came from his work, not from close friends or family.

Isaac Leeser was a remarkable human being. He was indefatigable in his drive to make Judaism flourish in the United States. He taught American Jews that they could be leaders in the wider Jewish world. He managed to influence the development of nearly every aspect of Jacksonian and antebellum Jewish life in the United states to the point where Henry Samuel Morais's observation that "the history of American Judaism and that of Isaac Leeser are one and the same" cannot be dismissed as hyperbole but is, in a very significant way, an accurate assessment of the American Jewish experience from the day Leeser first led a religious service at Mickveh Israel in 1829 to his death in Philadelphia in 1868.

Today, the American Jewish population is twenty-five times larger than when Leeser died. Tens of thousands of Jewish books have been written and published in America. Thousands of rabbis have been ordained in the United States. American Jews maintain approximately 2,500 synagogues. Scores of Jewish hospitals and retirement communities provide essential services to the Jewish and general communities. An active Jewish press keeps American Jews informed of news in their own communities and around the world. Jewish studies are taught in the most prestigious universities in the country. Jewish defense organizations carefully monitor judicial and legislative developments. In short, American Jews have created a thriving center of Judaism and Jewish culture in the United States.

But deep problems remain. Remarkably, many of them are the same ones that faced Leeser in his day. Only half of all Jewish children of school age receive any Jewish education. Ritual laxity remains a hallmark of American Jewish religious life. Denominationalism has become an accepted phenomenon, and clear, perhaps unmendable divisions exist among the various branches of American Judaism. Interfaith marriages are commonplace. It is even questionable that an "American Jewish community" can be legitimately discussed without the meaning of "community" being stretched beyond the borders of sociological theory and reality.

The long-term problems faced by American Jewry are the inevitable results of life in an open, democratic society. Perhaps they are not fully resolvable. A small ethnoreligious minority will always be torn between the poles of accommodation and resistance. Leeser suggested that a middle ground is possible and that both a dynamic Jewish community and a modernized version of Jewish religious Orthodoxy can flourish in American society. The great strengths of American Jewry today testify both to the efforts he made on its behalf more than twelve decades ago and to the viability of his dream for Jews and Judaism in the United States. In sum, Isaac Leeser, a poor orphan from rural Westphalia, was greatly responsible for the transformation and perpetuation of the Jewish heritage in America.

ABBREVIATIONS

AJA   American Jewish Archives
3101 Clifton Ave.
Cincinnati, Ohio 45220

AJA   *American Jewish Archives*

AJH   *American Jewish History*

AJHS   American Jewish Historical Society
2 Thornton Road
Waltham, Massachusetts 02154

AJHS-L   American Jewish Historical Society,
Leeser Papers

BB   Joseph L. Blau and Salo W. Baron, eds.
*The Jews of the United States, 1790–1840:
A Documentary History* (Philadelphia, 1975).

DIS   Isaac Leeser, *Discourses on the Jewish Religion*, 10 vols.
(Philadelphia, 1867).

D-L   Dropsie College (now Center for Judaic Studies, University of
Pennsylvania, Philadelphia). Leeser Collection.

EJ   *Encyclopedia Judaica* (Jerusalem, 1971).

256

ESC   Emily Solis-Cohen, unpublished manuscripts on Leeser.
                Copies at AJA and Annenberg Research Institute.

JE   *Jewish Encyclopedia* (New York, 1904).

JML   Isaac Leeser, *Jews and the Mosaic Law*
                (Philadelphia, 1834).

JRM-L   Jacob R. Marcus, Leeser Papers (private collection of negative
                photostats)

Morais   Henry Samuel Morais, *The Jews of Philadelphia* (Philadelphia,
                1894).

OCC   *The Occident and American Jewish Advocate*, 1843–1869. Isaac
                Leeser, editor.

PAJHS   *Publications of the American Jewish Historical Society*

WW   Edwin Wolf II and Maxwell Whiteman, *The History of the Jews
                of Philadelphia from Colonial Times to the Age of Jackson*
                (Philadelphia, 1956, 1975).

NOTES

INTRODUCTION

1. *WW*, 376–77.

2. Bertram W. Korn, "Isaac Leeser: Centennial Reflections," *AJA* 19 (1967):136.

3. Joseph Buchler, "The Struggle for Unity: Attempts at Union in American Jewish Life: 1654–1868," *AJA* 2 (1949): 21–46.

4. *OCC* 12 (1854): 412–13. On B'nai B'rith, see Julius Bien, "A History of the Independent Order of Bne B'rith," *Menorah* I–IV (July 1886–June 1889); Boris D. Bogen, "Historical Sketch of the B'nai B'rith," *B'nai B'rith Manual*, ed. Samuel S. Cohen (Cincinnati, Ohio, 1926); E. E. Grusd, *B'nai B'rith: The Story of a Covenant* (1966); Deborah Dash Moore, *B'nai B'rith and the Challenge of Ethnic Leadership* (Albany, N.Y., 1981).

5. *OCC* 11 (1854):589–602; Bertram W. Korn, "Judah Touro," *EJ* 15:1288–89; Leon Huhner, *The Life of Judah Touro, 1775–1854* (Philadelphia, 1946).

6. Jonathan D. Sarna, "Introduction: The American Rabbinate: A Centennial View," *AJA* 35 (1983):97. See also the bibliographies in Norman Linzer, ed., *Jewish Communal Services in the United States: 1960–1970* (New York, 1972), 128–248; Elliot L. Stevens, ed., *Rabbinic Authority: Papers Presented Before the Ninety-First Annual Convention of the Central Conference of American Rabbis* (New York, 1982), 111–18.

7. A partial listing of Leeser's literary works may be found in *PAJHS* 30 (1926): passim. On Leeser's sermons, see Robert V. Friedenberg, "Isaac Leeser: Pioneer Preacher of American Judaism," *Religious Communication Today* (September 1983):22–27. Friedenberg's article, however, contains several factual errors about Leeser's life.

8. On Leeser's educational activities, see David Urich Todes, "The History of Jewish Education in Philadelphia," doctoral thesis, Dropsie College, 1952, 43–56; Milton Feierstein, "Isaac Leeser: Founder of Jewish Education in the United States," doctoral thesis, SUNY-Buffalo, 1971. More broadly, see Lloyd P. Gartner, *Jewish Education*

in the United States: A Documentary History (New York, 1969; Judah Pilch, ed., *A History of Jewish Education in the United States* (New York, 1969). On Leeser's role in founding the first Jewish Publication Society in America, see Solomon Grayzel, "The First American Jewish Publication Society," *Jewish Book Annual* (1944–45).

9. On the Jewish community of Philadelphia, 1830–70, see *Morais*, passim.

10. Maxine S. Seller, "Isaac Leeser, Architect of the American Jewish Community," doctoral thesis, University of Pennsylvania, 1965, 136–75. On the Damascus Affair, see Joseph Jacobs, "The Damascus Affair of 1840 and the Jews of America," *PAJHS* 10 (1902): 119; Jonathan D. Sarna, *Jacksonian Jew: The Two Worlds of Mordecai Noah* (New York, 1981), 123–25, 200, n. 11, 13. On American Jews and the rise of public schools, see Lloyd P. Gartner, "Temples of Liberty Unpolluted: American Jews and Public Schools, 1840–1875," in *A Bicentennial Festschrift for Jacob Rader Marcus*, ed. Bertram W. Korn (New York, 1976), 157–90.

11. Leeser is neither mentioned in Sydney E. Ahlstrom, *A Religious History of the American People* (New York, 1975), nor listed in Frank Freidel, *Harvard Guide to American History* (Cambridge, Mass., 1974). A brief biography of him by Cyrus Adler appears in the *Dictionary of American Biography*.

CHAPTER ONE

1. For the first critical biography of Leeser, see Henry Englander, "Isaac Leeser, 1806–1868," *Central Conference of American Rabbis' Yearbook* 28 (1918): 213–52.

2. Maxwell Whiteman, "The Legacy of Isaac Leeser," in *Jewish Life in Philadelphia, 1830–1940*, ed. Murray Friedman (Philadelphia, 1983), 26.

3. H. H. Ben-Sasson, "The Middle Ages," in *A History of the Jewish People*, ed. H. H. Ben-Sasson (Cambridge, Mass., 1976), 394; "Westphalia," *EJ* 16:473–75, including bibliography; and Diethard Aschoff, "Geschichte original Beispal der Stadt Münster 5: Die Juden," n.d., copy at Leo Baeck Institute (New York). Otto's "Jewish policy" typified his use of the church as a counterweight to the independence of the great dukes. The alliance of the emperor and the Church was perpetuated by his successors. When Duke Henry the Lion of Saxony fell under the ban of the empire in 1180 and his duchy was divided, the archbishop of Cologne received lands that became the Duchy of Westphalia. The new duchy was awarded a constitution of its own and was governed for the archbishop by a marshall. This system lasted until 1803.

4. Selma Stern, *The Court Jew: A Contribution to the History of the Period of Absolutism* (Philadelphia, 1950), 179–83. On Jewish self-government, see Louis Finkelstein, *Jewish Self-Government in the Middle Ages* (New York, 1964), and Jacob R. Marcus, *The Jew in the Medieval World—A Source Book: 315–1791* (New York, 1974).

5. Michael A. Meyer, *The Origins of the Modern Jew: Jewish Identity in European Culture in Germany, 1749–1824* (Detroit, 1967), 13.

6. Stern, *Court Jew*, 182–83.

7. "Münster," *EJ* 12:504–505.

8. Herman Pollack, *Jewish Folkways in Germanic Lands (1648–1806): Studies in Aspects of Daily Life* (Cambridge, Mass., 1971), xvi. More broadly, see Jacob Katz, *Tradition and Crisis: Jewish Society at the End of the Middle Ages* (New York, 1977).

9. Mayer Sulzberger, "The Late Rev. Isaac Leeser," *OCC* 25:594. Republished in *AJA* 21 (November 1969): 140–48. On the *Haskalah*, see Meyer, *Origins*, 11–56, and Alexander Altmann, *Moses Mendelssohn: A Biographical Study* (Philadelphia, 1973).

10. Quoted in "Assembly of Jewish Notables," *EJ* 3:764. See also Simeon J. Maslin, *An Analysis and Translation of Selected Documents of Napoleonic Jewry* (Cincinnati, 1957), and Arthur Hertzberg, *The French Enlightenment and the Jews: The Origins of Modern Anti-Semitism* (New York, 1970).

11. "Westphalia," *EJ* 16:474. Censuses of Westphalian Jewry, 1821–1950, are reported in Arno Herzig, *Judentum und Emanzipation in Westphalen* (Münster, 1973), 62–65.

12. Jacob R. Marcus, *Israel Jacobson: The Founder of the Reform Movement in Judaism* (Cincinnati, 1972), reprinted from *Yearbook of Central Conference of American Rabbis* 30 (1928). See also David Philipson, *The Reform Movement in Judaism* (New York, 1907), 17–26.

13. Marcus, *Jacobson*, 52–105.

14. W. Gunther Plaut, *The Rise of Reform Judaism: A Sourcebook of its European Origins* (New York, 1963), 27–31. On opposition to Jacobson's reforms, see Marcus, *Jacobson*, 96–97; Mordecai Eliav, *Jewish Education in Germany During the Enlightenment and Emancipatory Periods* (in Hebrew; Jerusalem, 1960), 125; and Bernhard Brilling, "Das judische Schulweiser in Westfalia in 19. Jh.," *Udim* 5 (1974–75): 13.

15. Paul R. Mendes-Flohr and Jehuda Reinharz, eds., *The Jew in the Modern World, A Documentary History* (New York, 1980), 101–102, and especially item 19, 129. See also Jacob Katz, "The Term Jewish Emancipation: Its Origins and Historical Impact," in *Studies in Nineteenth Century Jewish Intellectual History*, ed. Alexander Altmann (Cambridge, Mass., 1964), 1–25.

16. "Germany," *EJ* 7:477; and Meyer, *Origins*, 182.

17. *BB* xvii–xxiii, 1–94.

18. Malcolm H. Stern, *Americans of Jewish Descent: A Compendium of Genealogy* (New York, 1971), 109. Stern incorrectly identifies Hyman as Leeser's father. Leeser's tombstone, located in West Philadelphia, names Uri as his father.

19. *ESC* 24 n.p. On "grandmother's religion," see *OCC* 25:538.

20. *OCC* 22:233 and 24:316–22.

21. Samuel Leeser to Isaac Leeser, Berlin to Philadelphia, October 6, 1847, JRM-L

22. *ESC*, n.p. Abraham Leeser to Isaac Leeser, Alpen to Philadelphia, March 1844, and Rehine to Philadelphia, August [?], JRM-L.

23. Samuel Leeser to Isaac Leeser, Berlin to Philadelphia, October 6, 1847, JRM-L.

24. *JML*, 239–40.

25. Leeser and his sister, Leah, corresponded on a regular basis. Leah and Tzvi-Hirsch Elkus, Denekamp, Holland to Philadelphia, June 16, 1834; September 29, 1835; February 10, 1849; June 18, 1849; July 12, 1853; April 12, 1855; June 30, 1862; July 28, 1863; JRM-L.

26. Lipman Leeser to Isaac Leeser, Dulmen to Philadelphia, March 21, 1833; Jacob Leeser to Isaac Leeser, Dulmen to Philadelphia, February 1827, JRM-L.

27. *DIS* 2:34.

28. Emily Solis-Cohen maintains that Leeser was four years old when he moved to Dulmen, n.p. Moshe Davis suggests that Leeser was already eight in *The Emergence of Conservative Judaism: The Historical School in Nineteenth Century America* (New York, 1963), 347.

29. *JML*, 233.

30. *OCC* 4:190; and Meyer Waxman, *A History of Jewish Literature* (New York, 1933, 1960), 2:635.

31. *OCC* 25:537.

32. *JML*, iii. The original manuscript of *Jews and the Mosaic Law* (Richmond, 1829, holograph) is simply dedicated to "Rabbi Cohen," D-L.

33. *OCC* 18:274.

34. Davis, *Conservative Judaism*, 347.

35. "Ezekiel ben Judah Landau," *EJ* 10:1388–91.

36. *DIS* 1:114, and *OCC* 4:190. On *The Vintage of Ephraim,* see Israel Bettan, *Studies in Jewish Preaching* (Cincinnati, 1939), 273–316.

37. Jakob J. Petuchowski, "Manuals and Catechism of the Jewish Religion in the Early Period of Emancipation," in Altmann, *Studies,* 48.

38. Herman Pollack, *Jewish Folkways,* 56.

39. Moshe Davis, *The Shaping of American Judaism* (in Hebrew, New York, 1951), 13–14.

40. Eliav, *Jewish Education,* 124–25.

41. Bernhard Brilling, "Das jüdische Schulweiser in Westfalen," 18.

42. Lawrence Grossman, "Isaac Leeser's Mentor: Rabbi Abraham Sutro, 1784–1869," in *Rabbi Joseph Lookstein Memorial Volume,* ed. Leo Landman (New York, 1980), 156. See also his "Tradition Under Fire: Isaac Leeser and Reform," *Gesher* 8 (1981/5741): 51–64; "Beitrage zur Biographie des letzer Landrabbiners von Münster, Abraham Sutro (1784–1869)," *Udim* 3 (1972): 31–64; and "Konsistoriums des Israeliten in Kassel an die Rabbiner Abraham Sutro und Marcus Baek Adler (1809–1812)," *Udim* 4 (1974): 39–57. A small collection of Sutro papers is housed at the Leo Baeck Institute (New York).

43. Brilling, "Jüdische Schulweiser," 15–19.

44. *DIS* 1:iii.

45. *OCC* 18:274.

46. Ibid.

47. *DIS* 1:iii.

48. *JML,* 67. On Sutro, see *OCC* 19:333.

49. Brilling, "Jüdische Schulweiser," 19.

50. Isaac Leeser to Abraham Sutro, Richmond to Münster, November 1825; Abraham Sutro to Isaac Leeser, Münster to Richmond, September 1829; Esther Sutro to Isaac Leeser, Münster to Philadelphia, July 17, 1864; Esther Sutro Faber to Isaac Leeser, Ochtending (near Koblenz) to Philadelphia, October 19, 1865; and Esther Sutro Faber to Isaac Leeser, Ochtending (?) to Philadelphia, December 2, 1866; negative photostatic copies, JRM-L. Mayer Sulzberger called Sutro Leeser's "constant friend" in *Isaac Leeser* (pamphlet, Philadelphia, 1881), 4.

51. *OCC* 25:538.

52. *JML,* 237–40.

53. *DIS* 2:396–97. Emily Solis-Cohen suggests that the benefactor was Rabbi Benjamin Cohen. This is plausible. See Benjamin (Katz?) to Isaac (Leeser?), Dulmen to Münster, December 1827, negative photostatic copy, JRM-L.

54. W. Engelkemper, "University of Münster," *Catholic Encyclopedia* (New York, 1911), 10:639. See also Maxine Seller, "Isaac Leeser: A Jewish-Christian Dialogue in Ante-Bellum Philadelphia," *Pennsylvania History* 35 (July 1968): 231–42.

55. *OCC* 10:524.

56. Noah H. Rosenbloom, *Tradition in an Age of Reform: The Religious Philosophy of Samson Raphael Hirsch* (Philadelphia, 1967), 56–65.

57. *JML,* 243. Original copies of Leeser's school notebooks can be found in the Leeser Papers at Dropsie College.

58. Quoted in *ESC.*

59. *JML,* 243.

60. "Alexander Haindorf," *EJ* 7:1141; Mordecai Eliav, *Jewish Education,* 286, 295–96, 310; and Diethard Aschoff, *Geschichte Original,* 7.

61. *JML,* iii.

62. Chaim Leeser to Isaac Leeser, Dulmen to Richmond, October 15, 1829,

negative photostatic copy, JRM-L. Chaim writes: "For a year now I have been at Mün-ster, where I hope to train myself in the Haindorf School to be a teacher. My studies and teachers will be: (1) Religion—Cohen, (2) Botany—Hackerdorff, (3) Pedagogy—Pickarius-Annagarn, (4) Mathematics-Schuler, (5) German composition and lan-guage—Pickarius-Annagarn, (6) Hebrew—Cohen, (7) French—Beidelbe, (8) Biblical History—Schuler, (9) German History—Pickarius-Annagarn, (10) Geography—Pickarius-Annagarn, (11) Penmanship—Cohen, (12) Logic—Antonio, (13) Drawing—Michaelis. The course is four years. I hope that all this study will contribute to the education of the youth of our people."

63. Diethard Aschoff, "Geschichte Original," 7.

64. Joseph L. Blau, *Modern Varieties of Judaism* (New York, 1966), 83.

65. *OCC* 10:524, and *JML*, 244.

66. Rosa Mordecai, "Personal Recollections of Rev. Isaac Leeser" (typescript, Washington, D.C., 1901). Englander Papers, *AJA*, 1–2.

67. Rehine's letter to Leeser is not extant. It is probable that he wrote to his nephew toward the end of 1823 and no later than January 1824. Leeser left Germany in February 1824.

68. E. Gans to Mordecai Manuel Noah, Berlin to New York, June 1, 1822, repub-lished in Morris U. Schappes, *A Documentary History of the Jews in the United States, 1654–1875* (New York, 1950), 159–60. More broadly, see Jonathan D. Sarna, *Jacksonian Jew: The Two Worlds of Mordecai Noah* (New York, 1981), 64–65.

69. Maldwyn Allen Jones, *American Immigration* (Chicago, 1960), 92–116. See also Oscar Handlin, *The Uprooted: The Epic Story of the Great Migrations That Made the American People* (Boston, 1951, 1973).

70. Quoted in *ESC*, n.p.

71. *OCC* 5:218, 11:355.

72. *DIS* 3:341, *OCC* 7:332.

73. Grossman, "Abraham Sutro," 151–52.

74. *JML*, vi. On the general nature of Jewish immigration and its role in shaping Judaism in the United States, see Arthur Hertzberg, *The Jews in America: Four Centuries of an Uneasy Encounter: A History* (New York, 1989).

CHAPTER TWO

1. Malcolm H. Stern, "The 1820's: American Jewry Comes of Age," in *A Bicen-tennial Festschrift for Jacob Rader Marcus*, ed. Bertram W. Korn (New York, 1976), 546.

2. *OCC* 10:163.

3. On John Quincy Adams, see Samuel F. Bemis, *John Quincy Adams*, 2 vols. (New York, 1949–56). On the Election of 1824, see James F. Hopkins, "Election of 1824," in *History of American Presidential Elections, 1789–1968*, ed. Arthur M. Schle-singer, Jr., and Fred L. Israel, vol. 1 (New York, 1971).

4. Marvin Meyers, *The Jacksonian Persuasion: Politics and Beliefs* (Stanford, Calif., 1957, 1960), 5, passim; Edward Pessen, *Jacksonian America* (Homewood, Ill., 1969).

5. John Ward, *Andrew Jackson: Symbol for an Age* (New York, 1955). Jacksonian-era historiography is particularly rich. See Frank O. Gatell, "The Jacksonian Era, 1824–1848," in *The Reinterpretation of American History and Culture*, ed. William H. Cart-wright and Richard L. Watson (Washington, D.C., 1973), 309–26.

6. Tyler Gregory Anbinder, *Nativism and Slavery: The Northern Know Nothings and the Politics of the 1850's* (New York, 1992); *Voting and the Spirit of American Democ-racy: Essays on the History of Voting and Voting Rights in America* (Urbana, Ill., 1992); Harry L. Watson, *Liberty and Power: The Politics of Jacksonian America*, 1st ed. (New

York, 1990); Marvin Meyers, *The Jacksonian Persuasion: Politics and Belief* (Stanford, Cal., 1968); Robert Vincent Remini, *The Age of Jackson* (New York, 1972); Arthur M. Schlesinger, Jr., *The Age of Jackson* (Boston, 1948); Edwin Charles Rozwenc, ed., *The Meaning of Jacksonian Democracy* (Boston, 1963); Carl N. Degler, *Out of Our Past: The Forces That Shaped Modern America*, rev. ed. (New York, 1959, 1970), 135–43.

7. Carl Bode, *The American Lyceum, Town Meeting of the Mind* (New York, 1956); Kenneth Walter Cameron, *The Massachusetts Lyceum During the American Renaissance: Materials for the Study of the Oral Tradition in American Letters* (Hartford, Conn., 1969); Willis D. Moreland, *Pioneers in Adult Education* (Chicago, 1985); Burke Aaron Hinsdale, *Horace Mann and the Common School Revival in the United States* (New York, 1898); Joseph Mayer Rice, *The Public-School System of the United States* (New York, 1969).

8. Alexis de Tocqueville, *Democracy in America*, ed. Phillips Bradley (New York, 1945), 1:303. On religion in American society, 1800–1830, see William G. McLoughlin, *Revivals, Awakenings, and Reform* (Chicago, 1978), 98–140; Donald G. Matthews, "The Second Great Awakening as an Organizing Process, 1780–1830: An Hypothesis," *American Quarterly* 21 (1969): 23–43. See also Winthrop S. Hudson, *Religion in America: An Historical Account of the Development of American Religious Life* (New York, 1965, 1973), 109–206; Sydney E. Ahlstrom, *A Religious History of the American People*, 2 vols. (Garden City, N.Y., 1972, 1975).

9. *JML*, 77–78.

10. *DIS* 6:185–88.

11. Schlesinger, *Age of Jackson*, 360.

12. *OCC* 12:561.

13. *OCC* 16:255; 17:185–86.

14. *DIS* 4:42.

15. Isaac Leeser, "Memorial at the Sunday School for Religious Instruction of Israelites in Philadelphia" (Philadelphia, 1840), 5–8, reprinted in *BB* 2:447–51. Also, see Lance J. Sussman, "Isaac Leeser and the Protestantization of American Judaism," *AJA* 38 (1986): 1–21.

16. Stern, "1820's," 539. For an excellent survey of the German period in American Jewish history, see Hasia R. Diner, *A Time for Gathering: The Second Migration, 1820–1880* (Baltimore, 1992).

17. Leon Jick, *The Americanization of the Synagogue: 1820–1870* (Waltham, Mass., 1978), 15–27.

18. Jonathan D. Sarna, *Jacksonian Jew* (New York, 1980), 61–76.

19. Hyman B. Grinstein, *The Rise of the Jewish Community of New York, 1654–1860* (Philadelphia, 1947), 58–80; *BB* 2:513–39; Jick, *Americanization*, 44–57. On the general nature of American Jewish leadership, see Jonathan D. Sarna, "The Spectrum of Jewish Leadership in Ante-Bellum America," *Journal of American Ethnic History* 1 (1982): 59–67.

20. Jonathan D. Sarna, "Introduction—The American Rabbinate: A Centennial View," *AJA* 35 (1983): 97. Also see the bibliographies in *Jewish Communal Services in the United States: 1960–1970* ed. Norman Linzer (New York, 1972), 128–248; *Rabbinic Authority: Papers Presented Before the Ninety-First Annual Convention of the Central Conference of American Rabbis* ed. Elliot L. Stevens (New York, 1982), 111–18.

21. Grinstein, *New York*, 81–102.

22. Jacob Rader Marcus, *The Handsome Young Priest in the Black Gown: The Personal World of Gershom Seixas* (Cincinnati, 1970), repr. from *Hebrew Union College Annual* 40–41 (1969–70).

23. Marcus, *Seixas*, 5.

24. On the Reformed Society of Israelites, see Lance J. Sussman, "Isaac Harby, Leadership and the Liturgy of the Reformed Society of Israelites, 1824–1833: A Reevaluation," typescript (*AJA*, 1979); Lou Silberman, "American Impact: Judaism in the United States in the Early Nineteenth Century," B. G. Rudolph Lecture in Judaic Studies, Syracuse, N.Y. 1964; Barnett A. Elzas, *The Reformed Society of Israelites: History and Constitution* (New York, 1916); L. C. Moise, *Biography of Isaac Harby with an Account of the Reformed Society of Israelites, 1824–1833* (Macon, Ga., 1931). On Harby, see the forthcoming Ph.D. dissertation by Rabbi Gary Zola (HUC-JIR). On Jewish life in Charleston, see James William Hagy, *This Happy Land: The Jews of Colonial and Antebellum Charleston* (Tuscaloosa, Ala., 1993).

25. *OCC* 9:210–11.

26. "Constitution of Mickveh Israel," Article II (Philadelphia, 1823); Jick, *Americanization*, 20–27.

27. Jick, *Americanization*, 15.

28. Grinstein, *New York*, 472–74.

29. Myron Berman, *Richmond's Jewry: 1769–1976, Shabbat in Shockoe* (Charlottesville, Va., 1979); Herbert T. Ezekiel and Gaston Lichtenstein, *The History of the Jews of Richmond: 1769–1917* (Richmond, Va., 1917).

30. Ezekiel, *Richmond*, 13–20.

31. Ibid., 238.

32. Ibid., 238–40; Berman, *Richmond*, 36–39.

33. Berman, *Richmond*, 101.

34. Ibid., 101–102.

35. Ibid., 64.

36. Ezekiel, *Richmond*, 238.

37. *OCC* 7:226; Berman, *Richmond*, 78.

38. Ezekiel, *Richmond*, 37–40.

39. Ibid., 72–75.

40. John C. Emmerson, *Chesapeake Affair of 1807* (Portsmouth, Va., 1954).

41. Ezekiel, *Richmond*, 72–75.

42. Joseph R. Rosenbloom, *Biographical Dictionary of Early American Jews: Colonial Ties to 1800* (Lexington, Ky., 1960), passim. On Leeser's private reading, see Maxwell Whiteman, "Isaac Leeser and the Jews of Philadelphia: A Study in National Jewish Influence," *PAJHS* 48 (1959): 218 n. 65: "Zalma Rehine presented Thomas Jefferson Randolph's *Memoir, Correspondence, and Miscellanies from the Papers of Thomas Jefferson* (4 vols.) (Charlottesville, Va., 1829) to Leeser while he was still in Richmond. Samson Levy's copy of Jefferson's *Notes on the State of Virginia* (Philadelphia, 1794) was acquired by Leeser in Philadelphia. These are in the Dropsie College Library." See also Cyrus Adler, *Catalogue of Leeser Library* (Philadelphia, 1883).

43. *DIS* 3:346.

44. Jacob Mordecai to Congregation Mickveh Israel, Richmond to Philadelphia, June 15, 1824, in *BB* 2:585.

45. David and Tamar de Sola Pool, *An Old Faith in the New World: Portrait of Shearith Israel, 1654–1954* (New York, 1955), 176–78.

46. Berman, *Richmond*, 120–25. Copy of Jacob Mordecai's "Remarks to Isaac Harby" can be found at *AJA*.

47. Quoted in Ezekiel, *Richmond*, 24–25.

48. Ibid., 23. See also Stanley F. Falk, "The Warrenton Female Academy of Jacob Mordecai, 1809–1818," *North Carolina Historical Review* 35 (1958): 281–98; Lance J. Sussman, "'Our Little World': The Early Years at Warrenton," typescript (*AJA*, 1974);

Edgar E. MacDonald, *The Education of the Heart: The Correspondence of Rachel Mordecai Lazarus and Maria Edgeworth* (Chapel Hill, N.C., 1977).

49. Berman, *Richmond*, 37.

50. *OCC* 10:162–67.

51. Gershom Kursheedt (1817–63) was born in Richmond and later settled in New Orleans. He was an early lay leader in the New Orleans Jewish community. Leeser and Kursheedt corresponded frequently. Many of Kursheedt's letters are still extant (D-L). Leeser published many of Kursheedt's reports in the *Occident*. See also David de Sola Pool, "Some Relations of Gershom Kursheedt and Sir Moses Montefiore," *PAJHS* 37 (1947): 213; Bertram W. Korn, *The Early Jews of New Orleans* (Waltham, Mass., 1969).

52. Pages from Leeser's diary can be found in the Leeser Papers at Dropsie College.

53. *DIS* 10:322n. Mayer Sulzberger edited vols. 9 and 10 of the *Discourses*. See also *DIS* 9:258.

54. Letter of Exemption from Military Service, April 13, 1826, D-L.

55. Isaac Leeser to Theodore Seixas, Elul 28, 5587 (August 1827), Richmond to New York, JRM-L.

56. *DIS* 10:322n. In his letter to Seixas, Leeser talks about his "last communication to the *New York* [probably *Richmond*] *Compiler*." Emily Solis-Cohen maintains: "He first launched into print in 1826 over a pen name. It was a letter refuting a defamatory statement about the Jews. 'Surprised by an acquaintance, I came out of the newspaper office,' he recorded, 'I acknowledged my temerity with burning cheeks.' "

57. *JML*, v.

58. *JML*, 220. "Joseph Wolff," *EJ* 16:611–12.

59. Rebecca Gratz to Maria G. Gratz, Philadelphia to Lexington, Ky., November 5, 1837, reprinted in *Letters of Rebecca Gratz*, ed. David Philipson (Philadelphia, 1929), 244–47.

60. Jonathan D. Sarna, "The American Jewish Response to Nineteenth-Century Christian Missions," *Journal of American History* 68 (1981): 36–38.

61. Jonathan D. Sarna, "The Freethinker, the Jews and the Missionaries: George Houston and the Mystery of *Israel Vindicated*," *AJS Review* 5 (1980): 101–114.

62. George L. Berlin, "Solomon Jackson's *The Jew*: An Early American Jewish Response to the Missionaries," *AJH* 71 (1981–82): 10–28; and his "Joseph S. C. F. Frey, The Jews and Early Nineteenth Century Millenarianism," *Journal of the Early Republic* 1 (Spring 1981): 27–50. On the American Jewish press in general, see Robert Singerman, "The American Jewish Press, 1823–1983; A Bibliographical Survey of Research and Studies," *AJH* 73 (1984): 422–44.

63. Sarna, "American Jewish Response," 39.

64. *JML*, 237.

65. Ibid., 238.

66. Quoted in Ezekiel, *Richmond*, 55–56.

67. "John Hampden Pleasants," *DAB* 8:7–8; and *Richmond Portraits in an Exhibition of Makers of Richmond, 1737–1860* (Richmond, Va., 1949), 155–56. On the rise of the Whig Party, see D. W. Howe, *The Political Culture of American Whigs* (Chicago, 1979).

68. Leeser strongly opposed dueling: see *DIS* 6:7–8. See also Maxwell Whiteman, "The Legacy of Isaac Leeser," 28.

69. *JML*, 246. An interesting example of contemporary interest in Jews and Judaism is found in Frances Trollope's *Domestic Manners of the Americas* (New York, 1960), which describes her visit to America, 1827–32: "The whole people appear to be

divided into an almost endless variety of religious factions; I was told in Cincinnati that to be well received in society it was indispensably necessary to declare that you belonged to some one of these factions—it did not matter much which—as far as I could make out, the Methodists were considered as the most pious, the Presbyterians as the most powerful, the Episcopalians and the Catholics as the most genteel, the Universalists as the most liberal, the Swedenborgians as the most musical, the Unitarians as the most enlightened, the Quakers as the most amiable, the dancing Shakers the most amusing, and the Jews the most interesting." See also Stern, "1820s," 545.

70. *JML*, 253.
71. Ibid., vi.
72. Ibid.
73. Jacob Mordecai to Raphael de Cordova, Richmond to Philadelphia, June 10, 1824, quoted in *ESC*.
74. *JML*, vi.
75. Ibid., iv.
76. Ibid., v.
77. Ibid.; and original manuscript (holograph) of *JML*, D-L.
78. John H. Pleasants to Isaac Leeser, Beaverdam, Va., to Philadelphia, August 27, 1829, D-L.
79. *JML*, vii.
80. Ibid., 21, 207.
81. Ibid., 7.
82. Ibid.
83. Ibid., 8.
84. Ibid., 9.
85. Ibid., 13.
86. Ibid., 21, 23. Leeser equated "Holy Spirit" with "inspiration" or "the endowment of superior knowledge proceeding from God as a special gift," 137.
87. Ibid., 65.
88. Ibid., 156.
89. Ibid., 177–78.
90. Ibid., 195–96.
91. See n. 73 above.
92. Raphael de Cordova to Isaac Leezer (sic), Philadelphia to Richmond, June 29, 1829, Korn Papers, AJA.
93. Isaac Leeser to Parnass and Members of Mickveh Israel, Philadelphia, May 15, 1840, typescript copy at AJA and Dropsie College.
94. *ESC*, 119.
95. *OCC* 7:614.

CHAPTER THREE
1. Sam Bass Warner, *The Private City: Philadelphia in Three Periods of its Growth* (Philadelphia, 1968), 5.
2. Michael Feldberg, *The Philadelphia Riots of 1844: A Study of Ethnic Conflict* (Westport, Conn., 1975), 12. Also, see his *Turbulent Era: Riot and Disorder in Jacksonian America* (New York, 1980).
3. Warner, *Private City*, 125.
4. Ibid., 49–50, 61.
5. Jacques I. Lyons and Abraham de Sola, *A Jewish Calendar for Fifty Years* (Montreal, 1854).

6. Murray Friedman, "Introduction: The Making of a National Jewish Community," in *Jewish Life in Philadelphia: 1830–1940* (Philadelphia, 1983), 2.

7. *WW*, 114.

8. Ibid., 41–42.

9. Ibid., 58–59, 117; *Morais*, 11.

10. *WW*, 76–113; Max Kohler, *Haym Solomon: The Patriot Broker of the Revolution* (New York, 1931); Samuel Rezneck, *Unrecognized Patriots: The Jews in the American Revolution* (Westport, Conn., 1975).

11. *WW*, 121.

12. *Morais*, passim.

13. *BB* l:xx suggests that the kosher food was actually provided by the public committee in charge of the event and not by an ad hoc committee of Philadelphia Jews. See also Morton Borden, *Jews, Turks and Infidels* (Chapel Hill, N.C. 1984), 23–51; Jonathan D. Sarna, "The Impact of the American Revolution on American Jews," *Modern Judaism* 1 (September 1981): 149–60.

14. On the Phillips family, see Joseph R. Rosenbloom, *A Biographical Dictionary of Early American Jews: Colonial Times through 1800* (Lexington, Ky., 1960); Sarna, *Jacksonian Jew*, 1–3; *Morais*, 567; Grinstein, *New York*, passim; Samuel Rezneck, *The Saga of an American Jewish Family Since the Revolution: A History of the Family of Jonas Phillips* (Washington, D.C., 1980).

15. *Morais*, 49.

16. *WW*, 360–71.

17. Ibid., 253.

18. *Morais*, 44, 46.

19. *OCC* 2:314.

20. Quoted in *ESC*, JRM-L.

21. John Hampden Pleasants to Isaac Leeser, Richmond to Philadelphia, August 27, 1829, D-L.

22. *Morais*, 45–46.

23. Quoted in *JE* 7:663.

24. Isaac Leeser to K.K.M.I., September 7, 1829, quoted in K.K.M.I. Minutebook, typescript, D-L.

25. Zalma Rehine to Isaac Leeser, Richmond to Philadelphia, October 14, 1829, D-L.

26. Isaac Leeser to K.K.M.I., May 15, 1840, D-L and AJA.

27. On Rebecca Gratz see Jacob R. Marcus, *The American Jewish Woman: A Documentary History* (New York, 1981), 87; Joseph R. Rosenbloom, "Rebecca Gratz and the Jewish Sunday School Movement in Philadelphia," *PAJHS* 48 (1958): 71; and his *And She Had Compassion* (D.H.L. thesis, HUC-JIR, 1957). See also Diane Ashton's Ph.D. thesis (Temple University).

28. Rebecca Gratz to Maria Gist Gratz, Philadelphia to Lexington, Ky., November 4, 1829, quoted in *Letters of Rebecca Gratz* (Philadelphia, 1929), 108.

29. Rebecca Gratz to Maria Gist Gratz, Philadelphia to Lexington, Ky., April 30, 1830, quoted in Bertram W. Korn, "Isaac Leeser: Centennial Reflections," 132.

30. Rebecca Gratz to Maria Gist Gratz, Philadelphia to Lexington, Ky., August 9, 1831, quoted in Philipson, *Letters*, 132–33.

31. Rebecca Gratz to Maria Gist Gratz, Philadelphia to Lexington, Ky., December 16, 1838, quoted in Philipson, *Letters*, 257.

32. *OCC* 2:318.

33. Louis Jacobs, "Preaching," *EJ* 13:1002–1006; Israel Bettan, *Studies in Jewish Preaching* (Cincinnati, 1939).

34. Alexander Altmann, "The New Style of Preaching in Nineteenth Century German Jewry," in his edited *Studies in Nineteenth Century Jewish Intellectual History* (Cambridge, Mass., 1964), 65–116. See also Abraham Milgrom, *Jewish Worship*.

35. *DIS* 3:vi.

36. On antebellum Protestantism, see Sydney E. Ahlstrom, *A Religious History of the American People* (Garden City, N.Y., 1975), pts. IV and VI; Winthrop S. Hudson, *American Protestantism* (Chicago, 1961); Martin Marty, *Righteous Empire: The Protestant Experience in America* (New York, 1970). See also Lewis O. Brastow, *The Modern Pulpit: A Study of Homiletic Sources and Characteristics* (New York, 1906). On lyceums, see Carl Bode, *American Lyceum: Town Meeting of the Mind* (New York, 1956); Vern Wagner, "Lecture Lyceum and Problem of Controversy," *Journal of the History of Ideas* 15 (1954).

37. *DIS* 1:1–2.

38. *OCC* 20:340–43; and quoted in Berman, *Richmond*, 42.

39. Maxwell Whiteman, "Isaac Leeser and the Jews of Philadelphia," 213 n. 34.

40. *DIS* 1:1–9. An annotated selection from "Confidence in God" appears in *BB* 2:578–82. Leeser does not explain why his text is neither the regular weekly portion for *Shabbat Naso* (Numbers 4:21–7:89) nor the *Haftarah* (Judges 13:2–25). It is possible he meant to give "public instruction" in Judaism and did not view himself as a "preacher" per se at this point in his career.

41. *OCC* 9 suppl.:xiv.

42. *DIS* 1:1–3.

43. Ibid., 9–10.

44. Ibid., x.

45. *DIS* 6:59. See also Robert V. Friedenberg, "Isaac Leeser: Pioneer Preacher of American Judaism," *Religious Communication Today* (September 1983): 22–27.

46. Mayer Sulzberger, "Isaac Leeser," pamphlet (Philadelphia, 1881), 5. Sulzberger read this short biography of Leeser before the Young Men's Hebrew Association of Philadelphia, 1881. Copy in Abraham de Sola Papers, AJA, and Mayer Sulzberger, "Isaac Leeser," *American Hebrew* 7 (May 27, 1881): 15–16 and (June 2, 1881): 28–29.

47. *OCC* 25:600.

48. Rosa Mordecai, "Personal Recollections of Rev. Isaac Leeser," AJA, Englander Papers, 1901, 6. Mordecai wrote this highly romaticized biography for the Washington, D.C., section of the (National?) Council for Jewish Women, December 30, 1901. Also, see her "Isaac Leeser," *Appleton's Cyclopaedia*, ed. James Grant Wilson and John Fiske (New York, 1889), 3:676.

49. *BB* 2:279.

50. On the frequency of Leeser's preaching and public speaking activities, see Sussman, " 'Confidence in God,' " 266–68.

51. "A Chronological Digest of Isaac Leeeser's Discourses," in Sussman, " 'Confidence,' " 240–65.

52. For example, "The Sorrows of Israel," *DIS* 3:10, was delivered on July 24, 1840, during the time of the Damascus Affair, when Jews in Damascus, Syria, and Rhodes were falsely accused of having committed ritual murder.

53. *DIS* 10:313.

54. *DIS* 4:vi.

55. Isaac Leeser to K.K.M.I., March 31, 1830, and April 21, 1831, JRM-L.

56. David Philipson, *The Reform Movement in Judaism* (New York, 1907), 149–50; *JE* 7:217–18.

57. Jakob J. Petuchowski, "Manuals and Catechisms of the Jewish Religion in the Early Period of Emancipation," in Altmann, *Jewish Intellectual History*, 48.

58. Isaac Leeser, *Instruction in the Mosaic Religion* (Philadelphia, 1830, 1866), iv.

59. On early Reform Judaism in Germany, see Alexander Guttmann, *The Struggle over Reform Judaism in Rabbinic Literature of the Last Century and a Half* (New York, 1976). See also Gunther W. Plaut, ed., *The Rise of Reform Judaism: A Sourcebook of Its European Origins* (New York, 1968); Philipson, *Reform Movement.*

60. Leeser, *Instruction*, vii.

61. Ibid., iv.

62. Ibid., 95–96, 99–100.

63. Ibid., 51–52.

64. Ibid., 46–47.

65. *DIS* 1:62–63.

66. Sulzberger, "Isaac Leeser," 5. See also Maxine Seller, "Isaac Leeser's Views on the Restoration of a Jewish Palestine," *PAJHS* 68 (1968): 118, 135.

67. Whiteman, "Isaac Leeser," 214 n. 39.

68. *Morais*, 52.

69. Leeser, *Instruction*, iii–iv.

70. Isaac Leeser to K.K.M.I., March 25, 1831, D-L.

71. Isaac Leeser to K.K.M.I., May 15, 1840, D-L and AJA; *OCC* 9:209.

72. *A Review of the Late Controversies Between the Rev. Isaac Leeser and the Congregation Mikveh Israel*, typescript extracts from K.K.M.I. Minutebook, D-L (Philadelphia, 1850), 5–6.

73. *Late Controversies*, 13; *Morais*, 535–36.

74. Sefton Temkin, "Isaac Mayer Wise: A Biographical Sketch," in *A Guide to the Writings of Isaac Mayer Wise*, ed. Doris C. Sturzenberger (Bell and Howell and AJA, 1981), 22; James G. Heller, *Isaac M. Wise: His Life, Work and Thought* (New York, 1965), 200; *OCC* 8:255–57.

75. Grinstein, *New York*, 334.

76. *Late Controversies*, 13.

77. Typescript extracts from K.K.M.I. Minutebook, April 8, 1832, D-L.

78. *DIS* 3:vii.

79. *DIS* 1:342.

80. Ibid., 342–43.

81. Ibid., 344.

82. On the text of *Jews and the Mosaic Law*, see ch. 2 above.

83. For a brief sketch of Abraham Hart's life (1810–85), see *Morais*, 53–58. See also Whiteman, "Isaac Leeser," 208 n. 3. Several years earlier, Hart was employed by the prestigious Carey and Lea Company at the invitation of Henry C. Carey, a senior member of the firm and a noted political economist. When the firm was divided in 1829, Hart associated with Edward L. Carey, brother of Henry C. Carey. Carey and Hart proved itself to be an outstanding publishing house. It was responsible for numerous important first editions and also printed works of many leading American authors, including Henry Wadsworth Longfellow and James Fenimore Cooper.

84. *DIS* 1:xi.

85. Zalma Rehine to Isaac Leeser, Baltimore to Philadelphia, December 18, 1832, D-L.

86. On S. Jane Picken Cohen, see *WW*, 237–48, 451. On Leeser's relations with Mrs. Deliah Nash Cozens, see Isaac Leeser to Mrs. D. Cozens, Charleston, S.C., to Philadelphia, February 27, 1867, D-L. Emily Solis-Cohen reports on Leeser's relations with three young women: Ellen Cozens, Simha Peixotto, and Louisa Hart, 181–85. Gershon Greenberg reports a conversation he had with Maxwell Whiteman on the

"affair" in "A German-Jewish Immigrant's Perception of America, 1853–54," *AJHQ* 67 (June 1978): 325 n. 30. Whiteman informed Greenberg that, in his opinion,

> Leeser was involved with a Christian woman: It is true that he lived in the household of Mrs. Ella Cozzens, a respectable Presbyterian lady considerably older than Leeser. She was widowed shortly after Leeser moved in their home for what was to have been temporary quarters. A series of events altered this plan, and when Leeser contracted smallpox . . . he was nursed by her when no one would come near him for fear of contagion. He continued to live there, was constantly chastized but stubbornly refused to move elsewhere. It was only to his uncle, Zalma Rehine, to whom he revealed that he maintained a separate kitchen for kosher food and religious rites and amenities. All of the details of what led to a major controversy have not been brought together. Actually, he was in love with Simha Peixotto, but the objections of her uncle overruled marriage between the two.

Bertrand W. Korn notes, "Leeser never married, and was deprived of the affection and strength that a wife and children can give a man, but he had a huge family of Jewish followers throughout the United States," in "Centennial Reflections," 136.

87. *DIS* 2:34.

88. Rebecca Gratz to Maria Gist Gratz, Philadelphia to Lexington, Ky., February 2, 1834, quoted in Philipson, *Letters*, 193.

89. "The Will of Isaac Leeser," Article 7, December 26, 1867, D-L and AJA. Leeser left Deliah Nash (Cozens) $400 annually as a token of appreciation for caring for him in 1834 when he was suffering from smallpox.

90. *DIS* 2:34. On Jacob Leeser's arrival in America, see Leah Lippman to Isaac Leeser, Denekamp, Holland, to Philadelphia, August (?) 1832, JRM-L. Emily Solis-Cohen also reports that Jacob Leeser came to America in 1832 to join Zalma Rehine. Rehine was then in the process of moving from Richmond to Baltimore.

91. *DIS* 2:35.

92. Ibid., 45–46.

93. Fredrick J. Streng, *Understanding Religious Man* (Belmont, Cal., 1969), 73–74.

94. *DIS* 1:ix.

95. *DIS* 2:112.

96. Ibid., 115.

97. *OCC* 16:347–50, 25:89. Solomon Munk to Isaac Leeser, Paris to Philadelphia, April 4, 1862, AJHS-L.

<h3 style="text-align:center">CHAPTER FOUR</h3>

1. Quoted in Carl N. Degler, *Out of the Past: The Forces that Shaped Modern America*, rev. ed. (New York, 1970), 157. See also Jonathan Messerli, *Horace Mann: A Biography*, 1st ed. (New York, 1972); Joel H. Spring, *The American School, 1642–1990: Varieties of Historical Interpretation of the Foundations and Development of American Education*, 2d ed. (New York, 1990); Frederick M. Binder, *The Age of the Common School: 1830–1865* (New York, 1974); David Madsen, *Early National Education: 1776–1830* (New York, 1974) and Harry Gehman Good, *A History of American Education* (New York, 1973).

2. According to Carl N. Degler, "there is a crying need for a broad, interpretative study of the ideas and forces behind the educational revival of the 1830's and 1840's," *Out of the Past*, 482. However, important work has been done by Lawrence Arthur Cremin. See his *American Education: The National Experience, 1783–1876* (New York, 1980). Earlier studies include Ellwood P. Cubberly, *Public Education in the United States*

(Boston, 1919); Paul Monroe, *Founding of the American Public School System* (New York, 1940); Sidney Jackson, *America's Struggle for Free Schools* (Washington, D.C., 1941).

3. For an excellent review of American Jewish opinion on the rise of the public schools, see Lloyd P. Gartner, "Temples of Liberty Unpolluted: American Jews and Public Schools, 1840–1875," in *A Bicentennial Festschrift for Jacob R. Marcus*, ed. Bertrand W. Korn (New York, 1978), 157–90.

4. Gartner, "Temples of Liberty," 167–69. On religion and public schools during the Antebellum Period, see Vincent P. Lannie, *Public Money and Parochial Education: New York* (New York, 1968); John W. Pratt, "Governor Seward and New York City School Controversy, 1840–1842," *New York History* 42 (1961): 351; Timothy L. Smith, "Protestant Schooling and American Nationality, 1800–1850," *Journal of American History* 53 (1967): 679.

5. Quoted in Winthrop S. Hudson, *Religion in America* (New York, 1965, 1973), 249.

6. John Tracy Ellis, *American Catholicism* (Chicago, 1956), and his *Documents of American Catholic History*, rev. ed. (Milwaukee, Wisc., 1962). See also Jay P. Dolan, *American Catholic Experience from Colonial Times to the Present* (New York, 1985); James J. Hennessey, *American Catholics: A History of the Roman Catholic Community in the United States* (New York, 1981).

7. Gartner, "Temples," 165–67.

8. Isaac Leeser, "To the Jewish Inhabitants of Philadelphia," March 8, 1835, p. 1 reprinted in *PAJHS* 30:303. Copy of p. 2 in box 1329, Fierman Collection, AJA.

9. Ibid.

10. Lance J. Sussman, "Jewish Intellectual Activity and Educational Practice in the United States: 1776–1840," typescript (AJA, 1978), 121–24, 230–31; Todes, "The History of Jewish Education in Philadelphia," 21–23; and WW, 210, 251, 255, 277, 304.

11. Leeser, "Jewish Inhabitants"; Chaim Leeser to Isaac Leeser, Dulmen to Richmond, October 15, 1829, typescript copy, JRM-L; see ch. 1, n. 62 above.

12. On Lomdai Torah, see Grinstein, *New York*, 232; "Circular of *Lomdai Torah*," February 1830, AJA.

13. Leeser, "Jewish Inhabitants."

14. Zalma Rehine to Isaac Leeser, Baltimore to Philadelphia, March 30, 1835, typescript copy, JRM-L.

15. Isaac Leeser to Parnass and Members of Mickveh Israel, April 10, 1835, typescript copy, D-L and JRM-L.

16. Ibid.

17. Isaac Leeser to President and Members of Mickveh Israel, Elul 19, 1836, typescript copy, D-L and JRM-L.

18. *DIS* 2:237, 444.

19. Malcolm Stern maintains that the child was born on November 16, 1834, in his *Americans of Jewish Descent* (New York, 1971), 49.

20. On Lewis Allen, Jr., see *Morais*, 243. See also Leeser's "Memorial" remarks, *DIS* 4:103; *OCC* 1:588.

21. Isaac Leeser to Lewis Allen, October 1834 (?), typescript copy, D-L. See also Isaac Leeser to David Meldola, Philadelphia to London, December 29, 1840, typescript copy, D-L

22. Zalma Rehine to Isaac Leeser, Baltimore to Philadelphia, November 13, 1835, typescript copy, JRM-L.

23. *DIS* 3:256. See also Hyman B. Grinstein, "The American Synagogue and Laxity of Religious Observance, 1750–1850," (master's thesis, Columbia University,

1936); Jeremiah J. Berman, "The Trend in Jewish Religious Observance in Mid-Nineteenth Century America," *PAJHS* 37 (1947): 31.

24. Quoted in Abraham J. Karp, *Haven and Home: The History of the Jews in America* (New York, 1985), 40.

25. The seven discourses on the Messiah were delivered on the following dates: October 30 and November 26, 1835; January 1, February 15, March 25, August 26, and December 3, 1836. All seven are in *DIS* 2:253–372.

26. *DIS* 2:372.

27. Ibid., 365–66.

28. Ibid., 270.

29. Ibid., 258.

30. Ibid., 274. A famous apologia for Judaism that contains a similar discussion on the word *Elohim, Hizzuk Emunah,* written by the Karaite scholar Isaac ben Abraham Troki (c. 1533–c. 1594), is not listed in Cyrus Adler's *Catalogue* of Leeser's library.

31. Leeser explained to his congregants that his knowledge of Christian doctrine was primarily based on the *Commentaries* of Matthew Henry. Henry, a seventeenth-century English Nonconformist, was widely read in antebellum America and his writings appeared in a variety of composite works of biblical interpretation (*DIS* 2:298). Additionally, Leeser corresponded with his old friend and teacher Jacob Mordecai, who also was involved in developing counterarguments to Christian theology on the basis of Hebrew grammar and biblical research. Mordecai's extensive writings, however, were not published (Jacob Mordecai, "Introduction to the New Testament," holograph, AJA, 5; Jacob Mordecai to Isaac Leeser, Richmond to Philadelphia, July 19, 1836, commentary on Job 2:9, JRM-L; on Mordecai's theological writings, see Berman, *Richmond's Jewry,* Charlottesville, Va., 1978), 120–24.

32. *DIS* 2:371.

33. *DIS* 1:xii.

34. *DIS* 1:xi, 3:v.

35. *Allgemeine Zeitung des Judentums* 3 (November 14, 1839): 53–54.

36. A. S. W. Rosenbach, "An American Jewish Bibliography . . . Until 1850," *PAJHS* 30 (1926).

37. *DIS* 1:v–vi, ix.

38. Charles Reznikoff and Uriah Z. Engelman, *The Jews of Charleston: A History of an American Jewish Community* (Philadelphia, 1950), 138.

39. *OCC* 1:253–61, 9:209.

40. Isaac Leeser to the Parnass and Members of Congregation Mickveh Israel, May 15, 1840, typescript copy, D-L.

41. Ibid.

42. Ibid. A "List of Subscribers" can be found at the end of vol. 1 of Leeser's *Form of Prayers According to the Custom of the Spanish and Portuguese Jews* (Philadelphia, 1838).

43. Isaac Leeser to Lewis Allen, August 23, 1837, typescript copy, D-L. A short biography of Jacques Judah Lyons can be found in *PAJHS* 21:xxiii–xxviii, 27:144–49. See also David and Tamar de Sola Pool, *An Old Faith in the New World: Portrait of Shearith Israel, 1654–1954* (New York, 1955), 178–82.

44. The ad hoc group comprised Isaiah Nathans, E. Hyneman, H. Polock, B. Eytinge, E. L. Cohen, F. Samuel, S. Dreyfous, Aaron Asch, and A. Ulhim. "To Lewis Allen," August 22, 1837, typescript copy, D-L.

45. Isaac Leeser to Lewis Allen, August 23, 1837, typescript copy, D-L.

46. Allen's note is not dated, typescript copy, D-L.

47. The twelve petitioners were John Moss, S. Dreyfous, B. Eytinge, E. L. Cohen,

D. Samuels, E. Hyneman, Jos. M. Ash, F. Samuels, Samuel Lyons, Jos. Phillips, Aaron Asch, and Jos. L. Moss. "To Lewis Allen," September 18, 1837, typescript copy, D-L.

48. Jacques Judah Lyons to the President and Members of Mickveh Israel, September 22, 1837, typescript copy, D-L. Leeser announced that he would stand for re-election on September 18, 1837, typescript copy, D-L. His note to the Parnass states: "To prevent all misapprehension I take this method to state that if the congregation again honours me with their confidence, as they have done hitherto, I shall think myself happy to be able to respond to their call."

49. Minutes of Meeting, Mickveh Israel, October 2, 1837, typescript copy, D-L.

50. Isaac Leeser to the Parnass and Members of Congregation Mickveh Israel, May 15, 1840, typescript copy. Gratz and Moses are mentioned in Isaac Leeser to Lewis Allen, December 1837 (?), typescript copy, D-L. "The Lyon is subdued" is quoted in ESC, JRM-L.

51. A Review of the Late Controversies between the Rev. Isaac Leeser and the Congregation Mickveh Israel (Philadelphia, 1850), 8–9. Leeser later unsuccessfully petitioned the congregation to restore his salary to $1,000 per annum, Isaac Leeser to Lewis Allen, September 20, 1839, typescript copy, D-L.

52. Isaac Leeser to Lewis Allen, December 1837 (?), typescript copy, D-L.

53. Late Controversies, 9.

54. Leeser to Parnass, May 15, 1840.

55. The exchange of letters is reported in ESC, JRM-L.

56. Late Controversies, 9.

57. Isaac Leeser to Lewis Allen, January 2, 1838, typescript copy, D-L.

58. PAJHS 27:144. Lyons applied for the position at Shearith Israel in 1839. According to Grinstein, he did not actually begin to work there until 1840, New York, 89.

59. Isaac Leeser, "Preface," The Form of Prayers According to the Custom of the Spanish and Portuguese Jews, vol. 1 (Philadelphia, 1837–38), vii.

60. Rosa Mordecai, "Personal Recollections of Rev. Isaac Leeser," typescript, 1901, Englander Papers, AJA.

61. Leeser, Form of Prayers, vol. 1, vii.

62. Ibid., vi.

63. Karp, Haven and Home, 38.

64. Leeser, Form of Prayers, vol. 1, vi. On David Levi, see EJ 11:78–79; Rev. S. Singer, "Early Translations and Translators of Jewish Liturgy in England," Jewish Historical Society of England, Transactions 3 (1896–98): 56–71; James Picciotto, Sketches of Anglo-Jewish History, rev. Israel Finestein (London, 1956), 219ff. Professor Sarna also shared with me an excellent paper by Richard Popkin, "David Levi, Anglo-Jewish Theologian," unpublished typescript (Washington University, St. Louis, Mo., 1984).

65. Leeser, Form of Prayers, vi. Leeser frequently refers to Rashi as "Yarchi" ("moon"), a reflection of Christian usage and based on an error by Christian Hebraists.

66. OCC 9 suppl. (1852):vi.

67. Leeser, Form of Prayers, v.

68. Bibliographical information is based on a computer check of the holdings of the Library of Congress.

69. OCC 9 suppl. (1852):xv.

70. On Gratz's Sunday school, see Joseph Rosenbloom, "Rebecca Gratz and the Jewish Sunday School Movement," PAJHS 48 (1958):71ff.; and the biographical dissertation by Diane Ashton (Ph.D. diss., Temple University). See also Diane A. King, "Jewish Education in Philadelphia," in Jewish Life in Philadelphia: 1830–1940, ed. Murray

Friedman, 239–40; Ruth Braude Sarner, "The Hebrew Sunday School Society of Philadelphia: Perspective and Promise," pamphlet (Philadelphia, 1964).

71. Mordecai, "Personal Recollections," n.p.

72. Abraham S. Wolf Rosenbach, "History of the Society," in *The Hebrew Sunday-School Society of Philadelphia: Celebration of the Seventy-fifth Anniversary* (Philadelphia, 1913), 17.

73. Joseph Rosenbloom, *"And She Had Compassion," The Life and Times of Rebecca Gratz* (unpublished D.H.L. thesis, Hebrew Union College, 1957), 243.

74. The rise of the Sunday school movement is reflected in the pages of the *Occident*: Baltimore, 15:201–202, 26:43; Boston, 6:154; Charleston, S.C., 5:313, 14:549, 24:47; Columbia, S.C., 2:59, 6:107, 10:173; 17:306; Cincinnati, 2:246, 10:48; Cleveland, 16:408, 16:551, 19:41, 19:568; Columbus, Ga., 17:209–210; Curaçao, 2:58, 8:107; Harrisburg, Pa., 25:213; Montreal, 6:620, 7:569, 9:119–20; New Orleans, La., 9:272; New York, 21:38; Philadelphia, 1:38–40, 6:105, 13:87, 17:36, 18:304, 21:89–90; Pittsburgh, Pa., 24:462; Richmond, Va., 4:405, 16:263; St. Thomas, Virgin Islands, 5:119, 5:216; Savannah, Ga., 10:574, 14:137–39, 18:54; and Washington, D.C., 26:94.

75. On the early history of the Sunday school in Great Britain, see Thomas W. Laqueur, *Religion and Respectability: Sunday Schools and Working Class Culture, 1780–1850* (New Haven, Conn., 1976).

76. On the general history of the Sunday school in America, see Jack Seymour, *From Sunday School to Church School: Continuities in Protestant Church Education, 1860–1929* (Washington, D.C., 1982); William B. Kennedy, *The Shaping of Protestant Education: An Interpretation of the Sunday School and the Development of Protestant Educational Strategy in the United States, 1789–1860*, Monographs in Christian Education 4 (New York, 1966); and Edwin W. Rice, *The Sunday School Movement and the American Sunday School Union* (Philadelphia, 1917). An important account of the development of Sunday schools in the context of women's history is Anne M. Boylan, "Women in Groups: An Analysis of Women's Benevolent Organizations in New York and Boston, 1797–1840," *Journal of American History* 71 (1984): 497–523.

77. Sussman, " 'Confidence,' " 101–102.

78. Jack J. Diamond, "A Reader in Demography," *American Jewish Yearbook* 71 (1977):231–319; Arthur M. Schlesinger, Jr., *The Age of Jackson* (Boston, 1945, 1948), 217–26.

79. *DIS* 2:383–84.

80. *DIS* 2:403.

81. *DIS* 3:328–39.

82. *WW*, 276ff.

83. Rosenbach, "History," 14.

84. Quoted from Miriam Gratz Mordecai, "Rebecca Gratz," in *Hebrew Sunday-School*, 6.

85. Rebecca Gratz to Maria G. Gratz, 1838, typescript, JRM-L.

86. Mordecai, "Rebecca Gratz," 6.

87. Rosenbach, "History," 15.

88. Quoted in Rosenbach, "History," 13–14. See also Isaac Leeser, *Memorial of the Sunday School for Religious Instruction of Israelites in Philadelphia* (Philadelphia, 1840), copy in Fierman Collection, box 1329, AJA; repr. in *BB* 2:447–51.

89. Rosa Mordecai, "Recollections," in *The American Jewish Woman: A Documentary History*, ed. Jacob R. Marcus (New York, 1981), 135–40.

90. Mordecai, "Recollections," 137–38.

91. Isaac Leeser, *Second Examination of Philadelphia Sunday School* (Philadelphia, 1840), 13.

92. Rosenbach, "History," 17.

93. Ibid., 17–18, 22.

94. See n. 76 above.

95. Jick, *Americanization*, 62–63.

96. Leeser, *Memorial* (1840), 5–6.

97. Rosa Mordecai, "Personal Recollections," n.p.

98. Rosenbach, "History," 15.

99. Isaac Leeser, *Catechism for Young Children* (Philadelphia, 1839).

100. Eduard Kley, *Catechismus der Mosaischen Religion* (Berlin, 1814). In 1840 Kley published a greatly expanded edition of the same work. On Kley's life and thought, see David Philipson, *The Reform Movement in Judaism*, 32, 42ff., 320; Gunther Plaut, *The Rise of Reform Judaism*, 31, 67; *EJ* 10:1108.

101. Leeser, *Catechism*, 132–34. See also *OCC* 1:157–62.

102. Ibid., viii.

103. Bibliographical information based on a computer check of the holdings of the Library of Congress.

104. Mordecai, "Rebecca Gratz," 7.

105. Rebecca Gratz to Miriam (Cohen?), March 29, 1840, *ESC* and JRM-L. Also quoted in Sussman, " 'Confidence,' " 107.

106. Ruth Braude Sarner, "The Hebrew Sunday School," n.p.; Todes, "Jewish Education," 63–64; Ben Yapko, "Jewish Elementary Education in the United States, Colonial Period to 1909," (Ed.D. thesis, American University, 1958), 106.

107. Isaac Leeser, *The Hebrew Reader: Hebrew and English, Designed as an easy guide to the Hebrew Tongue for Jewish children and self-instruction,* No. 1. *The Spelling Book* (Philadelphia, 1838).

108. William Chomsky, "Hebrew Grammar and Textbook Writing in Early Nineteenth Century America," in *Essays in American Jewish History,* ed. Bertrand W. Korn (Cincinnati, 1958), 123–46.

109. Isaac Leeser, *The Claims of the Jews to an Equality of Rights* (Philadelphia, 1841), was published both as a book and as a supplement to the first edition of vol. 3 of Leeser's *Discourses* (1841). Leeser published six letters in the *Philadelphia Gazette*: December 12, 19, and 29, 1839; January 27, February 7, and February 28, 1840. See also Jonathan D. Sarna, "The American Jewish Response to Nineteenth Century Missions," 41–42, for a brief analysis of *Claims*.

110. Grinstein, *New York*, 88. On Samuel M. Isaacs, see E. Yechiel Simon, "Samuel Myer Isaacs: A Nineteenth Century Jewish Minister in New York," (Ph.D. diss., Yeshiva University, 1974).

111. *DIS* 3:76.

112. Ibid.

113. Ibid., 3:365.

114. Isaac M. Wise, *Reminiscences*, trans. David Philipson (Cincinnati, 1901), 51–52.

Chapter Five

1. In a letter to the *Philadelphia Gazette* written on February 28, 1840, Leeser reported: "There are now five congregations in New York; two in Philadelphia; one in Hanover, Pa.; one (perhaps two) in Baltimore; one in Richmond; one in Charleston; one in Savannah; one in Cincinnati; one in Albany, and one in the interior of New York, besides a large number of individuals in Easton, Pottsville, Pittsburg, etc., Pa.; Frederic[k], Md.; Petersburg and Norfolk, Va.; Georgetown, Beaufort, Columbia, Camden, etc., S.C.; Augusta and Columbus, Ga.; Mobile, Ala.; Natchez, Vicksburg, Grand

Gulf, Miss.; New Orleans; Cleveland, Ohio; Louisville, Ky.; St. Louis, Mo.; and many other towns all over the Western States." Quoted from Isaac Leeser, *The Claims of the Jews to an Equality of Rights* (Philadelphia, 1841), 83–84.

2. Morton Borden, *Jews, Turks and Infidels* (Chapel Hill, N.C., 1984), 110; Stanley F. Chyet, "The Political Rights of the Jews in the United States: 1776–1840," *Critical Studies in American Jewish History*, vol. 3, ed. Jacob R. Marcus (New York, 1971), 27–88.

3. Leeser, *Claims*, 89–91.

4. Ibid., 51.

5. Ibid., 82.

6. Ibid., 19.

7. Sarna, *Jacksonian Jew* (New York, 1980), 123; Abraham J. Brawer, "Damascus Affair," *EJ* 5:1249–52.

8. Sarna, *Noah*, 124.

9. Ibid., 123.

10. Whiteman, "The Legacy of Isaac Leeser," 31.

11. *BB* 3:928; Cyrus Adler and Aaron Margolith, eds., *With Firmness in the Right: American Diplomatic Action Affecting American Jews, 1840–1865* (New York, 1948), 3–5. On the reaction of American Jews to the Damascus Affair, see Joseph Jacobs, "The Damascus Affair of 1840 and the Jews of America," *PAJHS* 10 (1902):122; Jacob Ezekiel, "Persecution of the Jews in 1840," *PAJHS* 8 (1900):141–44; Israel Goldstein, *A Century of Judaism in New York* (New York, 1930), 70–73; and Abraham J. Karp, *Haven and Home*, 41, 42–44.

12. *DIS* 3:168–69.

13. Sarna, *Noah*, 124–25; *BB* 3:930–32.

14. Jacob R. Marcus, "The Periodization of American Jewish History," in *Studies in American Jewish History* (Cincinnati, 1969), 8. The article originally appeared in *PAJHS* 47 (1958): 125–33.

15. Karp, *Haven and Home*, 42.

16. "Persecution of the Jews in the East, containing the proceedings of Meeting held at the Synagogue Mickveh Israel, Philadelphia, on Thursday evening, the 28th of Ab, 5600 [August 27, 1840]" (Philadelphia, 1840), reprinted in Abraham J. Karp, *Beginnings: Early American Judaica* (Philadelphia, 1975). Abraham Hart served as President of Mickveh Israel for thirty-five years, from 1841 to 1876.

17. *BB* 3:941.

18. *DIS* 3:347, 364.

19. *BB* 3:935.

20. Ibid., 934.

21. Jacobs, "Damascus Affair," 123.

22. *DIS* 3:357.

23. Ibid., 361–63.

24. John Moss to Lewis Allen, October 22, 1840, Morais Papers, Dropsie Library.

25. *BB* 3:955.

26. Jick, *Americanization*, 67; "Persecutions," passim.

27. Leeser owned stock in a local railroad. However, some of his congregants discouraged him from taking an active role in business outside the ministry. Hyman Gratz wrote to Leeser: "I regret to learn your determination to attend the meeting of the Rail Roads. Some of your congregation will be dissatisfied at your doing so, and observations will be made that will not be agreeable to you. If you desire your stock to

be represented, you can give your proxy to some person to vote for you." Hyman Gratz to Isaac Leeser, March 18, 1840, D-L.

28. *DIS* 3:208.

29. "Editor's Preface," Grace Aguilar, *The Spirit of Judaism*, ed. Isaac Leeser (Philadelphia, 1842).

30. *DIS* 2:161–82, repr. in part in Jacob R. Marcus, *The American Jewish Woman: A Documentary History*, 129–32.

31. *DIS* 3:266.

32. Ibid., 268–69.

33. Ibid., 280.

34. Ibid., 291.

35. Sarna, *Noah*, 142.

36. *DIS* 3:291.

37. Sarna, *Noah*, 142, 208 n. 63. See also Milton Matz, "The Meaning of Christmas to the American Jew," *Jewish Journal of Sociology* 3 (1961): 129–37; Jakob J. Petuchowski, "The Magnification of Chanukkah," *Commentary* 24 (January 1961): 38–43.

38. *DIS* 3:309.

39. Ibid., 321.

40. Ibid., 323.

41. Ibid., 318–319.

42. Ibid., ix, 321.

43. Isaac Leeser to Parnass and Members of the Congregation Mikveh Israel, Philadelphia, May 15, 1840, D-L and AJA.

44. Ibid.

45. Ibid.

46. Ibid.; and Isaac Leeser to Lewis Allen, Philadelphia, May 22, 1840, D-L.

47. In October 1840 a decision was made "to erect a building for school and vestry rooms in the rear of the synagogue. . . . John Moss offered to lend the amount needed [$2,150]," Memo, typescript copy, D-L, n.d. See also A. Dessen to Parnass, Philadelphia, October 18, 1840, typescript copy, D-L, on a dispute over the terms of membership at Mickveh Israel.

48. A copy of the contract proposed by the congregation is contained in *A Review of the Late Controversies Between the Rev. Isaac Leeser and the Congregation Mickveh Israel* (Philadelphia, 1850), 10.

49. *Late Controversies*, 9.

50. Isaac Leeser to Lewis Allen, Philadelphia, December 17, 1840, typescript copy, D-L; and "Contract offered by Leeser," December 17, 1840, typescript copy, D-L.

51. *Late Controversies*, 10–11.

52. Ibid.

53. *DIS* 3:vi–vii.

54. Ibid.

55. Ibid.

56. Isaac Leeser to Lewis Allen, Philadelphia, February 7, 1841, typescript copy, D-L.

57. Lewis Allen to Isaac Leeser, Philadelphia, February 8, 1841, typescript copy, D-L.

58. Isaac Leeser to Lewis Allen, Philadelphia, February 2, 1841, typescript copy, D-L.

59. On the early development of Reform Judaism in America, see Lou Silberman, "American Impact: Judaism in the United States in the Early Nineteenth Century,"

B. G. Rudolph Lectures in Judaic Studies, Syracuse University, Syracuse, N.Y., 1964. See also Alan Tarshish, "Charleston Organ Case," *AJHQ* 54 (1965): 411–49.

60. Historians of Reform Judaism have paid scant attention to Isaac Harby. See N. Bryllion Fagin, "Isaac Harby and the Early American Theater," *AJA* 8 (1956): 68; Max J. Kohler, "Isaac Harby, Jewish Religious Leader and Man of Letters," *PAJHS* 32 (1931): 35; L. C. Moise, *Biography of Isaac Harby with an account of the Reformed Society of Israelites, 1824–1831* (Macon, Ga., 1931). See also above, ch. 2, n. 24.

61. Alan Tarshish, "The Charleston Organ Case," *PAJHS* 54 (1965): 431.

62. *DIS* 4:1–12.

63. *OCC* 1:512–13; Tarshish, "Charleston," 439.

64. *DIS* 10:285.

65. Ibid., 28.

66. Rebecca Gratz to Miriam Gratz Moses, Philadelphia to Savannah, March 29, 1841, Miriam Gratz Moses Papers No. 2639, Southern Historical Collection, University of North Carolina Library, Chapel Hill, N.C.

67. *Late Controversies*, 11.

68. *DIS* 4:32.

69. Ibid., 39.

70. Ibid., 32; Jonathan D. Sarna, "Hebrew Poetry in Early America," *AJH* 69 (March 1980): 367–68, 375–77.

71. *Late Controversies*, 12.

72. *OCC* 3:175.

73. Ibid.

74. Isaac Leeser to Zalma Rehine, Philadelphia to Baltimore, July 21, 1841, holograph, D-L.

75. The "Plan of Union" was republished by Leeser in *OCC* 3:175–76, 222–27; and by Joseph Buchler, "The Struggle for Unity: Attempts at Union in American Jewish Life: 1654–1868," *AJA* 2 (21): 40–44.

76. *OCC* 3:176.

77. Ibid., 222–24. On Abraham Rice, see Israel Tabak, "Rabbi Rice of Baltimore," *Tradition* 7 (1965): 100–120.

78. *OCC* 3:222–24.

79. Ibid., 224–25.

80. Ibid., 225–27.

81. Ibid., 171–72.

82. Buchler, "Struggle," 27.

83. The "Resolution" is quoted in Buchler, "Struggle," 27.

84. Abraham Moise to Isaac Leeser, Charleston to Philadelphia, August 12, 1841, reprinted by Barnett A. Elzas in (Baltimore) *Jewish Comment* 23:18 (August 10, 1906): 1–2.

85. *DIS* 4:103–104.

CHAPTER SIX

1. Quoted in Carl N. Degler, *Out of Our Past*, 108; John A. Garraty, *The American Nation*, 263–64. On Manifest Destiny and westward expansion, see A. K. Weinberg, *Manifest Destiny* (Baltimore, 1935); Ray A. Billington, *Westward Expansion* (New York, 1949, 1967). For a general review of the history of the American city during the Antebellum Period, see David R. Goldfield and Blaine A. Brownell, *Urban America: From Downtown to No Town* (Boston, 1979), 98–197.

2. Leon Jick, *The Americanization of the Synagogue* (Hanover, N.H., 1976), 113.

See also Naomi W. Cohen, *Encounter with Emancipation: The German Jews in the United States, 1830–1914* (Philadelphia, 1984).

3. Grace Aguilar, *The Spirit of Judaism*, ed. Isaac Leeser (Philadelphia, 1842). The publication of Aguilar's work marked the beginning of the most creative period in her short life—she died in 1847 at the age of thirty-one. Her best-known work, a novel entitled *A Vale of Cedars*, was published posthumously in 1850. Her collected works, in 8 vols., appeared in 1861 and included numerous religious works addressed primarily to Jewish women. On Aguilar, see *Morais*, 12–15; *EJ* 2:428.

4. *Spirit of Judaism*, v-vi.

5. Ibid., i.

6. Ibid., vi–vii.

7. Ibid., 21.

8. Ibid., 104.

9. Ibid., 74–75.

10. Ibid., vii–viii.

11. Ibid., vii.

12. Ibid., 53.

13. *DIS* 4:210.

14. Isaac Leeser to Congregation Mickveh Israel, Philadelphia, August 28, 1842, typescript, D-L. Apparently, he wrote two letters on the same date to the congregation to discuss "improvements." Maxwell Whiteman, however, who saw the original documents at Mickveh Israel, claims they are undated but were written after September 21, 1842. See his "Isaac Leeser and the Jews of Philadelphia," 215 n. 45.

15. Ibid.; *DIS* 4:234.

16. *DIS* 4:234.

17. Ibid.

18. "Resolutions," Congregation Mickveh Israel, April 9, 1843, typescript copy, D-L. Leeser's response is reported in Whiteman, "Leeser and the Jews," 213 n. 34.

19. Morris U. Schappes, *A Documentary History of the Jews in the United States, 1654–1875* (New York, 1971), 606.

20. Grinstein, *New York*, 214. Only select details of Jackson's life are known. See George L. Berlin, "Solomon Jackson's *The Jew*: An Early American Jewish Response to the Missionaries," *American Jewish History* 71 (September 1981): 10–28; Grinstein, *New York*, passim; *EJ* 9:1189–90; Sussman, "Jewish Intellectual Activity and Educational Practice," 79–84 and Abraham J. Karp, *Beginnings: Early American Judaica* (Philadelphia, 1975), 37–40.

21. Grinstein, *New York*, 217; Malcolm Stern, "1820s," in *A Bicentennial Festschrift for Jacob Rader Marcus*, ed. Bertram W. Korn, 542; Jick, *Americanization*, 12.

22. Whiteman, "Leeser," 215ff. See also *OCC* 1:28–32.

23. On the development of the European Jewish press during the 1830s and 1840s, see *EJ* 13:1023–56; Meyer Wasman, *A History of Jewish Literature*, vols. 3 and 4 (New York, 1960).

24. *OCC* 1:2.

25. On the history of religious newspapers in the United States, see *The Religious Press in America*, Martin Marty et al. (Westport, Conn., 1963, 1973); Sussman, "Jewish Intellectual Activity," 80.

26. On the history of the general press in the United States, see Edwin Emery, *The Press and America: An Interpretive History of Journalism*, 2d ed. (Englewood Cliffs, N.J., 1962); Frank L. Mott, *American Journalism: A History, 1690–1960*, 3d ed. (New York 1962).

27. *OCC* 1:1.

28. *OCC* 4:1.

29. *The Voice of Jacob* 18 (May 27, 1842): 142–43; *Allgemeine Zeitung des Judentums* (October 1842): 618–19.

30. Subscription lists are printed in *OCC* 1:214, 515; 2:615–16.

31. *OCC* 2:616.

32. *OCC* 1:1.

33. Ibid., 4.

34. Ibid., 5. In vol. 1 alone, Leeser published "histories" of the Jews of Charleston, Savannah, and Ohio. Similarly, he included historical pieces on the Jews of China, Prussia, and Russia in the first year of his periodical.

35. *OCC* 15:3; Englander, "Leeser," 221.

36. The notion of symmetry is suggested by Elinor Grumet, "The Jewish Press in These States Before 1850," typescript (AJA, 1973), 3.

37. *OCC* 1:112.

38. Benjamin Dias Fernandes' *A Series of Letters on the Evidences of Christianity* had already appeared, in part, in Jackson's *The Jew*. Leeser began serializing the same in vol. 1 of the *Occident*. His original translation of Mendelssohn's *Jerusalem* appeared as a supplement to vol. 9 (1852) of the *Occident*.

39. The first piece written entirely in Hebrew to be published in the *Occident* was a letter (June 1847) by Menahem (Henry) Goldsmith of New York on the "fitness" of American-grown citrons for Jewish ritual purposes. Interestingly, Leeser attached a short note of his own, also written in Hebrew, to Goldsmith's correspondence (*OCC* 5:156–58).

40. Abraham Karp (University of Rochester) correctly suggested that the advertising supplement to the *Occident* be carefully examined for its valuable information about American Jewish life, 1843–69.

41. Bertram W. Korn, "Centennial Reflections," 136.

42. Jalonick's letter was published in *AJA* 8:75. See also the preface to bound copies of vol. 1 of the *Occident*.

43. *OCC* 1:304. For a comparison of Noah and Leeser as Jewish leaders, see Jonathan D. Sarna, "The Spectrum of Jewish Leadership in Ante-bellum America," *Journal of American Ethnic History* 1 (Spring 1982): 59–67; and his *Jacksonian Jew*, passim.

44. *OCC* 2:347–49, 407–408, 449–52, 552–56. Since olive oil was an important substance in the daily preparation of food, the discussion was not insignificant. Leeser generally favored innovations that would help preserve the integrity of traditional practice. If a suggested modernization created halachic problems, he would withdraw his support. He tried to make modern Orthodoxy appealing and available to the average American Jew but not at the expense of the *Halachah*. Thus, as the Orthodox community developed during the 1840s and 1850s, Leeser was pulled further and further to the right, in response to the ever-growing number of traditional rabbis who began settling in the United States in this period and in reaction to the appearance of increasingly radical reformers. See, for example, Leeser's equivocal response to the ritual fitness of American-grown citrons (*OCC* 5:106, 156–58, 210–12).

45. *OCC* 2:600–606; Sarna, *Jacksonian Jew*, 153–55.

46. *OCC* 2:604–606.

47. Maxine S. Seller's view that Leeser's proto-Zionism was not awakened unitl 1848 ignores his implicit approval of a modern Jewish state in his critique of Noah's "Restoration Address" (1844). See her "Isaac Leeser's Views on the Restoration of a Jewish Palestine," *AJHQ* 58 (1968): 118–35. Leeser's fully developed views are articulated in "The Future of Palestine," *OCC* 22:5–15. See also Peter Grose, *Israel in the Mind of America* (New York, 1983), 12–13, 21–22, 29–30, 102.

48. *OCC* 4:616; Salo W. and Jeanette Baron, "Palestinian Messengers in America, 1848–1879," *Jewish Social Studies* 5 (1943): 115–62, 225–92.

49. For an assessment of the history of American Zionism, see *AJH* 75 (December 1985).

50. *OCC* 2:544. On Leeser and reform, see Englander, "Leeser"; Lawrence Grossman, "Tradition under Fire: Isaac Leeser and Reform," *Gesher* 8 (1980): 73–89.

51. *OCC* 2:545.

52. *OCC* 1:209.

53. *OCC* 2:253–61.

54. *OCC* 1:253, 2:210, 297.

55. *OCC* 2:215. On the Brunswick Conference, see David Philipson, *The Reform Movement in Judaism*, 212–31; Gunther Plaut, *The Rise of Reform Judaism*, 74–90.

56. *OCC* 2:364.

57. Ibid., 370.

58. Ibid., 545.

59. Morton Borden, *Jews, Turks and Infidels*, 110.

60. *OCC* 2:496–510; Borden, *Jews, Turks*, 142 n. 2. See also *OCC* 3:561–67, 4:297–302 for a similar case in Virginia. Excellent source material on church-and-state issues involving American Jews during the nineteenth century is included in Schappes, *Documentary History*, 13, 63, 126, 168, 179, 235ff., 263, 279, 464, 520ff., 628, 631, 638, 719ff.

61. *OCC* 2:497–98.

62. Borden, *Jews, Turks*, 111–15.

63. *OCC* 4:596, 6:36–41.

64. Borden, *Jews, Turks*, 110. The debate over the South Carolina case continued in the *Occident* for several more years. Judge O'Neal also sent a letter to Leeser defending his view of the "Christian" Bible as the standard of morality. See *OCC* 6:186–93, 300–302.

65. Winthrop S. Hudson, *Religion in America* (New York, 1973) 440–41.

66. Sussman, " 'Confidence in God,' " 267–68.

67. *DIS* 4:308–367; *OCC* 1:7–21, 3:69–82, 3:115–29.

68. *DIS* 5:18–53, 239–58.

69. Isaac Leeser, "The Jews and Their Religion, *He Pasa Ekklesia. An Original History of the Religious Denominations at present in the United States containing Authentic Accounts of their Rise, Progress, Statistics and Doctrines written expressly for the work by eminent Theological Professors, Ministers, and Lay Members of the Respective Denominations*, ed. I. Daniel Rupp (Harrisburg, Pa., 1844), 350–69. Selections from the article also appear in *AJA* 7 (1955):82; Robert Handy, ed., *Religion in the American Experience: The Pluralistic Style* (Columbia, S.C., 1972), 46.

70. Leeser, "Jews and Their Religion," 350.

71. Ibid., 365.

72. Ibid., 367.

73. On Leeser's biblical work, see Lance J. Sussman, "Another Look at Isaac Leeser and the First Jewish Translation of the Bible in the United States," *Modern Judaism* 5 (1985): 159–90. Quote from Isaac Leeser, *The Twenty-four Books of the Holy Scriptures* (Philadelphia, 1853), iii.

74. Korn, "Centennial Reflection," 33; Isaac Leeser, *The Law of God*, vol. 1 (Philadelphia, 1845), viii.

75. Isaac Leeser, *The Form of Prayers*, vol. 1 (Philadelphia, 1838), vi; Joseph R. Rosenbloom, "Rebecca Gratz and the Jewish Sunday School Movement in Philadelphia," *PAJHS* 48 (1958): 71; *And She Had Compassion* (D.H.L. diss. Hebrew Union

College, 1957); Leopold Zunz, ed., *Die vier und zwanzig Bücher der Heiligen Schrift* (Berlin, 1838). On Leeser's indebtedness to Arnheim and Zunz, see *Law of God*, vol. 1, 146.

76. According to Maxwell Whiteman, Leeser's Pentateuch met with "even greater approval than he had anticipated . . . [and] a pirated edition appeared in Germany and was sold in England," in his "Leeser," *Jewish Life in Philadelphia*, Murray Friedman, ed. (Philadelphia, 1983) 35. However, Max Kohler reports: "Soon after Leeser's Bible translation appeared [1853], a pirated edition was also published and he brought suit for infringement of copyright in the Federal Court in Philadelphia. The claims of the defense were, of course, overruled, on the ground that there could be no copyright even in a new translation, made from the Hebrew, because the Bible itself is common property and the defendant could have made an independent translation of his own." The case is reported in the series entitled "Federal Cases," which is alphabeti-caly arranged, under the plaintiff's name "Leeser"; undated holograph (1919?), Englander Papers, AJA. See also Albert M. Friedenberg to Dr. Henry Englander, New York to Cincinnati, January 7, 1919, Englander Papers, AJA.

77. On the original (American) Jewish Publication Society, see Solomon Grayzel, "The First American Jewish Publication Society," *Jewish Book Annual* 3 (1944): 42–45; Morais, 175–76. More broadly, see Jonathan D. Sarna, *The Americanization of Jewish Culture, 1888–1988* (Philadelphia, 1989). A copy of the "Circular of the American Jewish Publication Society" (December 10, 1845) is in the Korn File, AJA. See also *OCC* 2:517–27.

78. *OCC* 3:35–40, 421–28; Myron Berman, *The Jews of Richmond*, 143–44. Brief biographies of these individuals can be found in *JE* and *Morais*. Solomon Solis was a "warm friend" of Leeser's and a frequent contributor to the *Occident*.

79. "Circular" (1845); *OCC* 6:411.

80. Grayzel, "First Publication Society," 42–45, offers an epitome of each publication.

81. *OCC* 10:42–43.

82. *OCC* 3:425.

CHAPTER SEVEN

1. On the general history of religion in antebellum America, see Winthrop S. Hudson, *Religion in America*, 4th ed. (New York, 1987), 127–94. For a more specialized treatment of Protestant developments, see Robert T. Handy, *A Christian America: Protestant Hopes and Historical Realities* (New York, 1971), 27–64. On trusteeism, see John Tracy Ellis, *American Catholicism*, 2d ed., rev. (Chicago, 1969); Hugh J. Nolan, "Francis Patrick Kenrick, First Coadjutor Bishop," in *The History of the Archdiocese of Philadelphia*, ed. J. Connelly (Philadelphia, 1976); John P. Marschall, "Kenrick and the Paulists, a Conflict of Structures and Personalities," in *Church History* 38 (1969): 88–105. On Bishop Kenrick of Philadelphia, see Hugh J. Nolan, *The Most Reverend Francis Patrick Kenrick, Third Bishop of Philadelphia, 1830–1851* (New York, 1948); Leonard W. Bacon, ed., *An Inside View of the Vatican Council* (New York, 1872); Gerald P. Fogarty, "American Catholic Translations of the Bible," in *The Bible and Bibles in America*, ed. E. Frerichs (New York, 1988), and "The Quest for a Catholic Vernacular Bible in America," in *The Bible in America*, ed. N. Hatch and M. Noll (New York, 1982).

2. Maldwyn Allen Jones, *American Immigration* (Chicago, 1960), 92–146.

3. *EJ* 15:1596; Robert E. Levinson, *Jews in the California Gold Rush* (New York, 1978); Norton B. Stern, *California Jewish History: A Descriptive Bibliography* (Glendale, Cal., 1967).

4. The basic issues are covered in Holman Hamilton, *Prologue to Conflict: The Crisis and the Compromise of 1850* (Lexington, Ky., 1964).

5. On Jewish emancipation in Europe, see *EJ* 6:696–718, esp. 707.

6. Bertram W. Korn, "Jewish 'Forty-Eighters' in America," *Eventful Years and Experiences: Studies in Nineteenth Century American Jewish History* (Cincinnati, 1954), 1–26.

7. *OCC* 10:371.

8. The growing diversity in American Jewish life in the 1840s is described by Leon A. Jick, *The Americanization of the Synagogue* (Hanover, N.H., 1976), 97–113.

9. Chaim I. Waxman, *America's Jews in Transition* (Philadelphia, 1983), 12–28.

10. Isaac Leeser, *Divrei Tzadikkim. The Book of Daily Prayers* (Philadelphia, 1848), introduction.

11. On Rabbi Wolf Heidenheim, see *EJ* 8:258–59.

12. Leeser, *Divrei Tzadikkim*, introduction.

13. At the same time Leeser published his Ashkenazic prayer book, he joined Isaac Mayer Wise in calling for a national meeting of American rabbis (1848). Thus, *The Book of Daily Prayers* may also be viewed as part of Leeser's effort to promote Jewish unity in the United States.

14. Isaac Leeser and Joseph Jacquett, *Biblia Hebraica* (Philadelphia, 1848). On Jacquett, see Franklin Spencer Edmonds, *History of St. Matthew's Church, Francisville, Pennsylvania, 1822–1925* (Philadelphia, 1925), 72–73, copy at Archives of the Episcopal Church, Austin, Tex. The Leeser-Jacquett *Biblia Hebraica* was probably based on a Hebrew Bible published by Samuel Bagster (London, 1824, 1833); see T. H. Darlow and H. F. Moule, *Historical Catalogue of Printed Editions of Holy Scripture*, vol. 2 (London, 1903), 725, 729. Leesser also edited a Hebrew edition of Job for the American Bible Union; see William H. Wyckoff to Isaac Leeser, New York to Philadelphia, March 11, 1857, D-L.

15. Isaac Leeser to Rev. Nathaniel Hewitt, Philadelphia to Bridgeport, Conn., July 11, 1839, Historical Society of Pennsylvania.

16. Jonathan D. Sarna, "The Politics of Scripture: Jewish Bible Translations and Jewish-Christian Relations in the United States," typescript (AJA, 1983), 12; Matitiahu Tsevat, "A Retrospective View of Isaac Leeser's Biblical Work," in *Essays in American Jewish History*, ed. Bertram W. Korn (Cincinnati, 1958), 297.

17. *The Twenty-four Books of the Holy Bible: Hebrew and English* (New York, 1912).

18. Jick, *Americanization*, 79–96; Jonathan D. Sarna, introduction, *The American Rabbinate: A Century of Continuity and Change: 1883–1983*, ed. Jacob R. Marcus and Abraham J. Peck (Hoboken, N.J., 1985), viii–ix.

19. *OCC* 4:406. On Abraham de Sola, see *EJ* 5:1562–63; *JE* 11:243–433; A.D. M. de Sola, *Jewish Ministers* (1905).

20. Jick, *Americanization*, 129–30.

21. Israel Goldstein, *A Century of Judaism in New York* (New York, 1930), 111–15, 148–53; *Morais* (Philadelphia, 1880), 287–91; Moshe Davis, *The Emergence of Conservative Judaism* (Philadelphia, 1963), 356–58.

22. Hyman B. Grinstein, *The Rise of the Jewish Community of New York* (Philadelphia, 1947), 214–16.

23. *OCC* 8:65.

24. Isaac M. Wise, *Reminiscences*, ed. and trans. David Philipson (Cincinnati, 1901), 62.

25. The history of the American rabbinate during its formative years has yet to be written. However, on the history of the American rabbinate during the last century,

see *The American Rabbinate: A Century of Continuity and Change, 1883–1983* (Hoboken, N.J., 1983), Jacob R. Marcus and Abraham J. Peck, eds.

26. *OCC* 2:515.

27. Bertram W. Korn, *American Jewry and the Civil War* (New York, 1970), 47–50; and his *Early Jews of New Orleans* (Waltham, Mass., 1969), 251–254.

28. David Philipson, *Max Lilienthal, American Rabbi: Life and Writings* (New York, 1915), 8.

29. Ibid.

30. For a general discussion of Russian Jewry during this period, as well as of Lilienthal's controversy with the regime, see Michael Stanislawski, *Tsar Nicholas I and the Jews: The Transformation of Jewish Society in Russia, 1825–1855* (Philadelphia, 1983).

31. *OCC* 3:471–72.

32. *OCC* 3:572, 576, 583–96; 4:259, 344–50.

33. Grinstein, *New York*, 52, 170, 296, 299, 303, 397, 404, 423.

34. *OCC* 5:110.

35. *OCC* 5:163.

36. Isaac Mayer Wise, *Minhag America* (Cincinnati, 1857).

37. A critical biography of Lilienthal is an important lacuna in the literature. See Philipson, *Max Lilienthal*: J. S. Raisin, *The Haskalah Movement in Russia* (Philadelphia, 1915).

38. For a new extensive, critical biography of Isaac Mayer Wise see Sefton Temkin, *Isaac Mayer Wise, Shaping American Judaism* (Oxford, New York, 1992). For a revisionist view of Wise as radical reformer, see Aryeh Rubinstein, "Isaac Mayer Wise: A New Appraisal," *Jewish Social Studies* 39 (Winter/Spring 1977): 53–74.

39. Jacob R. Marcus, ed., "The Americanization of Isaac M. Wise," *Studies in American Jewish History* (Cincinnati, 1969), and republished in pamphlet form by the AJA.

40. Isaac M. Wise to Isaac Leeser, Albany to Philadelphia, December 1849, typescript copy, D-L.

41. Marcus,"Americanization," 91–105. In a conversation with the author, Professor Marcus suggested that Wise was performing unauthorized weddings in Radnitz.

42. *OCC* 5:275.

43. Quoted by Jacob R. Marcus, *Memoirs of American Jews, 1775–1865* (Philadelphia, 1955), 2:64.

44. Wise, *Reminiscences*, 78.

45. Ibid., 78–79.

46. *OCC* 6:319.

47. Ibid., 435.

48. Ibid., 581.

49. Joseph Buchler, "The Struggle for Unity, Attempts at Union in American Jewish Life, 1654–1868," *AJA* 2 (1949): 21.

50. *OCC* 7:62.

51. Abraham Rice to Isaac Leeser, Baltimore to Philadelphia, December 15, 1848, AJHS-L.

52. Ibid.

53. *OCC* 7:140.

54. Ibid., 433–44.

55. *OCC* 8:257.

56. Ibid.

57. Wise, *Reminiscences*, 149.

58. Ibid., 165.
59. Ibid.
60. *OCC* 8:309.
61. Ibid., 424.
62. Mickveh Israel's Minutes, typescript copy, April 1, 1849, D-L.
63. *OCC* 7:569.
64. *OCC* 9:110.
65. Ibid.
66. Ibid.
67. *OCC* 7:377.
68. *A Review of the Late Controversies*, 16.
69. *OCC* 16:48.
70. *Late Controversies*, 17.
71. *A Review of "The Review"* (New York, 1850), 8.
72. Mickveh Israel's Minutes, typescript copy March 24, 1850, D-L.
73. Ibid.
74. *OCC* 8:61.
75. *Late Controversies*, 18.
76. *OCC* 8:431.
77. Ibid.; Joseph Schwartz, "Translator's Preface," *A Descriptive Geography and Brief Historical Sketch of Palestine*, trans. Isaac Leeser (Philadelphia, 1850).
78. *OCC* 16:47.
79. Ibid., 50.
80. *Morais*, 59–60.
81. Ibid.
82. *OCC* 8:371. 16:51.
83. *OCC* 12:164.
84. *Morais*, 105, 136, 155, 291–92. See also typescript copy of Mickveh Israel's Minutes, November 19, 1856, D-L.
85. *OCC* 8:371.

CHAPTER EIGHT

1. The nativist Know-Nothing Party aggravated relations between "native" Americans and the still-rising tide of immigrants, the largest segment being the poor Irish who sought refuge in America from the potato famine (1848–54). Nativism, also rooted in religious bigotry, was fiercely anti-Catholic. Although the Know-Nothing Party, later the American Party, was generally not anti-Semitic, it received very little support from American Jews, who as a group either philosophically opposed making political endorsements, or saw in nativism a distant threat to their security in the United States. See Bertram W. Korn, "The Know-Nothing Movement and the Jews," *Eventful Years and Experiences* (Cincinnati, Ohio, 1954), 58–78.

2. For a general review of developments in antebellum America, see Richard N. Current et al., *American History: A Survey,* vol. I: To 1877 (New York, 1987), 363–94; Carl N. Degler, *Out of Our Past: The Forces That Shaped Modern America* (New York, 1970), 160–87. See also John Higham, *Strangers in the Land: Patterns of American Nativism, 1860–1925,* 2d ed. (New Brunswick, N.J., 1988).

3. *EJ* 13:866–904.

4. The expansion of Jewish philanthropic and cultural activities in the United States during the 1850s occurred in cities throughout the country. The most dramatic developments, however, were in New York City. See Hyman Grinstein, *The Rise of the Jewish Community of New York*, passim; Jonathan D. Sarna, *Jacksonian Jew*, 119–42. See

also Daniel Elazar, *Community and Polity: The Organizational Dynamics of American Jewry* (Philadelphia, 1980), 32–69; Naomi W. Cohen, *Encounter with Emancipation: The German Jews in the United States, 1830–1914* (Philadelphia, 1984), passim.

5. On the *bet ha-midrash*, see Grinstein, *New York*, 12, 14, 93, 253, 263, 309, 347, 404, 412, 449, 474, 477, 486, 498, 575, 577. On Einhorn, see *EJ* 6:531–32; Bernard D. Cohn, "David Einhorn: Some Aspects of His Thinking," *Essays in American Jewish History*, ed. Jacob R. Marcus (Cincinnati, 1958), 315–25; Gershon Greenberg, "The Significance of America in David Einhorn's Conception of History," *AJHQ* (December 1973): 160–84.

6. Moshe Davis, *The Emergence of Conservative Judaism: The Historical School in Nineteenth Century America* (Philadelphia, 1965), 130–35, 156, 166, 201.

7. *OCC* 8:372.

8. *OCC* 10:403.

9. Abraham Kohn to Isaac Leeser, Chicago to Philadelphia, March 10, 1851, typescript copy, D-L.

10. Jacob R. Marcus, *Memoirs of American Jews*, (Philadelpia, 1955) 2:59.

11. *OCC* 8:262.

12. *OCC* 2:527, 9:380–83.

13. *OCC* 10:2.

14. Ibid., 49.

15. Ibid., 51.

16. Ibid., 50–55.

17. Ibid., 57.

18. Ibid., 55–57.

19. Ibid., 109–110.

20. Ibid., 110–12.

21. Ibid., 173–74.

22. Ibid., 174.

23. On Leeser's view of Mendelssohn, see Lance J. Sussman, "Another Look at Isaac Leeser and the First Jewish Translation of the Bible in the United States," *Modern Judaism* 5 (May 1985):174–75. See also *OCC* 9 suppl.: v. However, see "Revealed Truths" in *DIS* 9:216–17 and *OCC* 23:487. A comparison of Leeser's version of *Jerusalem* with the translation prepared by Moses Samuels, *Jerusalem: A Treatise on Ecclesiastical Authority and Judaism* (London, 1838) leaves little doubt that Leeser prepared his rendition of Mendelssohn's classic work independently. Leeser's rendition is "wordy" and also includes numerous translator's glosses.

24. *JML*, 228.

25. *OCC* 10:531.

26. *Pentateuch*, vol. 1, 146. On the general influence of German Jewish culture, see Bertram W. Korn, "German-Jewish Intellectual Influence on American Jewish Life," Syracuse University, B. G. Rudolph Lecture, 1972.

27. *Bible* (Philadelphia, 1853), iv; Rosa Mordecai, "Personal Recollections"; Israel Abrahams, "Isaac Leeser's Bible," *By-Paths in Hebraic Bookland* (Philadelphia, 1920), 256–57.

28. *Bible* (1853), x. On Anglo-Jewish translations of the Bible, see *EJ* 4:868–72. However, Leeser did correspond with Benisch; see A. Benisch to Isaac Leeser, London to Philadelphia, November 27, 1848, photostatic copy in the possession of Jacob R. Marcus.

29. *Bible* (1853), iv, and note to Exodus 25:17; *DIS* 2:272. The Raphael–de Sola version of Genesis was also published by Samuel Bagster and Sons.

30. *The Israelite*, February 14, 1868.

31. *OCC* 10:534. Leeser also occasionally consulted Dr. Gotthold Salomon's Bible, *OCC* 10:533.

32. *Bible* (1853), iii; *OCC* 10:525–35. Charges by Leeser's opponents from the Reform movement that he could not read unvocalized Hebrew are overblown. However, he often relied on Mendelssohn's *Biur* and Ludwig Philippson's biblical notes when he did not have access to select material in rabbinic literature.

33. Jakob J. Petuchoswki, "The Bible of the Synagogue," *Commentary* (February 1959): 150. Reprinted in his *Heirs of the Pharisees* (New York, 1970), 37.

34. *Pentateuch*, vol. 1, 147.

35. A quarto edition with notes was printed as late as 1914. Copy at Klau Library, Rare Book Room, HUC-JIR, Cincinnati.

36. *Bible* (1853), notes to Joshua 10:12 and II Kings 20:7. Following Philippson, Leeser explains in his note that the mode of hospitality discussed in Genesis 43:34 is "yet prevailing in Persia." See also notes to I Samuel 6:5, Jeremiah 25:10 and 35:2. For a complete discussion of Leeser's translation, see Sussman, "Another Look at Isaac Leeser," 159–90. In the *Occident*, Leeser also frequently reported on distant Jewish communities. For instance, on the Jews of Persia, see *OCC* 7:317, 504–507, 549–54, 596–601; and 8:43–48, 141–45.

37. *Bible* (1853), iii; *Pentateuch*, vol. 1, vii; Jonathan D. Sarna, "The Politics of Scripture: Jewish Bible Translations and Jewish-Christian Relations in the United States," typescript (AJA, 1983), 11.

38. *Bible* (1853), iv.

39. Rabbi Aryeh Kaplan, "Translator's Introduction," *The Living Torah* (New York, 1981), vii. On making translations conform with Jewish law, Kaplan adds that "this means following Maimonides's Code (the *Yad*) where law is concerned, literary considerations are secondary." On the problem of harmonization in the Leeser Bible, see *OCC* 10:527.

40. *JML*, 9, 13, 15–21, 137.

41. *Bible* (1853), iv; *OCC* 1:521–23; M. Tsevat, "A Retrospective View of Isaac Leeser's Biblical Work," in *Essays in American Jewish History*, ed. Bertram W. Korn (Cincinnati, 1958), 300.

42. *OCC* 11:521–22.

43. Isidore Kalisch, "English Versions of the Bible," *Israelite*, July 28, 1854: 21, 170; *OCC* 12:357–64.

44. *OCC* 12:520–21.

45. Ibid., 360; Mordecai, "Recollections." See also Alexander A. Hodge, *The Life of Charles Hodge* (New York, 1880, repr. 1969); Anna Robeson Burr, *Weir Mitchell, His Life and Letters* (New York, 1929).

46. *Bible* (1956), viii.

47. Ibid., iii–iv; Pocket Edition (1856, 1859), xii ff.

48. Steven A. Fox, "A Detailed Analysis of the Union of American Hebrew Congregations, Its Structure, Its Goals, and Its Accomplishments, 1873–1903" (ordination thesis, Hebrew Union College, 1980), 122–23. Moses Dropsie prepared an agreement to transfer the copyright of the Leeser Bible to Abraham de Sola on January 6, 1873. Subsequently, de Sola printed a public notice including a deed of transfer on May 1, 1875 (de Sola Papers, Misc. File, AJA). On how Leeser sold his Bibles, see Isaac Leeser to H. H. Kayton (?), Philadelphia to Baltimore, November 4, 1864, copy at Jewish Historical Society of Maryland.

49. Tzevat, "Retrospective," 302.

50. "Reforming and Deforming," *OCC* 8:61–73, 159–72.

51. All eight sections of "Progressive Reforms" appear in *OCC* 12 (1854).

52. *OCC* 12:127.
53. Ibid., 129, 177.
54. *DIS* 9:99n.
55. Heller, *Wise*, 258–82.
56. *DIS* 9:75, 95.
57. *OCC* 13, suppl.
58. *The Israelite*, August 17, 1855; and Heller, *Wise*, 286–87.
59. David Ellenson, "A Jewish Legal Decision by Rabbi Bernard Illowy of New Orleans and Its Discussion in Nineteenth Century Europe," *AJH* 69 (1979): 177–78.
60. *OCC* 13:407, 422.
61. Ibid., 410.
62. Heller, *Wise*, 290.
63. *OCC* 13:411.
64. Ibid., 413.
65. Ibid.
66. Wise, *Reminiscences*, (New York, 1901), 314–15.
67. *OCC* 13:413–14.
68. *OCC* 14:83.
69. Jick, *Americanization*, 163.
70. *EJ* 6:531–32.
71. David Einhorn's "Protest" was published in English and German and was also signed by A. Nachman, President of Har Sinai Verein (Baltimore, November 6, 1855), copy AJA and D-L.
72. *OCC* 14:511.
73. The Lilienthal-Leeser dispute is reported in detail by Cohen in *Encounter with Emancipation*, 175–80.
74. Ibid.
75. Jacques J. Lyons and Abraham de Sola, *A Jewish Calendar for Fifty Years* (Montreal, 1854); *OCC* 11:596–602.
76. *OCC* 2:616; 6:57–58; 14:387.
77. *OCC* 11:17–48.
78. *OCC* 14:239.
79. Ibid., 453.
80. *Morais*, 112.
81. Ibid., 154–55.
82. *OCC* 7:101–105, 169.
83. *OCC* 12:193–199; *DIS* 10:117–59.
84. *OCC* 16:52–57.
85. *OCC* 8:1–7.
86. Ibid., 5.
87. *OCC* 16:53.
88. Ibid., 57.
89. *Minutes* of Beth El Emeth (1857), typescript copy, D-L.
90. *Morais* 121–24.
91. Frank Fox, "Quaker, Shaker, Rabbi: Warder Cresson, the Story of a Philadelphia Mystic," *Pennsylvania Magazine of History and Biography* 95 (1971): 174–94; Abraham J. Karp, "The Zionism of Warder Cresson," in *Early History of Zionism in America*, ed. Isidore S. Meyer (New York, 1958), 1–20.
92. *OCC* 11:478.
93. Ibid., 433.

CHAPTER NINE

1. Among Leeser's publications after 1857 are: Archbishop of Crangor, *The Inquisition and Judaism: A Sermon Addressed to Jewish Martyrs on the Occasion of an Auto de Fe at Lisbon, 1705*, and Carlos Vero Nieto, *A Reply to the Sermon*, note by Isaac Leeser (both Philadelphia, 1860); Benjamin Dias Fernandes, *A Series of Letters on the Evidences of Christianity* (published privately by Isaac Leeser, Philadelphia, 1859); Ennery Jonas (?), *Meditations and Prayers*, trans. Hester Rothschild, revised and corrected by Isaac Leeser (Philadelphia, 1866); Ludwig Philippson, *The Crucifixion and the Jews*, trans. M. Meyer, preface by Isaac Leeser (Philadelphia, 1866).

2. Joseph Newhouse to Isaac Leeser, March 11, 1857, AJHS-L; *Morais*, 105–107.

3. *OCC* 15:151.

4. Ibid., 313.

5. Ibid., 326.

6. David H. Solis to Beth El Emeth, September 22, 1863, D-L.

7. *OCC* 16:351.

8. Mickveh Israel *Minutes*, April 5, 1857, typescript copy, D-L.

9. *OCC* 15:588–89; 16:29–43.

10. Bertram W. Korn, *The American Reaction to the Mortara Case: 1858–1859* (Cincinnati, 1957), 34.

11. Morton Borden, *Jews, Turks and Infidels* (Chapter Hill, N.C., 1984), 82–83, 86, 90–91; Morris U. Schappes, *A Documentary History of the Jews in the United Sates, 1654–1875* (New York, 1971), 315–24.

12. Schappes, *Documentary History*, 317.

13. *OCC* 15:295.

14. *EJ* 12:354–55.

15. Korn, *Mortara*, 6.

16. Ibid.

17. Ibid., 12.

18. *OCC* 16:381.

19. Korn, *Mortara*, 140.

20. *OCC* 16:452.

21. Korn, *Mortara*, 63.

22. Ibid., 57.

23. Ibid., 64–65.

24. Ibid., 65.

25. *OCC* 16:539.

26. Ibid., 539–40.

27. Ibid., 559–60.

28. Hyman Grinstein, *The Rise of the Jewish Community of New York* (Philadelphia, 1945), 433.

29. On the Board of Delegates of American Israelites, see Allan Tarshish, "The Board of Delegates of American Israelites (1859–1878)," *PAJHS* 49 (1959): 16–32; Max J. Kohler, "The Board of Delegates of American Israelites, 1859–1878," *PAJHS* 29 (1925): 75–128.

30. Grinstein, *New York*, 434.

31. Tarshish, "Board of Delegates," 19.

32. Minute Book of the Board of Delegates of American Israelites, holograph, AJA, box 952, 6.

33. "Minority Report," Minute Book of the Board of Delegates of American Israelites, 14–16.

34. Tarshish, "Board of Delegates," 20.

35. Ibid., 21–22. In 1878, the Board was absorbed by the Union of American Hebrew Congregations. Founded in 1873, the Union initially viewed itself as a broad, inclusive national organization. The merger of the Union and the Board was, in part, a rational attempt to avoid duplication of efforts and service in the American Jewish community. Ironically, the Union quickly evolved into an umbrella organization for Reform synagogues. Afraid that they would be dominated by the Board in 1859, the Reformers conquered the Board from within less than twenty years later and thereby expanded the scope of their movement's activities. See Tarshish, "Board of Delegates," 31.

36. Bertram W. Korn, *American Jewry and the Civil War* (New York, 1970), 30.

37. *OCC* 19:145.

38. *OCC* 20.8.

39. Bertram W. Korn, "Jews and Negro Slavery in the Old South, 1789–1865," *PAJHS* (March 1961): 151–201; Morris U. Schappes, *A Documentary History of the Jews in the United States* (New York, 1971), 405–428.

40. Korn, *Civil War*, 44.

41. Ibid., 254.

42. *OCC* 18:1.

43. Korn, *Civil War*, 32–55.

44. Ibid., 41.

45. *OCC* 19:93.

46. Isaac Leeser to Alexander Henry, mayor of Philadelphia, June 3, 1861, type-script copy, D-L.

47. Alexander Henry to Isaac Leeser, June 3, 1861, holograph, D-L.

48. Isaac Leeser's speech on Morris J. Raphall's "The Bible View of Slavery."

49. *OCC* 18:274.

50. *OCC* 23:274.

51. *OCC* 18:117; advertising suppl. to *OCC* 19:2; *OCC* (February 1862):3; *OCC* (October 1862):title page. See also Davis, *The Emergence of Conservative Judaism* (Philadelphia, 1963), 332.

52. *OCC* 19.2, advertising suppl.: 2.

53. The chaplaincy controversy is discussed in great detail in Korn, *Civil War*, 56–97.

54. Ibid., 60.

55. Ibid., 71–72.

56. *OCC* 20:362; Korn, *Civil War*, 77.

57. Korn, *Civil War*, 78.

58. Ibid.

59. Ibid., 96.

60. Ibid., 132.

61. Ibid., 152.

62. Borden, *Jews, Turks and Infidels*, 65.

63. Ibid., 67–68.

64. Ibid., 68.

65. Isaac Leeser to the Senate and House of Representatives, New York to Philadelphia, January 30, 1865, holograph, Board of Delegate Papers, AJHS.

66. Ibid.

67. Ibid.

68. A standard survey of the Civil War is J. G. Randall and David Donald, *The Civil War and Reconstruction* (Boston, 1961). See Carl N. Degler's "Bibliographical Note" in his *Out of Our Past*, (New York, 1920), 487–89.

69. Rosa Mordecai, "Recollections," n.p.
70. *DIS* 9:200–201.

Chapter Ten

1. *OCC* 24:239.
2. *EJ* 8:1033–1040; Jacob R. Marcus, *Communal Sick Care in the German Ghetto* (Cincinnati, 1947).
3. *WW*, 267.
4. Ibid., 275, 277.
5. *DIS* 2:279–93; *OCC* 8:259–61, 12:615, 13:558.
6. *Morais*, 91, 116, 275, 301.
7. Maxwell Whiteman, *Mankind and Medicine: A History of Philadelphia's Albert Einstein Medical Center* (Philadelphia, 1966), 5; *Morais*, 116–20.
8. Whiteman, *Mankind*, 9.
9. Quoted in Jick, *The Americanization of the Synagogue* (Hanover, N.H., 1976), 109.
10. Ibid., 169.
11. Ibid., 109–110.
12. *DIS* 12:412.
13. *OCC* 14:41.
14. Whiteman, *Mankind*, 7–8.
15. "Hospital for Israelites in Philadelphia," April 8, 1864, English and German, broadside, D-L. Partially reprinted in *Morais*, 117.
16. *EJ* 8:1035, 1039–1040.
17. Whiteman, *Mankind*, 14.
18. Ibid., 15–16.
19. *DIS* 10:170.
20. Leeser simply called his talk "The Hospital." *DIS* 10:159–73.
21. The only full-scale historical treatment of Maimonides College is Bertram W. Korn's "The First American Jewish Theological Seminary: Maimonides College, 1867–1873," in his *Eventful Years and Experiences* (Cincinnati, 1954), 151–213.
22. Ibid., 154.
23. *EJ* 13:1463–65.
24. Sydney E. Ahlstrom, *A Religious History of the American People*, vol. 2 (Garden City, N.Y., 1975), 84.
25. Winthrop S. Hudson, *Religion in America*, 2d ed. (New York, 1973), 154–57.
26. Ibid.
27. *OCC* 3:577. See also Lance J. Sussman, "Isaac Leeser and the Protestantization of American Judaism," *AJA* 38 (April 1986): 10–12.
28. *OCC* 24:200.
29. Korn, "Maimonides College," 152–63; Lance J. Sussman, "Jewish Intellectual Activity and Educational Practice in the United States," (typescript, HUC-JIR, Cincinnati, 1978), 104–115.
30. Michael A. Meyer, "A Centennial History of the Hebrew Union College–Jewish Institute of Religion," in *Hebrew Union College–Jewish Institute of Religion: At One Hundred Years*, ed. Samuel E. Karff (Cincinnati, 1976), 16.
31. Korn, "Maimonides College," 160.
32. Ibid., 161–62.
33. Ibid.
34. Korn, *Civil War*, 56ff.
35. Korn, "Maimonides College," 163.

36. *OCC* 7:105.
37. Korn, "Maimonides College," 164–66.
38. Ibid., 166–68.
39. *EJ* 9:1296–97; Moshe Davis, *The Emergence of Conservative Judaism*, 342–44.
40. Korn, "Maimonides College," 172.
41. Ibid., 196–98.
42. Robert E. Fierstein, "Sabato Morais and the Founding of the Jewish Theological Seminary," in *When Philadelphia Was the Capital of Jewish America*, ed. Murray Friedman (Philadelphia, 1993), 75–91. On the early history of the Hebrew Union College, see Meyer, "Centennial History," 1–283.
43. Leeser's interest in medieval Jewish literature paralleled that of his junior colleague Mayer Sulzberger.
44. Preface, *DIS* 4:v.
45. Ibid., vi.
46. Ibid.
47. *DIS* 9:258.
48. *OCC* 25:599.
49. Ibid., 593.
50. *OCC* 26:606.
51. Ibid.
52. Ibid., 607.
53. Ibid.
54. *OCC* 25:593–611. Partially reprinted in *AJA* 21 (1969): 140–48.
55. *OCC* 25:610–11.
56. *Israelite*, February 14, 1868, 4ff.
57. Ibid.
58. Broadside, Board of Delegates Papers, AJHS.
59. Inscription on Leeser's tombstone, located in Beth El Emeth's cemetery in West Philadelphia (see illustrations).
60. Sulzberger, an attorney, also handled Leeser's estate. Copies of Leeser's will are available at the American Jewish Archives (Cincinnati) and the National Museum of American Jewish History (Philadelphia).

CONCLUSION

1. Henry Samuel *Morais*, 195–96.
2. Hyman Gratz (1776–1857), a close personal friend of Isaac Leeser, left a provision in his will for the founding of a college. Also, see *Publications of the Gratz College* (1897). A large dedicatory plaque in memory of Isaac Leeser once graced the main entrance to Dropsie College. Solomon Solis-Cohen, "The Jewish Theological Seminary: Past and Future, Address Delivered at the Twenty-fifth Annual Commencement, New York, June 2, 1918" (New York, 1919), 18–21; Henry Englander, "Isaac Leeser," *Yearbook of the Central Conference of American Rabbis* 28 (1918): 213–52. Englander reports that "appreciations of Leeser's life appeared in the *American Israelite*, January 31, 1918, by G. Deutsch, also in the *Bnai Brith News* by the same writer; [and in the] *Jewish Exponent*, February 8, 1918 by Mayer Sulzberger." Subsequently, the *Jewish Exponent* ran a favorable review of Englander's monograph, February 14, 1919, and a "Centennial Appreciation" by Maxine S. Seller, January 26, 1968. See also "Rev. Isaac Leeser: The Man Who Labored Indefatigably for Israel and Judaism," *The Hebrew Watchword and Instructor*, March 1897, and "Isaac Leeser and Isaac M. Wise," *The Hebrew Standard*, March 7, 1919.

3. Emily Solis-Cohen's work on Leeser is described in the essay section of the Bibliography below. For a sympathetic view of Leeser, see Ralph Alfred Habas, "Isaac Leeser: The Great American Conservative," *The Jewish Layman*, September 1930.

4. Lance J. Sussman, "Another Look at Isaac Leeser and the First Jewish Translation of the Bible in the United States," *Modern Judaism* 5 (May 1985): 180–81.

5. A select bibliography of secondary works on Isaac Mayer Wise is offered by Jeffrey Gurock, *American Jewish History: A Bibliographical Guide* (New York, 1983), 34. On Wise's own writings, see Doris C. Sturzenberger, *A Guide to the Writings of Isaac M. Wise* (Cincinnati, 1981).

6. Moshe Davis, *The Shaping of American Judaism* (New York, 1951, in Hebrew) and *The Emergence of Conservative Judaism: The Historical School in 19th Century America* (New York, 1963). Davis's 1951 study was based on his doctoral dissertation at the Hebrew University, the first Ph.D. thesis at the Jerusalem school in the field of American Jewish history. See also Herbert Parzen, *Architects of Conservative Judaism* (New York, 1964), and Arthur Hertzberg, "Conservative Judaism," *EJ* 5:901–902.

7. The "Orthodox" historiographical counterclaim began with Charles Liebman, "Orthodoxy in Nineteenth Century America," *Tradition* 6 (Spring-Summer 1964): 132–40, a review of Davis's *Emergence of Conservative Judaism*. More recently, see Lawrence Grossman, "Tradition Under Fire: Isaac Leeser and Reform," *Gesher* 8 (5741/ 1980): 73–89, and "Isaac Leeser's Mentor: Rabbi Abraham Sutro, 1784–1869," in *Rabbi Joseph H. Lookstein Memorial Volume*, ed. Leo Landman (New York, 1980), 151–62.

8. The "Philadelphia school" has published six articles on Leeser: Bertram W. Korn, "Isaac Leeser: Centennial Reflections," *AJA* 19 (1967): 127–41, and "The First American Jewish Theological Seminary: Maimonides College, 1867–1873," in his *Eventful Years and Experiences* (Cincinnati, 1954), 151–213; Maxine S. Seller, "Isaac Leeser's Views on the Restoration of a Jewish Palestine," *PAJHS* 68 (1968): 118–35, and "Isaac Leeser: A Jewish-Christian Dialogue in Ante-Bellum Philadelphia," *Pennsylvania History* 35 (1968): 231–42; and Maxwell Whiteman, "Isaac Leeser and the Jews of Philadelphia," *PAJHS* 48 (1959): 207–244, and "The Legacy of Isaac Leeser," in *Jewish Life in Philadelphia, 1830–1940*, ed. Murray Friedman (Philadelphia, 1983), 26–47. More recently, see *When Philadelphia Was the Capital of Jewish America*, ed. Murray Friedman (Philadelphia, 1993).

9. Maxine S. Seller, "Isaac Leeser: Architect of the American Jewish Community," (Ph.D. diss., University of Pennsylvania, 1965), 180.

10. For a history of the Union of American Hebrew Congregations (Reform), see Sefton Temkin, "A Century of Reform Judaism in America," *American Jewish Yearbook* (1973): 3–75. The founding and early years of the Union of American Hebrew Congregations is discussed by Steven A. Fox in "The Union of American Hebrew Congregations" (ordination thesis, HUC-JIR, Cincinnati, 1980). On the United Synagogue (Conservative), see Abraham J. Karp, *A History of the United Synagogue of America 1913–1963* (New York, 1964). On the early history of the Union of Orthodox Jewish Congregations of America, see Eugene Markovitz, "Henry Pereira Mendes: Architect of the Union of Orthodox Jewish Congregations of America," *AJHQ* (March 1966): 364–84; and Jeffrey Gurock, "Resistors and Accommodators: Varieties of Orthodox Rabbis in America, 1886–1983," *AJA* 35 (1983): 100–187.

11. No complete history of the Jewish Sunday school in America has yet been written. A partial review of developments in the nineteenth century can be found in Kerry Olitzky, "Sunday Schools: The Beginning," *Jewish Education* (Fall 1985): 6–11. On the post–World War II day school, see Walter I. Ackerman, "Jewish Education," in *Movements and Issues in American Judaism: An Analysis and Sourcebook of Developments Since 1945*, ed. Bernard Martin (Westport, Conn., 1978), 184–205.

SELECTED BIBLIOGRAPHY

The following is intended to serve as a general bibliographical guide in the area of studies of Isaac Leeser. It is not an exhaustive listing of all materials used in this study. Additional references may be found in the notes.

Archival Sources

The largest collection of Leeser archival materials is housed at the Center for Judaic Studies (formerly Dropsie College), a division of the University of Pennsylvania in Philadelphia. For the Center's holdings, see Arthur Kirow, *The Isaac Leeser Collection, MS 2: Finding Aid* (Center for Judaic Studies, Philadelphia, 1994) with a "Preface" by Lance J. Sussman. Unfortunately, when the research for this study was conducted, the Dropsie Collection was in considerable disarray. The bulk of the Leeser Collection at the Center for Judaic Studies, approximately fifteen linear feet, revolves around Leeser's activities as editor of the *Occident*. Relatively few items from before 1843 were found. Numerous letters from Leeser's friends and literary agents, including Abraham de Sola (Montreal), R. Lindo (New York), and Gershom Kursheedt (New Orleans), contain valuable information about Leeser's personal life.

The Center's collection also includes manuscripts of Leeser's sermons (both drafts of original texts and scriveners' copies), items for the *Occident*, unpublished biblical studies, and the handwritten manuscript of *Jews and the Mosaic Law*. Three unfinished and incomplete works by Emily Solis-Cohen, Jr., are also scattered throughout the Dropsie materials. They include *Leeser: A Beginner in America*, *Leeser: A Man and His Destiny*, and a general work on American Jewry during the Early National Period. Solis-Cohen received help from Solomon Grayzel in translating much of Leeser's Hebrew, Yiddish, and Judeo-German correspondence. Much of his work is still available in typescript. The Dropsie Collection also includes Leeser's school notes from Germany, letters from Moses Montefiore and the Office of the Chief Rabbi of England, and even a letter from a child, Isaac Leeser Cohen, asking the hazzan to save his foreign stamps. Additionally, the Center for Jewish Studies Annenberg Research Institute has large collections of both Sabato Morais and Mayer Sulzberger papers.

The American Jewish Archives on the campus of the Hebrew Union College—Jewish Institute of Religion in Cincinnati, Ohio, also has an extensive collection of Leeser papers. Microfilms 199, 200, and 201, a sampling of materials found at Dropsie thirty years ago, contain items no longer available in the original as well as selections from the Morais papers. Original Leeser materials are contained in boxes 1071, 2326, and 2333 as well as in the Bertram W. Korn Collection, the Floyd Fierman Collection (box 1329), the Jacob Ezekiel Scrapbook (box 1734), and the Marcus Jastrow Collection (box 1278). Materials from Congregation Mickveh Israel are in boxes 872, 886, 889, and 899. Additionally, Beth El Emeth (microfilm 3001) and Board of Delegates of American Israelites (microfilm 478) materials are available at the archives. Currently, the archives is in the process of consolidating its Leeser papers, which will greatly facilitate the work of future research.

The American Jewish Archives also houses a considerable collection of unpublished secondary materials, including some of Emily Solis-Cohen's manuscripts (microfilm 2966) and Uriah Todes's dissertation on Jewish education in Philadelphia (box 1797). Additional studies are listed in the *Manuscript Catalog of the American Jewish Archives* (1971) and *Supplements* (1977). Mention has already been made of Abraham Shinedling's massive index to the *Occident*, which is housed in the American Jewish Archives. References to Leeser in the European Jewish press can be found in the Deutsch Catalog at the Archives. Also, the indexes to *The American Hebrew*, *Deborah*, and *Sinai* are valuable research tools.

Professor Jacob R. Marcus, director of the American Jewish Archives, allowed me to examine his private collection of Leeser materials. Composed largely of negative photostats, Marcus's files contain correspondence between Leeser and his family in Europe, including letters from his sister, Leah, as well as letters from his maternal uncle, Zalma Rehine, who lived in Baltimore and Richmond. Marcus also has copies of numerous documents that involve Leeser's work as editor of the *Occident* and hazzan at Mickveh Israel.

The American Jewish Historical Society (AJHS) on the campus of Brandeis University (Waltham, Massachusetts) has a small but important collection of Leeser papers (P-20) as well as five items on the Board of Delegates of American Israelites (I-20). A partial index to American Jewish periodicals at the AJHS contains many references to Leeser, especially from *The American Israelite*, *Asmonean*, and *Jewish Messenger*. J. Kutnick's index to the general American press was also helpful. An exhaustive search of the secular press would undoubtedly yield still further materials on Leeser.

Additional Leeser and background materials were found at the Historical Society of the Episcopal Church, Historical Society of Pennsylvania, Library of the Jewish Theological Seminary, Leo Baeck Institute (New York), Maryland Jewish Historical Society, New York Public Library, and Philadelphia Jewish Archives. The Klau Library (HUC—JIR) staff assisted in a computer check on the Library of Congress holdings of books authored by Leeser.

Unfortunately, three collections of Leeser papers were not made available to me. Mickveh Israel (Philadelphia) refused access to their archival holdings, which also include papers from Beth El Emeth (1857–84), Leeser's second pulpit. Photocopies of some of this material were found in other institutions. Professor Abraham Karp has a small collection of Leeser materials, as does Maxwell Whiteman. Although neither private collection was actually made available for this study, both individuals answered specific questions about Leeser.

Selected Bibliography

Isaac Leeser's Published Materials

Biblia Hebraica. Philadelphia: J. W. Moore [Printer], 1848.

The Book of Daily Prayers for every day in the year. According to the custom of the German and Polish Jews. Philadelphia: C. Sherman [Printer], 1848.

Catechism for Younger Children. Designed as a Familiar Exposition of the Jewish Religion. Philadelphia: Adam Waldie [Printer], 1839.

The Claims of the Jews to an Equality of Rights. Philadelphia: C. Sherman [Printer], 1841.

Discourses, Argumentative and Devotional, on the Subject of the Jewish Religion. 2 vols. Philadelphia: Haswell and Fleu [Printer], 1837.

Discourses, Argumentative and Devotional, on the Subject of the Jewish Religion, 2d ser. Vol. 3. Philadelphia: C. Sherman [Printer], 1841.

Discourses on the Jewish Religion. 10 vols. 3d ser. Philadelphia: Sherman and Company [Printer], 1867.

The Form of Prayers According to the Custom of the Spanish and Portuguese Jews. Philadelphia: Haswell, Barrington, and Haswell [Printer], 1837–38.

The Hebrew Reader: Hebrew and English, Designed as an easy guide to the Hebrew Tongue, for Jewish children and self-instruction. No. 1. *The Spelling Book.* Philadelphia: Haswell, Barrington, and Haswell [Printer], 1838.

Instruction in the Mosaic Religion. Translated from the German of J. Johlson. Philadelphia: Adam Waldie [Printer], 1830.

"To the Jewish Inhabitants of Philadelphia." Philadelphia: [Broadside], 1835.

The Jews and the Mosaic Law. Philadelphia: E. L. Carey and A. Hart [Printer], 1834.

"The Jews and Their Religion." In *He Pasa Ekklesia,* ed. I. Daniel Rupp, 350–69. Harrisburg, Pa.: Clyde and Williams, 1844.

The Law of God [Pentateuch]. 5 vols. Philadelphia: C. Sherman [Printer], 1845.

The Occident and American Jewish Advocate. A Monthly Periodical Devoted to the Diffusion of Knowledge on Jewish Literature and Religion. 26 vols. Ed. Isaac Leeser. Philadelphia: 1843–69.

Persecution of the Jews in the East, Containing the Proceedings of a Meeting held at the Synagogue Mickveh Israel. Philadelphia: C. Sherman [Printer], 1840.

The Twenty-four Books of the Holy Scriptures. Philadelphia: L. Johnson, 1853–54.

Other Books Edited or Translated by Isaac Leeser

Aguilar, Grace. *The Spirit of Judaism,* ed. Isaac Leeser. Philadelphia, 1842.

Archbishop of Crangor. *The Inquisition and Judaism: A Sermon addressed to Jewish Martyrs on the Occasion of an Auto de Fe at Lisbon, 1705.* And Carlos Vero Nieto. *A Reply to the Sermon.* Note by Isaac Leeser. Philadelphia: Barnard and Jones, 1860.

Fernandes, Benjamin Dias. *A Series of Letters on the Evidences of Christianity.* Philadelphia: published privately by Isaac Leeser, 1859 (and in serial form in the *Occident*).

Meditations and Prayers. Trans. Hester Rothschild. Rev. and corrected by Isaac Leeser. Philadelphia, 1866.

Mendelssohn, Moses. *Jerusalem: A Treatise on Religious Power and Judaism.* Trans. Isaac Leeser. Published as a supplement to *Occident* 9 (1852).

Philippson, Ludwig. *The Crucifixion and the Jews.* Trans. M. Meyer. Preface by Isaac Leeser. Philadelphia, 1866.

Salomon, Louis. *The Mosaic System in its Fundamental Principles.* Trans. G. Remak. Ed. Isaac Leeser. Philadelphia: E. G. Dorsey, 1841.

Schwartz, Joseph. *A Descriptive Geography and Brief Historical Sketch of Palestine.* Trans. Isaac Leeser. Philadelphia: A. Hart, 1850.

Select Sentences: Designed as a Moral Guide-Book for Young Israelites. Philadelphia: published privately by Isaac Leeser, 1854.

SECONDARY WORKS ON LEESER

Published

Abrahams, Israel. "Isaac Leeser's Bible." *By-Paths in Hebraic Bookland*, 254–59. Philadelphia: Jewish Publication Society, 1920.

Adler, Cyrus. *Catalogue of the Leeser Library.* Philadelphia: E. Hirsch and Company, 1883.

———. "Isaac Leeser." *Dictionary of American Biography* 11:137–38. New York: Scribner's, 1933.

Englander, Henry. "Isaac Leeser." *Yearbook of the Central Conference of American Rabbis* 28 (1918):213–52.

Friedenberg, Robert V. "Isaac Leeser: Pioneer Preacher of American Judaism." *Religious Communication Today* (September 1983):22–27.

Grossman, Lawrence. "Tradition Under Fire: Isaac Leeser and Reform." *Gesher* 8 (5741/1980):73–89.

———. "Isaac Leeser's Mentor: Rabbi Abraham Sutro, 1784–1869." In *Rabbi Joseph H. Lookstein Memorial Volume*, ed. Leo Landman, 151–62. New York: Ktav, 1980.

Isaacs, Moses L., and Nancy I. Klein. "Isaac Leeser and The Occident." *Guardians of Our Heritage*, ed. Leo Jung, 247–62. New York: Bloch, 1958.

Korn, Bertram W. "Isaac Leeser: Centennial Reflections." *American Jewish Archives* 19 (1967):127–41.

———. "The First American Jewish Theological Seminary: Maimonides College, 1867–1873." *Eventful Years and Experiences*, 151–213. Cincinnati: American Jewish Archives, 1954.

Mordecai, Rosa. "Isaac Leeser." *Appletons' Cyclopaedia*, ed. John Fiske and James Grant Wilson. Vol. 3, 676. New York, 1889.

Riemer, Jack. "Isaac Leeser." *Encyclopedia Judaica* (Jerusalem, 1971) 10:1561–62.

Seller, Maxine. "Isaac Leeser's Views on the Restoration of a Jewish Palestine." *Publications of the American Jewish Historical Society* 68 (1968):118–35.

———. "Isaac Leeser: A Jewish-Christian Dialogue in Ante-Bellum Philadelphia." *Pennsylvania History* 35 (1968):231–42.

Solis-Cohen, Jr., Emily. "Isaac Leeser." *Universal Jewish Encyclopedia* 6 (New York, 1939):588.

Sulzberger, Mayer. "Isaac Leeser." *Jewish Encyclopedia* 7 (New York, 1904): 662–63.

Sussman, Lance J. "Another Look at Isaac Leeser and the First Jewish Translation of the Bible in the United States." *Modern Judaism* 5 (1985): 159–90.

———. "Isaac Leeser and the Protestantization of American Judaism." *American Jewish Archives* 38 (April 1986):1–21.

Tsevat, Matitiahu. "A Retrospective View of Isaac Leeser's Biblical Work," In *Essays in American Jewish History*, ed. Bertram W. Korn, 295–313. Cincinnati: American Jewish Archives, 1958.

Whiteman, Maxwell. "Isaac Leeser and the Jews of Philadelphia." *Publications of the American Jewish Historical Society* 48 (1959): 207–244.

———. "The Legacy of Isaac Leeser." In *Jewish Life in Philadelphia, 1830–1940*, ed. Murray Friedman, 26–47. Philadelphia: ISHI, 1983.

Unpublished

Akselrad, Sidney. "A Comparison of Isaac Leeser and Isaac Mayer Wise." Ordination thesis, Hebrew Union College, 1947.

Bennet, E. "An Evaluation of the Life of Isaac Leeser." Ph.D. diss., Yeshiva University, 1959.

Cohen, Malcolm. "Introduction to the Occident." Ordination thesis, Hebrew Union College–Jewish Institute of Religion, 1952.

Feierstein, Milton. "Isaac Leeser: Founder of Jewish Education in the United States." Ph.D. diss., State University of New York, Buffalo, 1971.

Lehrman, Linda. "A Native of Germany, Isaac Leeser: A Biographical Sketch, 1824–1840." Typescript, American Jewish Archives, 1979.

Levy, Theodore S. "The Place of Isaac Leeser in American Life." Ordination thesis, Hebrew Union College, 1951.

Plaut, Jonathan. "Isaac Leeser and *The Occident*." Ordination thesis, Hebrew Union College–Jewish Institute of Religion, 1970.

Seller, Maxine. "Isaac Leeser: Architect of the American Jewish Community." Ph.D. dissertation, University of Pennsylvania, 1965.

Solis-Cohen, Emily. "Isaac Leeser: A Beginner in America." Typescript [incomplete manuscript], Dropsie College Library, Philadelphia, n.d.

———. "Isaac Leeser: A Man and His Destiny." Typescript (incomplete manuscript), Dropsie College Library, Philadelphia, n.d.

Sussman, Lance J. " 'Confidence in God': The Life and Preaching of Isaac Leeser, 1806–1868." Ordination thesis, Hebrew Union College–Jewish Institute of Religion, 1980.

NEWSPAPERS

Allgemeine Zeitung des Judentums, Leipzig, 1837–1922

Archives Israélites de France, Paris, 1840–60

The Asmonean, New York, 1849–57

Die Deborah, Cincinnati, 1855–1903

Der Israelit, 1839–48

The Israelite, Cincinnati, 1854–present

Israel's Herald, New York, 1849

The Jew, New York, 1823–25

Jewish Messenger, New York, 1857–1902

Der Orient, Leipzig, 1840–51

San Francisco Gleaner, 1855–62

Sinai, Baltimore and Philadelphia, 1856–63

SUPPLEMENTARY PRIMARY LITERATURE

Adams, Hannah. *A Dictionary of All Religions and Religious Denominations*. Boston, 1817.

———. *The History of the Jews From the Destruction of Jerusalem to the Present Time*. London, 1818.

Benjamin, Israel Joseph II. *Three Years in America, 1859–1862*. Trans. Charles Reznikoff. Philadelphia: Jewish Publication Society, 1956.

Berk, Matthew A. *History of the Jews up to the Present Time*. 3d ed. Boston, 1844.

Carvalho, Solomon Nunes. *Incidents of Travel and Adventure in the Far West, 1857*. Repr. Philadelphia: Jewish Publication Society, 1957.

Charter and By-Laws of Kaal Kadosh Mickve Israel. Philadelphia, 1841.

Dropsie, Moses A. "Discourse on Thanksgiving Day." Philadelphia, 1864.

———. "Panegyric on Life, Character and Services of the Rev. Isaac Leeser." Philadelphia, 1868.

Elzas, Barnett A. "A Letter to Leeser: An Important American Jewish Historical Document." *Jewish Comment* August 10, 1906.

Herxheimer, Salomon. *Der Pentateuch oder Die fünf Bücher Moses.* Berlin, 1840.

Hirsch, Samuel R. *The Nineteen Letters on Judaism.* Trans. Bernard Drachman. New York: Feldheim Publishers, 1969.

Jenks, William. *The Comprehensive Commentary of the Bible.* 2 vols. Philadelphia: Fessender and Company, 1848.

Johlson, Joseph. *Alumei Josef, Unterricht in der Mosaischen Religion.* Frankfurt, 1819.

———. *Die Lehren der Mosaischen Religion.* Frankfurt, 1829.

Jones, Alfred T. "Address at Mortuary Service in Memory of Rev. Isaac Leeser." Philadelphia: Beth El Emeth, 1868.

Kalisch, Isidore. *A Guide on Rational Inquiries into Biblical Writings.* Trans. M. Mayer. Cincinnati: Bloch, 1857.

———. "English Versions of the Bible." *Israelite* 1 (July 28, 1854): 21ff.

Keith, Rev. Alexander. "Evidence of the Truth of the Christian Religion." Holograph, n.d., American Jewish Archives.

Kley, Edward. *Catechismus der Mosaischen Religionslehre.* Leipzig, 1838–1840.

———. *Predigten in dem neuer Israelitischen Tempel zu Hamburg: Erste Sammlung.* Hamburg, 1819.

Kley, Edward, and Gotthold Salomon. *Sammlung der neuesten Predigten gehalten in dem neuer Israelitischen Tempel zu Hamburg.* Hamburg, 1826.

Lilienthal, Max. "Rev. I. Leeser and Reform." *Asmonean* 10 (1854): 85.

Luntshits, Ephraim. *The Vintage of Ephraim* (in Hebrew), Amsterdam, 1779.

Lyons, Jacques J., and Abraham de Sola. *A Jewish Calendar for Fifty Years.* Montreal, 1854.

Morais, Sabato. "Isaac Leeser." *Philadelphia Enquirer* February 13, 1868.

Mordecai, Jacob. "Introduction to the New Testament." Holograph, American Jewish Archives, n.d.

———. "Critique of Harriet Martineau's *Providence as Manifested Through Israel* [1832]." Holograph, American Jewish Archives, n.d.

Mordecai, Rosa. "Personal Recollections of Rev. Isaac Leeser." Typescript, American Jewish Archives, Englander Papers, 1901.

Philipson, David, and Louis Grossman, eds. *Selected Writings of Isaac M. Wise with a Biography.* Cincinnati: Robert Clarke Co., 1900.

Philippson, Ludwig. *Der Israelitische Bibel.* Leipzig, 1844.

A Review of the Late Controversies Between the Rev. Isaac Leeser and the Congregation Mickveh Israel. Philadelphia, 1850.

A Review of "The Review." New York, 1850

Rupp, I. Daniel. *He Pasa Ekklesia. An Original History of the Religious Denominations at present Existing in the United States.* Philadelphia: J. Y. Humphreys, 1844.

Samuels, Moses. *Jerusalem: A Treatise on Ecclesiastical Authority and Judaism.* London, 1838.

Solis-Cohen, Solomon. *The Jewish Theological Seminary: Past and Future* (an address, June 2, 1918). New York Jewish Theological Seminary, 1919.

Sulzberger, Mayer. "The Late Rev. Isaac Leeser." *Occident* 25 (1868): 593–611. Partially reprinted in *American Jewish Archives* 21 (1969): 140–48.

———. "Isaac Leeser" (pamphlet). Philadelphia, 1881. Reprinted in *American Hebrew* May 27, 1881, 15–16, and June 2, 1881, 28–29.

———. *Address on the 50th Anniversary of the Hebrew School of Philadelphia.* Philadelphia, 1888.

Sutro, Abraham. *Des Land-Rabbiners Sutro Widerlegung der Schrift des Herrn H. B. H. Cleve.* 1824.

———. *Wars of the Lord* [Hebrew]. 1836.

———. "An meine Glaubensgenössen in meinem Rabbinate, in der Fürsten-Thuemern Münster und Paderhorn." Münster, 1863.

Wise, Isaac M. *History of the Israelitish Nation from Abraham to the Present time,* Albany, N.Y., 1854.

———. *Reminiscences,* ed. and trans. David Philipson. Cincinnati: Leo M. Wise and Co., 1901.

———. *Minhag America.* Cincinnati: Bloch, 1857.

Wolf, Simon. "Address on the Life and Services of Isaac Leeser." IOBB (International Order of Bnai Brith), 1868.

———. *Selected Addresses and Papers of Simon Wolf.* Cincinnati, 1926.

Zunz, Leopold. *Die vier und zwanzig Bücher der Heiligen Schrift.* Berlin, 1838.

———. *Die gottesdienstlichen Vorträge der Juden historisch entwickelt.* Frankfurt, 1832.

INDEX

301

BOOKS IN THE AMERICAN JEWISH CIVILIZATION SERIES